AF334804

WOMEN PHOTOGRAPHERS

WOMEN PHOTOGRAPHERS

EDITED BY

CONSTANCE SULLIVAN

ESSAY BY

EUGENIA PARRY JANIS

HARRY N. ABRAMS, INC., PUBLISHERS, NEW YORK

Library of Congress Cataloging-in-Publication Data
Women photographers / compiled and edited by Constance Sullivan ;
essay by Eugenia Parry Janis.
p.   cm.
ISBN 0–8109–3950–9
I. Photography, Artistic. 2. Women photographers. I. Sullivan,
Constance. II. Janis, Eugenia Parry.
TR650.W65 1990
779'.082—dc20   90–30722
CIP

Published in 1990 by Harry N. Abrams, Incorporated, New York
A Times Mirror Company

Printed and bound in Switzerland

CONTENTS

Preface

7

Her Geometry
Eugenia Parry Janis

9

Plates

29

Acknowledgments

256

List of Plates

257

PREFACE

The detective story, points out Raymond Chandler in his essay *The Simple Art of Murder*, "has a way of minding its own business, solving its own problems, and answering its own questions. There is nothing left to discuss except whether it was well enough written to be good fiction."

This book (a fiction of sorts) attempts to explore the questions, concerns, and considerations raised in looking at a selection of photographs by women, to suggest how that work has affected, influenced, and shaped the language of photography, and to reveal a fascinating episode in the development of the medium. Assembling such a body of work required the tenacity of a private eye—relentlessly ferreting out and searching through collections, tracking down leads, examining evidence, and shamelessly preying upon knowledgeable people. My intention was to bring to light relatively obscure names like Marie Chambefort, Lady Filmer, Anna Atkins, Lucy Fleming, and Louise Deshong Woodbridge from the last century, and Madame Yevonde, Margaret Watkins, Alma Lavenson, Marjorie Content, and Aenne Biermann from the earlier part of this century. I wanted to publish lesser known work by such famous artists as Gertrude Käsebier, Imogen Cunningham, Margaret Bourke-White, Berenice Abbott, and Dorothea Lange, as well as present the landmark modern work of Helen Levitt and Diane Arbus with important and emerging contemporary photography.

The two hundred pictures reproduced here are arranged chronologically and sequenced visually. Most photographers are represented with several works, which meant excluding others who would have been part of a broader survey. I chose to emphasize a particular period of work or series by each rather than attempting, with so few examples, to outline the scope of a unique accomplishment or describe the visual ideas explored throughout a lifetime. For instance, Margaret Bourke-White's industrial imagery of the twenties and thirties is featured rather than the documentary magazine work for which she is better known. Some, like Tina Modotti and Lee Miller, are given lavish attention because I surrendered to unabashed admiration.

The slow process of distillation that occurs while editing a photographic survey creates a kind of narrative that takes on a life of its own. Considerations of context, inflection, and pacing take precedence, and fine pictures that don't sit well within that framework must sometimes be omitted. Painfully. Nonetheless, every enthusiast of the discipline could list what they consider to be unforgivable omissions. I trust that not too many of these can be blamed on my ignorance or lack of awareness.

A single quality persistently asserts itself in these compelling images. The arresting gaze and ardent contact with which each photographer captures her subjects imbues the pictures with a sensation of intimacy. While reflecting a personal point of view, I hope my selection conveys the power of that vision. Critical analysis and scholarly evaluation of the works and their makers were entrusted to the formidable intellect and writing skill of Eugenia Parry Janis. Her insight greatly enhances our understanding and appreciation.

Others made essential contributions to the preparation of this book. Susan Weiley edited the text with characteristic intelligence and grace. Katy Homans's elegant design is perfect. The quality of reproduction is due in large part to Robert Hennessey, who made fine tritone separations, many from original vintage prints, and provided invaluable production supervision. Paul Gottlieb and Robert Morton at Harry N. Abrams, Inc. encouraged and supported the book from the earliest stages through publication.

CONSTANCE SULLIVAN

HER GEOMETRY

Last spring I talked here, and one of the girls asked me, "Miss O'Connor, why do you write?"
and I said, "Because I'm good at it."
Flannery O'Connor, *Mystery and Manners*

STARTING FROM WITHIN

Photography by women is a loaded subject, replete with every issue that has plagued or glorified the sex, from its sacrifices and confusions, to its sensing powers and sense of destiny. Categorizations lead to dubious expectations, such as whether we can recognize and discuss per se female visual intelligence, female curiosity, female observation, female affirmation, female narcissism, female passion, female search for the sacred, female sense of mystery, female metamorphosis, female bizarre, female sense of family, female self-destruction, female goofiness, female declaration of perversity, female charity, female courage, female recognition of injustice, female horror of suffering, female fly on the wall, and so forth. Looking at the present selection of images the answer to these implied questions would have to be yes. Collectively, the women represented here demonstrate all these qualities, and more. Yet the answer conveys little of interest, because such questions already have answers; and anyhow, these have never been the interesting issues about anyone's work. Happily, the photographs themselves allow their makers to escape the tightrope of fatuous speculation. The images offer revelations that have little to do with women as a classification. Each picture proposes a compelling aspect of the woman's gaze that can be subsumed in what Eudora Welty, attempting to characterize her years of sheltered existence as a writer, called so gently the "serious daring" that "starts from within."[1]

From the beginning the camera obscura, and its related realms of dark room and dark cloth, invited seclusion. Working with early photographic chemistries has been compared to entering a secret society of Paracelsians—exclusively male alchemists in their laboratory lairs. Many women were experiencing parallel situations in the very lives assigned to them by most nineteenth-century social constraints, of course. But the situation was much more complicated for those who declared themselves photographic artists, which meant yet another degree of existence in a world apart.

Few of them articulated their trials as women through their photographing, at least not at first, although the *Ladies' Pool* (c. 1890) by Louise Deshong Woodbridge (pl. 6), a prominent club woman in Chester, Pennsylvania, for all its lighthearted charm, epitomizes this sequestered state, and certainly may be seen to represent an oblique appeal from the sector of privilege. Fewer women still found the language with which to convey their awareness of the terrible difficulties encountered in trying to concoct images with a machine, a matter that gives Julia Margaret Cameron's jubilant "My First Success," written on her 1864 portrait of *Annie,* the poignancy of a note in a bottle.

In the paradoxical detached engagement essential to mastering a new medium each female practitioner may have fancied herself some kind of heroine, not only in the age-old struggle to work and move freely in the world, but in the more mysterious struggle of the artist involved in turning inward, collecting oneself. In the process of making photographic pictures and becoming "good at it," each discovered in the self an unexpected other, with formidable powers of concentration and command.

Perhaps this is why a rare and little-known photograph by Gertrude Käsebier (pl. 21) of a woman playing billiards has the power to rivet attention like the opening scene of a long and beautiful novel. With this simple record of daily life,[2] Käsebier brings us into her interior in every sense, allowing us to witness, through a form of popular family entertainment, an exercise of will that may be seen to stand for the ways in which women decide to exploit their capacities.

Around 1909 Käsebier, by then a successful portrait photographer in New York, printed in platinum a modest picture that shows her oldest daughter Gertrude Elizabeth Käsebier O'Malley, playing pocket billiards in the Käsebier home in Oceanside, Long Island. Engulfed in shadow, young Gertrude dominates the dimly lit billiard room, from which we see a sequence of parlors that open up like a bellows, and into which apertures admit streams of light. In one of these rooms stands the player's opponent, her brother-in-law William Mason Turner.[3] With eight balls on the green felt, Gertrude O'Malley has presumably called the shot and positions her cue for a center hit on the cue ball,[4] her body aligned along the cue as a singular directing force. The man does not hover over her, anxious to see what "impossible shots" she will bequeath him. He has planted himself in the adjoining foyer, a position permitting her full command of the table, and as far as we can tell, the entire billiard room. As he waits his turn, slender and solemn in the open doorway, he leans on one foot, his cue a measure against his notable height. The sun grazes his face, dreamy and preoccupied with something behind the confines of the house; light puddles around his ankles, its entry sufficient to illuminate the entire scene without obscuring the meticulous delineation of the receding lines of floors, walls, and ceilings of the foyer and parlors, for Käsebier's camera registers even an oil lamp with an opaline glass shade in the distance. Thus in this seamless rendition of domestic serenity, the photographer completely accounts for the space. Enclosing, delineating, receding in her arrangement, it forms the perfect geometrical analogue of "home."

Young Gertrude's glance along the cue's line of sight is meant to be the scene's definitive vector. Through this gaze her mother has her define an arena of influence. How incongruous seem the corseted bodice and flounced sleeve, standing for centuries of feminine guile and coquetry, now in league with the aligning cue, pocket call, and follow through. Writing in 1907 the photographer suggested the edges of her intentions: "From the first days of dawning individuality, I have longed unceasingly to make pictures of people, not maps of faces, but pictures of real men and women, *as they know themselves*, to make likenesses that are biographies.[5]

More than one biography is conveyed by the billiard player's intensity and clarity of purpose. Her namesake is a perfect generic substitute for the photographer's own indomitable will. Perhaps Käsebier regarded her daughter's roundly acknowledged delight in pool as akin to her own devotion to the camera's aligning art, for this family tableau is rich with parallels to the mentality of photography. Also, like photography—which Käsebier and other pictorialists then practiced with much renewed flair for technical experimentation, as if to prevent the medium from being ossified into mere formulas—the scene exudes ardor for the game.

Resonating beyond its ostensible rendition of daily life, the image is charged with Käsebier's entirely personal and ever-present "symbolism," in which her subjects, besides playing themselves, seem to allude to the photographer's own artistic independence and self-conscious heroism.[6] The scene's representation of intimacy and skill boldly shows how one might possess mental as well as physical space in exercising an art or gift. As she concentrates on her game the billiard player quietly commands the table. By extension, with the staged withdrawal of her partner she claims the entire space around her as well. We feel it intensely. The mirror at her back holds what remains of his space; by reflecting a sideboard along the wall behind us, it completes the survey of the woman's gaze.

Käsebier's subject is a paragon of preoccupation. It proposes a mystique of female vision, performance, and control. This attitude had rivals in other strong voices of the time that added more typical variations on the theme. These were individuals such as Frances Benjamin Johnston, who promoted photography as some sort of cure-all, and even tried to lay down rules through which disenfranchised women might somehow redeem themselves. The patronizing advice given by Johnston, Käsebier's admirer and herself a portrait photographer and journalist, was of course considered progressive. In articles such as "Ever Try Photography? A Good Profession for Women Says Miss Johnston" or "What a Woman Can Do with a Camera," she reassures readers that a photograph can be produced by any person of average intelligence.[7] Käsebier had proven to herself what she could "do" with a camera in the portrait trade alone and was recognized for the "tact" with which she united art and business.[8] Her pictures show that photography to her was more than a profession or even an art: it offered a means by which she might perceive and know others "as they know themselves." Through photographing she felt she established contact with others' deepest desires, afflictions, and triumphs. Besides, in the process she seems to have discovered the supreme mental pleasure—evidenced in every aspect of the billiard picture's conception and execution—of lining things up.

Alignment is natural to photography's spatial language, especially since the medium is essentially a mechanical refinement of the art of perspective. When Frances Benjamin Johnston photographed at the Hampton Institute in Virginia at the turn of the century, she turned the view camera's potential for expressive alignment to a moral purpose. She had her sitters, exemplars of "the right path" prescribed for black America, adjust their bodies to repeat invisible parallel lines receding from the ground-glass back of the camera. How strangely self-conscious, and yet how eloquent, are these idealistic tableaux where "hearts beat, breath is held, time ticks. Eyelids barely flutter."[9] What a peculiar rhetoric of betterment Miss Johnston's aligning art stands for here. In her maneuvered theater of self-improvement, she is content to dwell upon externals, not unlike the make-over she exhorted from women using the camera.

Käsebier's aligning image forces us to turn inward with the player. Its power lies in suggesting more than it actually records. With one ritual of contemplation Käsebier reaches toward others in which women might discover not a pastime but the very limits of their ardor, not the least of these the discipline of photography itself.

The inventors of photography, and later its practitioners, consistently held high hopes for the medium, placing its purpose somewhere between science and art. But in 1839, when it was introduced to the world, there were hardly the standards for photographic practice or results to equal those of other disciplines. No one yet knew what the standards needed to be. Rewards went simply to those who succeeded and who were able to make their success known. The discourse was in terms of photography's potential, and enthusiasts published lists of what photography might do. How it would occur remained to be seen. At this stage both sexes were on equal footing. Neither knew exactly where the photographic quest would take them or what it might mean in the larger schemes of progress and self-discovery. For everyone, photography was the quest of the amateur, a category within which women were immanently comfortable. Hardly expected to succeed at anything, except as amateurs, they already knew the joy of doing things for the love of it.

Who were among the first? Names float to the surface like fragments of memory. Among the French daguerreotypists, who was Marie Chambefort (active c. 1850), the "itinerant" artist in the Department of Saône-et-Loire?[10] Did this woman, who made the portrait of Stéphanie Poyet, aged seven years, also hand-color this still-life arrangement of books, basket of roses, hat, and nunlike doll that surround the dour little sitter? What kind of nineteenth-century woman would have been "itinerant," roaming the countryside with a camera and a pharmacy of daguerreotype equipment? The notion is almost inconceivable for the time. The woman would have been a perfect freak, as fully suspect as the most dejected *fille folle de son corps* or *fille sans nom* to be rounded up among the "hysterics" or the "insane" for the Paris women's prison of Saint-Lazare. Would the parents of the little subject have considered the child safe with such a practitioner? How doll-like the little girl seems, more so than the doll beside her. How wooden her pose is, how piquant the strangely crimped points on her petticoat.

Among the British we find the most distinctive female group of early photographic personalities, all of whom seemed to belong to an extended family. First there was Constance Talbot, wife of the English inventor of photography, William Henry Fox Talbot. As early as May 1839 she was setting some of her husband's "mousetraps," as she called his many cameras placed around the buildings and grounds of Lacock Abbey, and making pictures following her husband's recipes.[11] And in Scotland, where Talbot's patent on his process was inoperative, Frances Dunlop Monteith, wife of an Edinburgh lawyer, in 1845 made calotype (paper-negative) portraits in the photographic circle of Sir David Brewster.[12]

Another of these early enthusiasts with fierce single-mindedness seized on photography on paper as a tool to promote her botanic interests. Anna Atkins's scientist father, John George Children, had nurtured her passion for science and art from childhood. They were close friends of Sir John Herschel, the great astronomer and natural philosopher who, among his many contributions to photography, invented the cyanotype (blueprint) process. Thus by late 1841 she had access to an exquisitely simple means by which to collect and systematically illustrate the many specimens known to her.[13] Using cyanotype she produced thousands of photograms with the confidence of those who know their subject well. Atkins arranged the plants on light-sensitive paper to make them instantly recognizable and to give the impact of their individuality the greatest force. Hers is an art of precision and discrimination, dependent on the viewer's ability to clearly discern specimens by the distinctiveness of their contours and relative density of their material substances. By October 1843 she had selected from these gorgeous silhouettes material for the first photographically illustrated book. Called *Photographs of British Algae: Cyanotype Impressions* and privately published from 1843 to 1853, it predates even Talbot's *The Pencil of Nature*, which began to appear in installments in June 1844. Atkins found the saturated hue of cyan dye "beautiful," not overly intense, as we might imagine; garish aniline dyes had begun to invade the wardrobes and appurtenances of many Victorian households. What a perfect artificial "sea" cyan blue was for her seaweeds from the Sussex shore, pond scums, and stone worts.[14]

It was Atkins's passion for learning that led her to photographic chemistries. Herschel had welcomed women to the fold of scientists and freely acknowledged their contributions in many fields, including photography, where he experimented so successfully. He credited Atkins's photographic predecessor Elizabeth Fulhame's work with light-sensitive compounds in his first photographic paper. Despite Herschel's fairness, Fulhame's brutal directness in assessing the male scientific community generally shows where most innovative women of "serious daring" found themselves. Of the men in her world she wrote: "Some are so ignorant that they grow sullen and silent and are chilled with horror at the sight that bears the semblance of learning in whatever shape it may appear; and should the spectre appear in the shape of a woman, the pangs they suffer are truly dismal."[15]

Many Victorians found learning not only distasteful but downright unbecoming for either sex. Few early photographs by women are as "learned" as those of Anna Atkins, and if Botany was a field where Atkins and her associate Anne Dixon received restrained welcome, the more sentimental "secret language of flowers" had fervent devotees of its arbitrary meanings. Would that we could reassemble the playful parlor albums of Mary Georgiana Caroline, Lady Filmer. Next to Anna Atkins's visions of precision, how charming and superficial these album leaves seem. Lady Filmer's humor attracts us, especially united with her powers of free association, which have a flagrant psychological directness.

Lady Filmer was close to Queen Victoria's court circles, and her pictures use many carte-de-visite portraits of court members, which she cut and pasted into designs enhanced with watercolor. Her strange liberties in exaggerating space, scale, and disjointed figures parallel the dreamlike configurations of other fanciful Victorian image-makers such as Lewis Carroll—in pictures as in text, for Filmer's abstracting art is notably literary. Using a handsome man's head, elongated with a top hat, she envisions a sexually attractive floral center, with this dandy the "pistil," in an imaginative reconstitution of a flower. Around him a series of identified "Misses" and "Ladies" wearing sumptuous crinolines (two women hold a photographic album like some kind of *Wonderland* self-referent) play the equivalents of "petals." Filmer intersperses watercolor drawing, no more skilled than that of any competent amateur, between the photographs to express more directly flowers' tender language of emotion. We have the forget-me-not, the rose, the pansy (I'm thinking of you) accompanied by tremulous butterflies (pl. 4).

Artists closer to our own time with well-established Victorian roots, such as Imogen Cunningham, enjoyed the affinities between flowers and sexual allusion. Her studies of calla lilies in the late 1920s, in which the camera eye caresses the waxy petals and seems to peer into a flower's intimate cavity, are sensual parallels to her explorations of the female nude. The aloe bud's thrust in this regard plays an obviously complementary role.

Flowers aside, for modern eyes the deeper significance of Lady Filmer's *découpage* would have to wait for the politically and artistically tumultuous era in which Hannah Höch lived—the 1920s and 1930s— in order to give full value to the Dada/Surrealist exposition of the female unconscious that this Victorian amateur awakens. Lady Filmer's art thus establishes a traditional photographic way of thinking that continues to attract the medium's more literary adherents, who are drawn to combine and superimpose images in order to delve into illusory visions of dreams and multiple personalities. Hannah Höch worked with equally pointed meaning regarding her sense of self, as in *Russiche Tanzerin (Mein Double)*. Others who worked this vein include Aenne Biermann in *Portrait mit Champs-Elysées, Paris* (pl. 94), Alice Lex-Nerlinger in *Näherlin* (pl. 90) and Wanda Wulz in *Lo & Gatto (I and Cat)* (pl. 87). We should not exempt from this idiom of juxtaposition more recent work, including the still-life arrangements with animals (from pigeon to muskrat, whether stuffed or real) by Barbara Norfleet (pl. 199) or the pointed, theatrical absurdities of *Radioactive Cats* by Sandy Skoglund (pl. 198), or even Jan Groover's deviations from Cubist spatial play by adding wee figurines and their implied narratives to her tabletop fancies (pl. 173).

We are only beginning to discover how many Victorian women did camera work in the relative obscurity of the closed family circle. This too constitutes the basis for a vigorous photographic tradition upheld today. The world of Lady Clementina Hawarden was that of the cloistered manor house, with its parapets, balconies, and sun-drenched interiors. Relying on her daughters and other intimates, she composed pictures to reveal the sultry dramatics, the passion in preoccupied glances that lay thinly veiled beneath camisole and crinoline. How successfully she conveys the invisible web of female exclusivity in two girls who form a veritable garland with their embrace. One meets our gaze with unmitigated effrontery, certain that the photographer's intrusion in no way violates their bond of sisterhood (pl. 7).

Clementina's passionate atmospheres illuminate the work of contemporary artists such as Andrea Modica and Sally Mann, especially since they, like the Victorians, draw inspiration from the virtues of the narrow scope, finding in "the local" sources of "the universal."[16] In Lexington, Virginia, where she examines and reexamines her near and dear, Mann finds dramas in the everyday that stand for the great themes that others feel they must travel widely to discover. Like Lady Hawarden she explores the fluctuating moods of the young, and documents the emergence of conscious sexual power and its origins in childhood. *Jessie at Six* (pl. 149), an Eve against a tree entwined with Virginia Creeper that grows through the great porch, shoots a glance that contains the entire history of woman's capacity to bedazzle. Hawarden expressed it through a language of dressing up and *déshabille*; Mann updates it with the contemporary "naturalness" of nudity. But both artists, linked across centuries, have understood well that grand ideas are to be found not in mere everydayness but, more pointedly, as Anthony Trollope recognized, in "the way we live now."

Having entered this stay-at-home tradition more recently, W. Snyder MacNeil takes the issue of "now" and distills it into an examination of digital moments, monumental glimpses from life seen as an unending river's flow. Earlier images were of stunning body fragments meant to stand for family ties and genetic linkage, or to equate human infancy with the dawn of early cultures, as in the portrait head of *Jazimina* (pl. 164), which has the durability of a megalith. Today she chooses images from endless ribbons of home videos featuring the lives of her family in a white bungalow in Lincoln, Massachusetts. Again, from the narrow scope appear countless opportunities for a deep exploration of daily existence. Now, the same child, crying, in a huge cibachrome transparency of 40 x 50 inches, is a dematerialized tragedienne lifted from the infinitesimal number of seconds it takes to dramatize a feeling. Again we have a fragment, carefully chosen from many, which the photographer continually plays and replays in order "to think about it some more, to understand it further."[17]

Connoisseurs of passion and drama among the Victorians had delighted in elevating members of their circle to transcendent actors. The family and friends of Julia Margaret Cameron became part of her galaxy of greatness. The titles *Stella* and *Cassiopeia* are clear enough in naming each steadfast glance. These disembodied gazes seem to hold immeasurable time. Cameron wrote that she sought in the immortal human face the "mighty influence of the mystery of beauty . . . its secret, swift, and subtle . . spell."

She turned all of her sitters into spellbinders, even her vicar, the merry Rector of Freshwater, Reverend J. Issacson, in whom in 1864—her first year of photographic achievement—she sought a "subtler magic" by softening the delineation of his face by having it protrude slightly in front of the lens's focal plane (pl. 10).[18] To honor her son's marriage she portrayed *The Bride* (*Our Beautiful Birdie, My Ewen's Bride of 18 Nov. 1869*) wearing a seasonal fur-trimmed gown. Birdie's sad expression fulfills Cameron's sacred program: "I would . . . for the sake of any one of my sons sacrifice anything I could sacrifice at the Altar of Marriage with any girl noble in mind and nature. That is, you know, the real nobility I prize above all things."[19] Infants before Cameron's lens were equally sacred, emulating the infancy of Christ, at times portrayed in compositions that fracture and dislocate previous conceptions of the theme in all media, for example *Prayer and Praise/Freshwater* (pl. 12). Thus it is not surprising to see Cameron's art capture inconceivable radiance in the strange 1867 portrait of *Hallam Tennyson* (pl. 11), the son of her hero, who becomes a mysterious specter dissolving into incandescence before our eyes.

Cameron's work is the quintessence of the idealizing Victorian frame of mind. It is unlikely that anyone of her stature will suddenly appear from obscurity, but work by Victorian women continues to emerge steadily. There are the cool architectural photographs by Lucy Fleming (active 1860s), about whom we know next to nothing. Hers is simply the name on eight architectural images of Castle Hedington, Essex, found in the collection of Gertrude Elizabeth Rogers, a similarly obscure photographer, and part of a small group of women doing camerawork together near Sevenoaks in England. Fleming and the others may have been taught by Rogers, who was photographing by the 1850s. Similarly, we can only surmise that the platinum print of the *Ladies' Pool* by Woodbridge stands for a spirited body of pictorialist work.[20] Its exclusivity recalls a bathing scene by an earlier pictorialist, the French photographic pioneer Henri Le Secq, who around 1850 defined the masculine domain with considerably more sobriety. This derived from the difficulties of his chemistries, rather than the somnambulance of his models. Perhaps a hierarchy of greater and lesser photographic energies has begun to form, but despite a continual emergence of new names, it is embarrassing how little we know, and most significantly, how few of the right questions we have asked about the images we have found.

POETIC INTERVALS

Even current photographic studies remain primitive in many ways. Where women are concerned, the literature has been dedicated to restoring lost artists to the history,[21] recognizing women's supernal contributions, whether they practiced photography as a profession, a pastime, or an art.[22] But these studies still do not fully address how women used photography as a means by which to think and to imagine. This does not mean the ways women have thought to express their widely felt despair and vulnerability as perennial objects of the disenfranchising male gaze, a subject that has engaged so many among the politically correct practitioners of "the new art history" and of so much excellent related scholarly writing that one feels justifiably relieved from dealing with it here.[23] Thinking women are increasingly using photography to politicize the history of the indignities suffered through male dominance in Western society as a whole. Today a certain corner of this photography marinates in the continued politicizing of the deplorable history of women's subjugation. The problem with the imperative in this powerful, if at times deadly, work is that it implies that all legitimate art by women must either treat feminist issues, in one way or another, or else be rejected as "modernist" or politically and artistically retrograde.[24]

Few photographs in the present selection are actively concerned with demonstrating art political affinities or correctives. Rather the images show us something more refreshing, inspiring, enriching because they cast a wider net. Through the range of interests expressed, they reflect the intensity with which certain artists observe and acknowledge the mysterious relationships between things.

Already familiar subject matter emerges here renewed by a profound sensing power. If Anna Atkins's solution to illustrating botanic specimens was through a kind of radar vision, rather than in common illustration, others have found solutions to the problem of how to make things "tell" through vantage points established without fear of coming up with nothing, or what seems like nothing, because the artist is consumed by the relationships of things to the spaces surrounding them. Much exciting work in the present selection involves sensing the potential within the poetic interval. Margaret Watkins's (active 1920s) kitchen still lifes are interesting not because they dramatize the lowly shower hose, eggs, or a clutter of dishes in a sink; rather, we are drawn to her acknowledgement of the rare beauty of the spaces that hold these objects, embrace them in radiance. Beauty is the wrong word. Imaginative potential perhaps is better. There is a short story by Isaac Bashevis Singer that opens with something like, "In the forgotten space that lies between the back of a stove and the wall . . . ," riveting us to an unlikely place and sharpening our appetite for what might happen there. Watkins's cluttered sink, for all its pictorial attractiveness, stimulates similar thoughts.

The interval was a topos of modernist composition. Ilse Bing found it in the potent fragment of a poster of Garbo, where it becomes the resting place between the surrounding cracked walls. Berenice Abbott found it by turning from the compelling alignments and geometries in vernacular architecture that she loved so well, toward the swags of clothes lines against a New York sky. As a connoisseur of practically everything graphic that she could find along a street, Abbott discovered in the space between buildings an explosion of contemporary hieroglyphics, ragged and damp, but as optimistic as a weed seen through a crack in the pavement.

The eloquence of the interval is a leading theme in the still lifes of Florence Henri. For all of their self-conscious modernism, there is excitement in the mysterious journey one is forced to take between the object and its reflection in the surrounding space, made more ambiguous as a mirrored surface that creates continual questions as to which is the original and which its *semblable*. For theorists of design in the 1920s and 1930s the spaces in between were given renewed formal attention. But this did not occur without a concomitant recognition of their effect on the feelings. Henri's still life with lemon and the enigmatic presence of fur—or is it grass?—that leads to the thin strip of land in the distance is a queer elision from one subject genre to another, but also between two different states of mind (pl. 66).

Spaces were full of psychic interest to Bauhaus theorists themselves. Lucia Moholy's famous portrait of her protesting husband from 1925–26 (pl. 86) includes his interfering hand, a blurred barrier between him and her camera, but also a pointed reference to the psychological space between them, if only at that instant. László Moholy-Nagy's photograph *At Coffee* is in a parallel way almost novelistic. We see only the trousers and shoes of two male conversationalists, a finished demitasse cup and saucer on the terrace floor. Moholy-Nagy makes the space between the men intensely palpable through these objects that practically hold the substance of their conversation, such as we can imagine it. A Bauhaus dictum of finding new, modern vantage points is insufficient to explain the imaginative promise of *At Coffee*, or of Lucia's portrait of László. Other German photographers such as Ellen Auerbach pursued this potential with the same devotion to ordinariness that suggests the Surrealist's domain of incipient events through the "intelligence" that resides in the furniture. Her view of an empty hallway in a searing light (pl. 93) brings to mind a detective thriller or a story by Kafka. Here is space you would hardly notice, with its wall sink, single faucet, umbrella, and fedora on a hook. Empty of preconceptions or desire, it seems to conceal feelings and events still unnamed.

There are rare photographers for whom the almost magical array of objects or events thrown by chance into a field of play allows them to recognize certain narrative possibilities that emerge from the sheer coincidence. From the middle of the nineteenth century, street photography had reveled in these randomly achieved configurations. From that time one of photography's fascinations has been to propose psychological connections between forms and figures in space, however fragmented they may be, to suggest a rich sense of ambiguity that has come to be associated with modernism.

In Henri Cartier-Bresson's 1930s vision, which united disparate people and objects on the street, what counted was the illusion of things coalescing by virtue of their proximity in space and time. While this photographic mode has its multitude of followers, others have refined the idea in which the artist sees more broadly by exploiting the geometrical arrangement for its layers of puzzlement, not as a detached stroller but as an impassioned participant.

Helen Levitt displayed this quality of visual imagination in 1941 in Mexico, where she had gone to look for Cartier-Bresson's effects.[25] The circumstances that led to her explosive picture of the revolted little girl (pl. 125) are not known, except that the photographer found her on a busy street, much like those in the New York neighborhoods that became Levitt's principal arena for showing that children's games convey the ultimate in unselfconscious physical grace, and that this play encapsulates all significant moments to come in our life stories.

Did Levitt mean simply to record her discovery of the man with broken teeth and shredded clothing about to tear into his tortilla? What a grotesque face he makes in the instant, like some mythical mask from an ancient fountain or baroque theater. In pressing the shutter Levitt captured a scene that surpassed her French mentor's tableaux of pleasing forms. Rather she proposed startling connections among the three figures that seem to implicate the viewer. Levitt does not want to be alone in having recognized the impact of the ugly man in the street. He becomes significant insofar as she can include others within the image to stand for her amazement, as Käsebier fixed upon her daughter's zeal to parallel her own. Levitt, like Käsebier, builds her recognition into the image's very fabric. The man, more grotesque for being caught off guard, gapes into the aperture just as the little girl, carrying a small bowl, moves past with the weightless stride of Botticelli's Judith. Holding her possession, as if to protect it from what she sees, she turns only her head to drink in the man's face, to which we, of course, are being treated head on. Nonetheless, her vantage point is good enough to produce an expression that spans disapproval, alarm, and revulsion.

Levitt's configuration does not end with the man and girl: a third figure, which neither of them notices, grazes their alignment like a "kiss shot" in billiards. A boy, younger than the girl, rushes into the foreground, breaking our view of the man. He sticks his finger into his nose, a gesture, despite its softer focus, destined to further exacerbate the girl's scorched sense of dignity. Without this boy, the equation is too theatrical, too easily grasped. With his accidental appearance Levitt retrieves something complete, utterly genuine, infinitely puzzling.

A distant wall shows two paintings, a still life with compote and a landscape, rendered with ubiquitous Mexican illusionism. On either side are café doors, at the threshold of which stand men in white shirts; two, at least, witness the events in the street, such as they were before the photographer "made something of them." What has Levitt made? Simply a secure structure against which there is no comeback, a scaffolding that aligns photographer, little girl, and viewer.

In the 1980s certain photographers continue to explore this eloquent ineloquence of the interval, but they face it deadpan, as a domain of the strange and inexplicable within the familiar. Tina Barney shows in her monuments to take-for-granted American bourgeois life that the spaces of this form of existence are often odd, even exotic, a recognition she asserts with unstrived for, quotidian flatness. In her family groups the interval is often temporal. There's a lull, an interruption. Someone has said something, maybe several people are talking at once. Maybe no one is saying anything. What is the moment? There is none.

THE EDGE OF AN INSTINCT

Contemplation of the way certain photographers explore a recognition of the psychological potential in spatial relationships, as they might stand for other kinds of recognition, brings up thoughts of other intervals, such as the margin, and all that the word implies. From the beginning much photography sought to manifest what lay outside of the familiar. To find it photographers simply left homes, countries, continents, a matter to which we shall return. But women have done this in ways that acclaimed the "other" without always traveling far and wide.

A New Yorker of wealth, Doris Ulmann from 1918 until her death surveyed the American east coast for hidden colonies of artisans, people in obscurity upholding undescribed craft traditions and religious practices. She discovered some 400 Gullah Negroes of the Lang Syne Plantation in South Carolina who came from what is now Liberia, their own language of Gullah setting them farther apart even from mainstream rural blacks. In their religious ceremonies she found moments that captured their habits, beliefs, and values. She idealized their every gesture as standing for something America had lost—or perhaps proposing a life of grace it had never known. Thus her images have the poignancy of disbelief, of a wish come true through her photographic fabrications.[26]

Blacks were an integral part of Eudora Welty's sheltered Mississippi life, but existed in a world apart just the same. When the young writer worked as a publicity agent in the mid-1930s for the Works Progress Administration, taking pictures and writing news stories for county papers, she recognized in the camera "a hand held auxiliary of wanting to know." Photography she regarded as crude in itself, but she continued, "when we look at the little prints that come of it, we get a fine unproportional satisfaction as if we had netted a prize."[27] Welty's little photographs helped her discover "that every feeling waits upon its gesture." But also that "the fictional eye sees in, through, and around what is really there."[28] If her image of Negroes of the Church of God in Christ Holiness with their preacher (pl. 107) has imposing visual force, compare it with her description:

> The preacher, shown here at the top, was a little man, jet black, with monkey features and antics.
> He played the banjo, both solo and as an accompaniment, and as a sort of gong—with single,
> abrupt twangs when he wanted attention or appreciation. He preached strolling around, up and
> down the aisle. He was nimble and nimble witted, he never let his flock get bored, and when he
> saw it getting restless, he would interrupt himself in the middle of a sentence to suddenly click
> his heel down sharply on the floor, call a word or a name—'Lazarus! Holy Lamb!'—and start a
> dance. He could also do a dance himself with the cymbals, and handle a tambourine, rap it
> behind him with a neat kick of the heel. It was said he had two wives, one for sorrow and one
> for joy.[29]

Netting photographically is one thing. For Welty it would be words with which she would see "in, through, and around."

Exploring the margin in the 1930s and 1940s led to Photo-League photographer Consuelo Kanaga's "sober and profound" descriptions of the "external world," which often meant black New York. She made documents that surpass the League's pretensions to record the poor. Stepping back to understand the racial particularity of a girl in terms of the outline her form cuts against the sky, or in earlier work getting so close to a black subject's face that her skin becomes unfamiliar terrain, like the moist respiring earth in a tropical rain forest, Kanaga observes with curiosity that obliterates stereotypes, wishes, or "others'" strange antics.

More recently Nancy Hellebrand used the face of a black woman in six rapidly changing aspects to turn racial structure and demeanor into a similarly unfamiliar, malleable substance, like putty shaped in light to convey an ineffable poetics of expression. The faces in the sequence connect like handwriting; each expression exists only to give rise to the next, reinforcing the observation that the moods a face may display are not simply still shots separating instantaneous revelations of character. By dwelling on the idea, Helle-brand sees the face as all transition, like shifting storm clouds in unsettled weather(pl. 168).

Poverty was the first exotic "other" for those who could afford cameras in 1839. Before the nine-teenth century was over, the plight of the poor proved to photographers, as Lincoln Kirstein observed, that their subject could be indignation.[30] Well before the mid-twentieth century, photographic indignation was an institution explored with varying degrees of concern that some masked with skilled, stylized detach-ment that elevated their subjects to indelible symbols. Dorothea Lange's physical handicap, a leg withered from polio, made it impossible for her to "pounce on an exposure or leap from subject to subject."[31] Pre-sumably her subjects saw her coming, which makes the men of the *White Angel Kitchen*, *San Francisco* (pl. 117) who eat so intently, quite ignorant of the photographer's presence, doubly poignant. Other jobless men she made stand for all of the nameless and homeless. Blocking the face, the man's hat stands for his palpable existence, where dignity is questionable, misery a certainty. Similarly, *Damaged Child*, *Shacktown*, *Elm Grove*, *Oklahoma* (pl. 119) is the portrayal of a withered shell, the misshapen result of obscure inflictions, revealed in the filthy garment, and the shadow that hides an eye that cannot make contact.

In New York Lisette Model let the street people she photographed in the 1940s loom over her like giants of despair. Even the dwarf in front of a hotel seems an oversized paradox, as if Model had photo-graphed him from down on her knees. Despite her obvious proximity, the subjects ignore her. Gigantic, high-toned women stampede past Model's lens as well. Looking like blind monsters in unidentifiable fur coats, their forms nearly squeeze out the milquetoast dandy between them. At Sammy's Bar on the Bowery, quintessentially on the fringe (in the 1940s it was a favorite haunt of Weegee too), Model moves in close to the sailor murmuring to the girl (pl. 127). She gets not a clear sense of personality as much as a space molded by their glances through the force of their attraction, leaving all others on the periphery.

Model and Weegee inspired Diane Arbus's investigations along the margin. The intensity of her quest led to discoveries such as *Albino Sword Swallower at a Carnival*, *MD* (pl. 130), who seems to sacrifice her-self in the name of some greater spiritual force. Her body makes a splendid cruciform; her hands balance like the wings of a bird. If anyone who entered the margin reveled in the marvelous there, it was Arbus. We still have not absorbed the full extent of her subjects' messages to us from the interior. By comparison, Wee-gee's art, for all of its open-city bravura, is manic craving. Model and Arbus saw, in worlds apart, mythical heroes on heroes' journeys. Weegee did not. In this context Arbus's photographs of young people and children resonate with parallel sensitivity. With eyes that glow like fireflies, they are all some version of Arbus's own "I am curious."

What we learn from the work in the present selection of photographs by women we learn through endless comparison, which may be the only valid tool available to seekers of visual knowledge. Certain artists serve us well by providing one sort of conception of a subject, as Margaret Bourke-White did in the spring of 1945 in photographing the aftermath of the "final solution," showing carts at Buchenwald piled with victims to convey the grossest possible horror, as only Bourke-White knew how to do. Against this we have here the lesser known, and perhaps more complex, mentality of Lee Miller, who entered the concen-tration camps of Buchenwald and Dachau in April 1945 as an independent photographer with no assignment, curious to see it all, but for some reason fixing upon how the perpetrators ended up. At Dachau she found an S.S. officer in a shallow river, his body dumped there by prisoners. At Buchenwald, other guards had died by suicide with ropes; young guards on their knees, beaten to a pulp by their half-alive victims, plead for mercy before Miller's camera, before the anonymous woman who had entered on the coattails of a U.S. Army raid on Buchenwald and the Rainbow Company of the 45th Division that liberated Dachau.[32]

What a release such pictures provide, as if every victim from Bourke-White's Buchenwald cart had miraculously arisen and like some ghostly army saw that justice was done. What a difference in the way we must henceforth think of this period, by virtue of Miller's need to confront the enemy directly, to find barbaric visual equivalents through which to show the barbarity of the acts, the enormity of the sacrifice, the guilt, the collective insanity. "I implore you to believe this is true," she cabled to her editor.[33] "Believe it" was the title given to her article in the June 1945 issue of *Vogue*, which first published the work.[34] The pictures showed her fanatical need to get behind the more obvious manifestations of the horror and to examine, with the greatest discernment, the very fabric of the crime. What a Goldilocks Miller was, as well. She took her "first bath in weeks" in the Münich house where Hitler had spent so much time during the Third Reich. This is a more obvious note than the nap she took on the bed of Eva Braun, after studying the appalling contents of her medicine chest in a villa a few blocks away.[35] We are comparing two journalists' responses in April 1945 when both crossed unspeakable thresholds. The differences in what they decided to bring out with them on film were in part dictated by their differing assignments. (Miller was essentially acting on her own, though many of her stories ended up in *Vogue*.) But ultimately the issue between them is one of temperament and imagination.

"Believe it!" Miller's pictures cried out. The phrase lies behind the revelations that Susan Meiselas brought out of Nicaragua in 1978–79, captioned: *Children rescued from a house destroyed by a 1000-pound bomb in Managua. They died shortly thereafter,* or *Cuesta del Plomo. Hillside outside Managua, a well-known site of many assassinations carried out by the National Guard. People searched here daily for missing persons* (pl. 138–139). It lies behind the image of a Peruvian shepherdess giving suck to a motherless lamb by Rosalind Solomon or the stump of a man Solomon found at the Swayamanboth Temple in Kathmandu, Nepal, (pl. 135) whose glance holds us in a grip stronger than that of the one good hand he has left. "Believe it" is sufficient to explain the work of Mary Ellen Mark at Mother Teresa's Missions of Charity in Calcutta. In the *Home for the Dying, Calcutta, India* (pl. 141–143), those *in extremis* pierce you, involuntarily take your picture, as if by remote control, their lidless eyes blind apertures.

In such places abject misery runs the paradoxical risk of being stereotyped by the camera. The condition is inherently repetitious; the sensing powers of the photographer are crucial in being able to arouse a response. In Mark's picture of the *Blind Orphan at Shishu Bhawan, Calcutta, India* (pl. 140), the child's ability to know and trust are shown to have evolved from smell and touch, senses completely outside the realm of what the photographer has the power to convey. It is a rare symbol that recognizes the helpless position in which all visual recorders ultimately find themselves.

In the fierce desire to make contact, and recognizing the inadequacy of the mechanism available, artists such as these have lingered with their subjects. I don't know if this is a quality peculiar to the way women photograph, but it is a feature of many pictures in the present selection. Mark returned to the Home for the Dying in 1981 after *Life* first sent her there in 1979. But it is worth noting that since 1968 she has been to India some fourteen times.[36] Rosalind Solomon has traveled there five times. All return—to India, Central America, Peru—to examine more closely, to understand more than what the camera eye alone can provide. As Solomon put it, to "stare into ourselves."[37]

I don't know how many times Linda Connor has been to India. Her work suggests the hero's journey, the myth of eternal return. There are some women whose belief in who they are and what they have to offer as artists emerges through the demands and isolation imposed by traveling great distances. They are the polar opposites of those who find all the richness they need simply by charting a familial routine. Connor's travel alludes to the restless curiosity of such journeying male Victorians as Francis Frith, John Thomson, or Samuel Bourne. There is in her work with the 8 x 10-inch view camera homage paid to her predecessors, but also evidence, in the kind of light that appeals to her, of the period she spent exploring the pictorial perfections of the imperfect Diana camera. This sensibility serves her well. Composing the vistas of Ladakh, her eye suspends sites in a glowing cocoon out of time that speaks eloquently of phantom India. What leads this solitary traveler to seek evidence of the sacred? To let the wash of space enfold her like a ragged sari? As with the billiard player ensconced in her Victorian parlor, Connor surveys instinctively with a cue's clear line of sight. Her instrument embraces infinities that take on qualities of divine mystery. Since she fully accepts the partiality of what her camera is able to retrieve, each picture is an act of faith, as resonant with prayer as the oracles, monks, prayer flags, and Chörtens that govern her holy subjects.

We are following the edge of an instinct, the urge to make contact, not through notes made in passing, after which one is sped away by a cab at the door. The feeling here is of being fully enveloped. If Connor's work records a place through its sacred signs, it also penetrates the outer skin. The light dissolves barriers, infiltrates an inner sanctum. Not many seek this kind of intimacy. It is too perilous, confusing, exhausting.

The *dream* of travel is something else again. Contemplation without having to go anywhere was one of the first lessons photography taught in 1839. Armchair travelers safe with lithographic views could continue with daguerreotypes, or better yet *excursions daguerriennes*. Thinking about the journey is enough for some, as the pinhole camera images of Ruth Thorne-Thomsen point out. Approximations of romantic longing, the primitive technical status of these pictures associates them markedly with the works of photography's earliest moments. Every image turns backward referring to the first, and perhaps quintessential, photographic exotics, Maxime Du Camp and Gustave Flaubert in Egypt in 1850. Each picture is a philosophical meditation, hardly a record of anything making us reflect on the history of exoticism, and the camera's fictive role in the traveler's quest.[38]

WHAT BEAST MUST I ADORE?

There was a time when visitors to the studio of New York painter Lee Krasner could find scrawled on the wall these lines from Rimbaud's *A Season in Hell*: "To whom shall I hire myself? What beast must I adore? What holy image is attacked? What hearts shall I break? What lie must I maintain? In what blood tread?"[39] The ravings of the adolescent poet of Charleville suggested to Krasner, a strong woman, something potent. Perhaps they represented the pitfalls she felt she faced in a man's world. In a way the lines place Krasner within a generation of women for whom Rimbaud's fears had real bearing on the way they saw they must conduct their lives as artists. It had a lot to do with compromise, acknowledgments, and the treachery in hero worship.

Always exquisitely sincere, Mrs. Cameron probably started it by giving Sir John Herschel all the credit as her "priest and teacher."[40] Others have happily knelt at the feet of guiding masters and put their testimonials in writing. The masters were not necessarily male, as the English portrait photographer Mrs. Edith Middleton, called Madame Yevonde, made clear in the 1920s in describing the fame of her illustrious tutor. "The great" Madame Lallie Charles had

> *. . . attained a huge success. With characteristic boldness she swept away all preconceived notions in portrait photography, and won fame by placing her sitters against a plain white background, softly vignetted. This also had never been done before with any notable success. She was the possessor of a very brilliant personality which must have contributed largely and aided her considerably."*[41]

Madame Charles only fueled Madame Yevonde's passionate belief that: "Women as a rule make better photographers than men, possessing to a greater degree . . . personality, tact, patience, and intuition . . . and of course, their inherent knowledge of clothes and eye for detail is a great asset in a profession."[42]

In a different vein, there is Tina Modotti, writing in 1928 to Edward Weston:

> *You don't know how often the thought comes to me of all I owe to you for having been* the one important *being at a certain time of my life, when I did not know which way to turn, the one and only vital guidance and influence that initiated me in this work that is not only a means of livelihood but a work that I have come to love with real passion and that offers such possibilities of expression . . . Really Edward dear—my heart goes out to you with such a deep feeling of gratitude . . . I would like you to know how genuine and deep my appreciation is and will always be!*[43]

Citing these acknowledgments is not meant to detract from the truths they contain. Every artist can ascribe his or her success to the influence of guiding spirits who were there at the right moment. Madame Yevonde was only seventeen when she apprenticed herself to Lallie Charles. It is almost too obvious to mention that for all his technical genius, Herschel could have done very little to turn Julia Margaret Cameron into the titanic original who completely transformed the idea of photographic portraiture. Equally, Madame Yevonde's "world" of socialites and noble women turned into "Goddesses" with the trichrome carbro or Vivex color process was stunningly innovative in itself. This is not to mention the photographer's extraordinary ability to entice her sitters into becoming mythical presences before the lens, which may have been influenced by Madame Charles's "very brilliant personality." But we have to credit Yevonde herself for eliciting the intense femininity from her subjects, whether they played themselves, faked tears to play Niobe, or caressed a cow for the part of Europa yearning for union with a white bull.[44]

What Modotti leaves unsaid—and why not? although perhaps she was unable to acknowledge it to herself at the time—is that for all his "vital guidance," Weston could not have made her into the artist she ultimately became, for it is clear enough how unlike Weston's her work is. That it stems from a very different kind of ego emerges in a letter she wrote to him in 1925, which shows how tortuous she found her artistic path: "I have not been very 'creative' Edward as you can see—less than a print a month. That is terrible! And yet it is not lack of interest as much as lack of discipline and power of execution. I am convinced *now* that as far as creation is concerned (outside the creation of species) women are negative—They are too petty and lack power of concentration and the faculty to be wholly absorbed by *one* thing."[45]

That year Modotti produced the *Telephone Wire Composition in Mexico* (pl. 48) and in 1926 the *Hands of a Marionette Player* (pl. 49). She seems to have regarded the power lines less as a symbol of technological progress, as Margaret Bourke-White would do with cables on the George Washington Bridge, than as a variable symmetry, elegant and spare, yet tremulous in the details like the awkward phrases of her writing. Characteristic of Modotti, the *Marionette Player* makes a good pendant to the telephone wires' yielding tautness. In relaxing the strings, the hands communicate like creatures at rest. In the same spirit her attraction to roses past their prime (pl. 44) reminds us of an over-ripe nudity, a fleshly sensuality that probably would have overwhelmed Weston's pristine sensibility.

Indebtedness, and how women artists express it, is tricky. Krasner sensed the problem as the way in which women find that acknowledgment compromised them, locked them in. When Margaret Bourke-White is caught saying things like "I can do anything I want to do with these men," it sounds like sexual bragging, but it also has overtones of a survivor's self-coaching.[46] Which beasts did Bourke-White feel she had to adore? What hearts break? To whom should she hire herself? She had her masters, but she wouldn't let them imprison her. If her capacity to escape the shackles of Modotti's kind of ambivalence makes her slightly repulsive, at the same time we have a very clear idea of who she thought she was as an artist, for better or worse. This is less true for others. Look at the work of Helen Levitt, whose achievement most still link to that of her master Cartier-Bresson, a notion she is responsible for promoting. It is clear that to identify the differences between these artists is to acknowledge Levitt's profound originality.

Similarly, how far does it take us in examining the work of Graciela Iturbide to see her simply as a student of Manuel Alvarez Bravo?[47] She uses her sense of the bizarre, of the incongruous, almost as a weapon, against which Bravo's work seems tepid. Perhaps Iturbide's art is too theatrical, strives too much after surrealistic effects; but where women are concerned she pursues with insistent direction a theme that concerns us here. In posing women next to reptiles, as if the animals were trophies, or showing women wearing veritable "crowns" of iguanas (pl. 136–137), we have the same uneasy feeling that Goya conveyed in portraying ruthless *majas* plucking their victims like chickens. Iturbide's women associate comfortably with monsters in a way that likens them to monsters themselves, heroines of tooth and claw. This is not to put them in a strictly dangerous category. Or is it? Iturbide acknowledges something that women rarely confront and men run from in terror (Goya's fascination had a moral purpose): the idea of the monster within the woman. By this is not meant their destructive power, but rather the opposite—the powers of concentration that allow a woman, or anyone, to be an artist, Modotti's contrary claim notwithstanding. Iturbide sees that female generative powers are not necessarily maternal and nurturing. They can exist with the rapaciousness of a crocodile.

If Lee Krasner had to continually ask herself what beast she should adore, there are artists today who might respond: the beast within ourselves. We are familiar enough with the way Cindy Sherman uses herself as a filter, assuming the roles of a history of female incarnations, not only stereotypes but a full palette of what has been thought about women by men and by women themselves, from the self-deprecating neurotic, to the fatuous I-don't-know-myself-do-you? type. After years of trying on various personas, in 1989 Sherman turned to a related theme, showing a lugubrious "self" concealed beneath theatrical hair and plastic breasts (pl. 200). We hardly see "her" anymore. The woman gives way to a monster, a beast *with one live eye.* Sherman's vision of the ridiculous serves a purpose, for her experiments in depicting feminine debilitation force us to recall the former role of female archetypes in which monstrousness, creative inspiration, and spiritual power were forcibly united.

Today, more than ever before, considering photography by women means compensating for decades of ignorance and neglect. It means beginning at the beginning, seeking out obscure or lost careers in order to reconstruct a pantheon. But our interest in women's photography goes more deeply than verifying the art historian's task or the imperatives of the feminist corrective, or even in determining whether an artist is being true to the medium in terms of the age of progress that invented it. What matters in camera art by women is whether they can bring to it the emotional weight carried by the other arts, whether women can give broader evidence of the feminine in terms of an awareness of the enormous psychic privilege that the human imagination has granted them since the beginning of time. Käsebier accomplishes this so modestly with her billiard player, by the sheer force of the glance that commands an arena of influence.

The work of many other women continues to redefine the limits of this arena with relentless energy that recognizes the intervention of an overwhelming spiritual presence in all that is associated with The Feminine. Women have discovered in the camera—paltry toy—a vehicle of the feminine spirit in which awareness is inextricably involved with the exploitation of space, intimate and immense, and with "the stream of time."[48] Should we not continue to demand images that explore the primordial mysteries and inspire us to levels of mythic imagination where women's power is in the grandest sense guaranteed, through not only the archetypal "good mothers" but through "terrible" ones as well? In photography's brief history women have helped show us that the camera can be made to yield images that nourish many conflicting desires of the unconscious mind, transport us beyond the confines of the document into more uncertain confrontations with possibility, with facts' dark secrets and terrible truths. Such pictures of complexity are the ones we seek, images of meditation to ponder at the end of our century, to console us in the next millennium.

EUGENIA PARRY JANIS

NOTES

1. Eudora Welty, *One Writer's Beginnings* (Cambridge: Harvard University Press, 1984), p. 104.

2. Probably never exhibited at the time of its making, the image was hardly known until recently and exists in three documented copies: one is in the J. Paul Getty Museum, Malibu; another was sold at Christies, New York in the spring of 1989; another belongs to Gertrude Käsebier's granddaughter, Elizabeth (O'Malley) MacFarland, who in a telephone conversation with Barbara L. Michaels on July 27, 1989, positively identified the work as depicting her "mother (Gertrude Elizabeth Käsebier O'Malley) and Uncle Billy." In the same conversation, Mrs. MacFarland stressed how much her mother had loved billiards, and that the game being played was not actually billiards but a variant called "telephone."

3. Barbara L. Michaels, who is preparing a monograph on Gertrude Käsebier, generously consulted with me regarding this scene's date, location, and players; she is in no way responsible for any false conclusions I may have drawn from our discussions.

4. Willie Mosconi, *On Pocket Billiards*, New York, Crown Publishers, Inc., 1975, pp. 22-32. I am indebted to Bunny Harvey for this source and for her insights into the art of pool.

5. William Innes Homer, et al., *A Pictorial Heritage: The Photographs of Gertrude Käsebier* [exhibition catalogue] (Wilmington: The University of Delaware and the Delaware Art Museum, 1979), p. 17. (Italics mine.)

6. Regarding the fact that some have identified the billiard player as Käsebier herself, Barbara Michaels has made known to me several portraits by Käsebier of Gertrude Elizabeth (b. December 16, 1878) from 1899 (playing the piano; and her wedding portrait), both of which show off a well-corseted middle. (Käsebier was renowned for rejecting such restrictions and wearing Chinese-style smocks that concealed her waist.) A photograph of young Gertrude from around 1909 playing Cat's Cradle with her two children shows that she has filled out to match exactly the more matronly form of the billiard player, which suggests a date of c. 1909 for that image and confirms that its central figure can only be that of the daughter and not the more matronly, and by then corsetless, mother.

7. Respectively in *The Press*, October 13, 1895; and in *The Ladies Home Journal*, vol. 14, no. 10 (September 1897). Both are cited by Constance W. Glenn and Leland Rice in *Frances Benjamin Johnston: Woman of Class and Station* (Long Beach: The Art Museum and Galleries and the Center for Southern California Studies in the Visual Arts, California State University), pp. 16, 18.

8. Charles Caffin, "Mrs. Käsebier's Work—An Appreciation," *Camera Work*, no. 1 (January 1903), p. 17.

9. Lincoln Kirstein, "Introduction," *The Hampton Album* (New York: The Museum of Modern Art/Doubleday, 1966), p. 11.

10. This information comes from Gérard Lévy, Paris.

11. Hans P. Kraus, Jr., "Anna Atkins," *Sun Pictures: Early British Photographs on Paper*, Catalogue One (Hans P. Kraus, Jr., Fine Photographs, n.d.), unpaginated. Lady Talbot's work has not survived.

12. This derives from Gordon Baldwin's examination of the Sir David Brewster Album in the Department of Photography at The J. Paul Getty Museum, Malibu.

13. Larry J. Schaaf, *Sun Gardens, Victorian Photograms by Anna Atkins* (St. Andrews: Crawford Centre for the Arts of the University of St. Andrews, 1988), unpaginated. Schaaf goes into Atkins's father's close connections with Talbot.

14. Ibid., unpaginated. In Atkins's circle was another amateur botanist, Anne Dixon (1799–1864). A Vicar's wife and Atkins's childhood friend, she contributed to many parts of *British Algae*. Virtually nothing is known about her photographic pursuits except that she played an important role in Atkins's projects even after the work on algae in 1854, when she turned to ferns. Some impressions attributed to Atkins may well be by Dixon.

15. Schaaf cites Mrs. Fulhame's *An Essay on Combustion with a View to a New Art of Dying and Painting* (London: J. Cooper, 1794) as the source.

16. *Sally Mann: Still Time*, text and photographs by Sally Mann (Clifton Forge, Virginia: Allegheny Highlands Arts and Crafts Center, Inc., 1988), unpaginated.

17. From my conversation with W. Snyder MacNeil, August 10, 1989.

18. Mike Weaver, "A Divine Art of Photography," *Whisper of the Muse, The Overstone Album and Other Photographs* by Julia Margaret Cameron (Malibu: The J. Paul Getty Museum, 1986), p. 57. Quoted are extracts from her poem "On a Portrait."

19. Ibid., p. 66. From a letter to her son Hardinge Hay Cameron, in the Archives of the History of Art, The Getty Center for the History of Art and the Humanities, Los Angeles.

20. Mary Panzer provides the fullest discussion of Louise Deshong Woodbridge presently available, in *Philadelphia Naturalistic Photography 1865–1906* [catalogue] (New Haven: Yale University Art Gallery, 1982), pp. 48–49. I am grateful to Barbara L. Michaels for this source.

21. Striking examples of this process of restoration abound. See for example the revelatory monographs on Lee Miller by Antony Penrose *The Lives of Lee Miller* (New York: Holt, Rinehart and Winston, 1985), and by Jane Livingston (see note 32), but they can take minimalist forms. Jill Quasha, a New York photography dealer, announced her discovery of the exquisite work of Marjorie Content describing the photographer's career in hardly more than fifty words on a postcard announcement sent through the mail like a haiku: "Marjorie Content. . . close friend of Alfred Stieglitz and Georgia O'Keeffe . . . started photographing in the 1920s . . . influenced by the artists at '291' . . . photographed images of New York streets and Washington Square Park, flowers, clouds, New Mexico . . . brought great craftsmanship to her mostly unique prints . . . stopped photographing in the 1930s . . . lives in Pennsylvania."

22. A recent exhibition catalogue discussing the work of photographer Barbara Morgan at the International Center of Photography in New York elicited the following "what's that again?" response from a glib *New Yorker* magazine reviewer: "The catalogue says that Morgan turned to photography in order to have time for her children, suggesting that other mediums, which she abandoned for a while, required more of her. That's a plug the advertising industry missed—photography as a time-saving medium for Mother. It sounds less lazy than 'You push the button, we do the rest.'"—"Photography," *The New Yorker*, June 19, 1989, p. 15.

23. For example, in Richard Thomson's *Degas: The Nudes* (London: Thames and Hudson, 1988), which I have reviewed for *The Burlington Magazine* (forthcoming), female nudity is discussed to verify Degas's "conventional male views" (p. 11), his "actively scabrous curiosity" (p. 82) "consistent with his class and upbringing" (p. 12). Women in Degas's art, says Thomson are "under a threat . . . from the intrusive male gaze" (p. 207). But nowhere does Thomson give the artist credit for having actively conferred on female nudes the monumental strength that comes from the very power of their preoccupation, their passionately expressed detachment from all eyes upon them. And in an astonishing collection of provocative essays, *Fragments for a History of the Human Body*, ed. by Michel Feher with Ramona Naddaff and Nadia Tazi, 3 vols. (New York: Zone, 1989), an essay questioning patriarchal portrayals of primitive societies introduces the subject with a classic feminist summation of women's position in Western society:

> *No observer of Western society will deny the emphatic male domination by which it is marked . . . the recognized and valued activities are those that men carry out . . . there is a major sex and a minor sex . . . a "strong" spirit and a "weak" spirit. The natural, congenital weakness of women implies and legitimizes the subject even of their bodies. (Françoise Héritier-Augé, "Older Women, Stout-Hearted Women, Women of Substance," pp. 281–82).*

24. The best critical summary of this consciousness is by Griselda Pollock, *Vision and Difference, Femininity, Feminism and Histories of Art* (London and New York: Routledge, 1988), in which she states, "Thus feminist artists concerned to explicate the character of women's oppression within classed and racially divided patriarchal societies cannot be content to describe its appearances and symptoms. Structural determinations need to be excavated and tracked through their articulation in representation." This introduces *Post Partum Document* and other photography by Mary Kelly and others, pp. 165–66ff.

25. From my conversation with Maria Morris Hambourg, August 11, 1989.

26. Robert Coles, *The Darkness and the Light: Photographs by Doris Ulmann* (Millerton, NY: Aperture, 1974), pp. 8–12.

27. Eudora Welty, "Literature and the Lens," *Vogue*, August 1, 1944, p. 105.

28. Eudora Welty, *One Writer's Beginnings*, p. 85.

29. Welty, "Literature and the Lens," p. 105.

30. Kirstein, p. 11.

31. Daniel Dixon, "A Universal Language," *Dorothea Lange, Eloquent Witness, An Exhibition of Vintage Photographs* (Chicago: Edwynn Houk Gallery, 1989), p. 7.

32. See Jane Livingston, *Lee Miller, Photographer* (London and New York: Thames and Hudson, 1989), pp. 76–77, 82.

33. Ibid., p. 77.

34. Ibid., p. 82.

35. Ibid., p. 89.

36. David Featherstone, *Mary Ellen Mark Photographs of Mother Teresa's Missions of Charity in Calcutta India* (Carmel: The Friends of Photography, 1985), Untitled 39, p. 6.

37. Arthur Ollman, *Rosalind Solomon, Photographs 1976–1987* (Tucson: Etherton Gallery, 1988), from statement by Solomon on back cover of catalogue.

38. Similarly, "The mental theater" of Barbara Ess, as in her 1986 series, "Food for the Moon," also relies on the obfuscating poetry of pinhole camera work.

39. *Eleanor Munroe, Originals, American Women Artists* (New York: Simon and Schuster, 1982), p. 111. For the original French see Wallace Fowlie, *Complete Works of Rimbaud* (1966): "A qui me louer? Quelle bête fait-il adorer? Quelle sainte image attaque-t-on? Quels coeurs briserai-je? Quel mensonge dois je tenir?—Dans quel sang marcher?"

40. Weaver, p. 15.

41. Ron Callender, "Madame Yevonde's World," *The British Journal of Photography*, January 21, 1988, note ii, p. 15. Perhaps Irving Penn should look into this claim for priority regarding the "plain white background."

42. Ibid., p. 12.

43. Letter 28.1, given a date of January 8, 1928, reproduced in full in Amy Stark, "The Letters of Tina Modotti to Edward Weston," *The Archive* (University of Arizona, Tucson: Center for Creative Photography), research series no. 22 (January 1986), pp. 54–55.

44. Callender, "Madame Yevonde's World," p. 14.

45. Letter 25.4, dated July 7, 1925 in Stark, "Letters of Tina Modotti," p. 39.

46. Vicki Goldberg, *Margaret Bourke-White: A Biography* (Reading: Addison-Wesley Publishing Company, Inc., Radcliffe Biography Series, 1987). The author makes this line the title of chapter 8.

47. See *Sueños de Papel: Graciela Iturbide*, presentación de Veronica Volkow (México, D.F.: Fondo de Cultura Económica, 1985), p. 9.

48. Erich Neumann, *The Great Mother: An Analysis of the Archetype* (Princeton, N J: Princeton University Press, Bollingen Series XLVII, 1972), pp. 226–27.

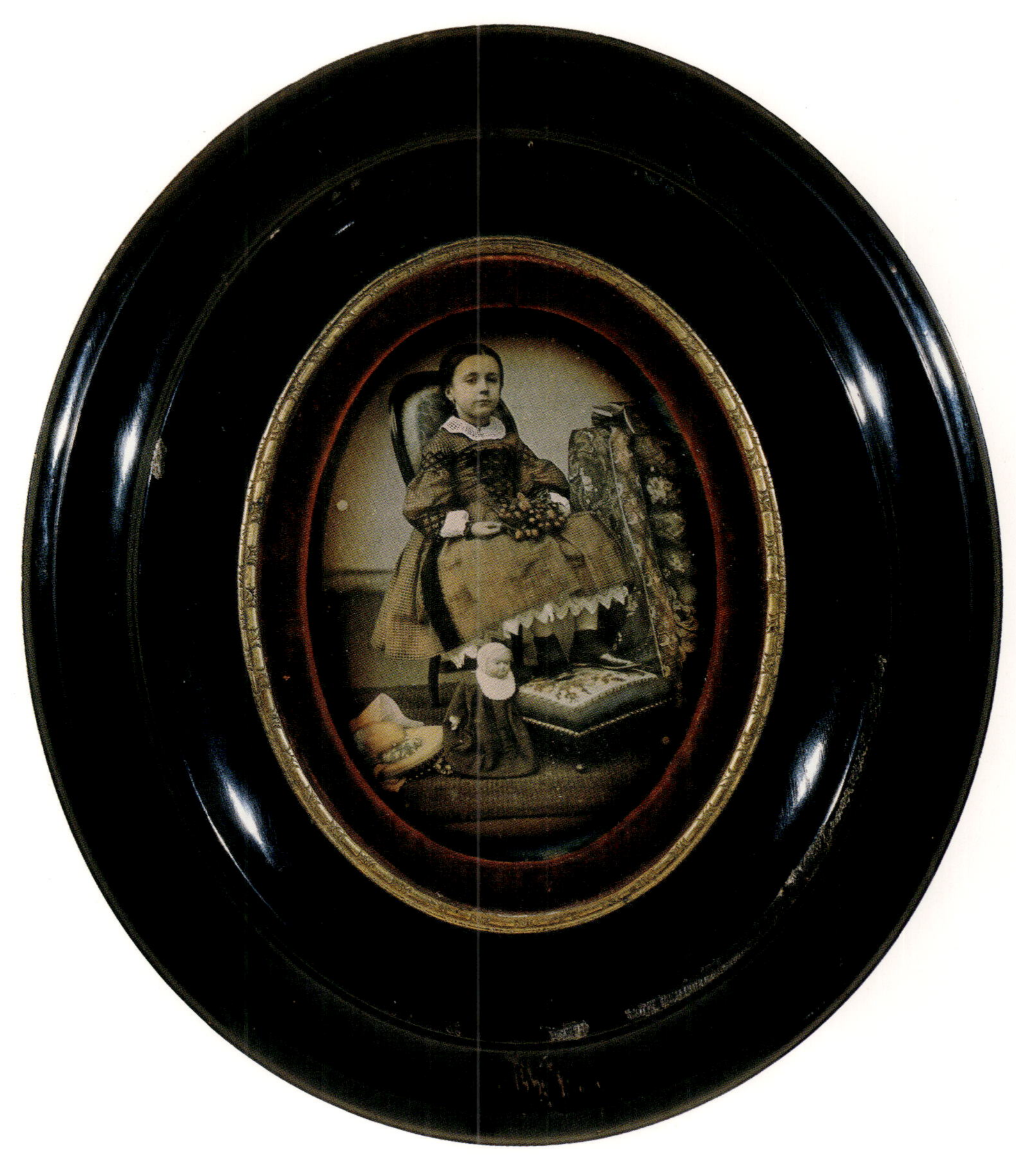

1 · Maria Chambefort · **Stéphanie Poyet, agée de 7 ans** · c. 1850

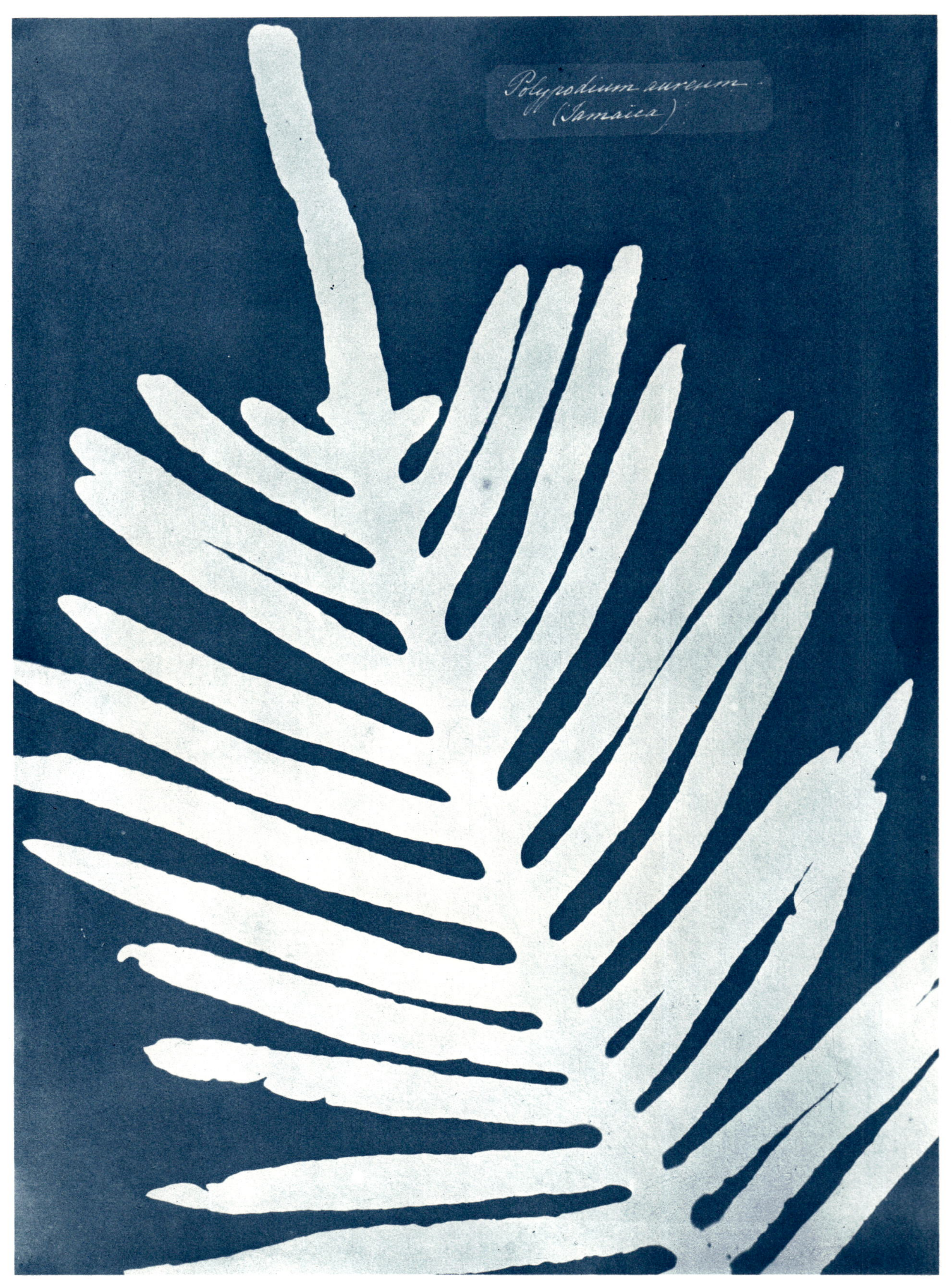

2 · Anna Atkins · **Polypodium aureum (Jamaica)** · c. 1854

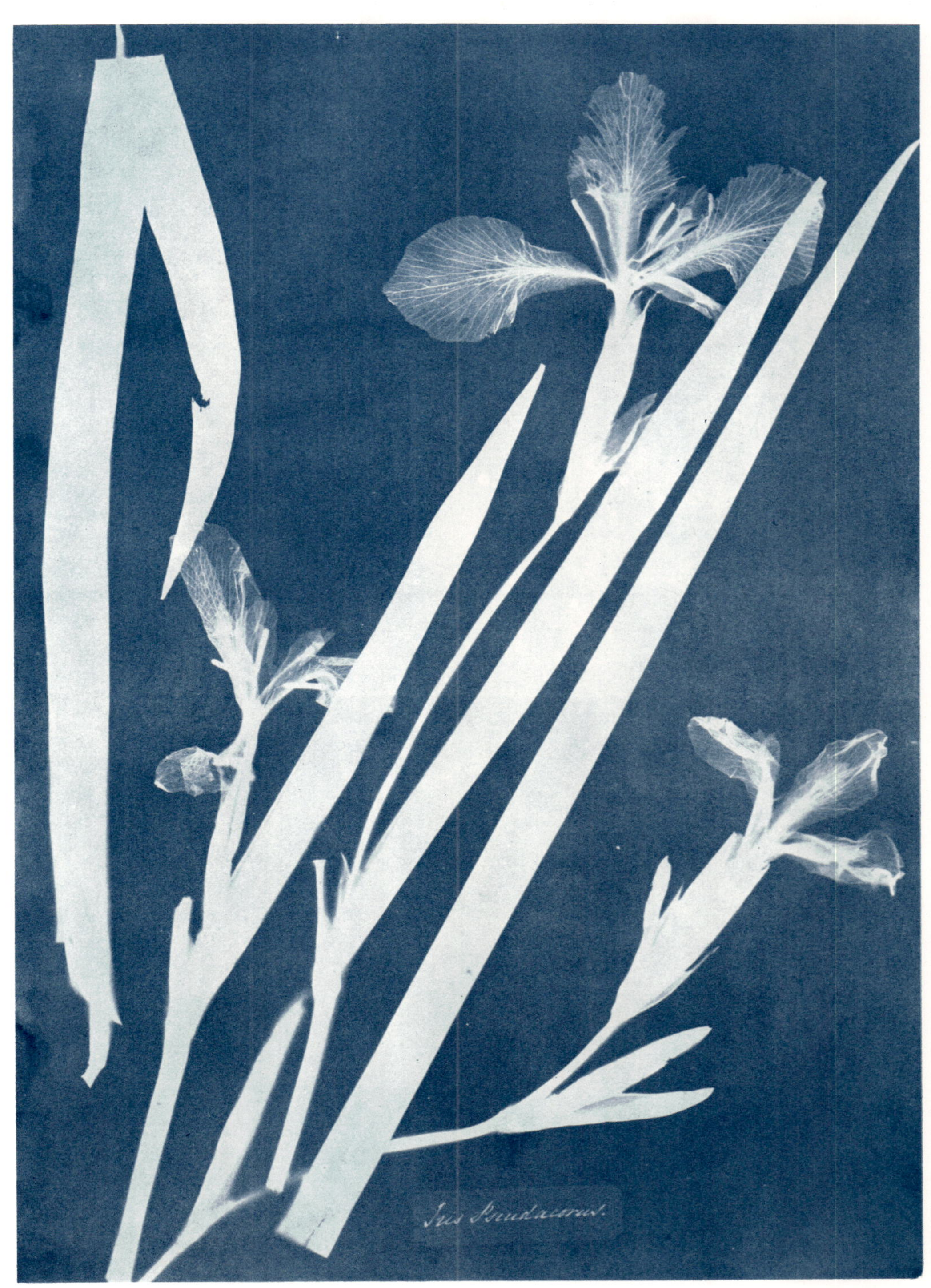

3 · Anna Atkins · **Iris pseudacorus** · c. 1861

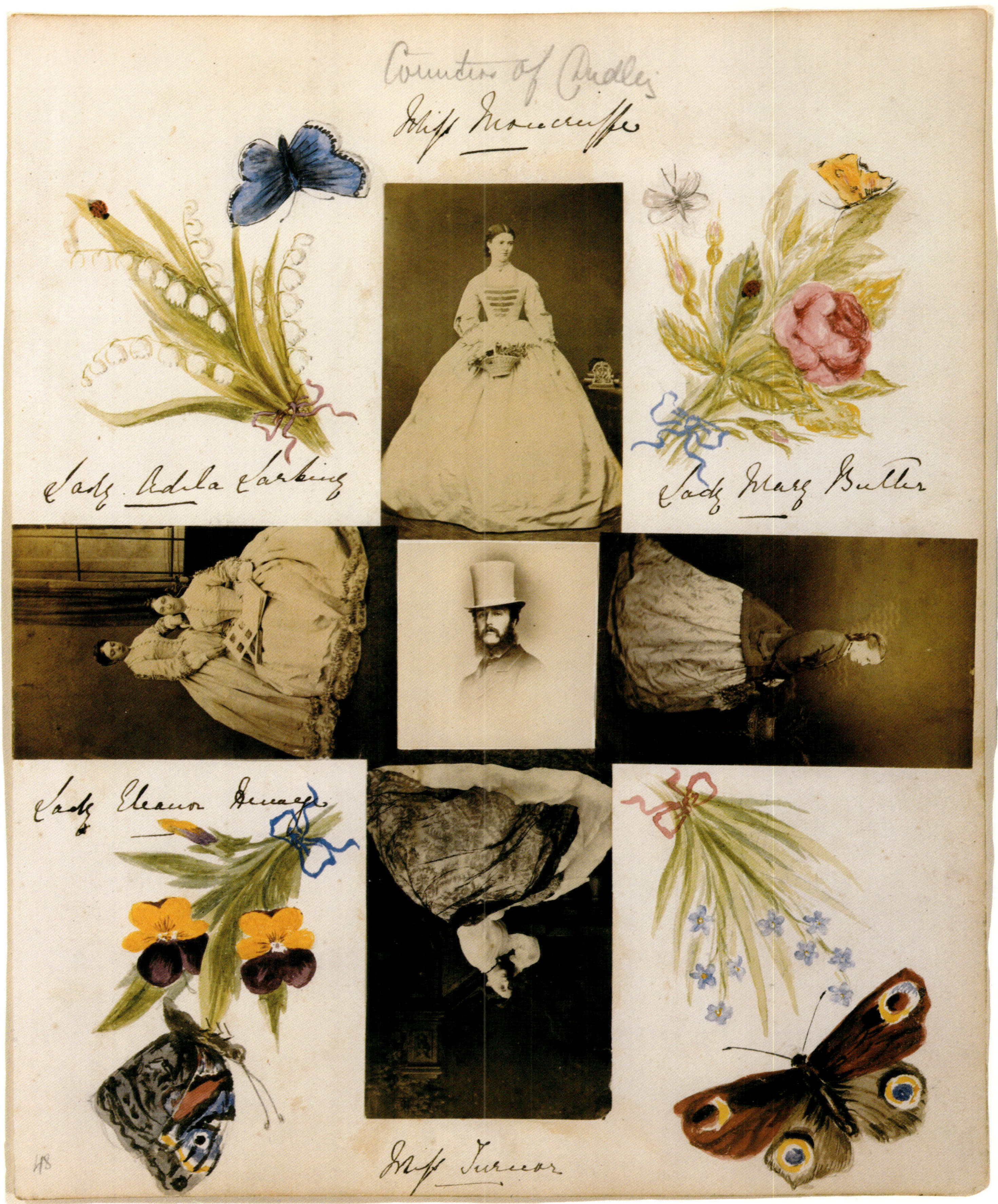

4 · Lady Filmer · Untitled · c. 1864

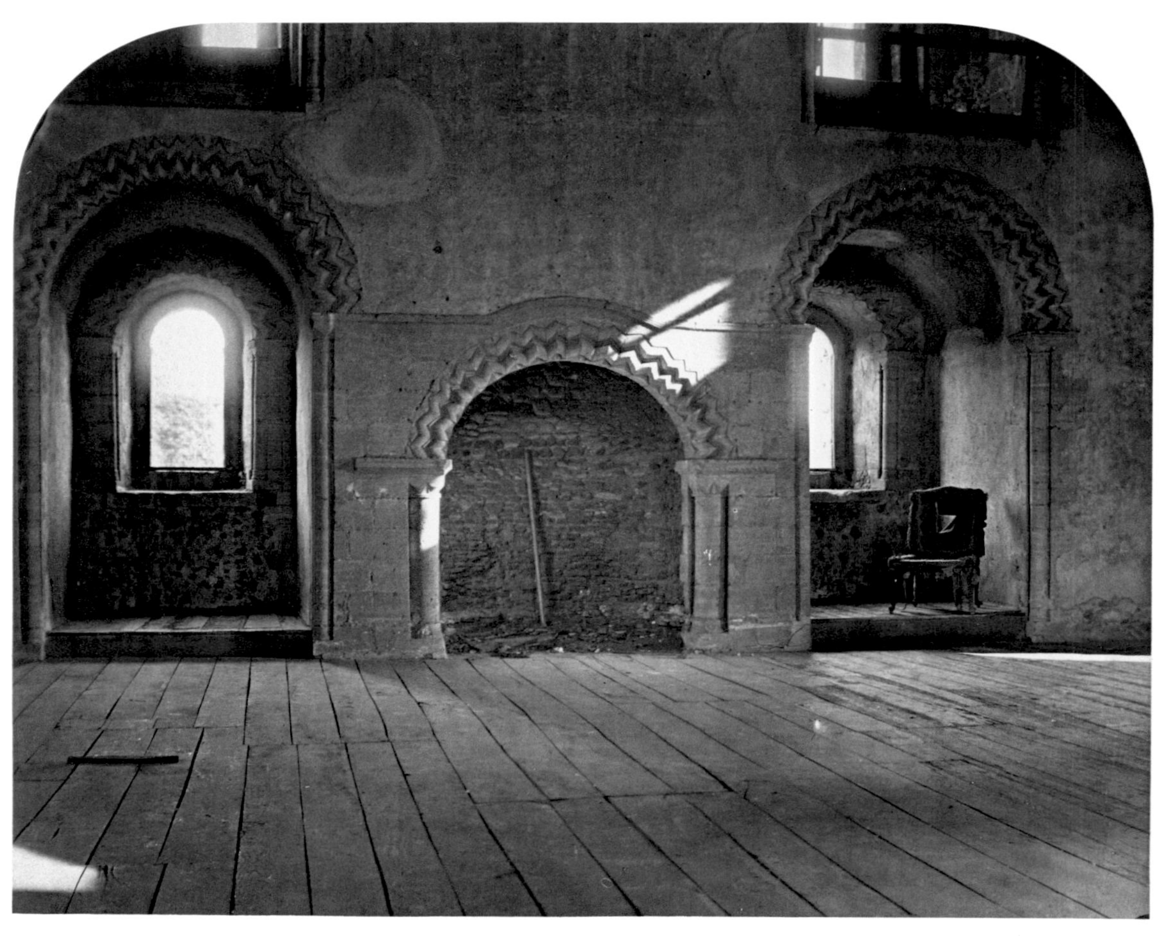

5 · Lucy Fleming · **Interior, Castle Hedington, Essex** · c. 1864

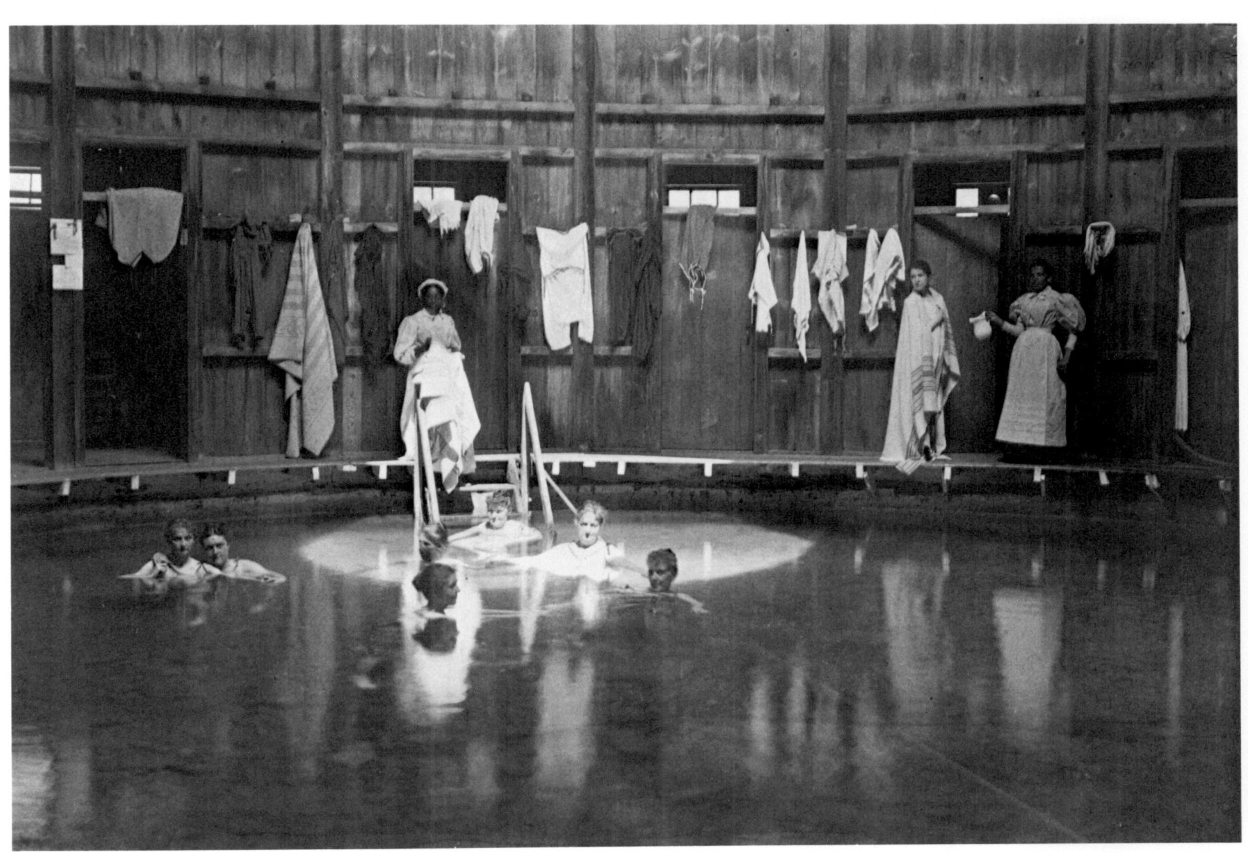

6 · Louise Deshong Woodbridge · **Ladies' Pool** · c. 1890

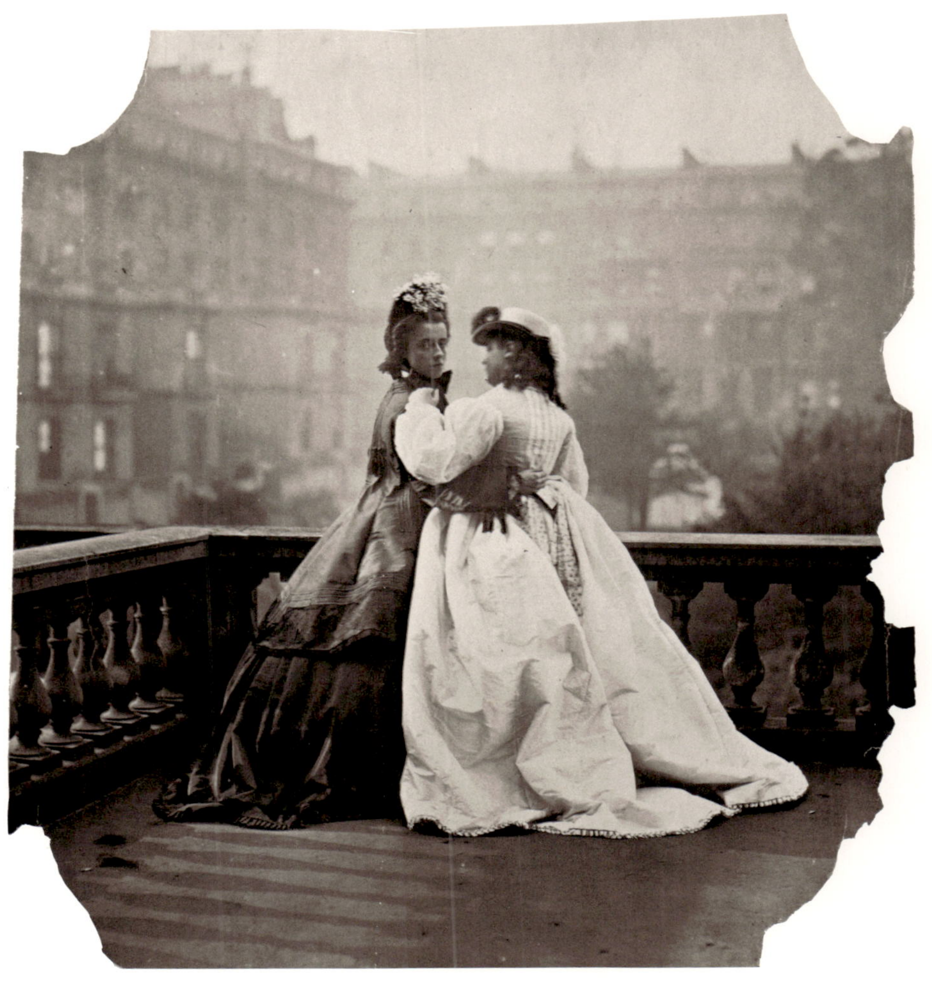

7 · Lady Clementina Hawarden · Photographic study · c. 1862–63

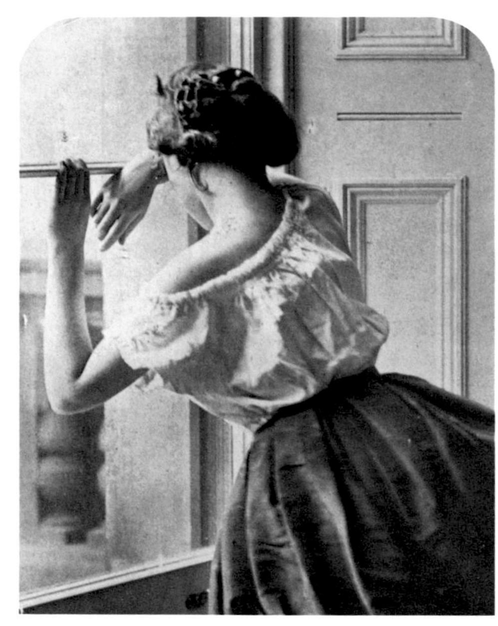

8 · Lady Clementina Hawarden · Photographic study · Early 1860s

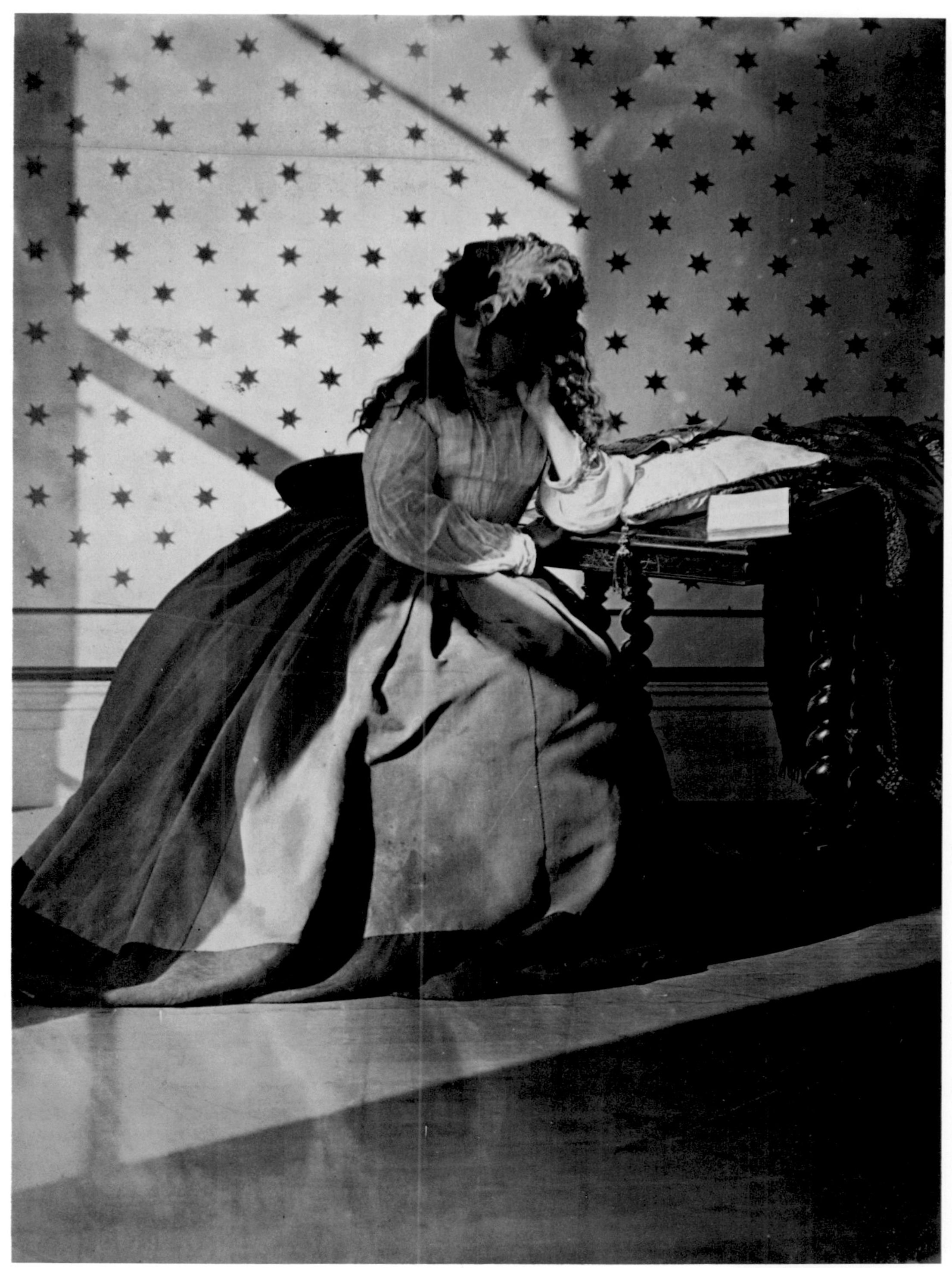

9 · Lady Clementina Hawarden · Photographic study · Early 1860s

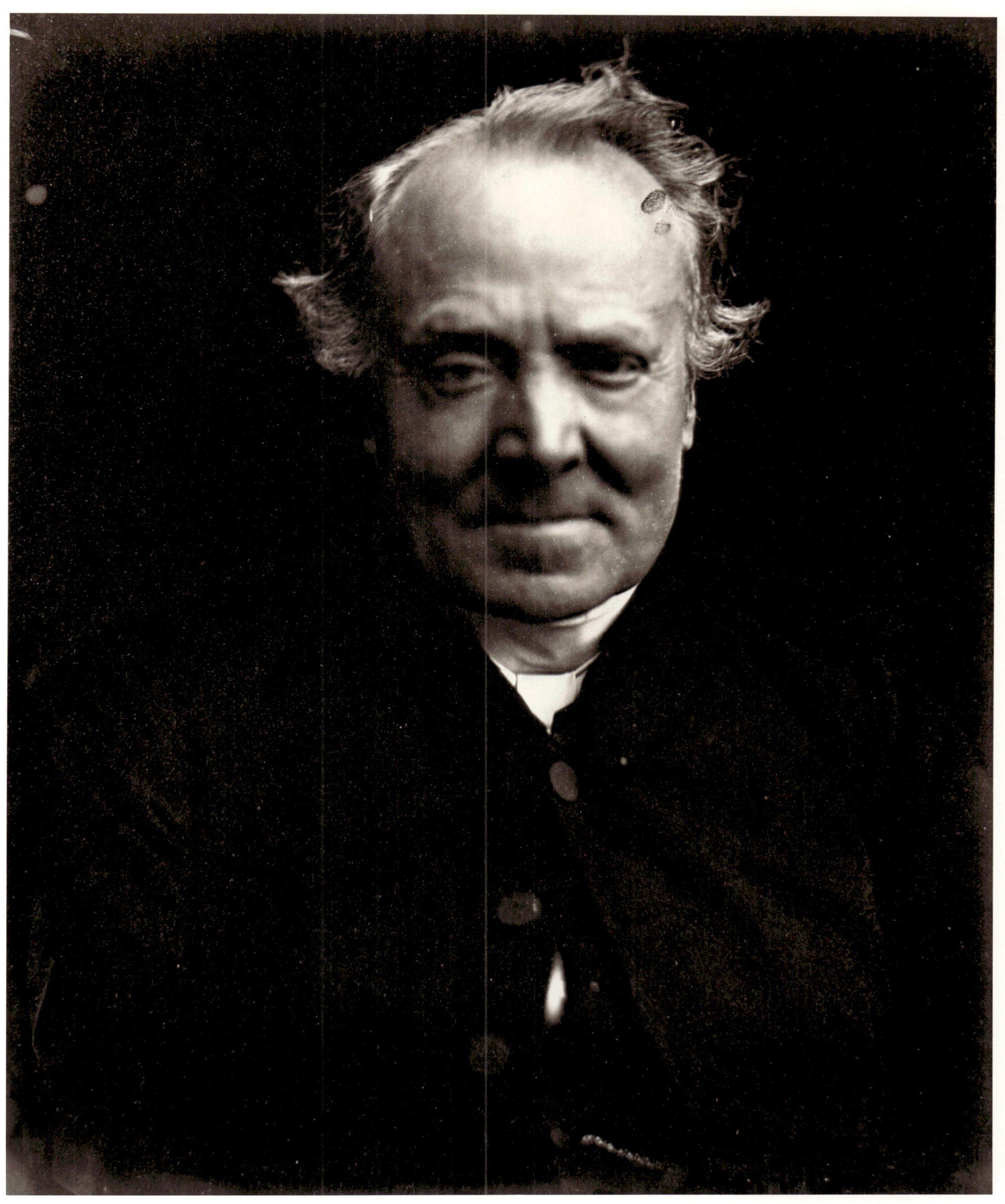

10 · Julia Margaret Cameron · **Rev. J. Isaacson, Rector of Freshwater** · 1864

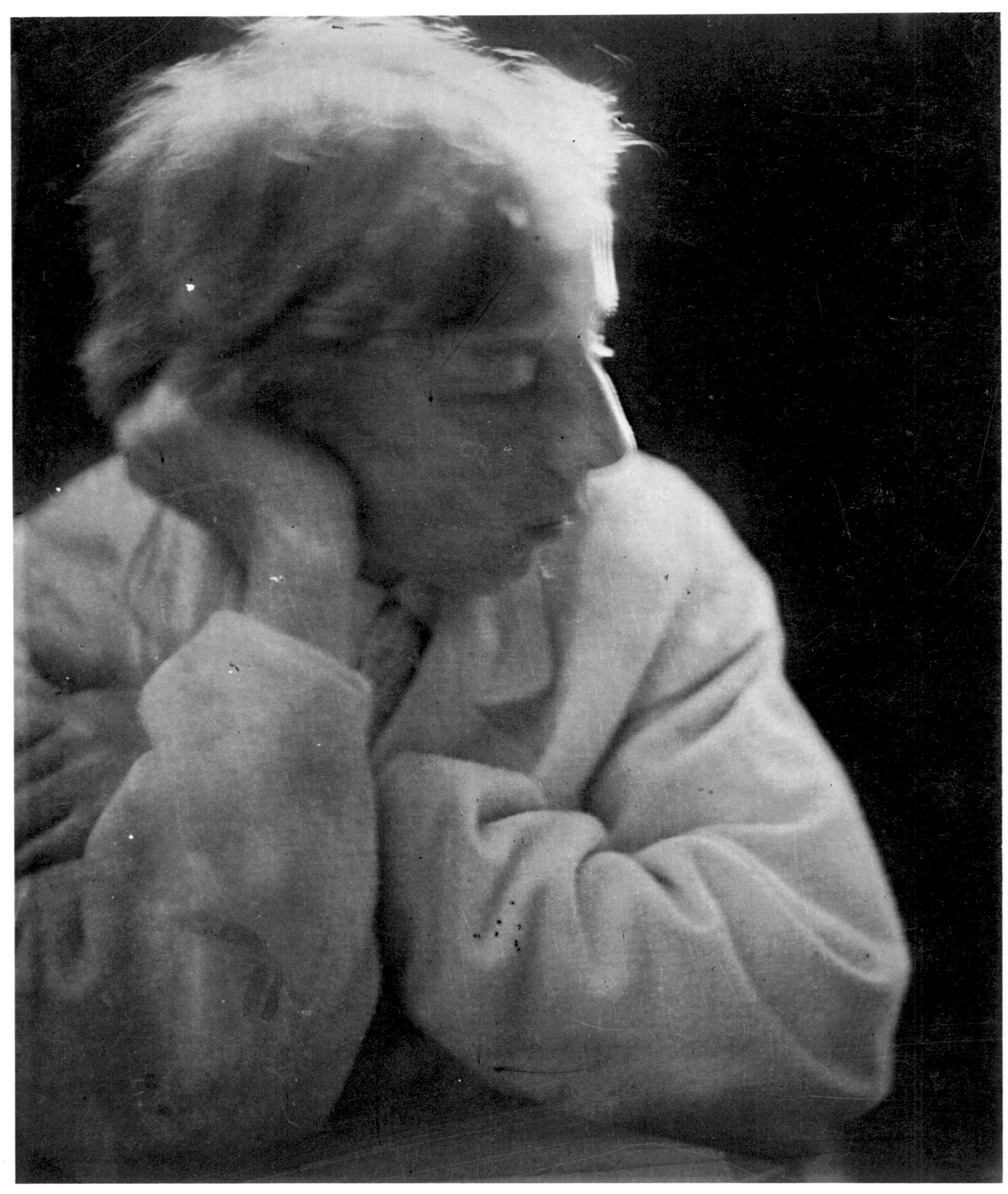

11 · Julia Margaret Cameron · **Hallam Tennyson** · 1867

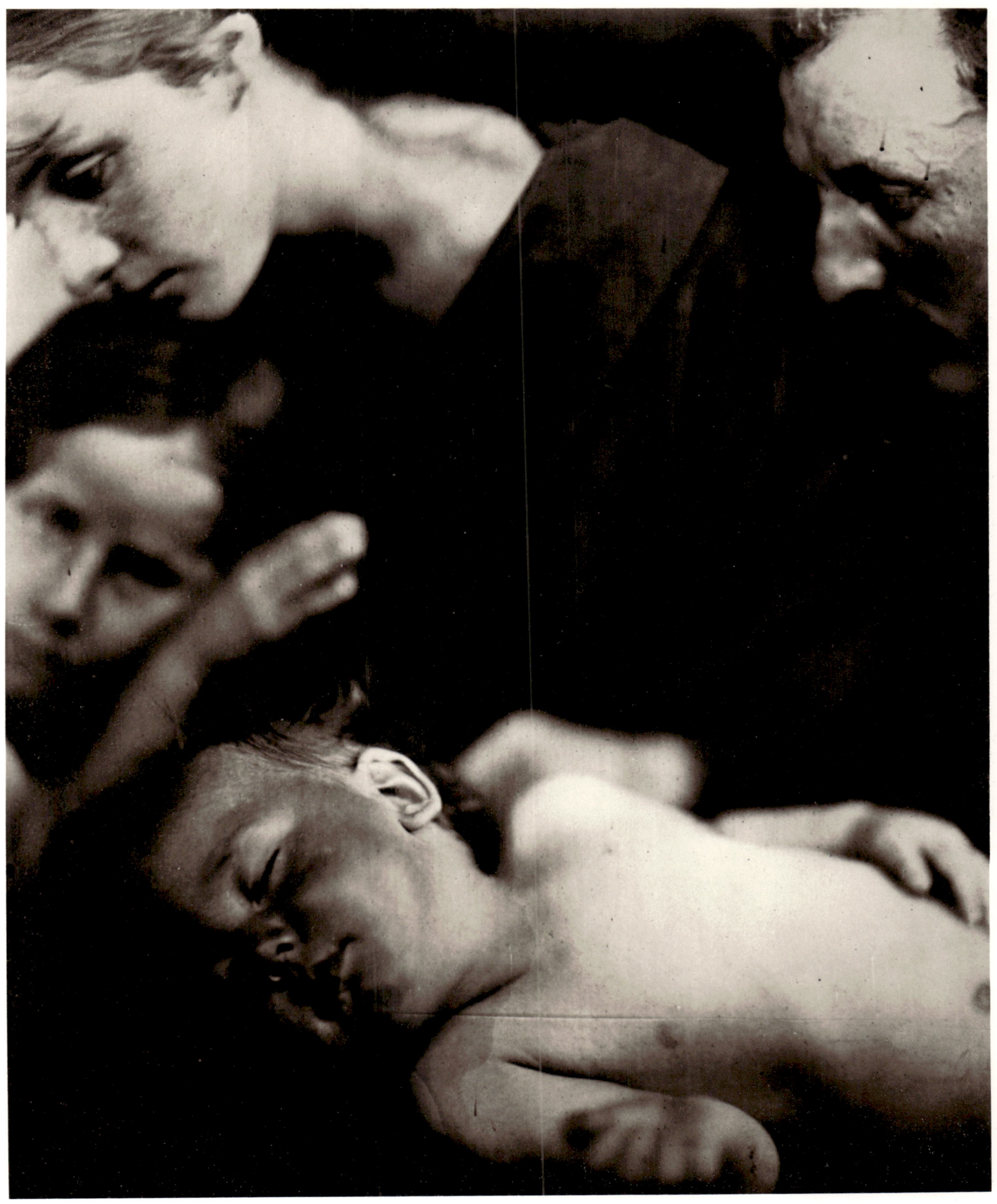

12 · Julia Margaret Cameron · **Prayer and Praise**/**Freshwater** · 1865

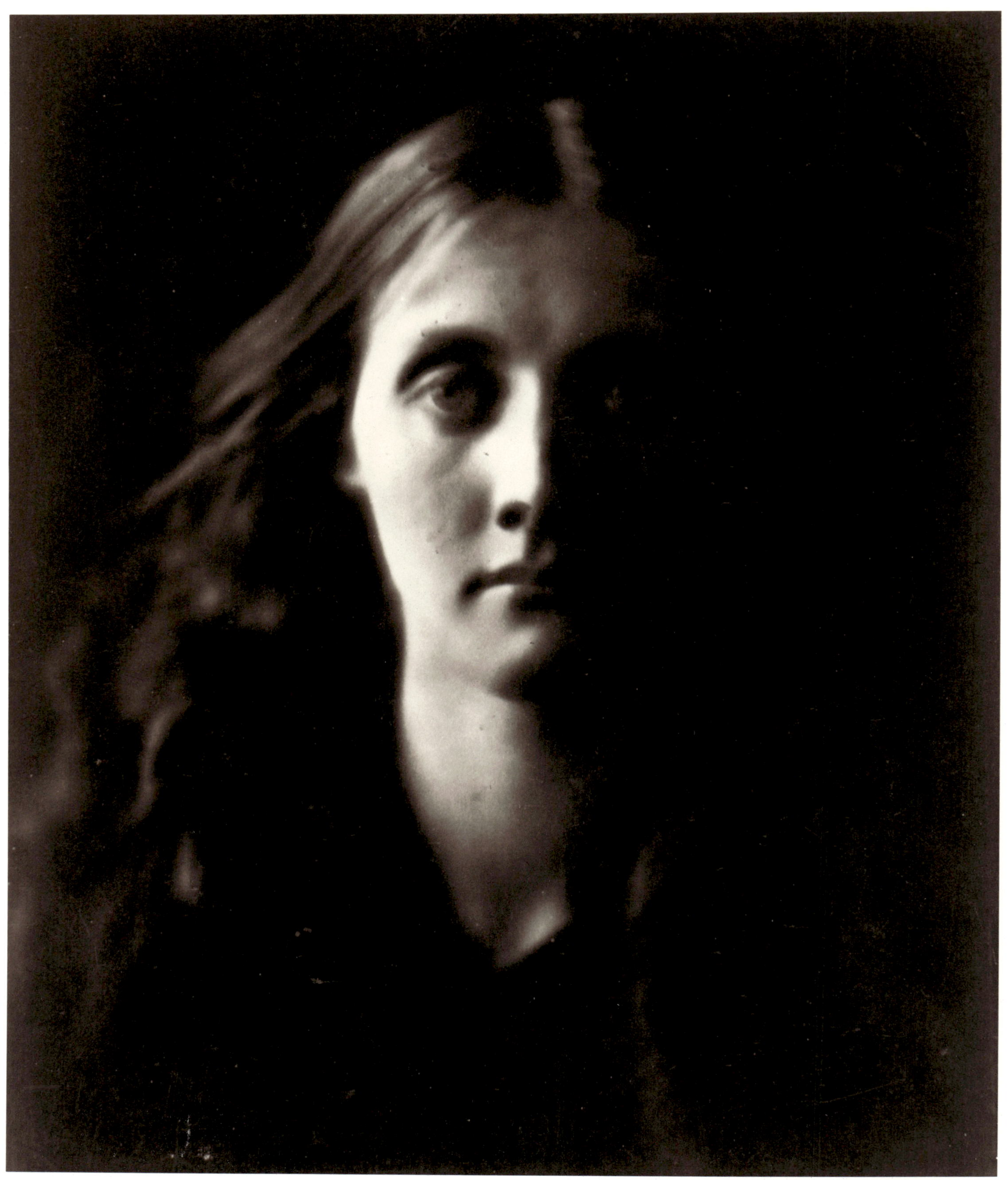

13 · Julia Margaret Cameron · **Stella** · 1869

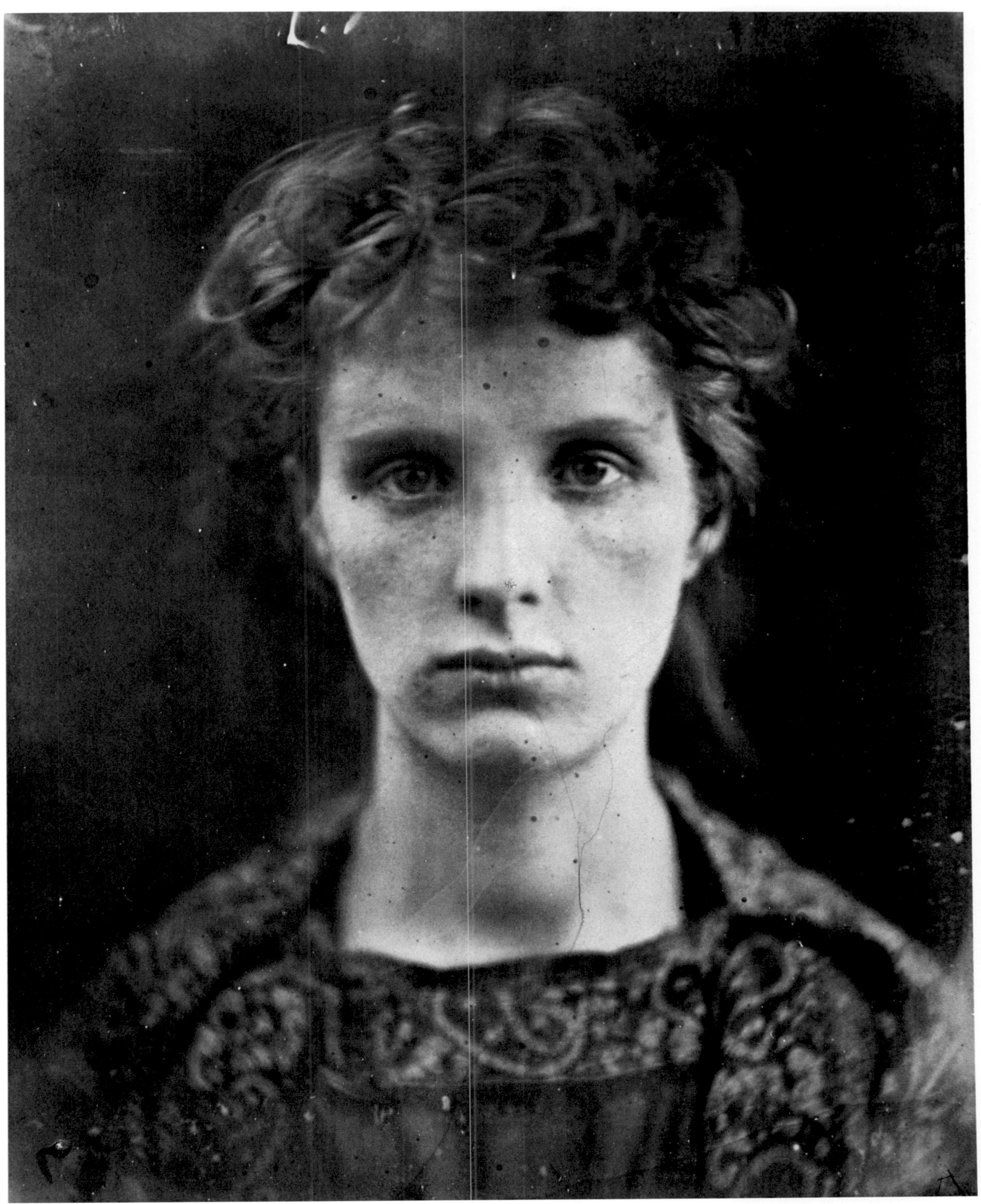

14 · Julia Margaret Cameron · **Cassiopeia** · 1866

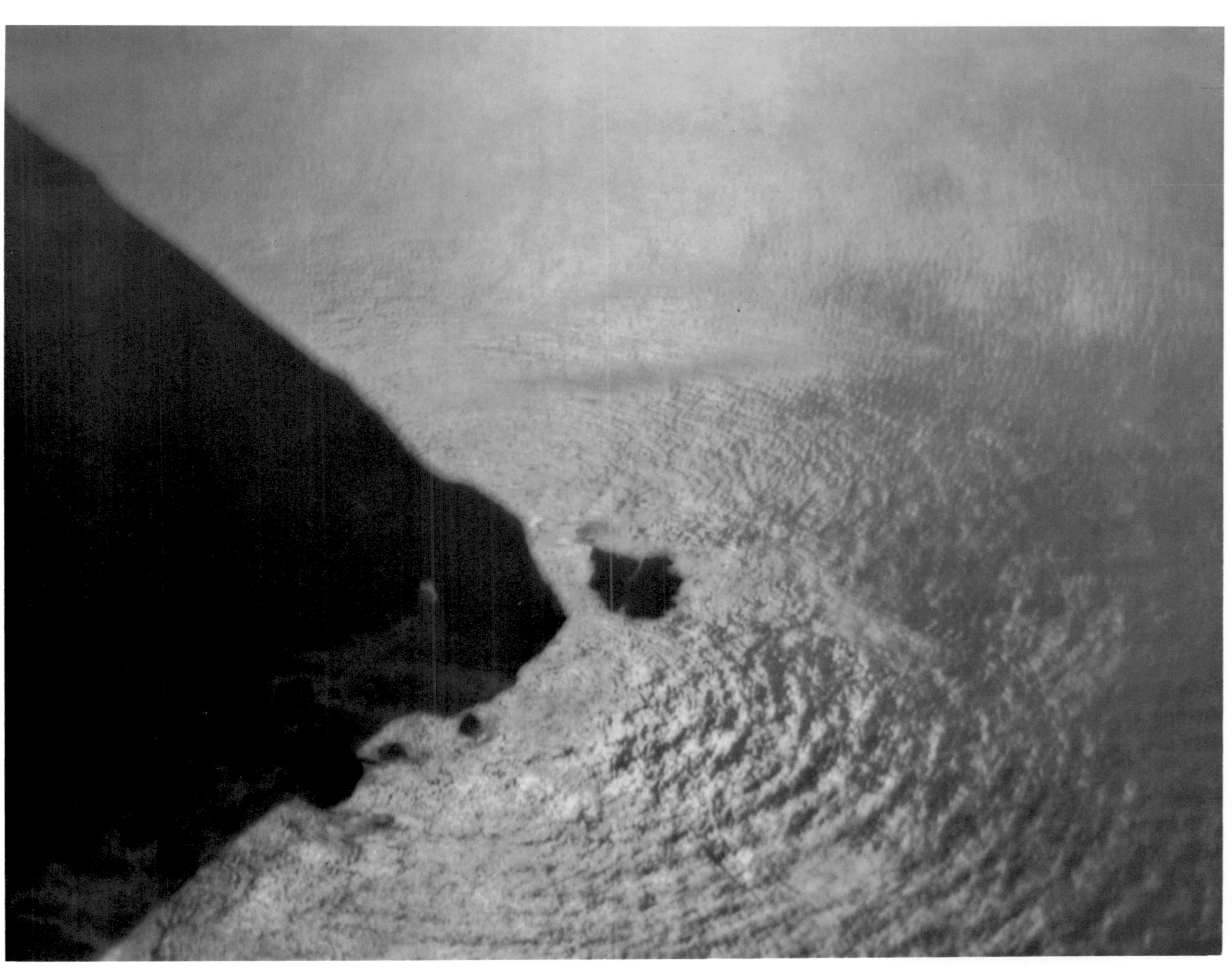

15 · Anne Brigman · **A Study in Radiation** · 1924

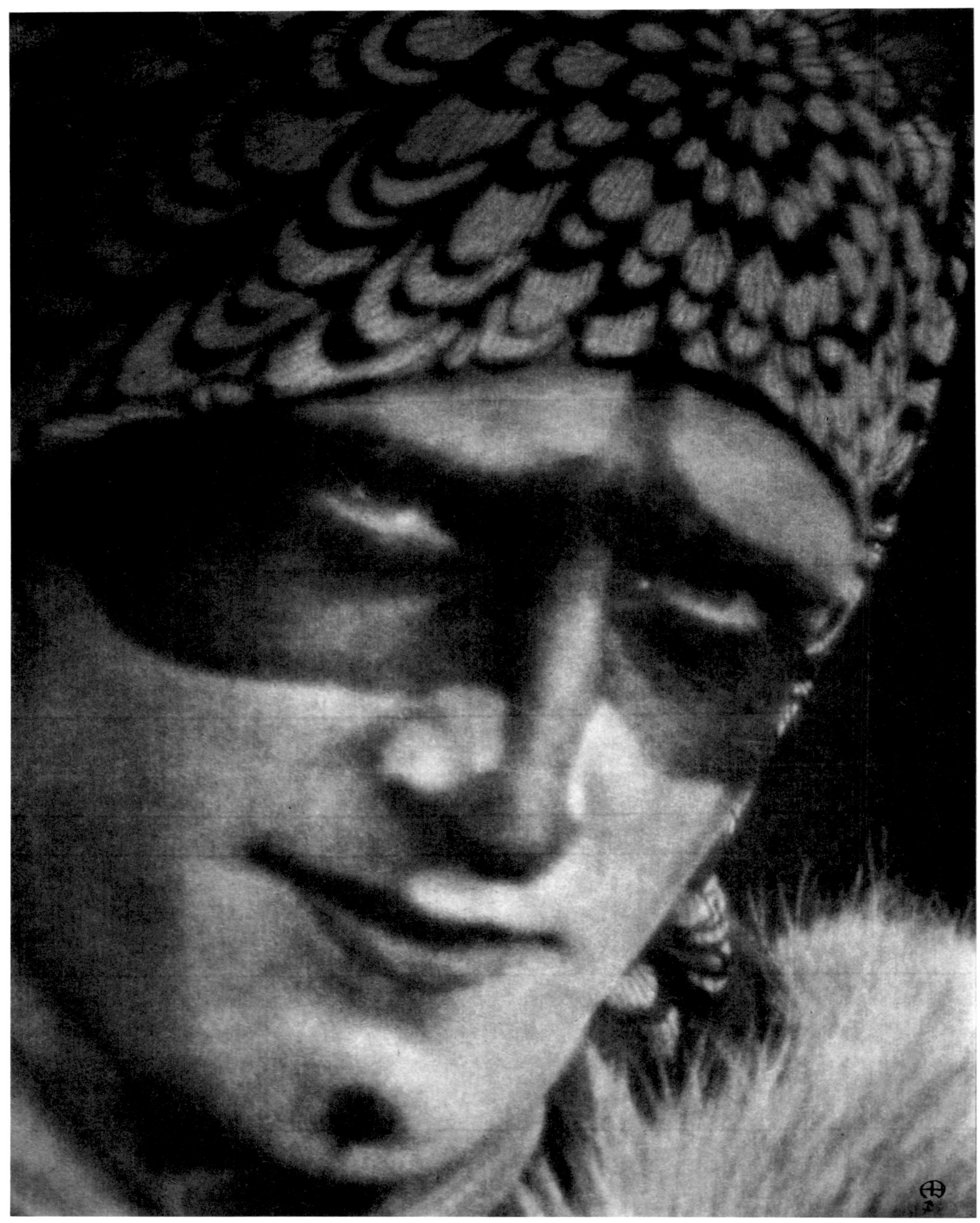

16 · Anne Brigman · **Saga—The Golden Fleece** · 1924

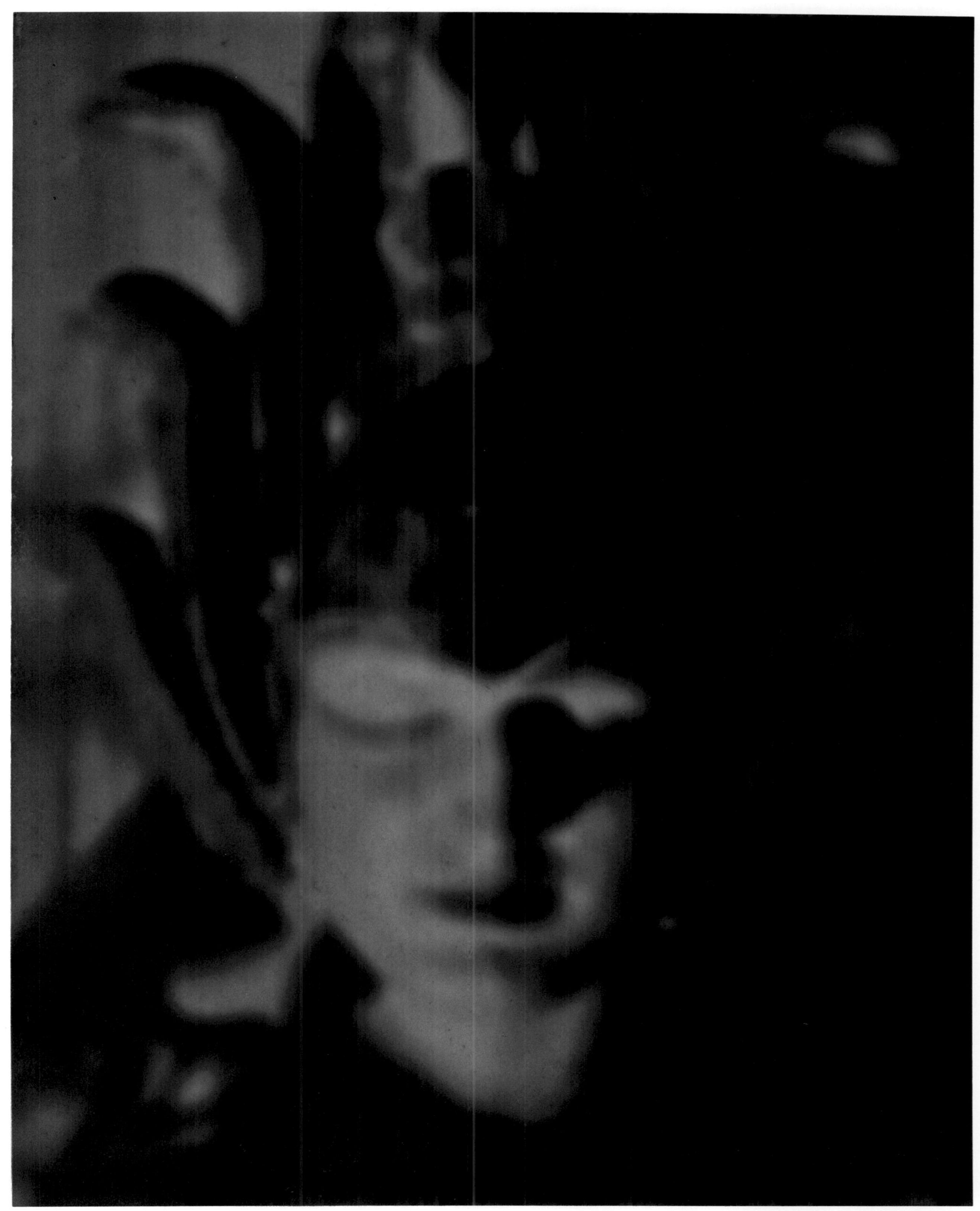

17 · Anne Brigman · Untitled · 1922

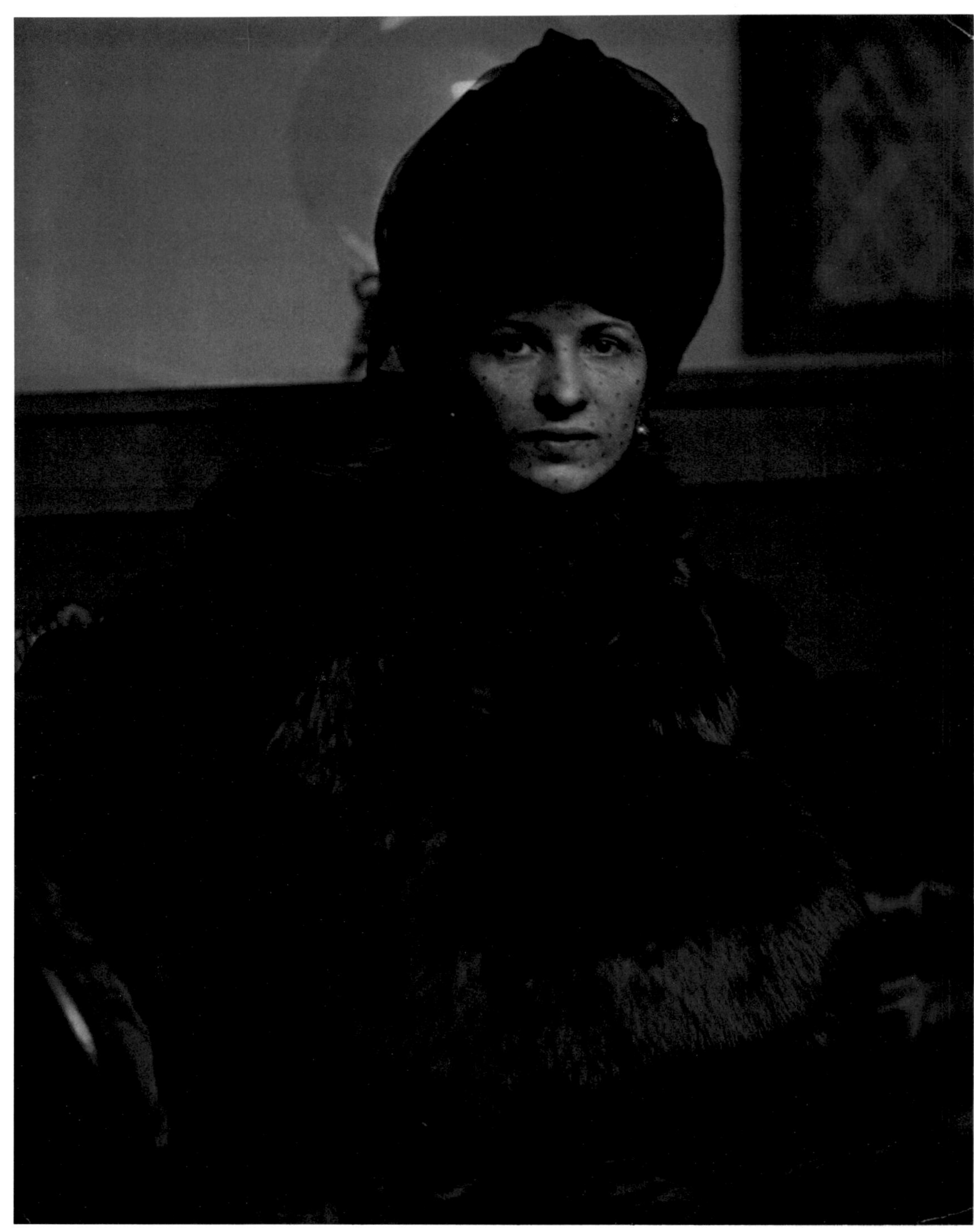

18 · Gertrude Käsebier · **Miss Dix** · n.d.

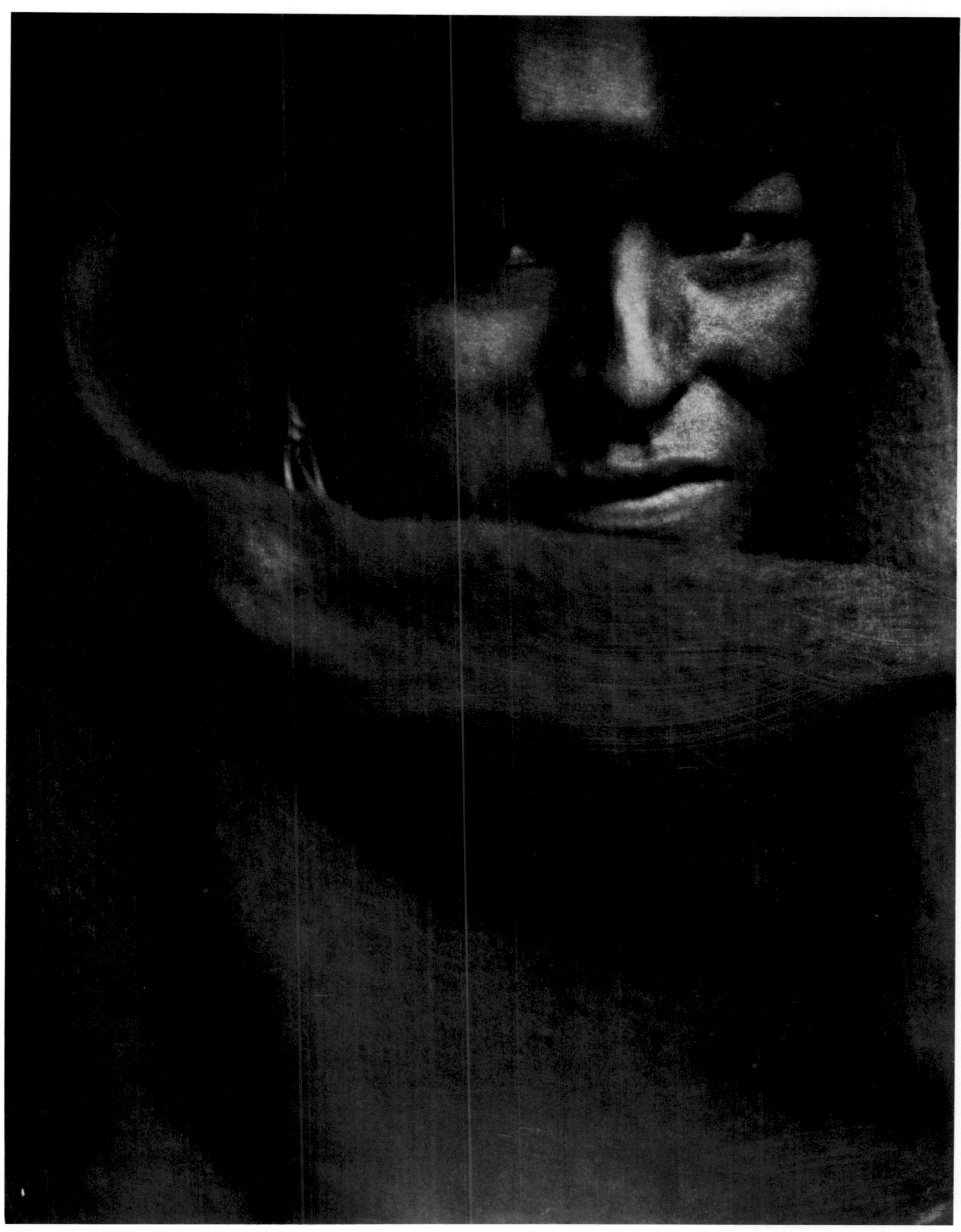

19 · Gertrude Käsebier · **Indian Portrait** · c. 1905

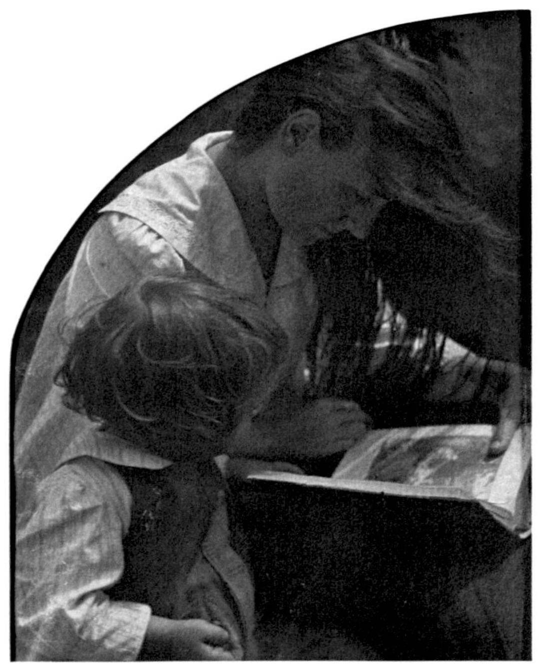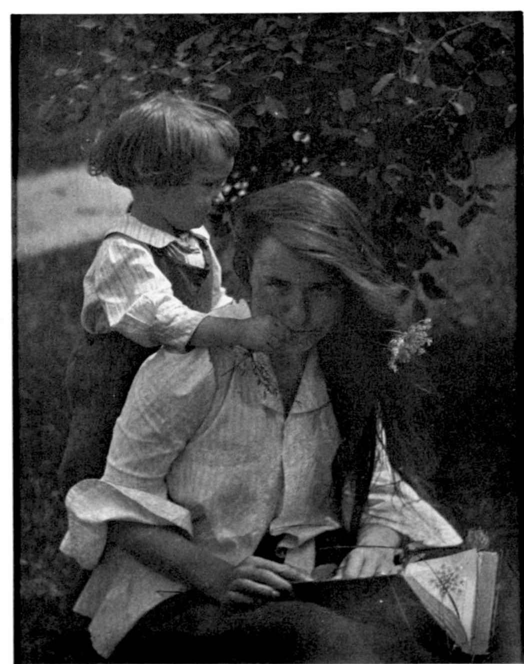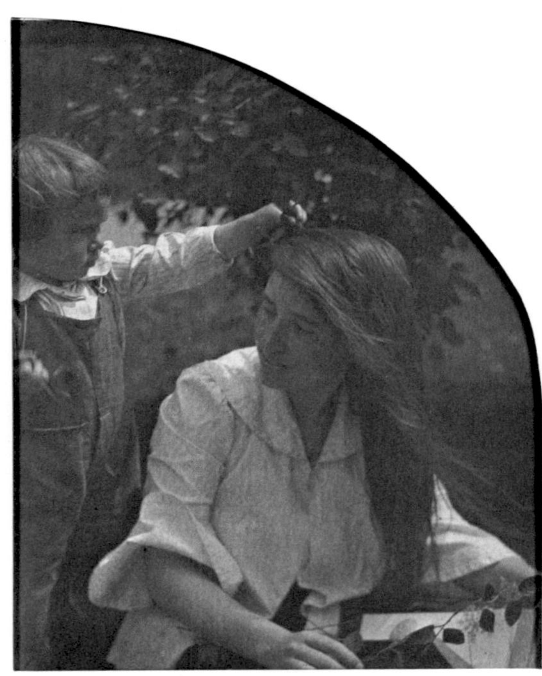

20 · Gertrude Käsebier · **Gertrude and Charles O'Malley,
Newport, Rhode Island: A Triptych** · 1902

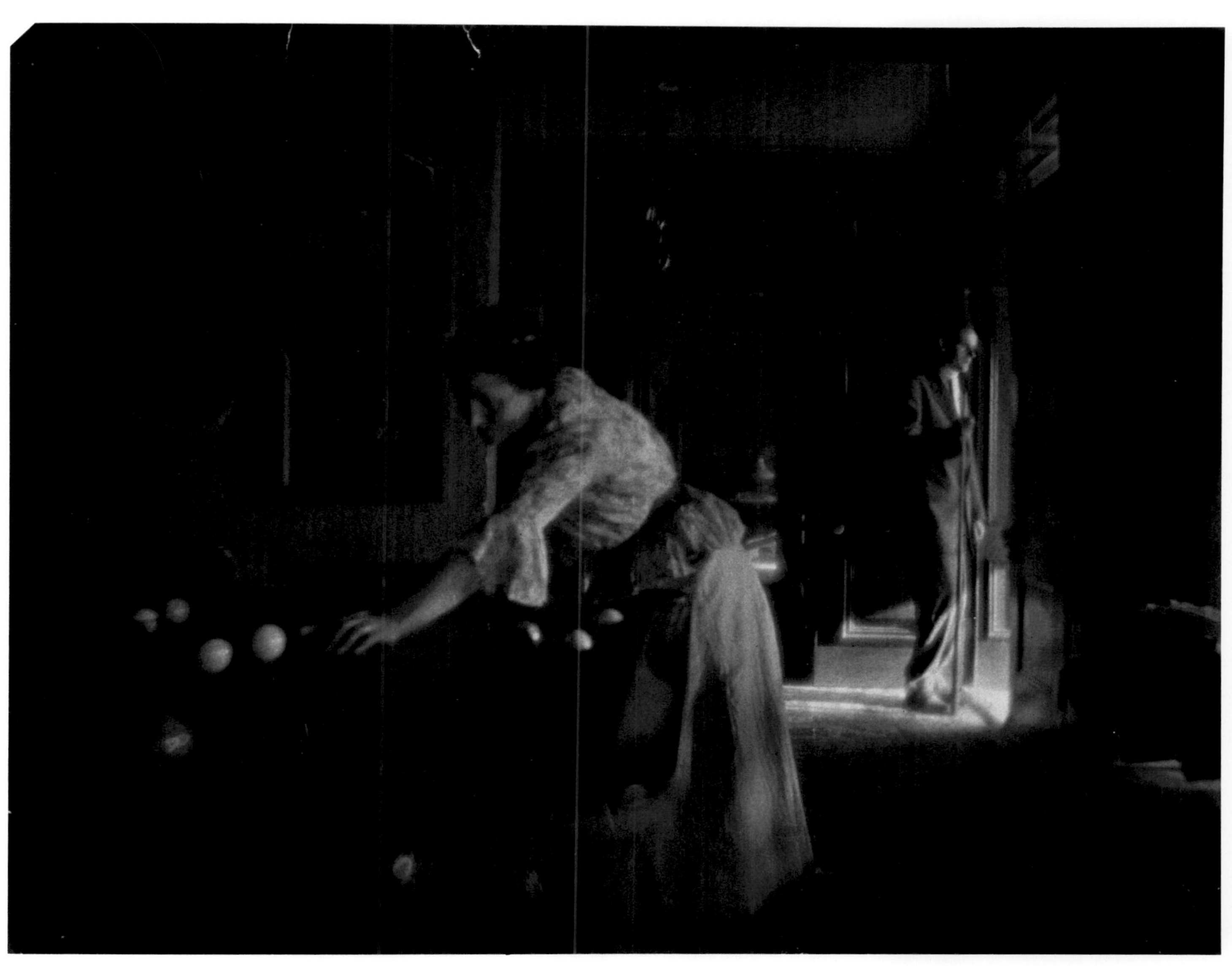

21 · Gertrude Käsebier · **Gertrude Käsebier O'Malley at Billiards** · c. 1909

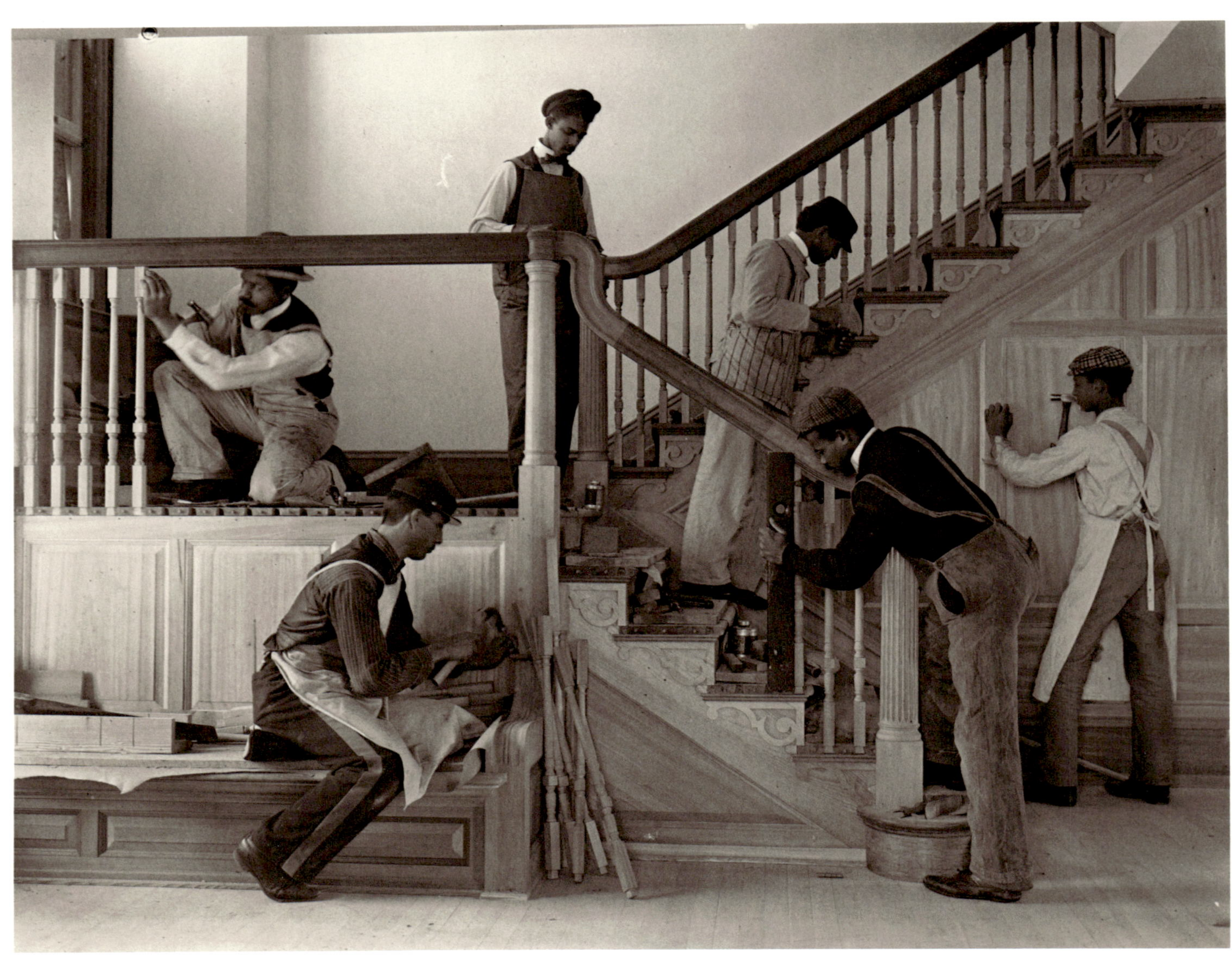

22 · Frances Benjamin Johnston · **Stairway of Treasurer's Residence. Students at Work** · 1899–1900

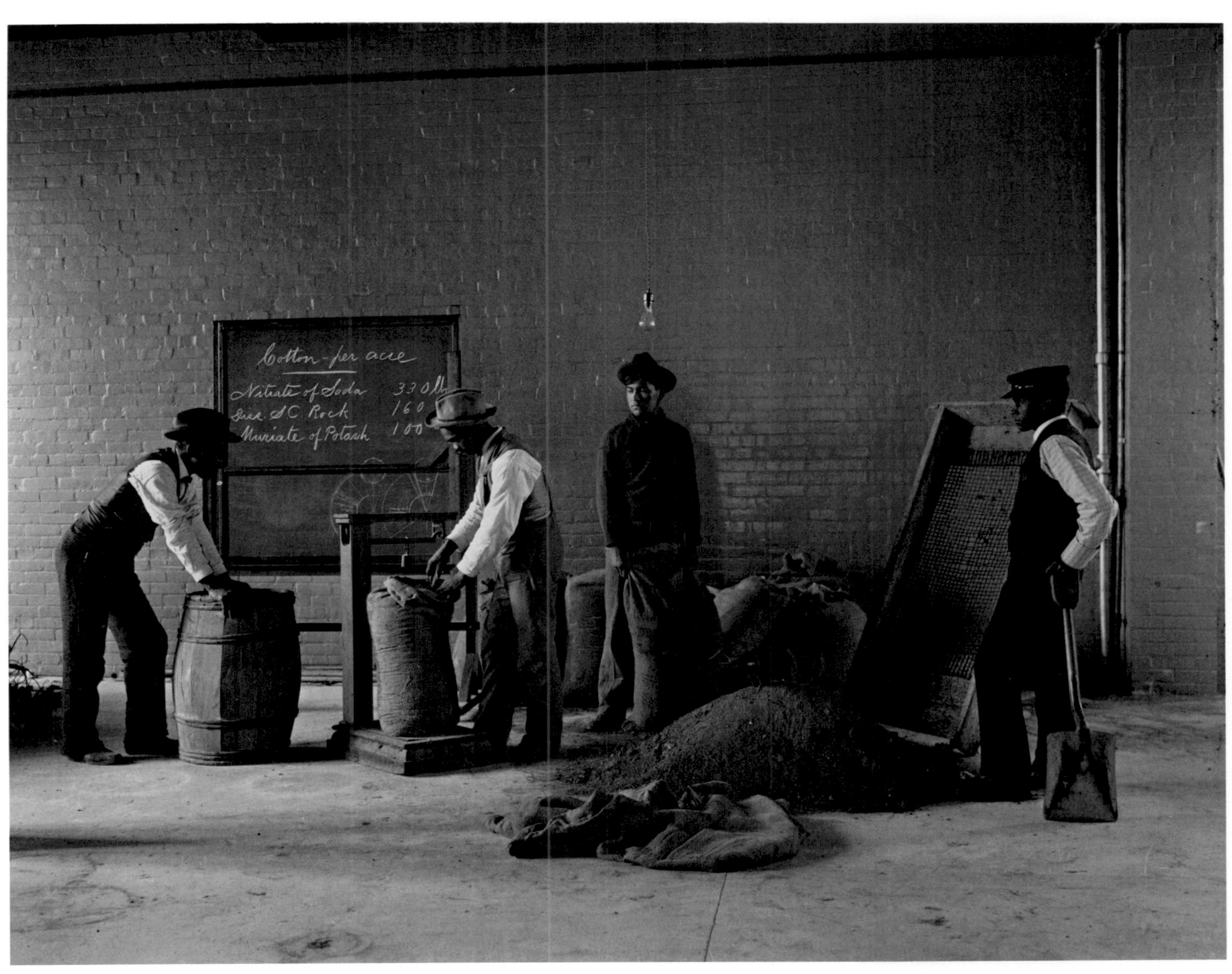

23 · Frances Benjamin Johnston · **Agriculture Mixing Fertilizer** · 1899–1900

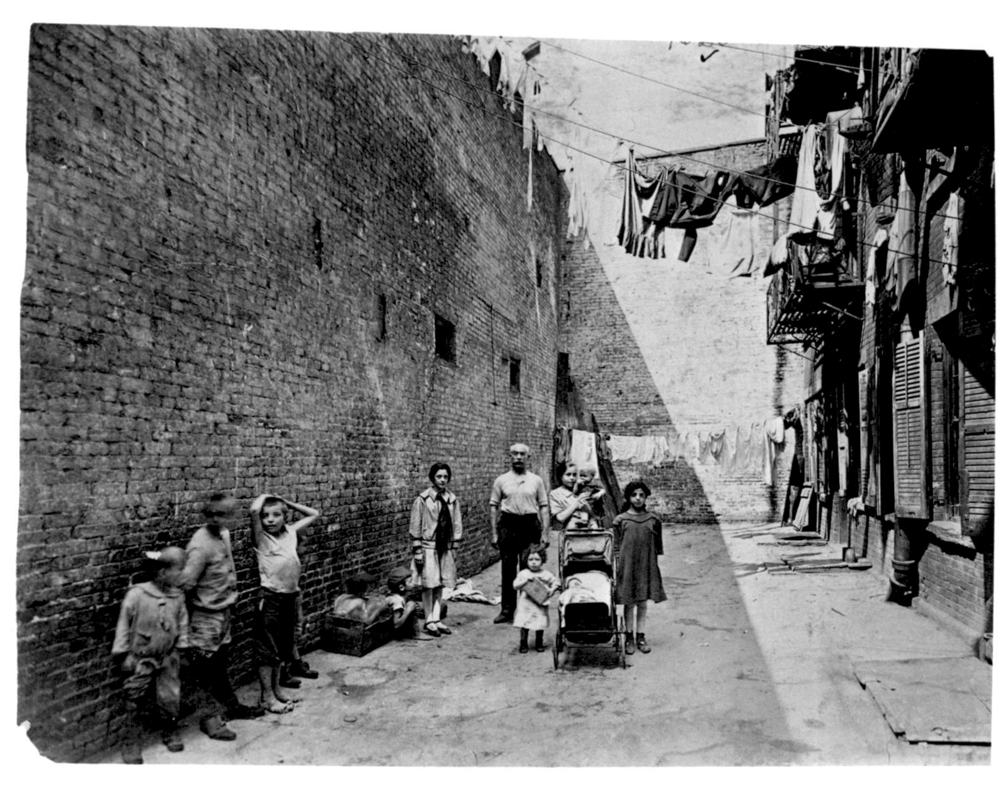

24 · Jessie Tarbox Beals · **Man and Children in Tenement Back Yard, New York** · n.d.

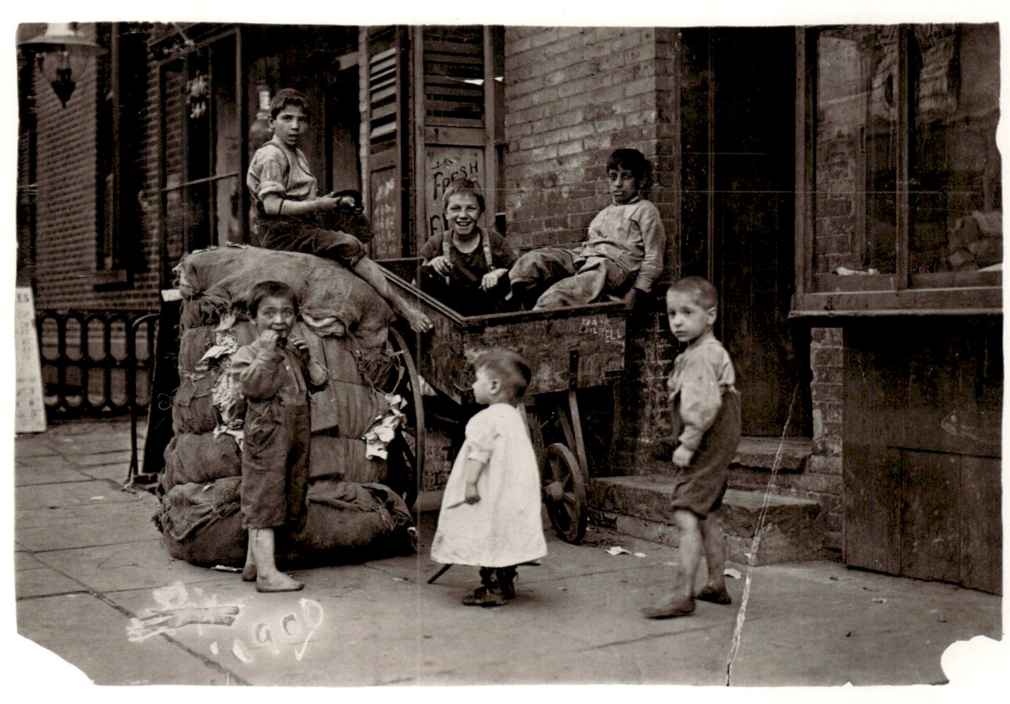

25 · Jessie Tarbox Beals · **Children with Burlap Sacks and Wheelbarrow** · n.d.

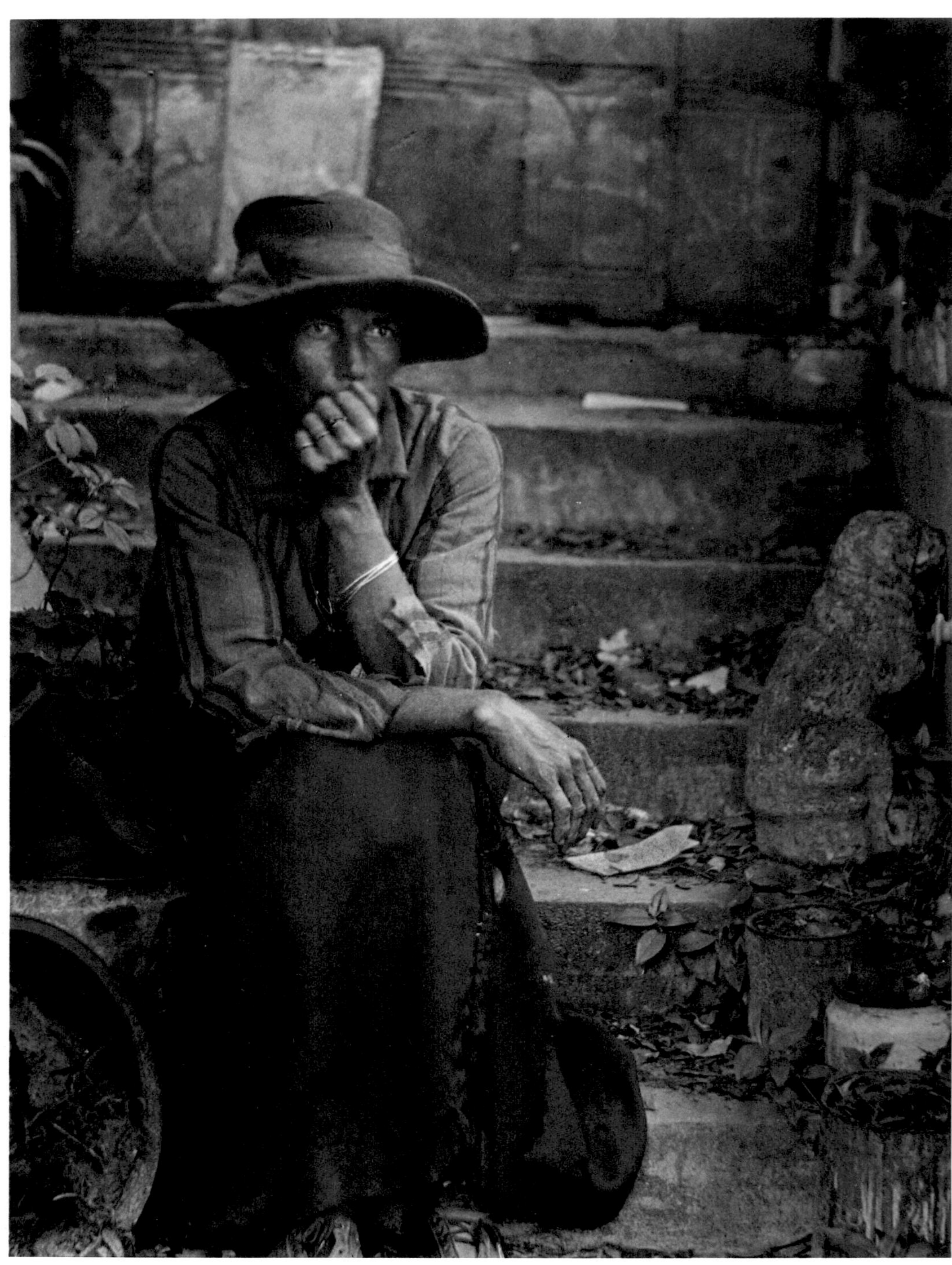

26 · Doris Ulmann · **Woman Seated on Steps** · c. 1930

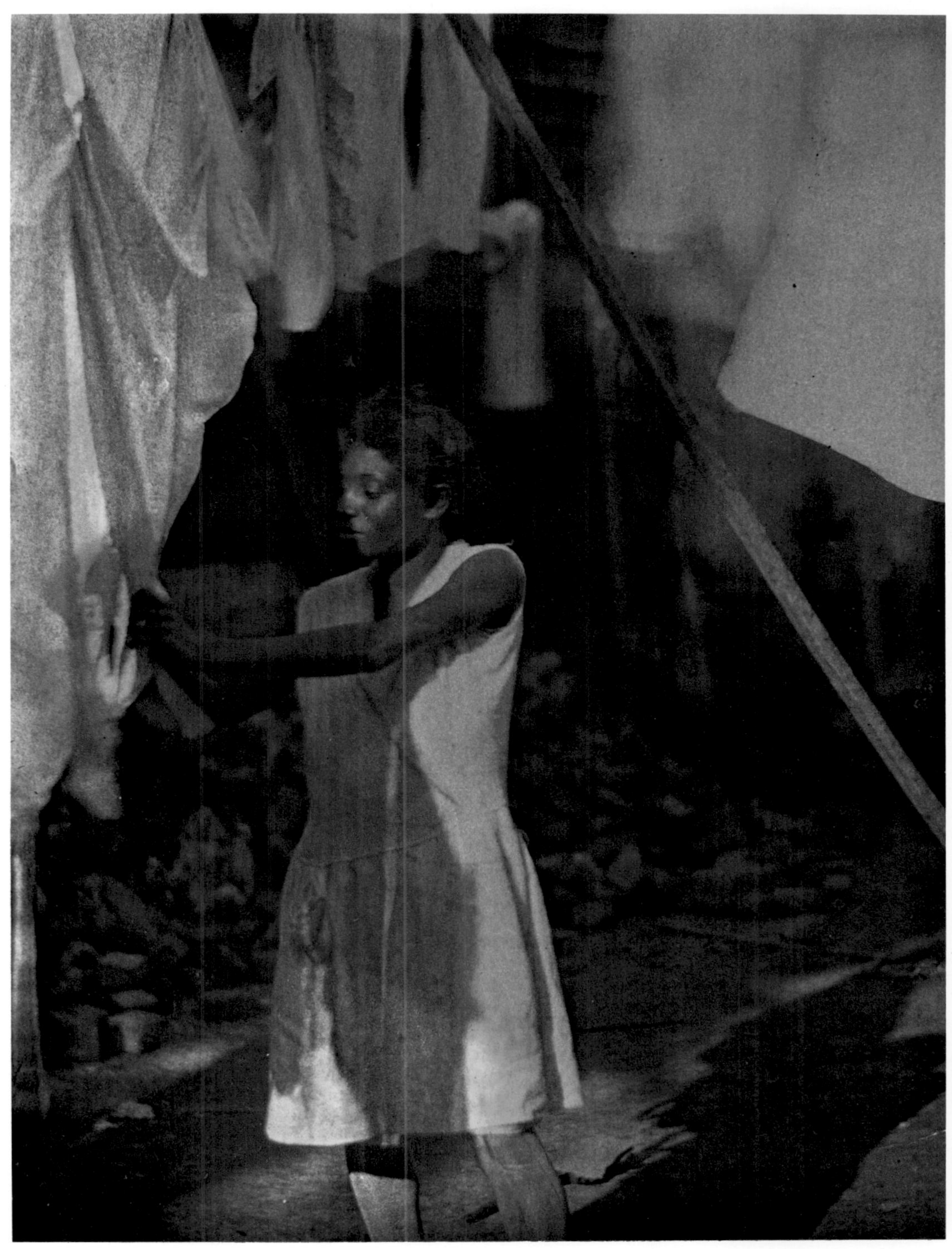

27 · Doris Ulmann · **Laundress, Peterken Farm, South Carolina** · 1929

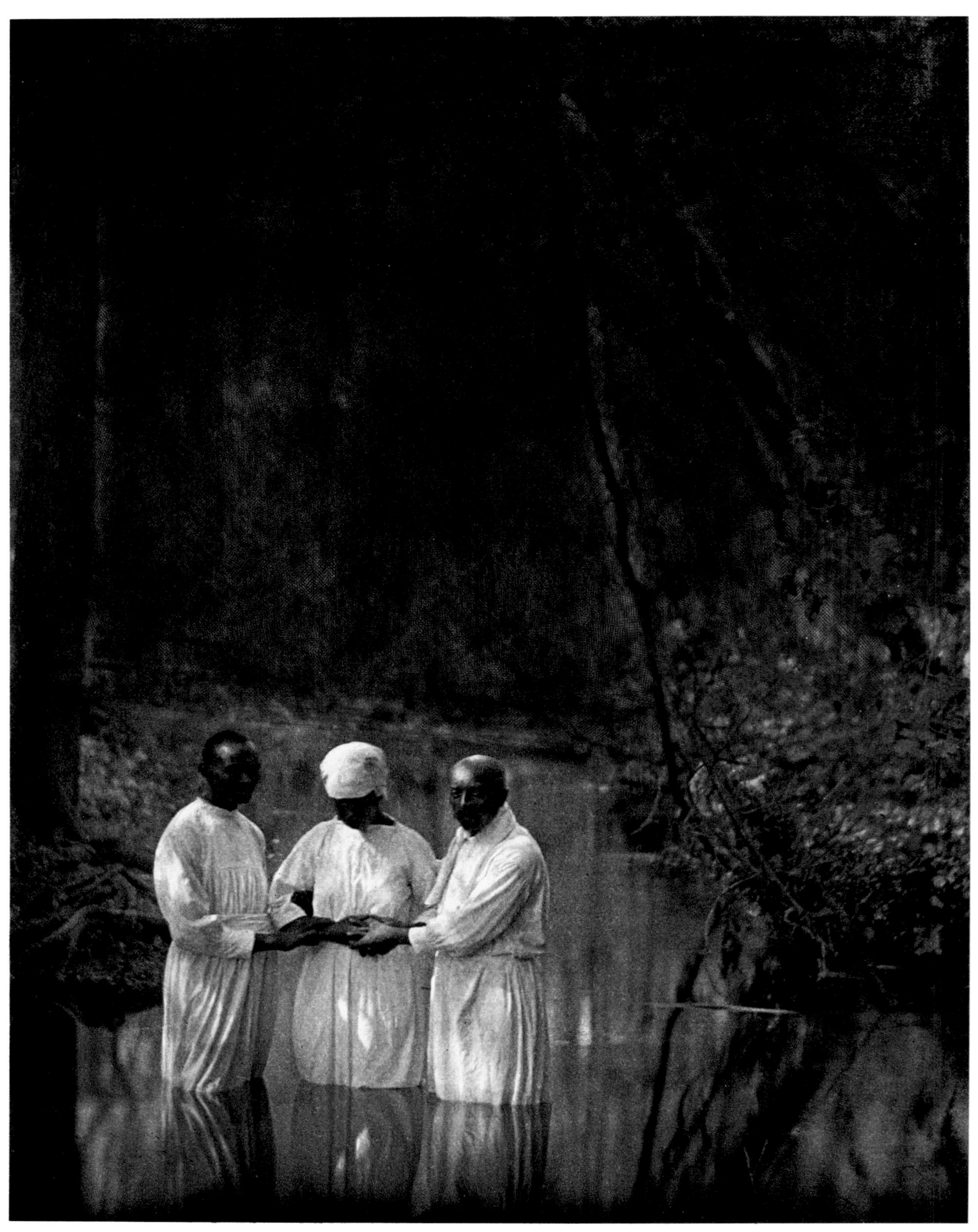

28 · Doris Ulmann · **Baptism, South Carolina** · c. 1930

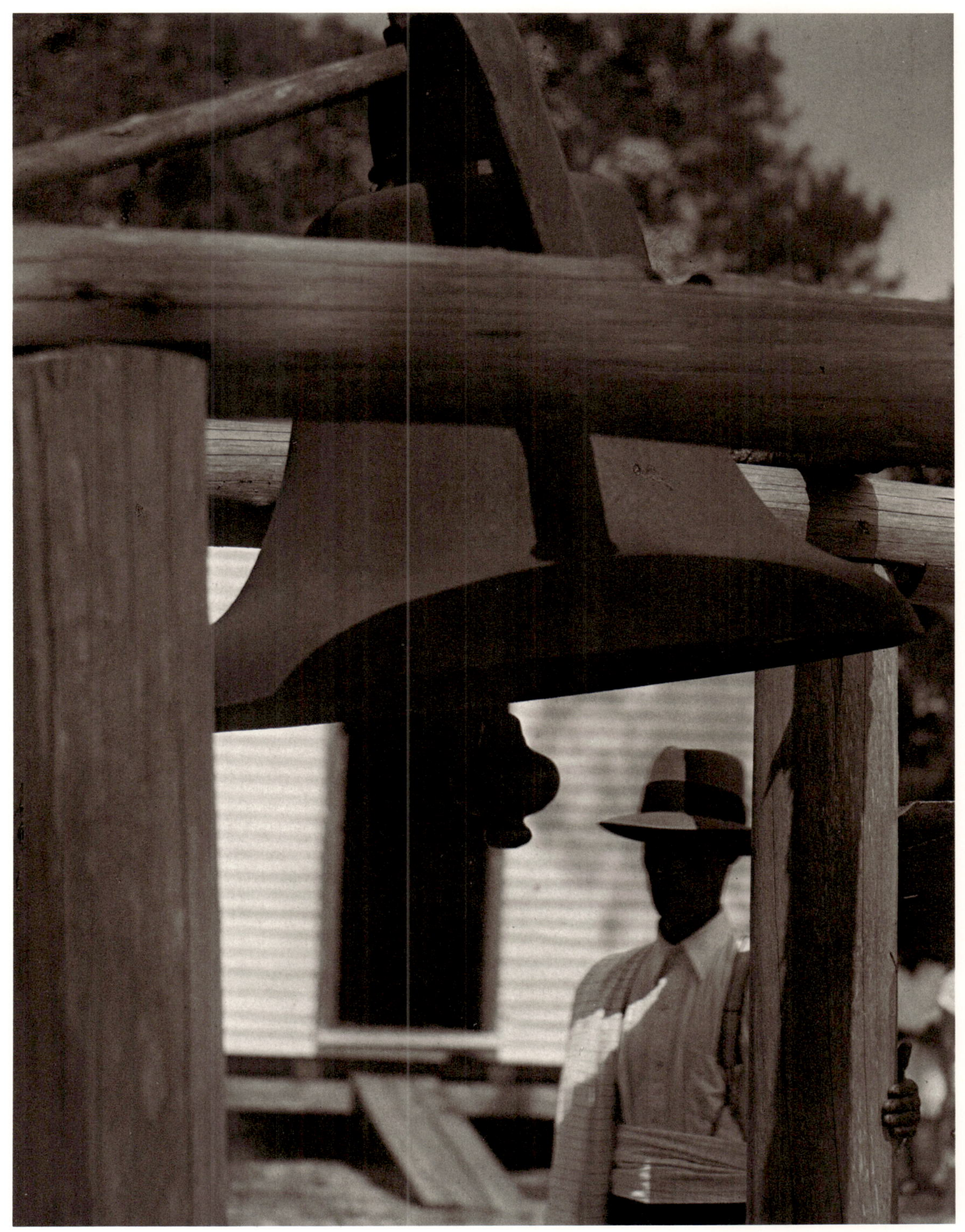

29 · Doris Ulmann · **Bell Ringer, South Carolina** · c. 1930

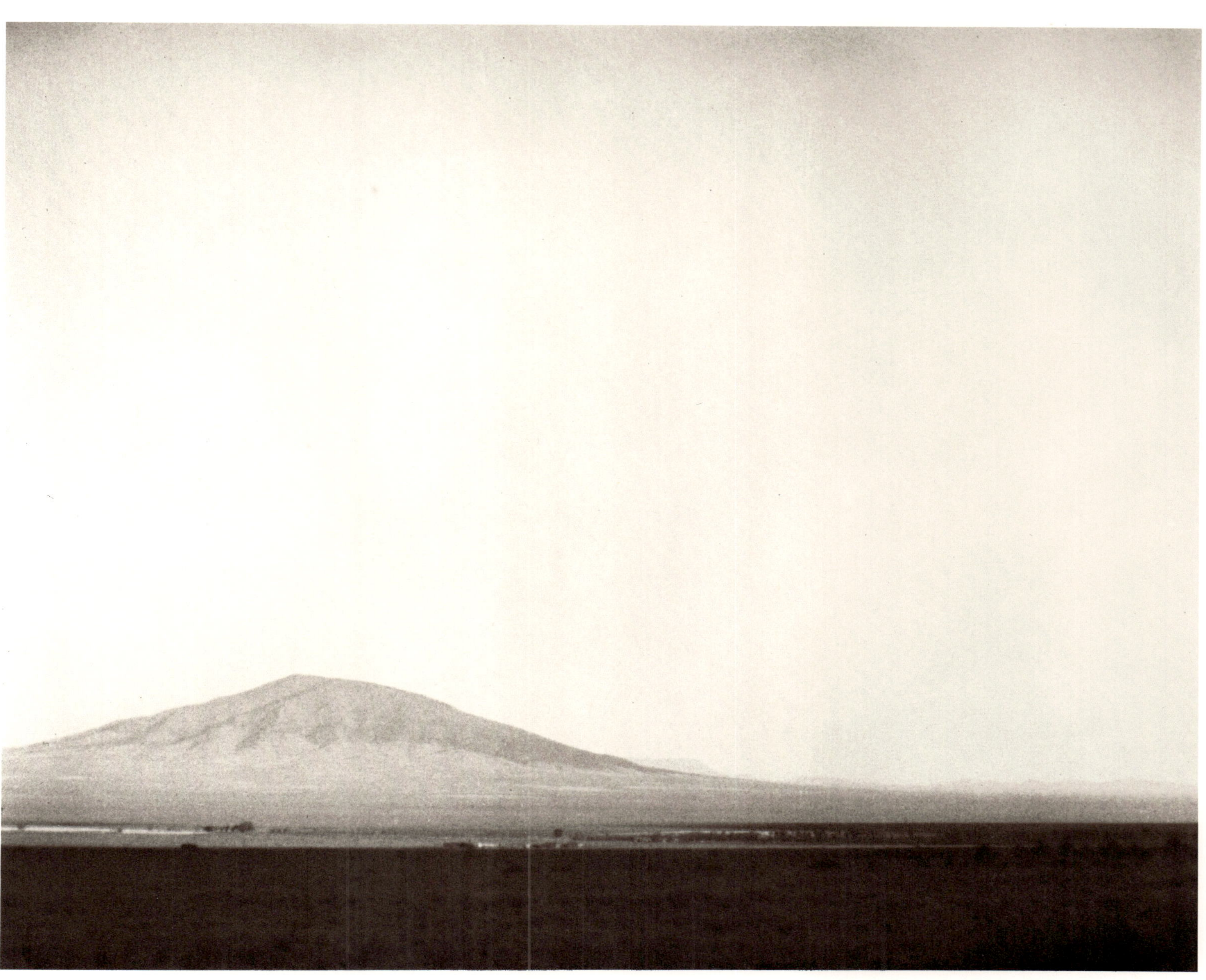

30 · Laura Gilpin · **Sunrise, San Luis Desert** · 1921

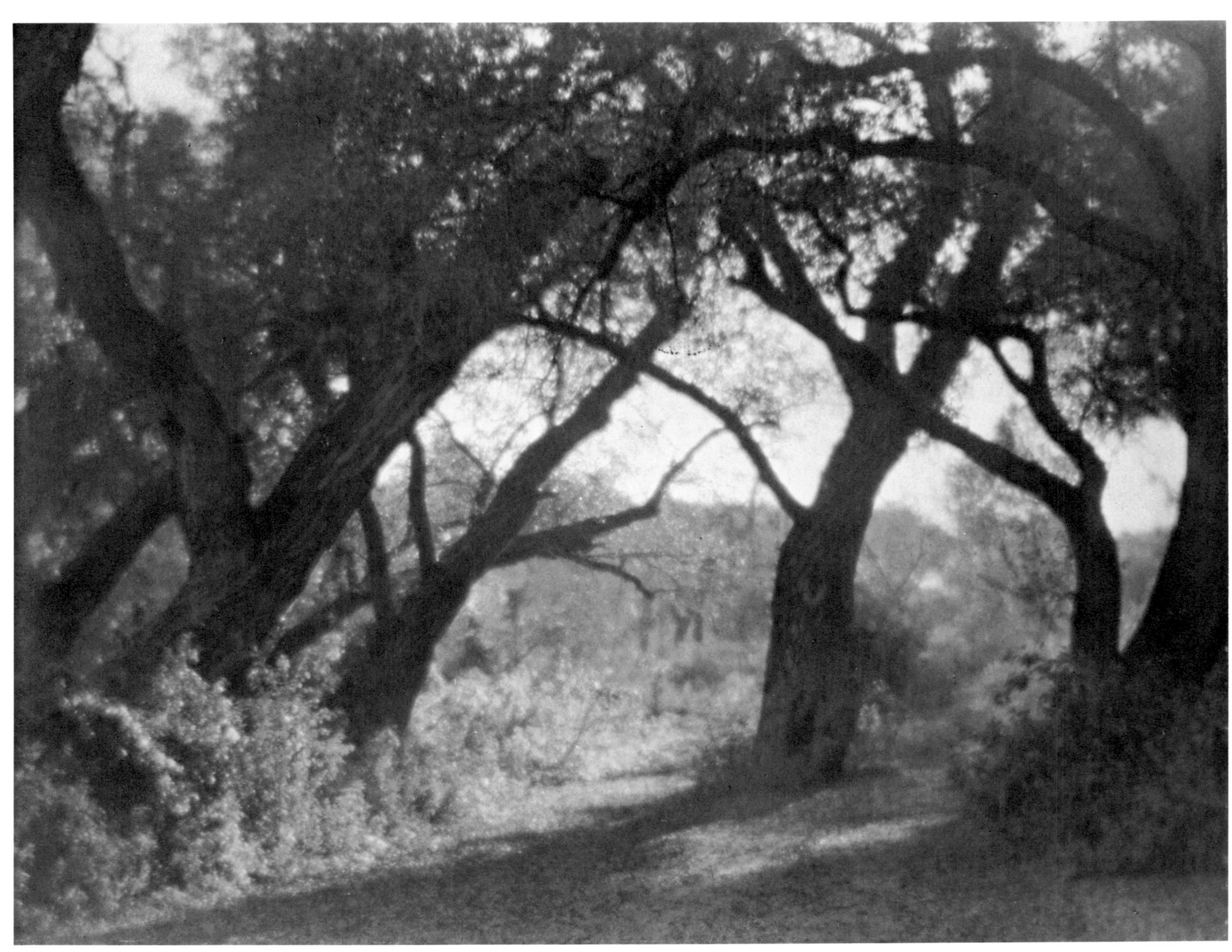

31 · Laura Gilpin · **Cottonwoods, Taos Pueblo** · 1923

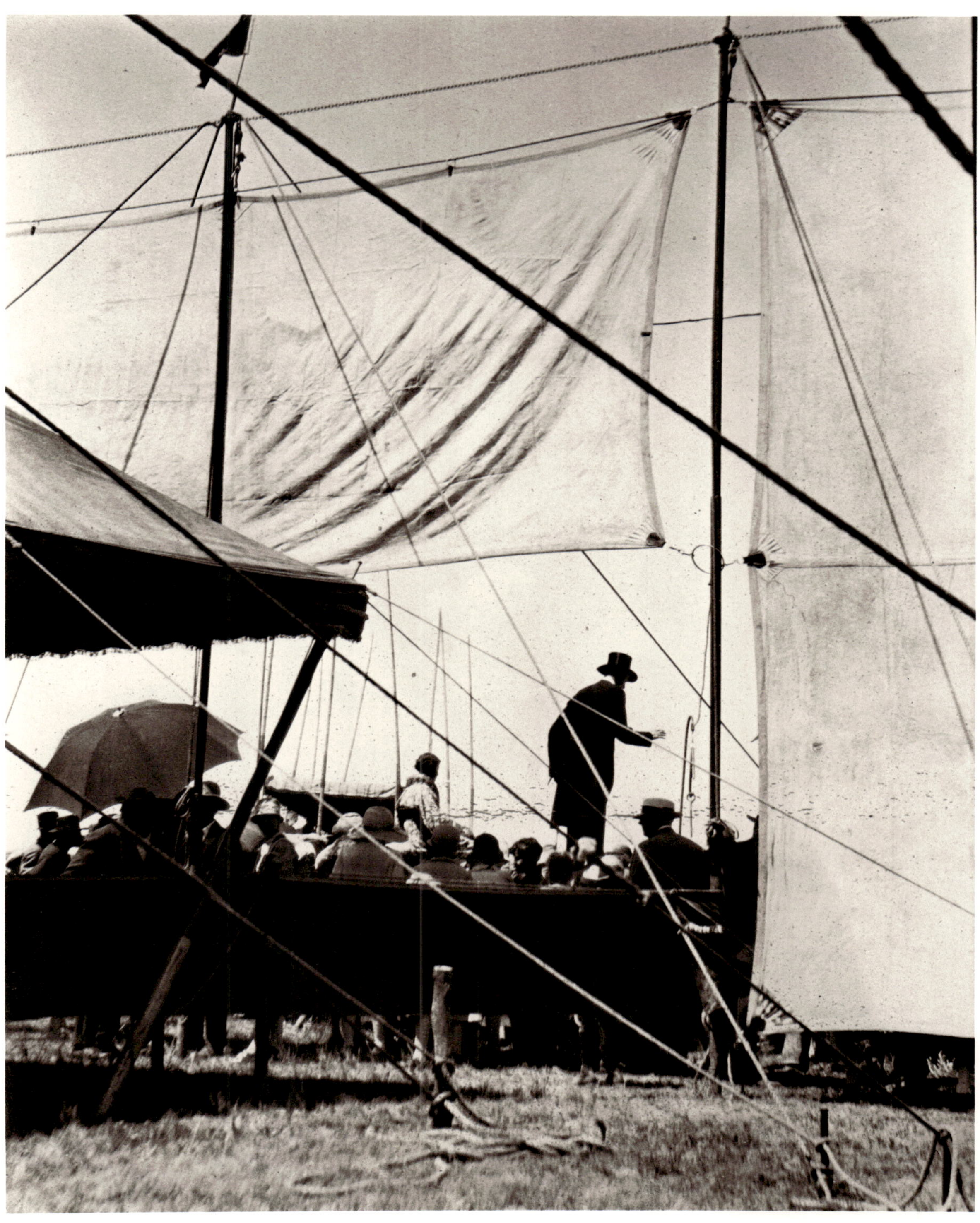

32 · Laura Gilpin · **The Tall Man at the Circus** · c. 1920s

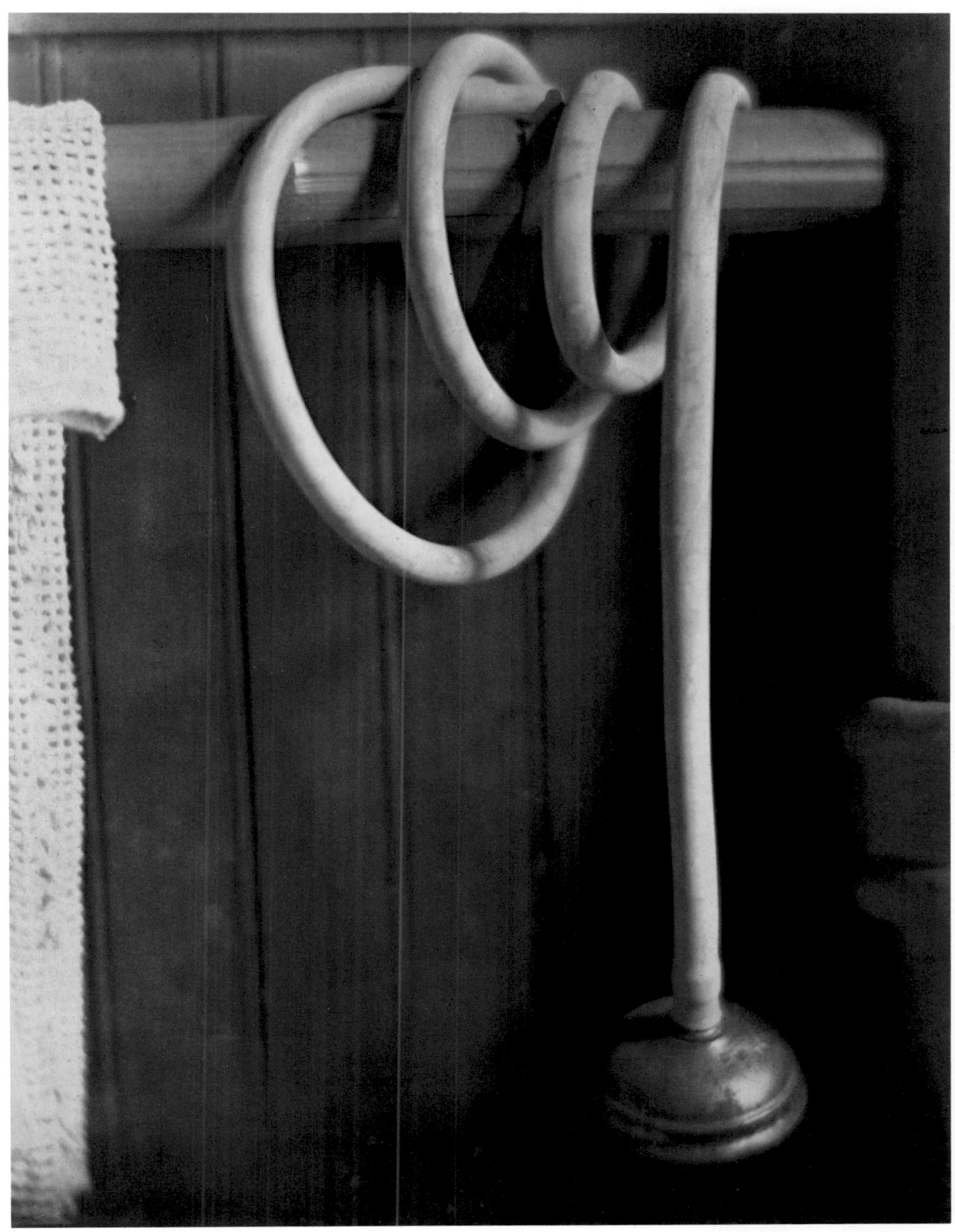

33 · Margaret Watkins · **Still-life—Shower Hose** · 1919

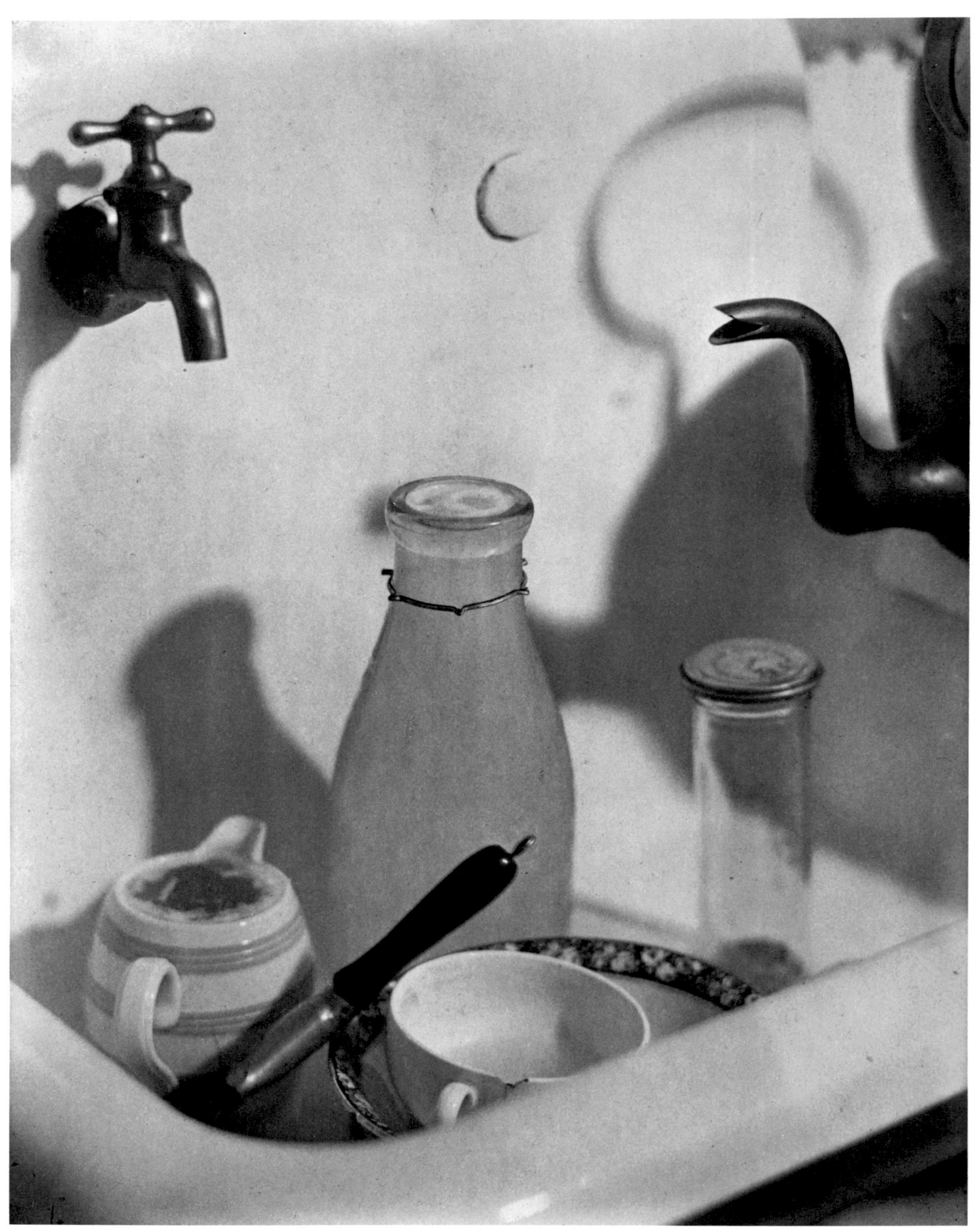

34 · Margaret Watkins · **The Kitchen Sink** · c. 1919

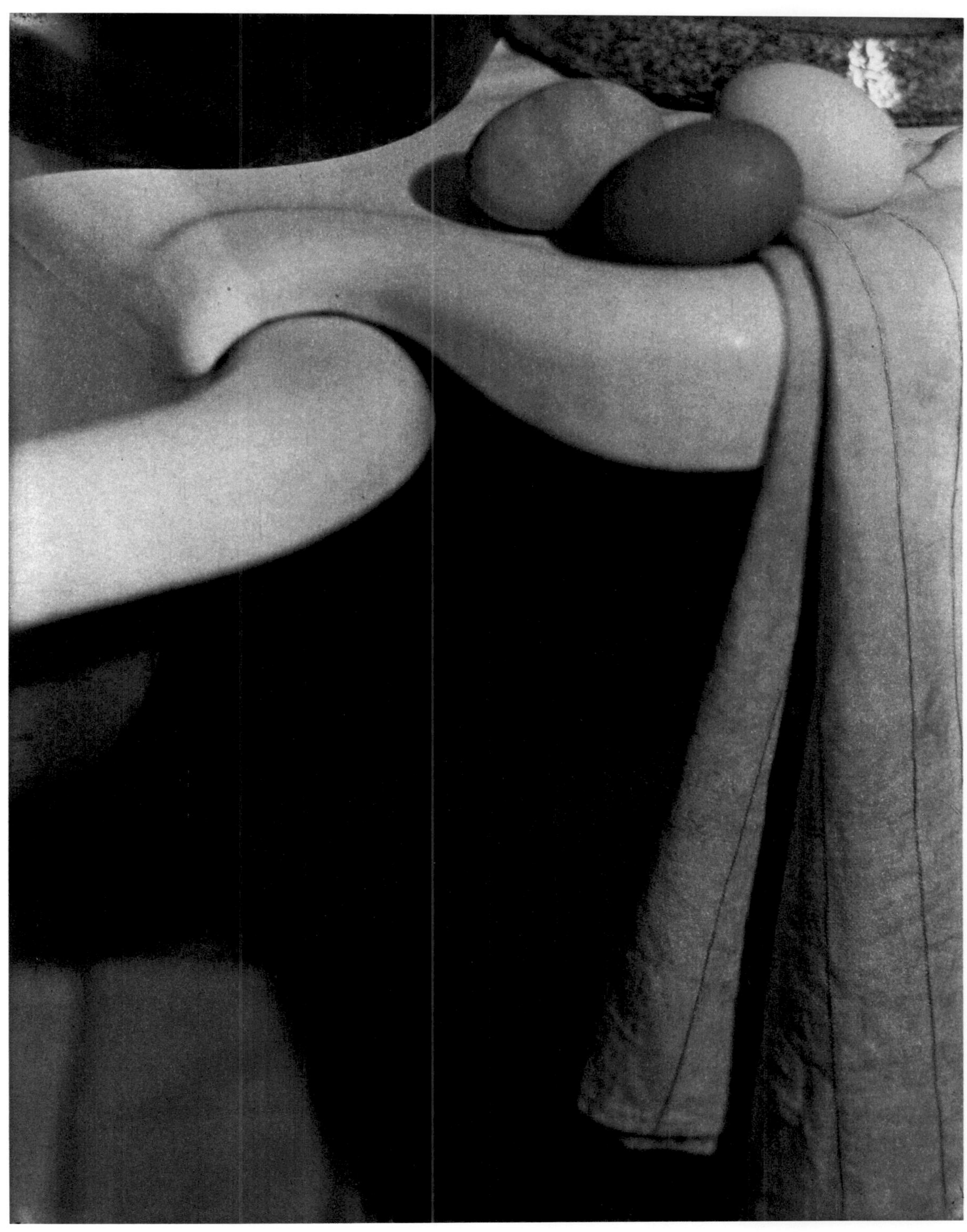

35 · Margaret Watkins · **Domestic Symphony** · 1919

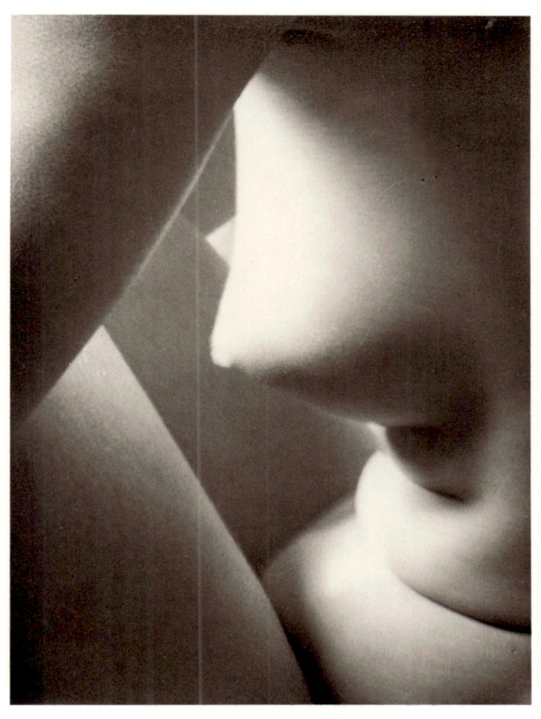

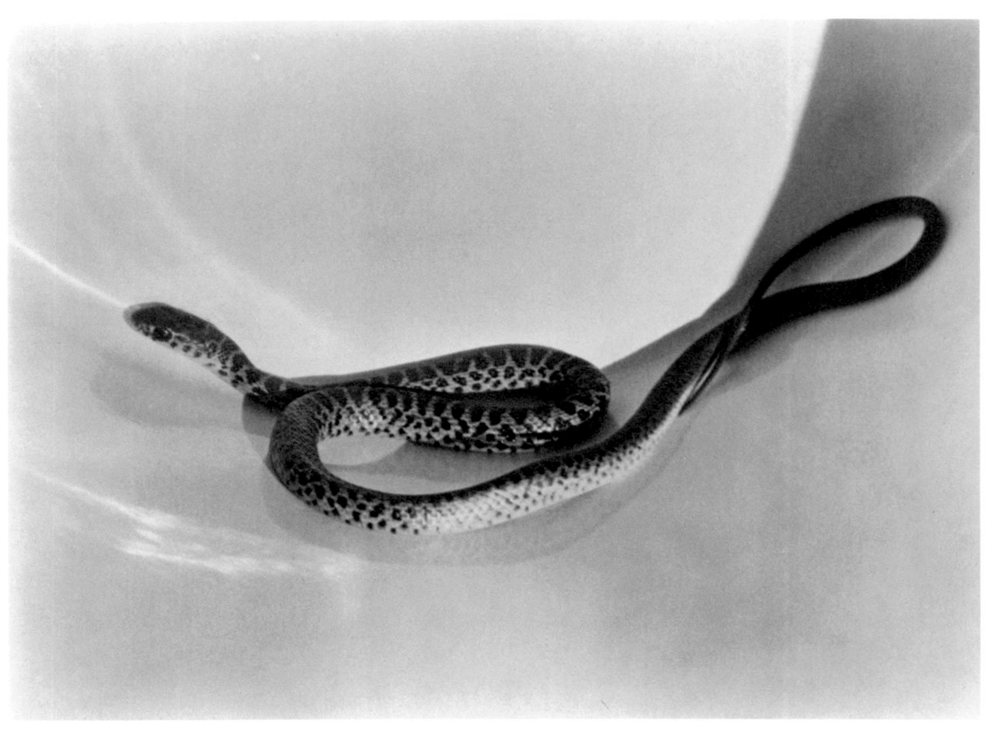

37 · Imogen Cunningham · **Snake in Bucket** · 1929

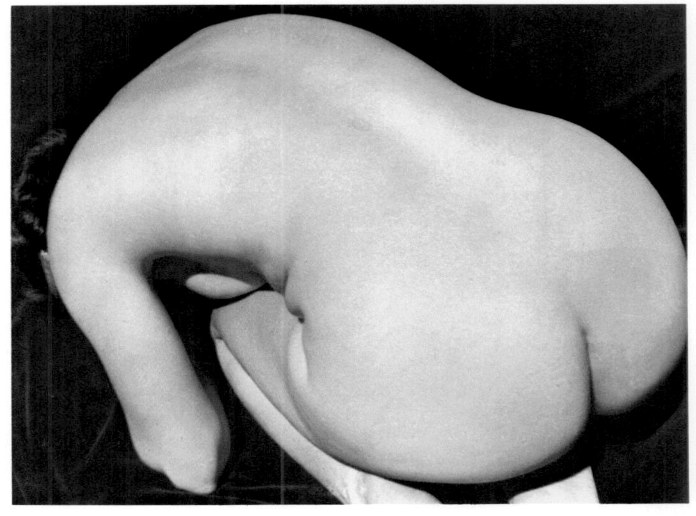

38 · Imogen Cunningham · **Nude** · 1932

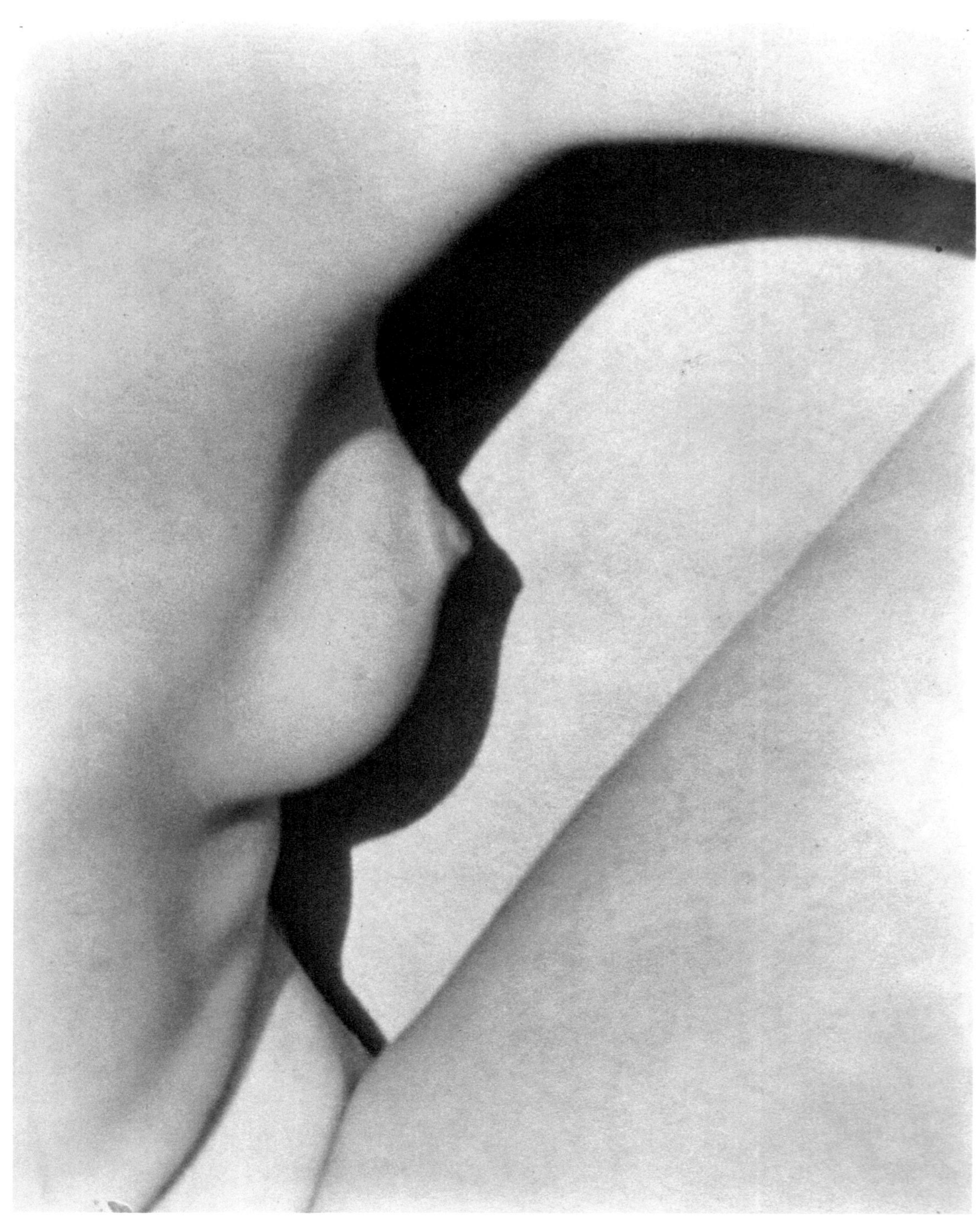

39 · Imogen Cunningham · **Breast** · c. 1927

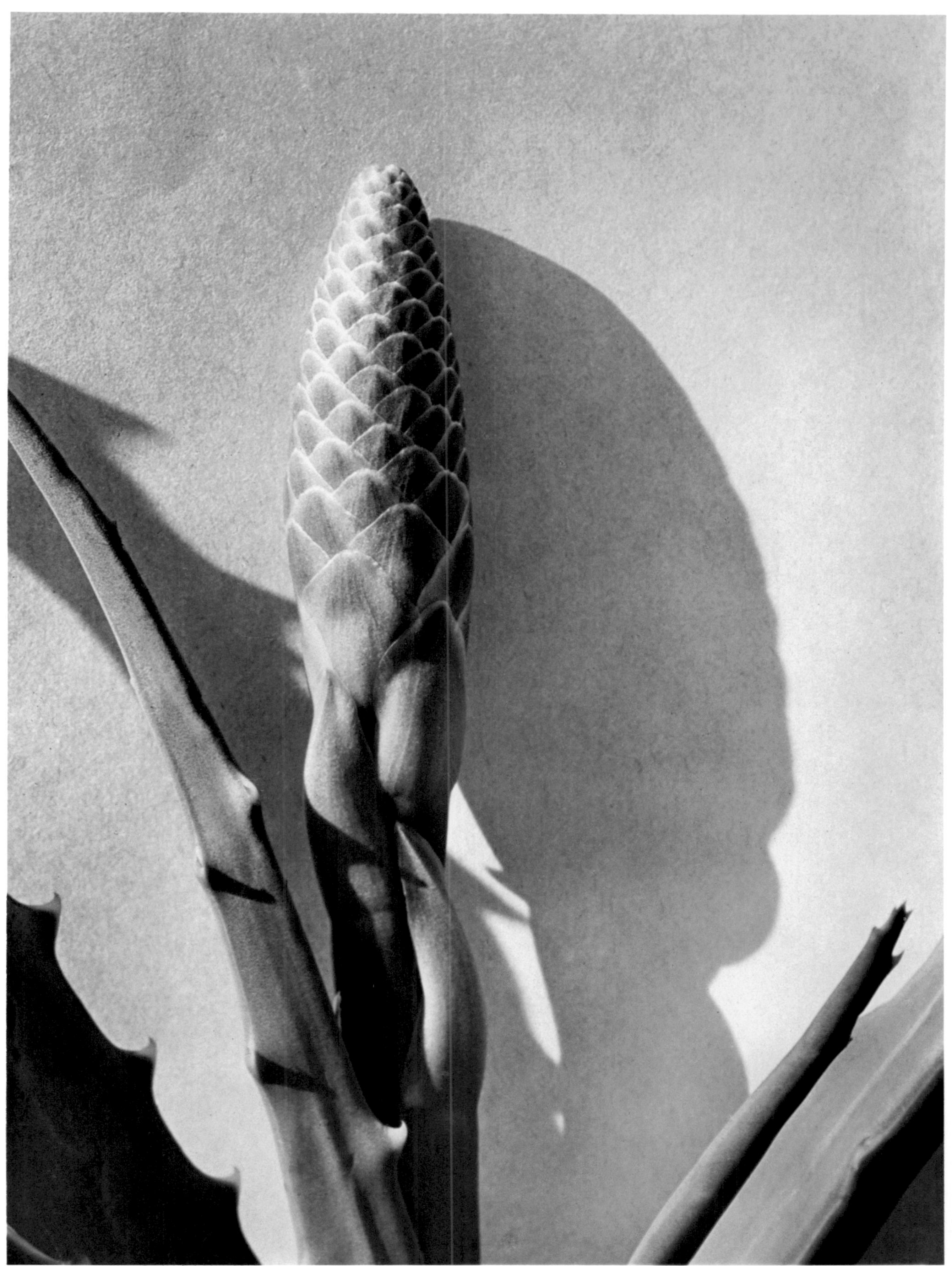

40 · Imogen Cunningham · **Aloe Bud** · c. 1926

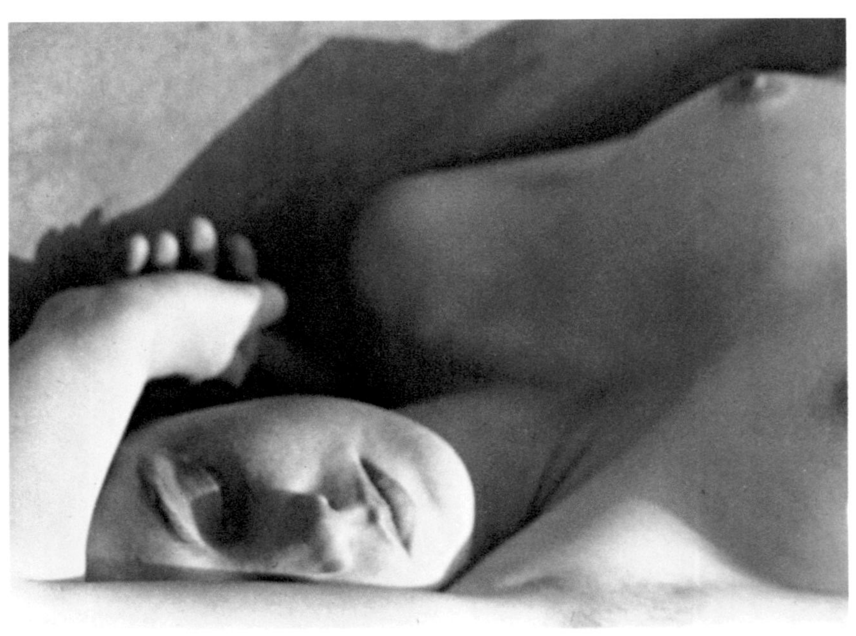

41 · Imogen Cunningham · Untitled (Portia Hume) · c. 1930

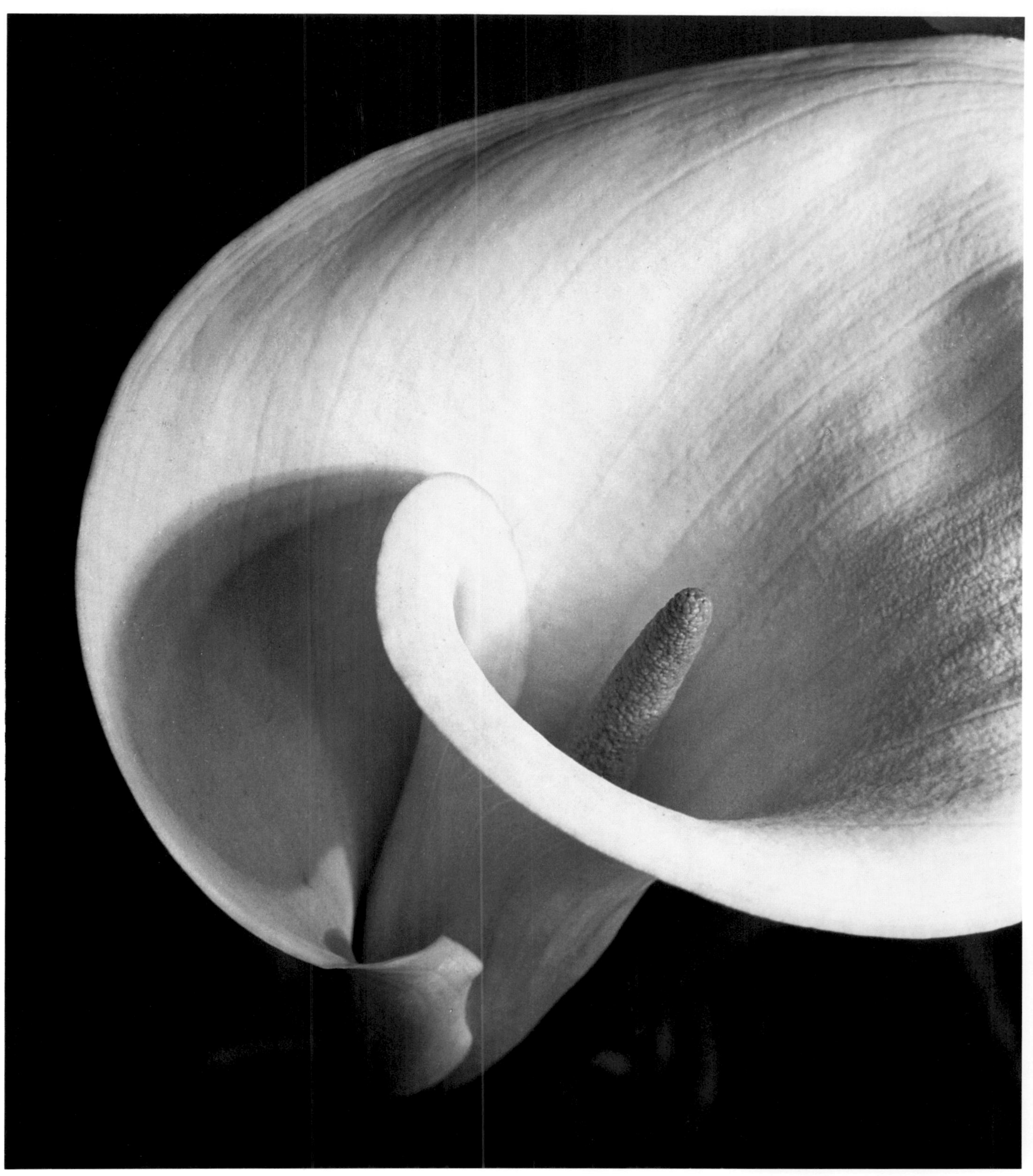

42 · Imogen Cunningham · **Calla** · c. 1929

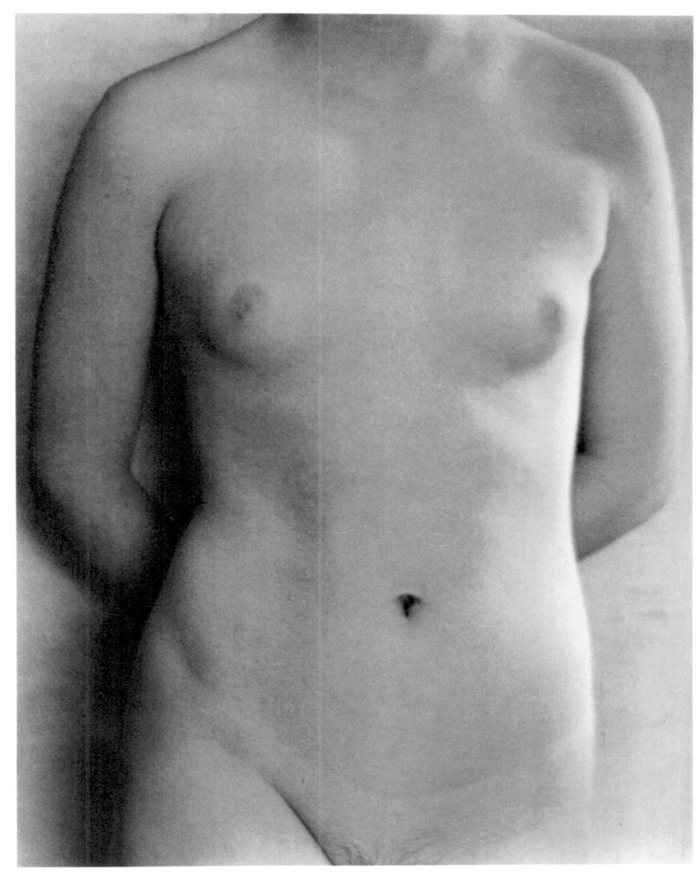

43 · Dorothea Lange · **Torso, San Francisco** · 1923

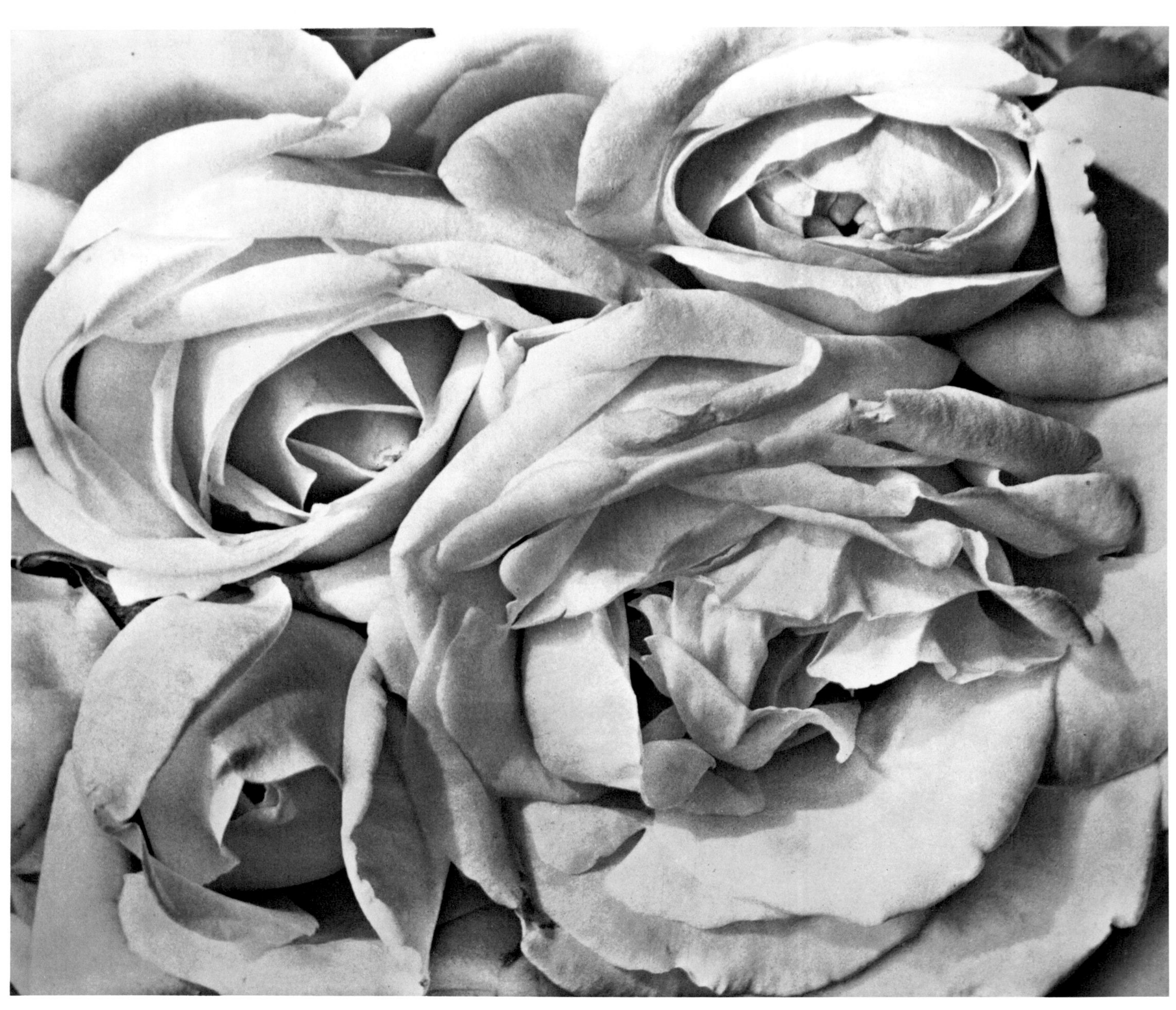

44 · Tina Modotti · **Roses** · 1924

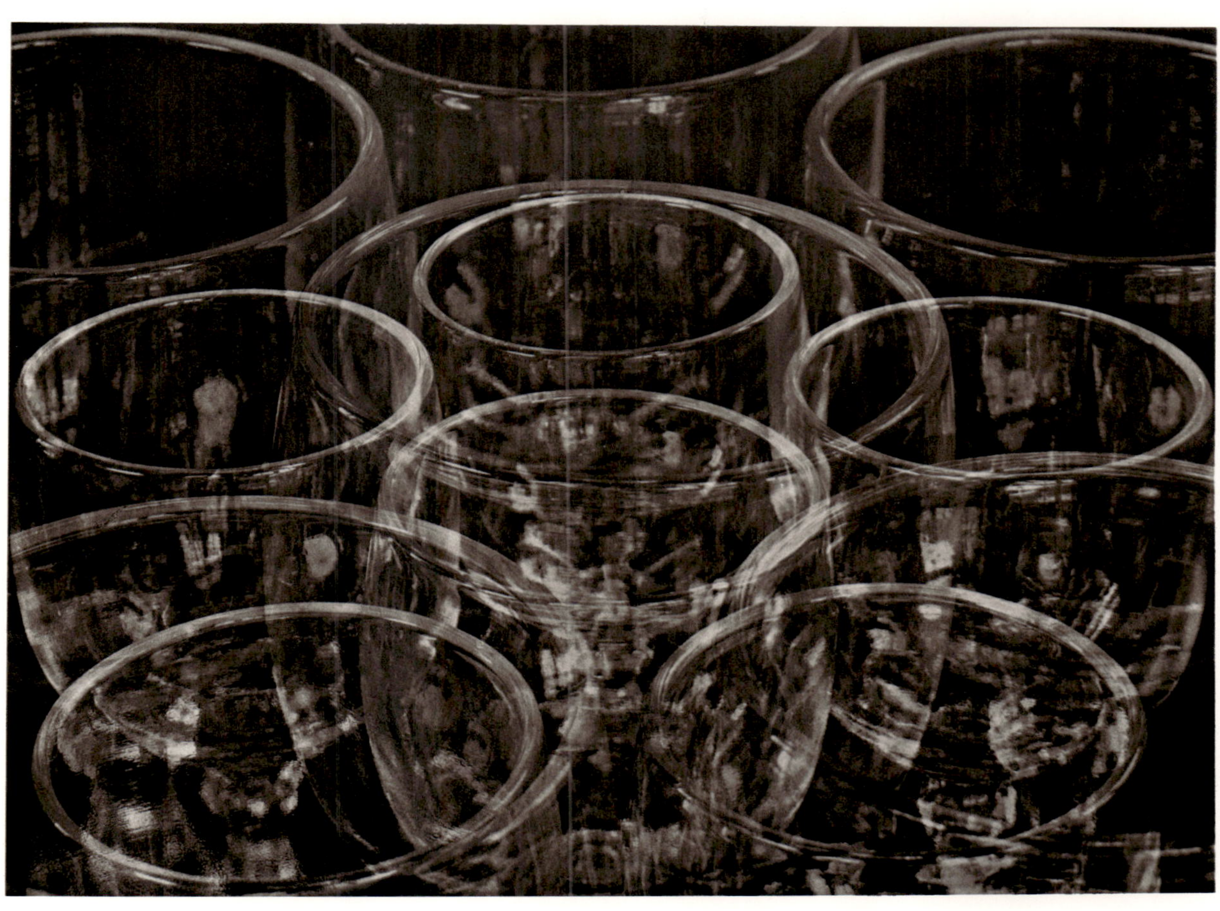

45 · Tina Modotti · **Experiment in Related Forms** · 1924

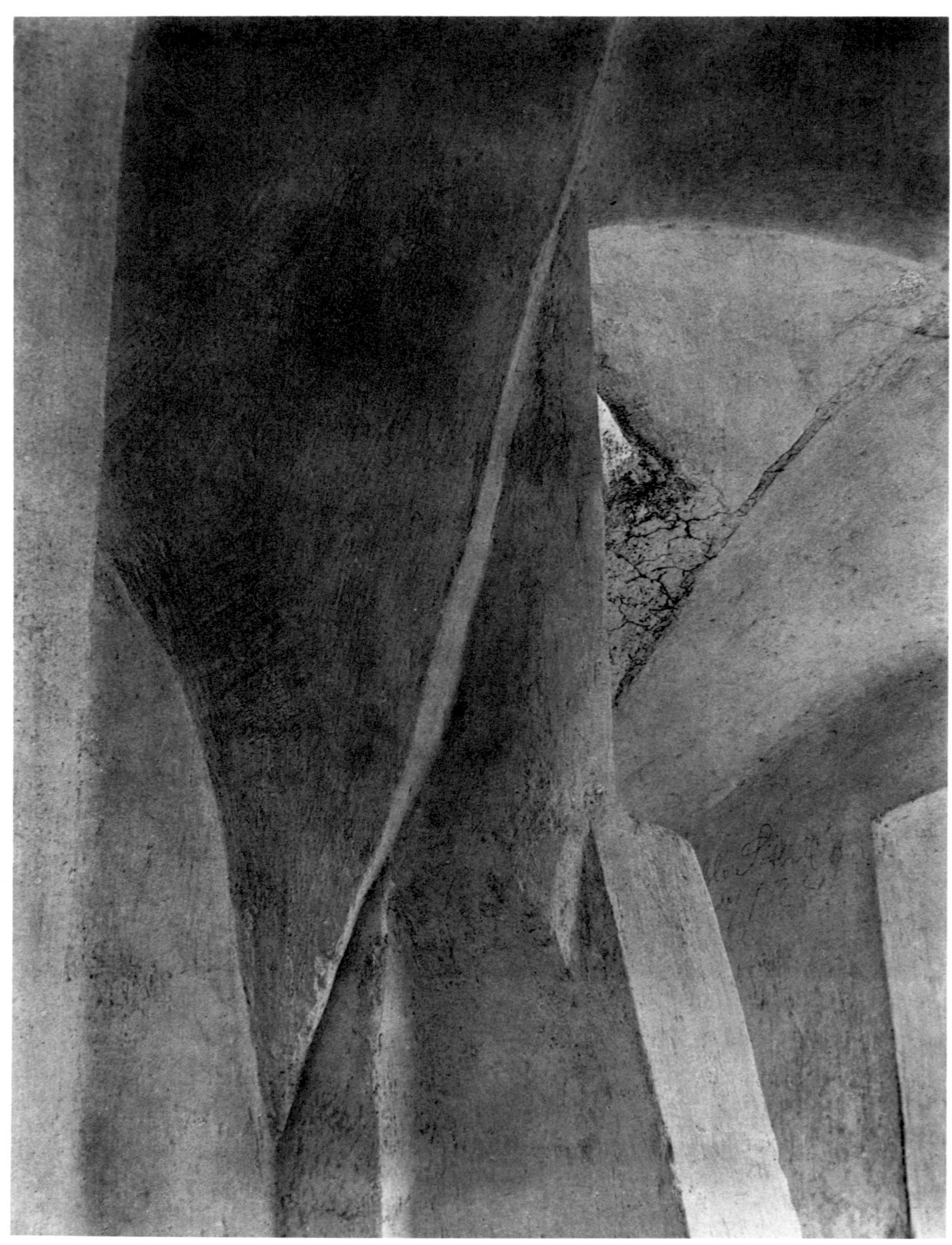

46 · Tina Modotti · **Interior of Church Tower, Tepotzotlan, Mexico** · 1924

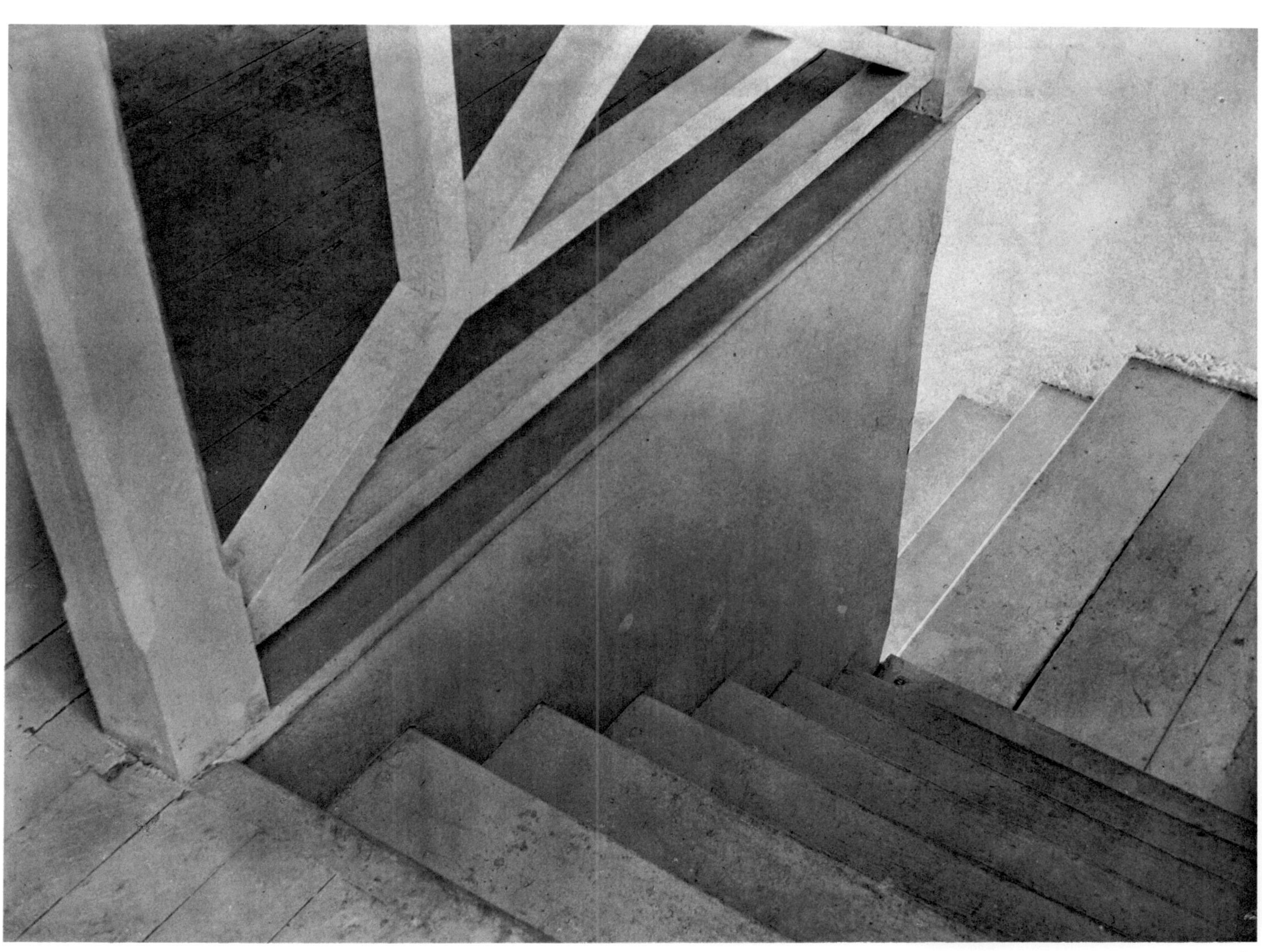

47 · Tina Modotti · **Stairs, Mexico City** · 1923–26

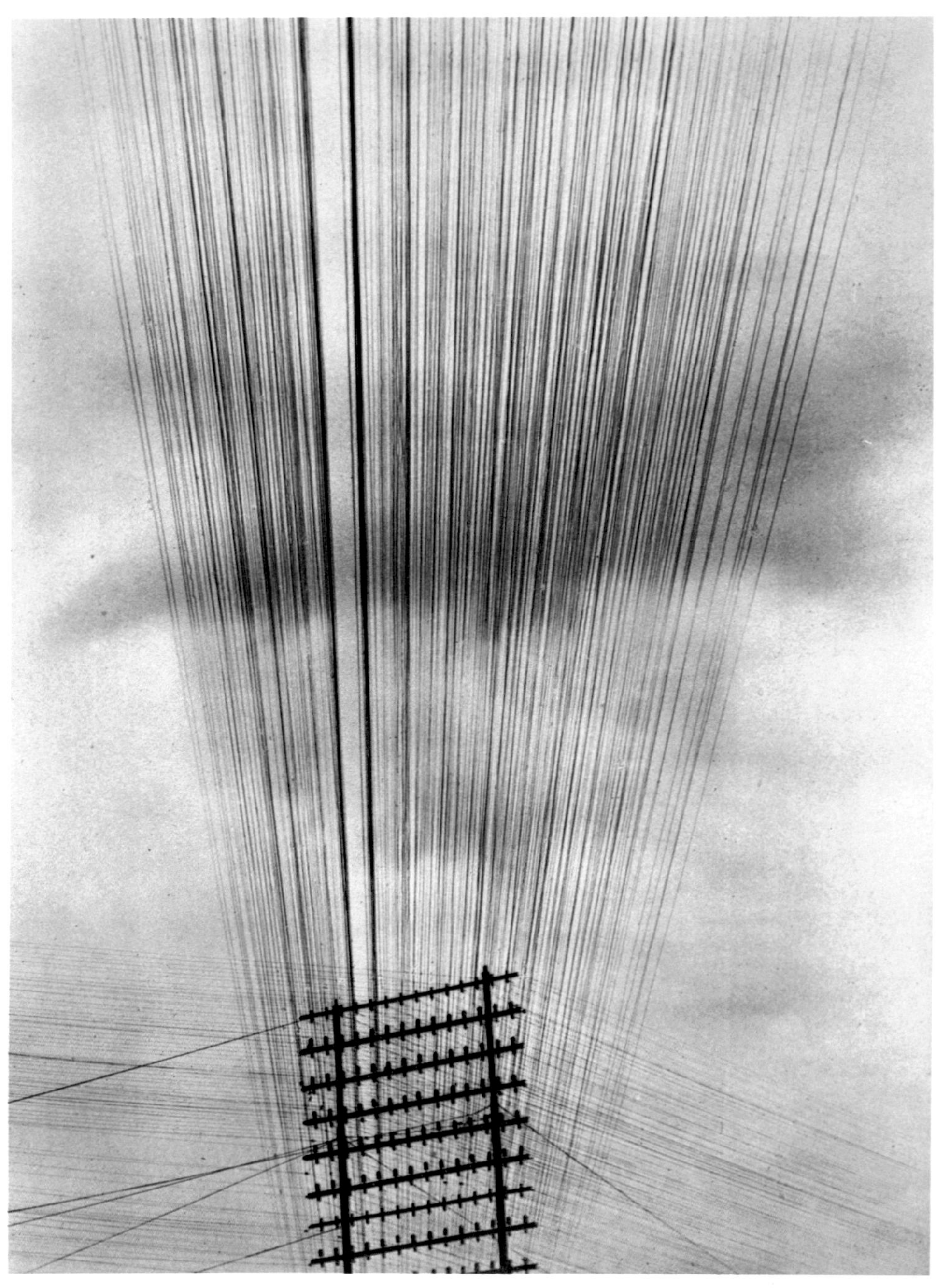

48 · Tina Modotti · **Telephone Wire Composition, Mexico** · 1925

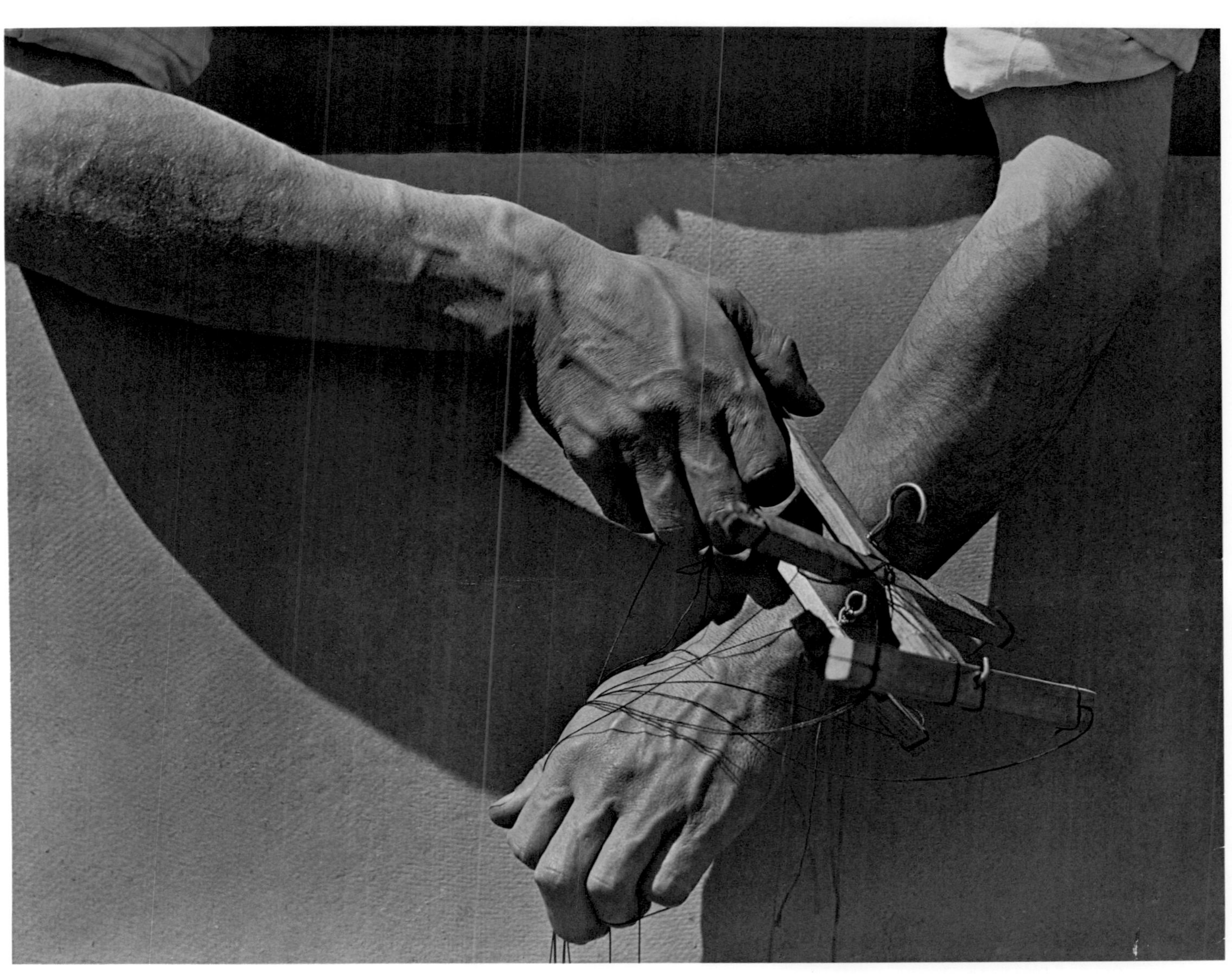

49 · Tina Modotti · **Hands of a Marionette Player** · Mexico, 1926

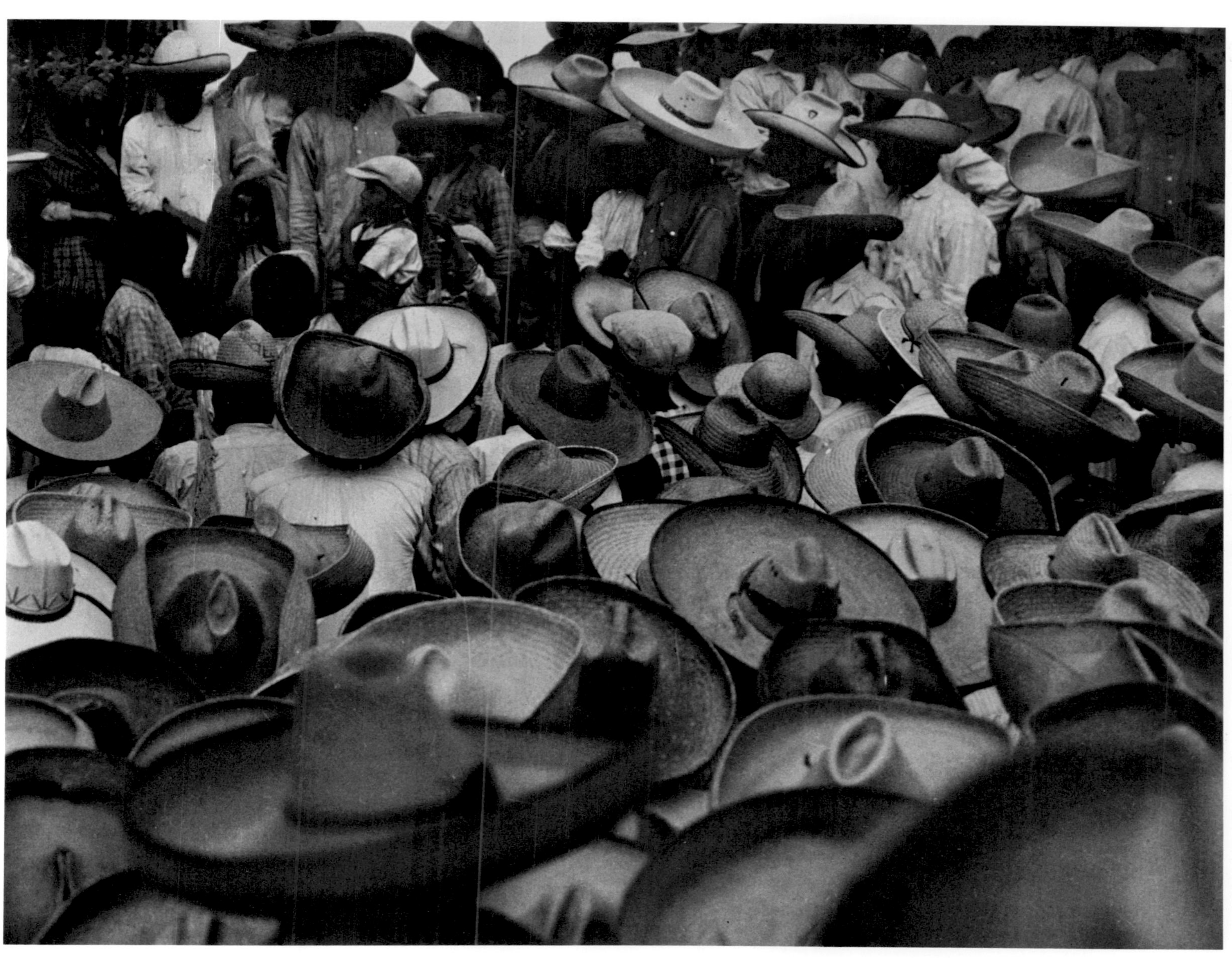

50 · Tina Modotti · **Demonstrations by Campesinos, Mexico** · c. 1928

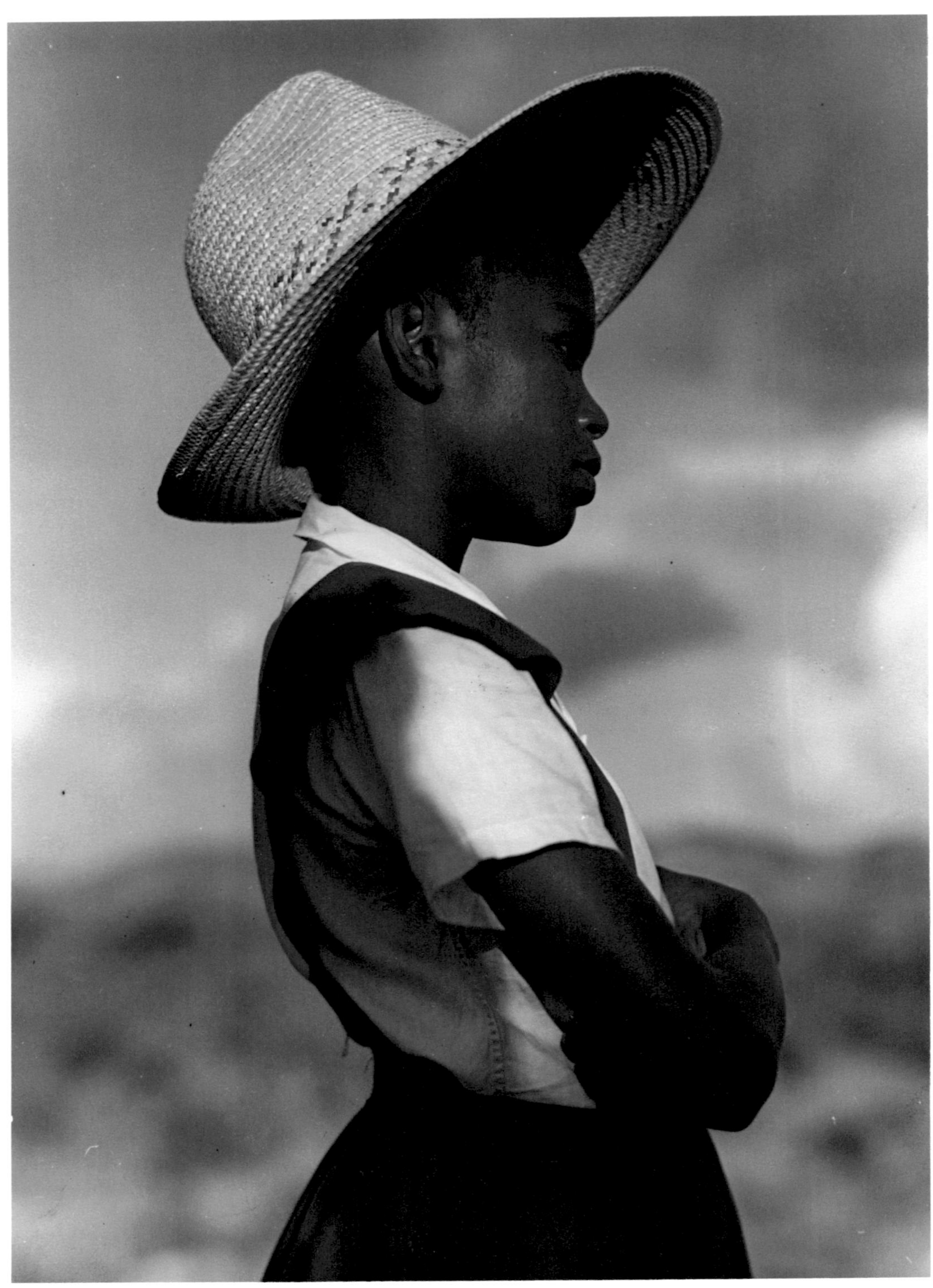

51 · Consuelo Kanaga · **Girl in Straw Hat** · c. 1940

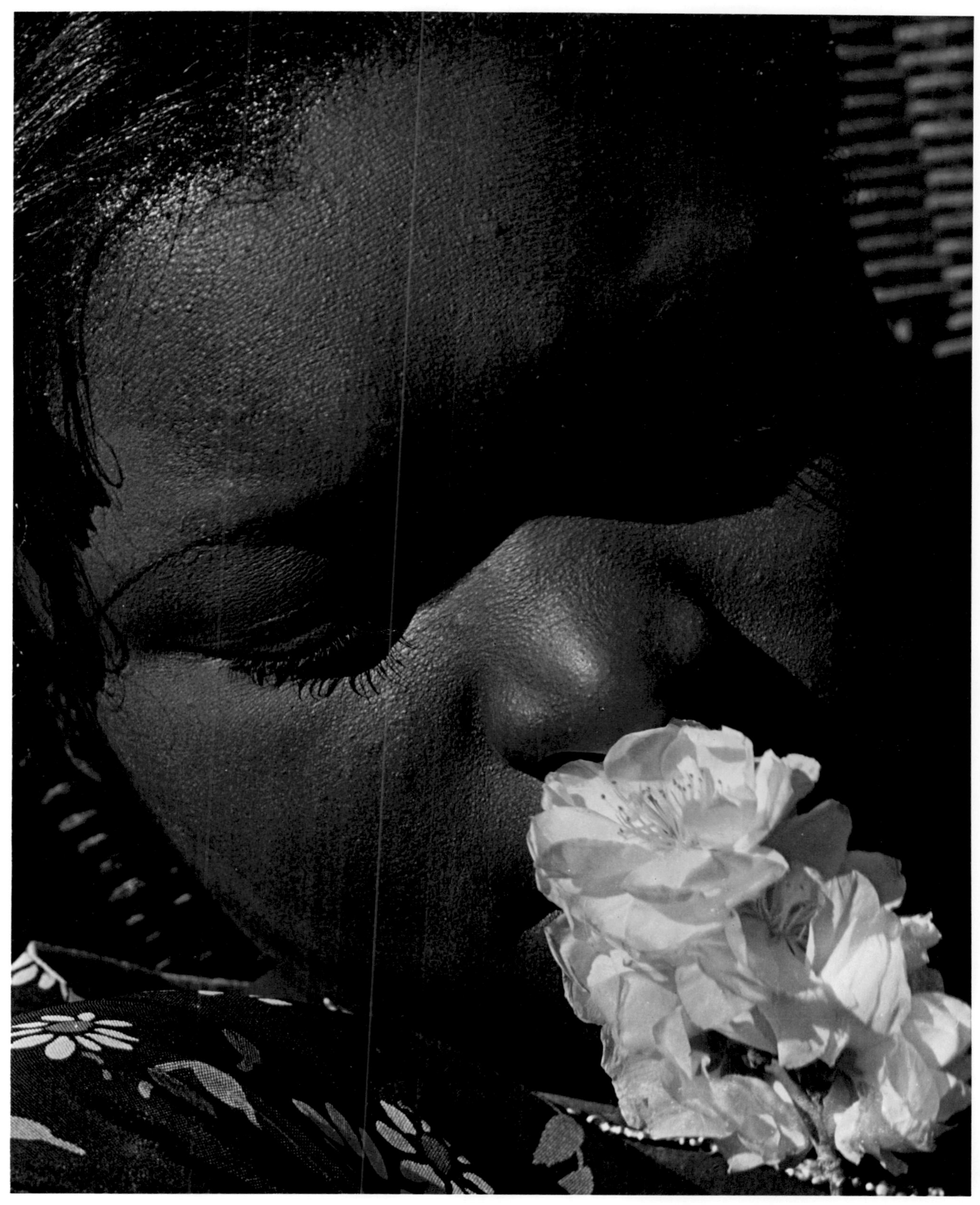

52 · Consuelo Kanaga · **The Girl with a Flower (Francis)** · 1928

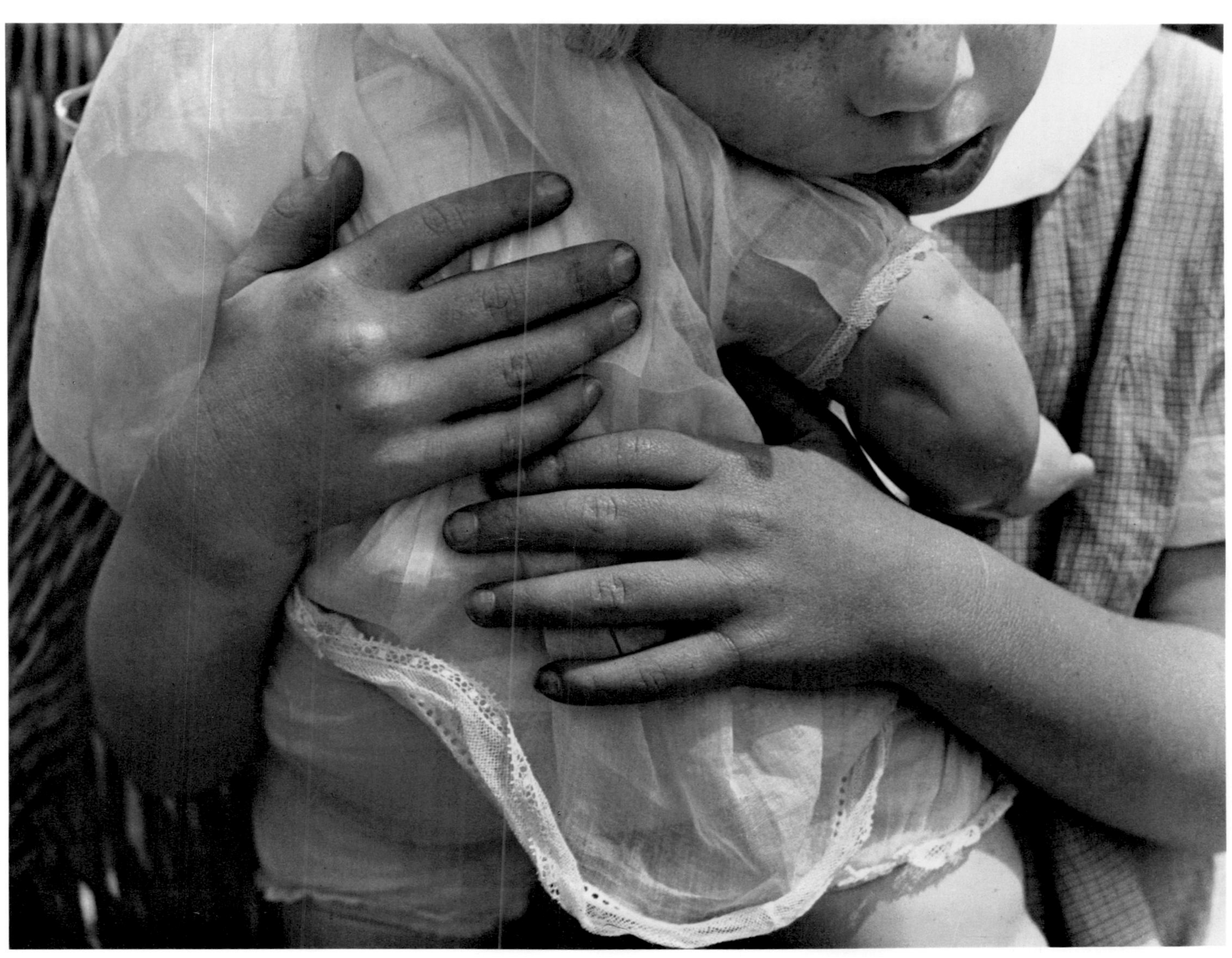

53 · Alma Lavenson · **Child with Doll** · 1932

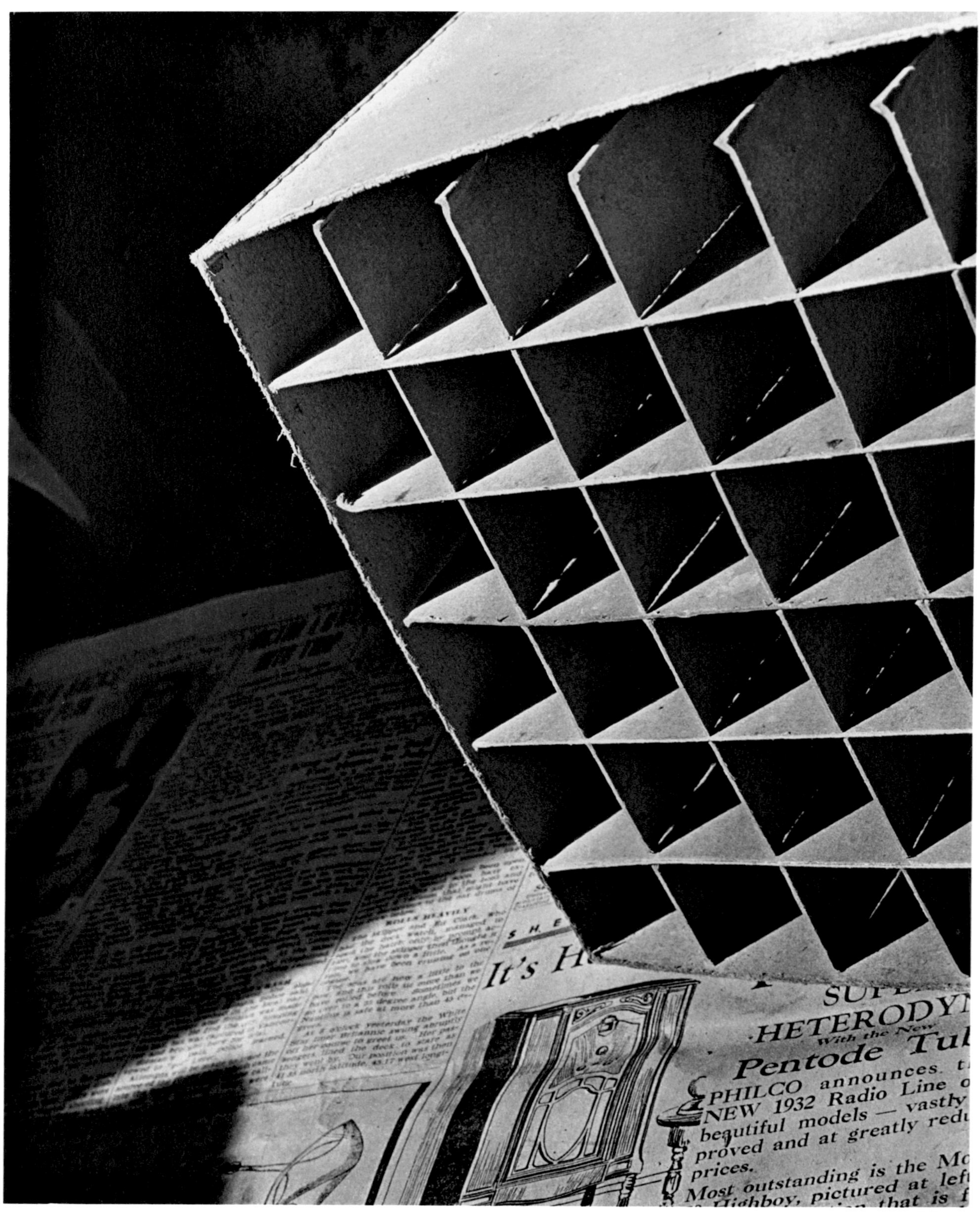

54 · Alma Lavenson · **Egg Box** · 1931

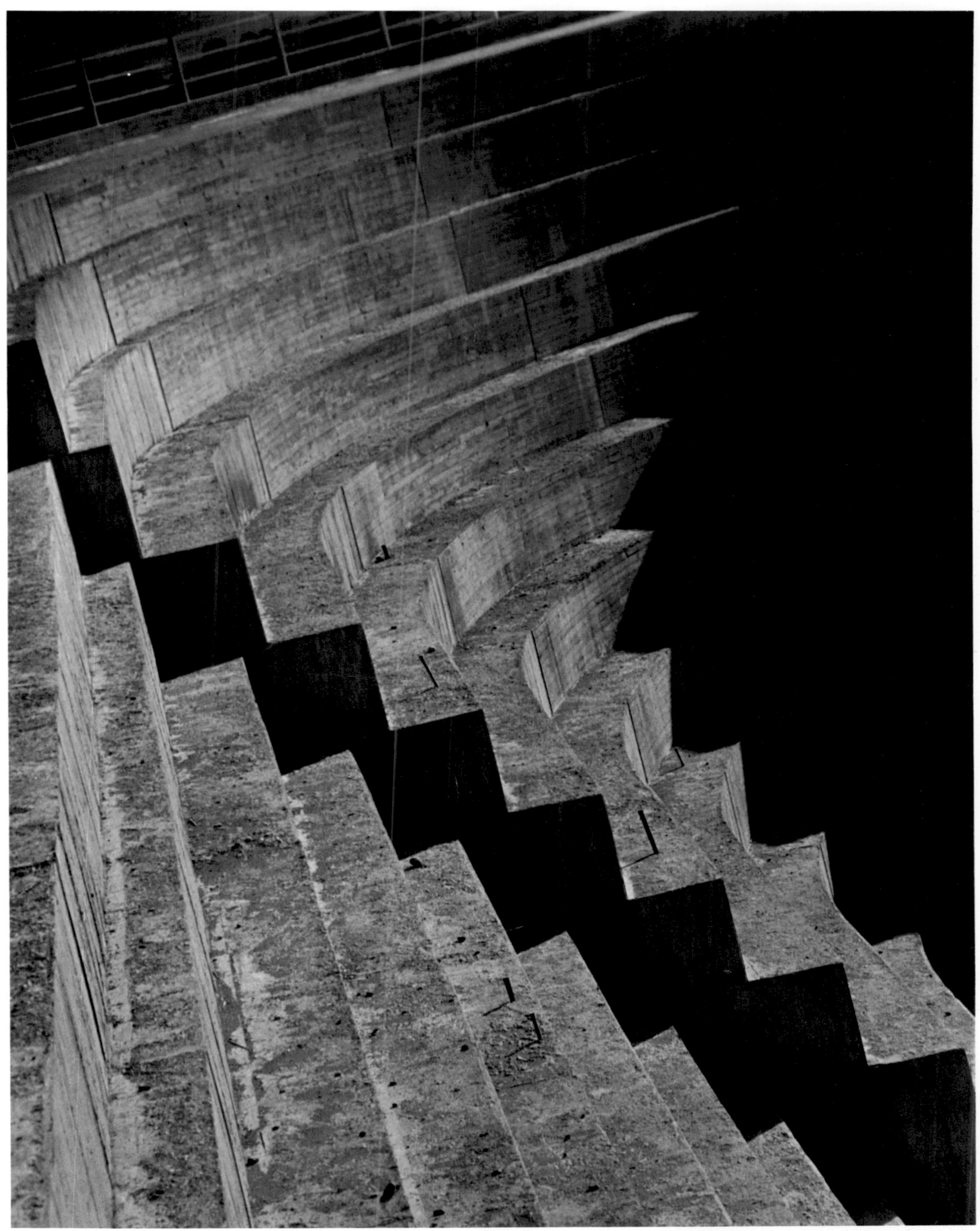

55 · Alma Lavenson · **Calaveras Dam II** · 1932

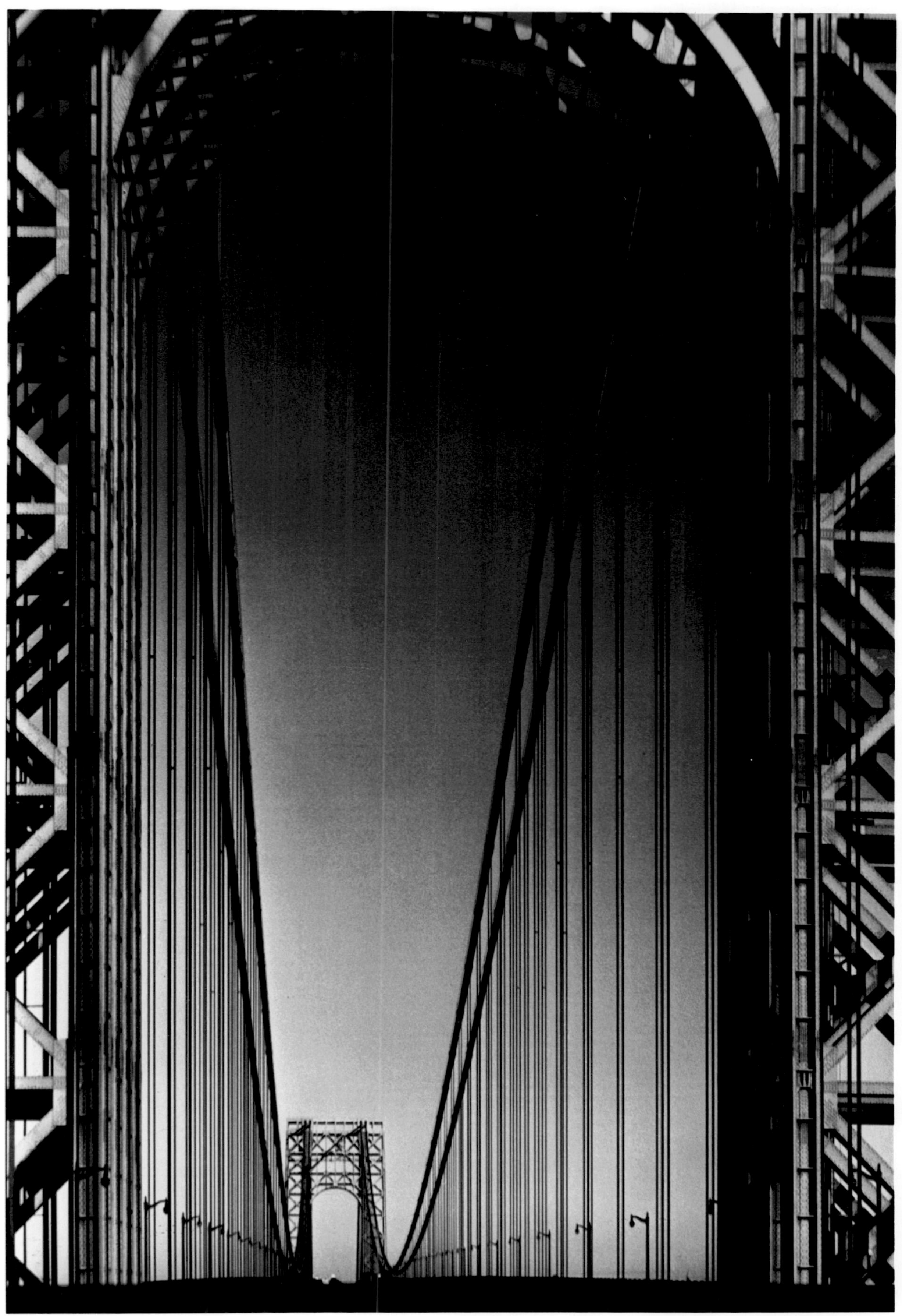

56 · Margaret Bourke-White · **George Washington Bridge** · c. 1930s

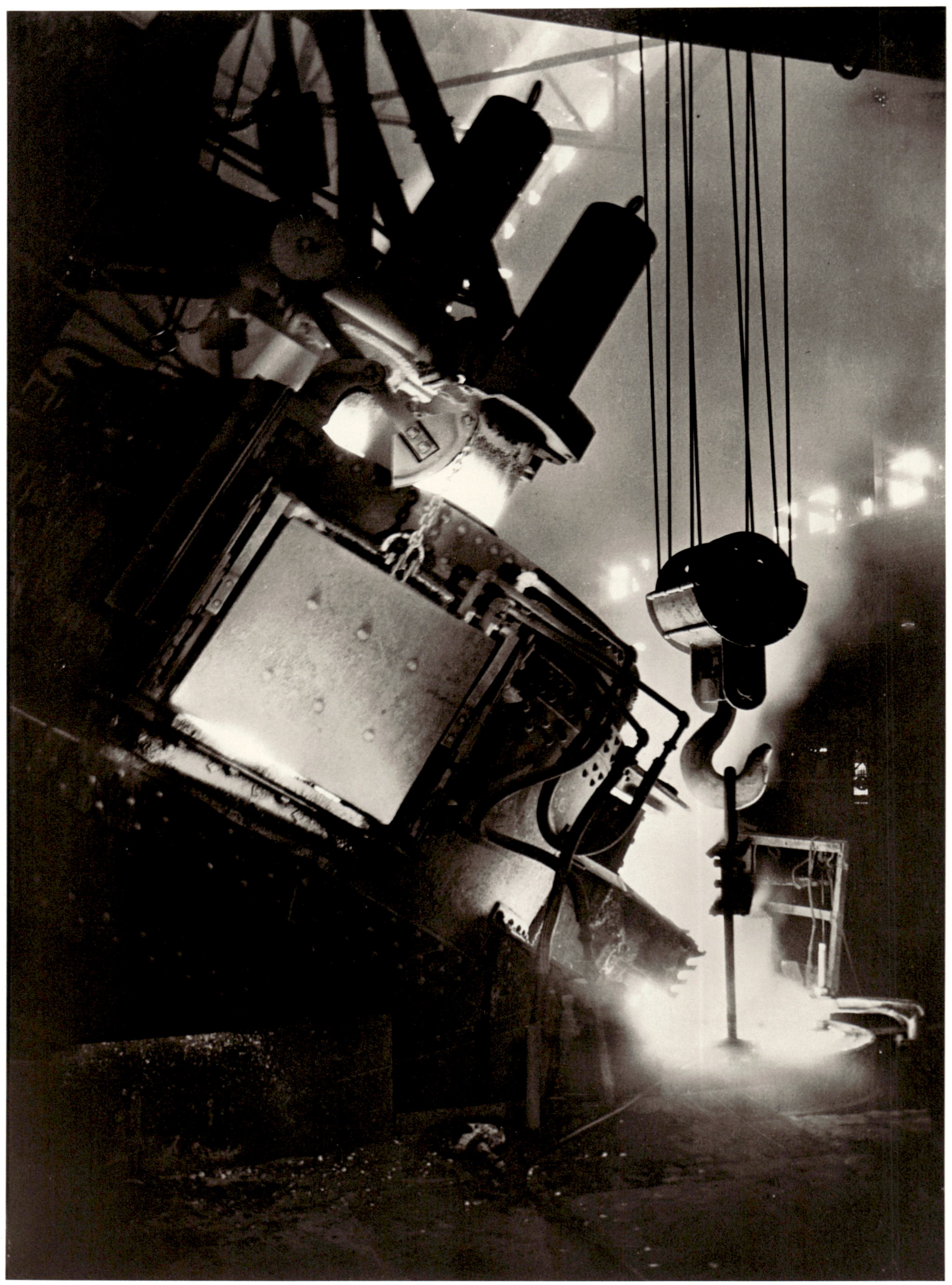

57 · Margaret Bourke-White · Untitled · Late 1920s

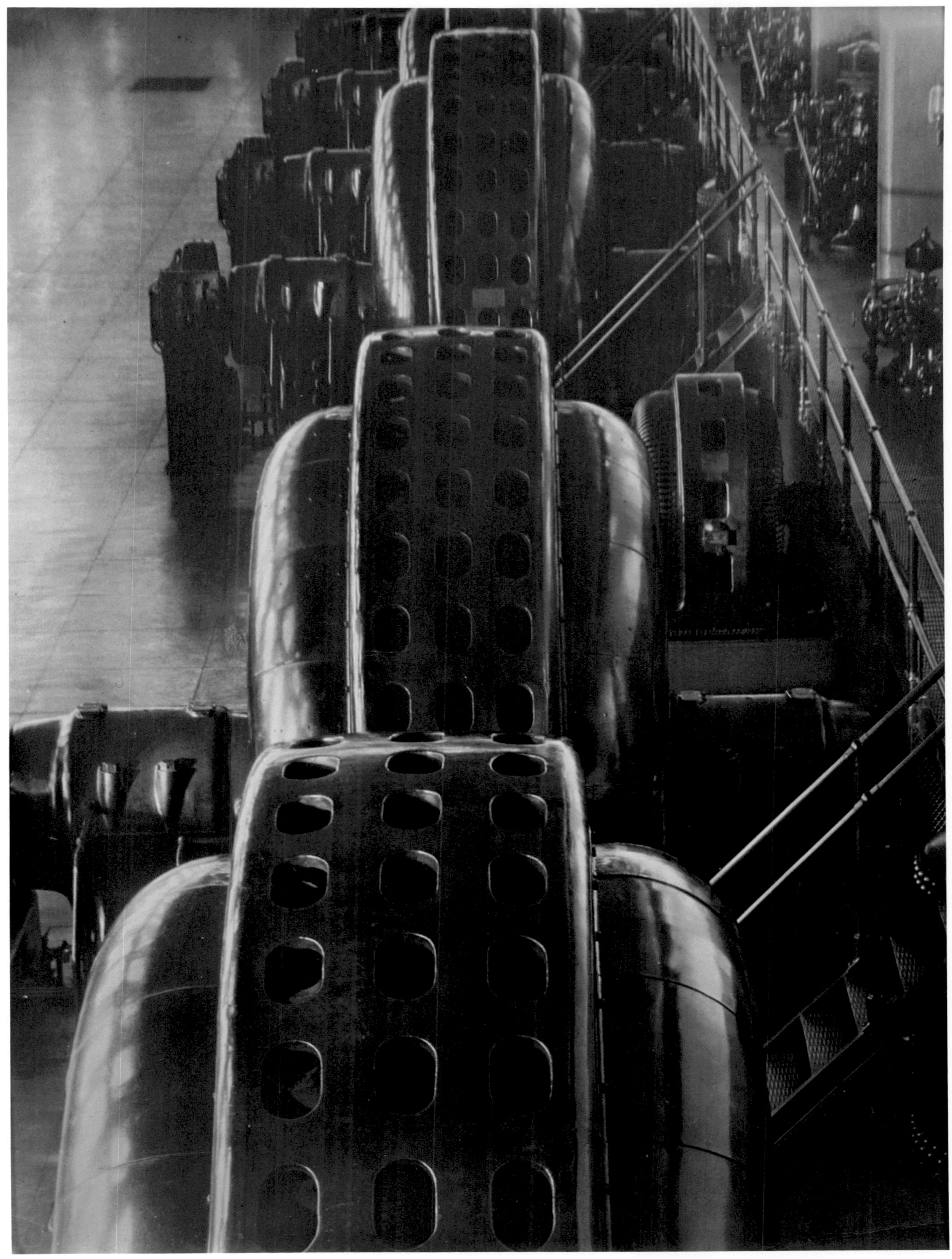

58 · Margaret Bourke-White · **Hydro Generators, Niagara Falls Power Co.** · 1928

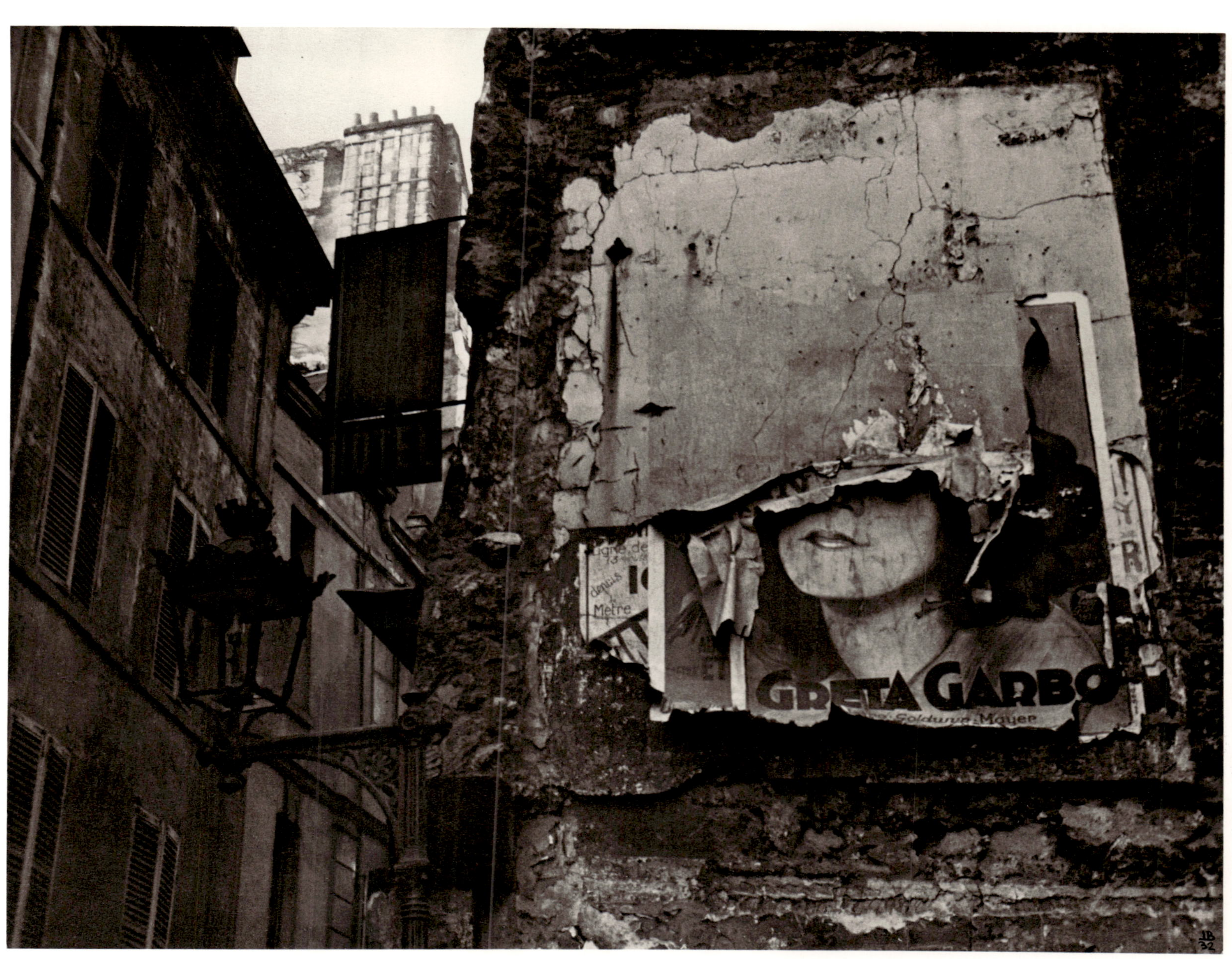

59 · Ilse Bing · **Paris** · 1932

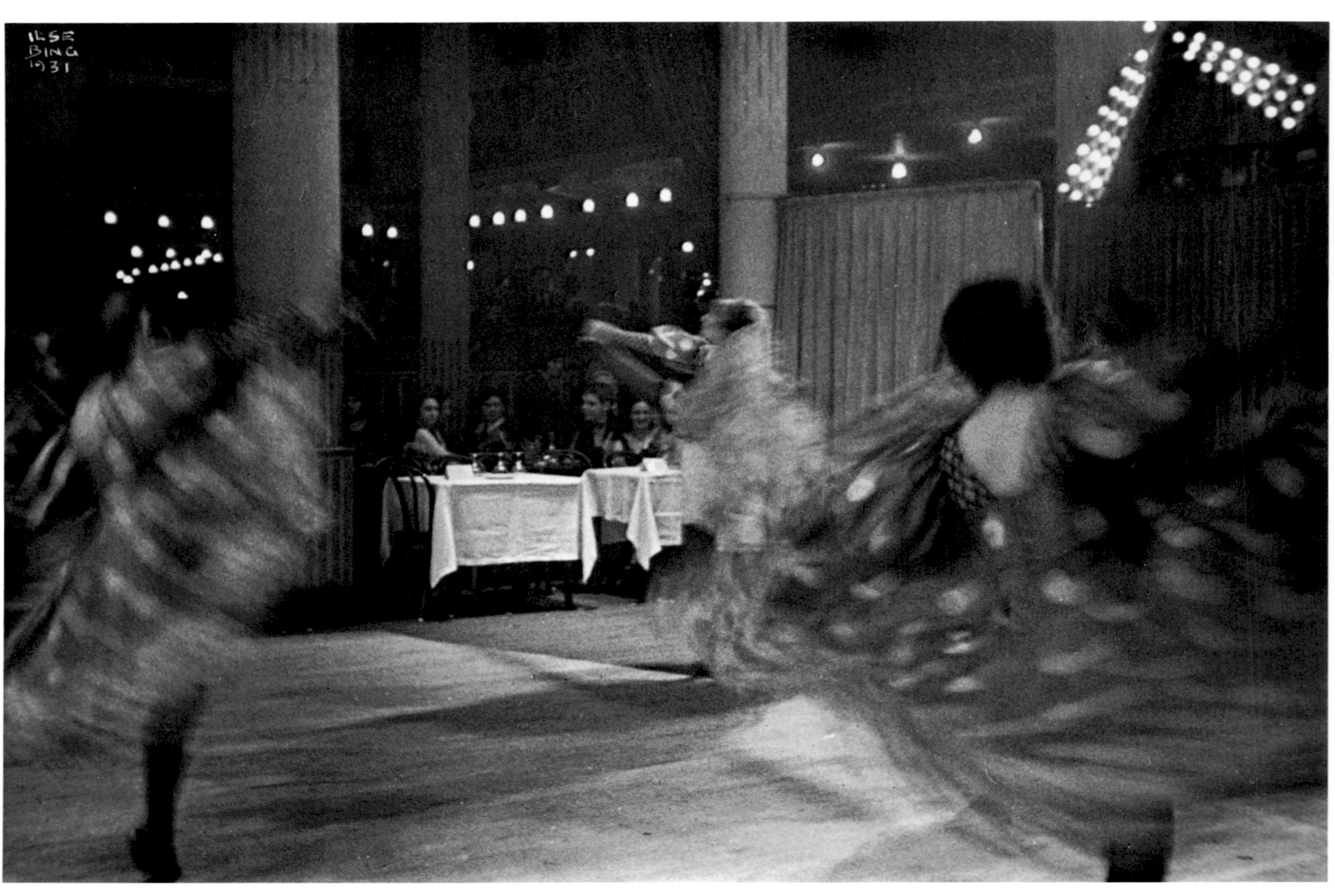

60 · Ilse Bing · **Can-Can Dancers at the Moulin Rouge** · Paris, 1931

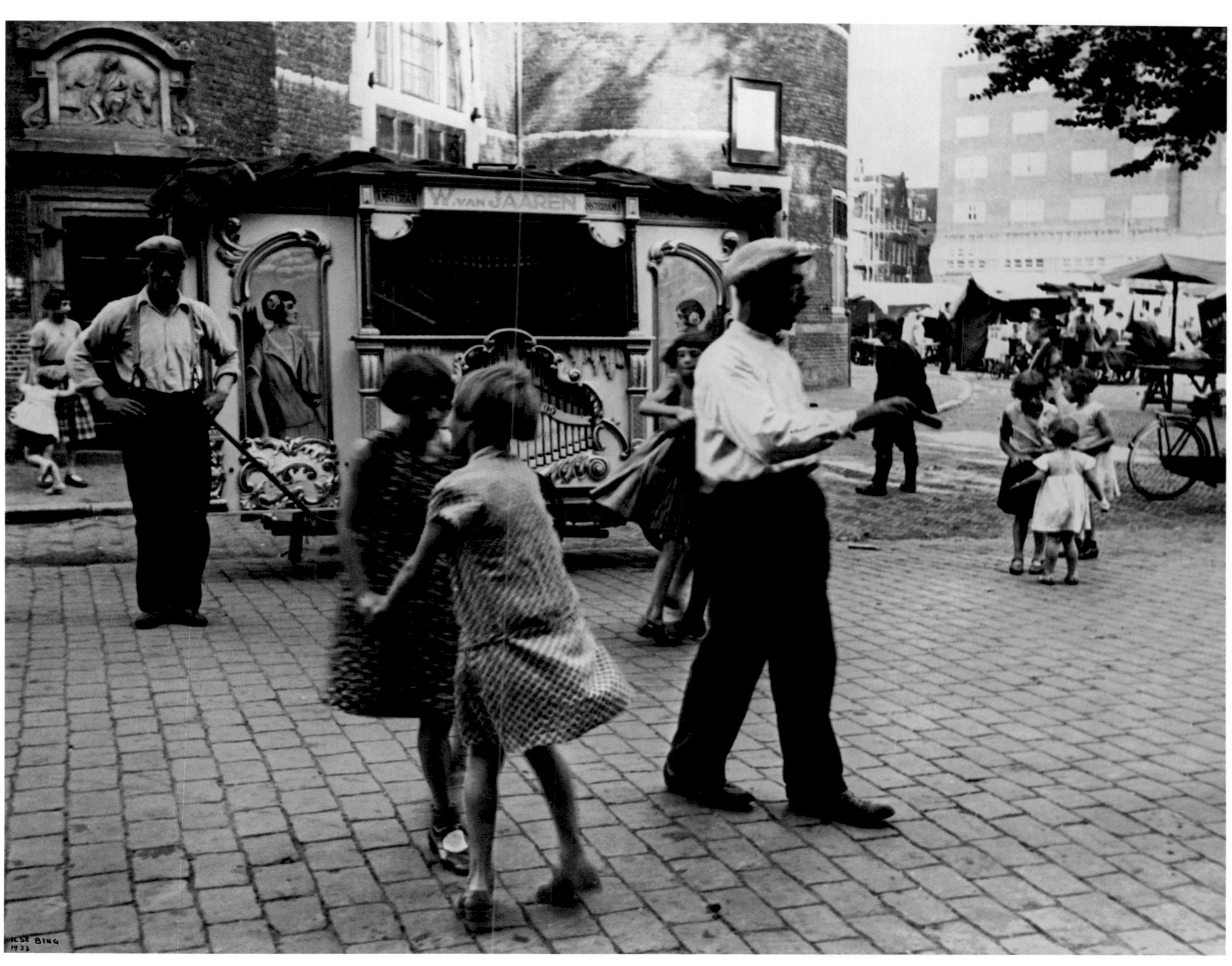

61 · Ilse Bing · **Street Organ** · Amsterdam, 1933

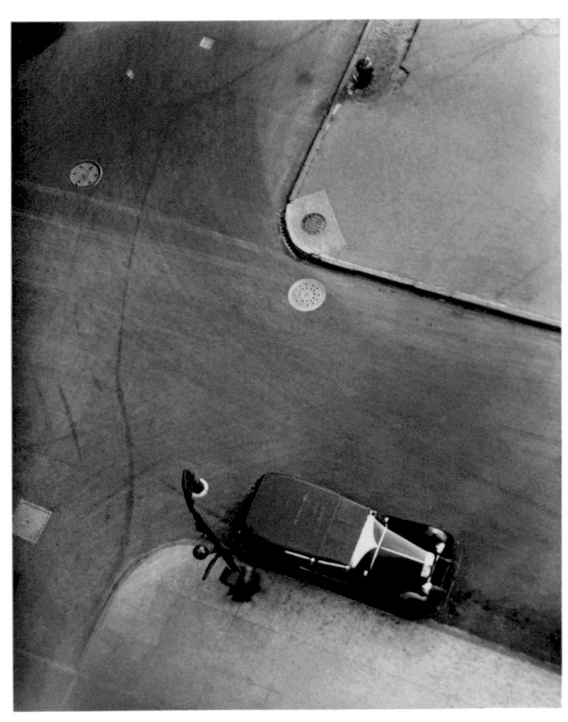

62 · Marjorie Content · **From 29 Washington Square** · c. 1928

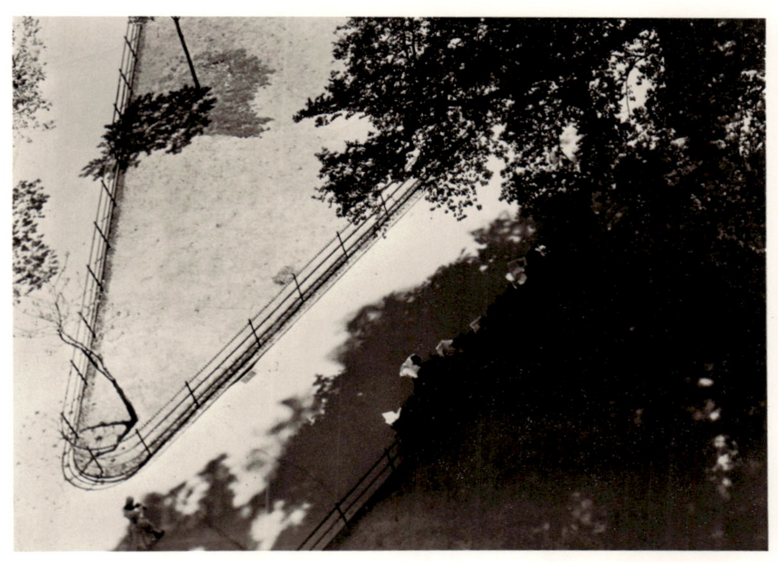

63 · Marjorie Content · Untitled · c. 1928

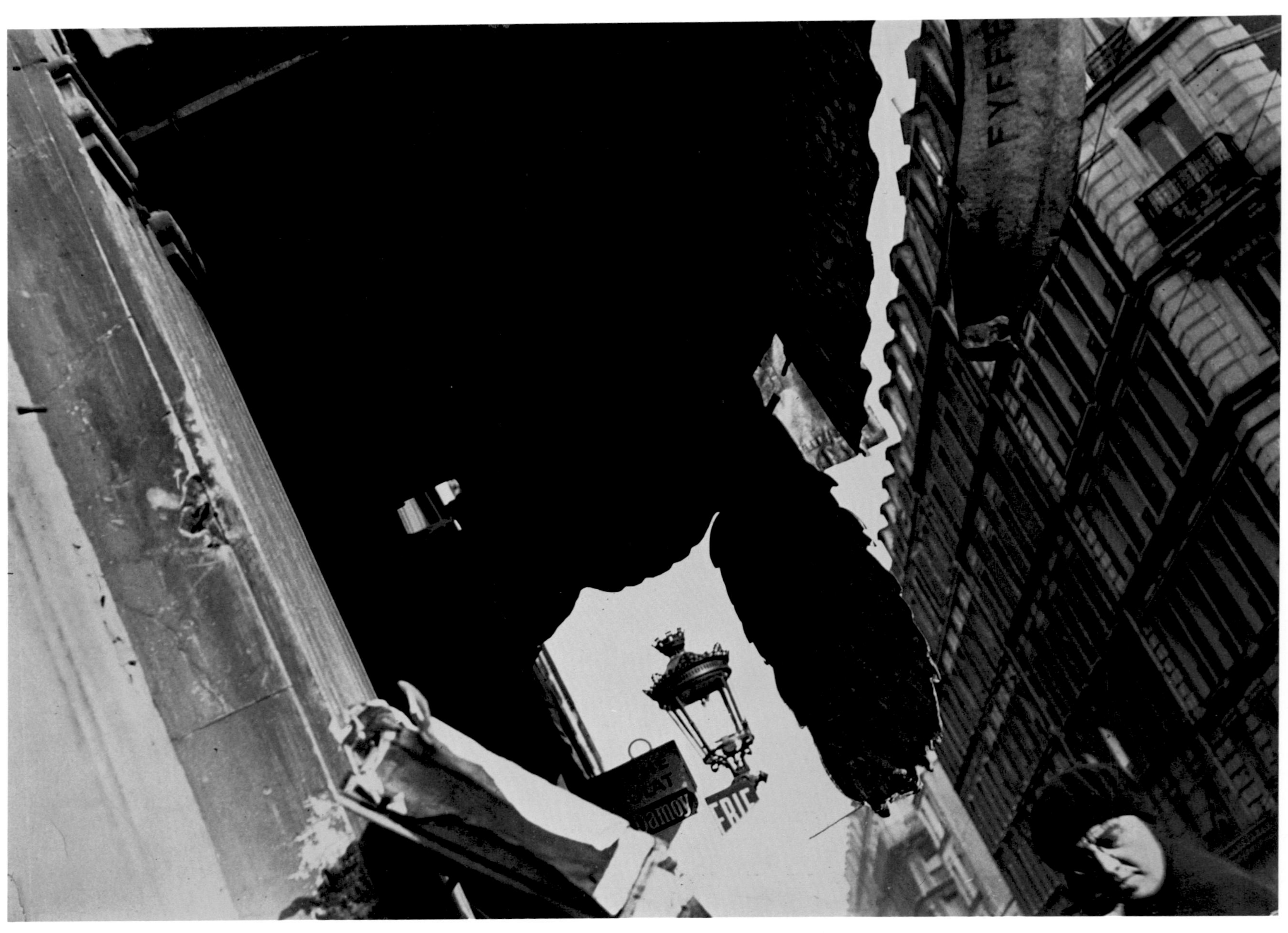

64 · Florence Henri · **In der Strasse** · 1930

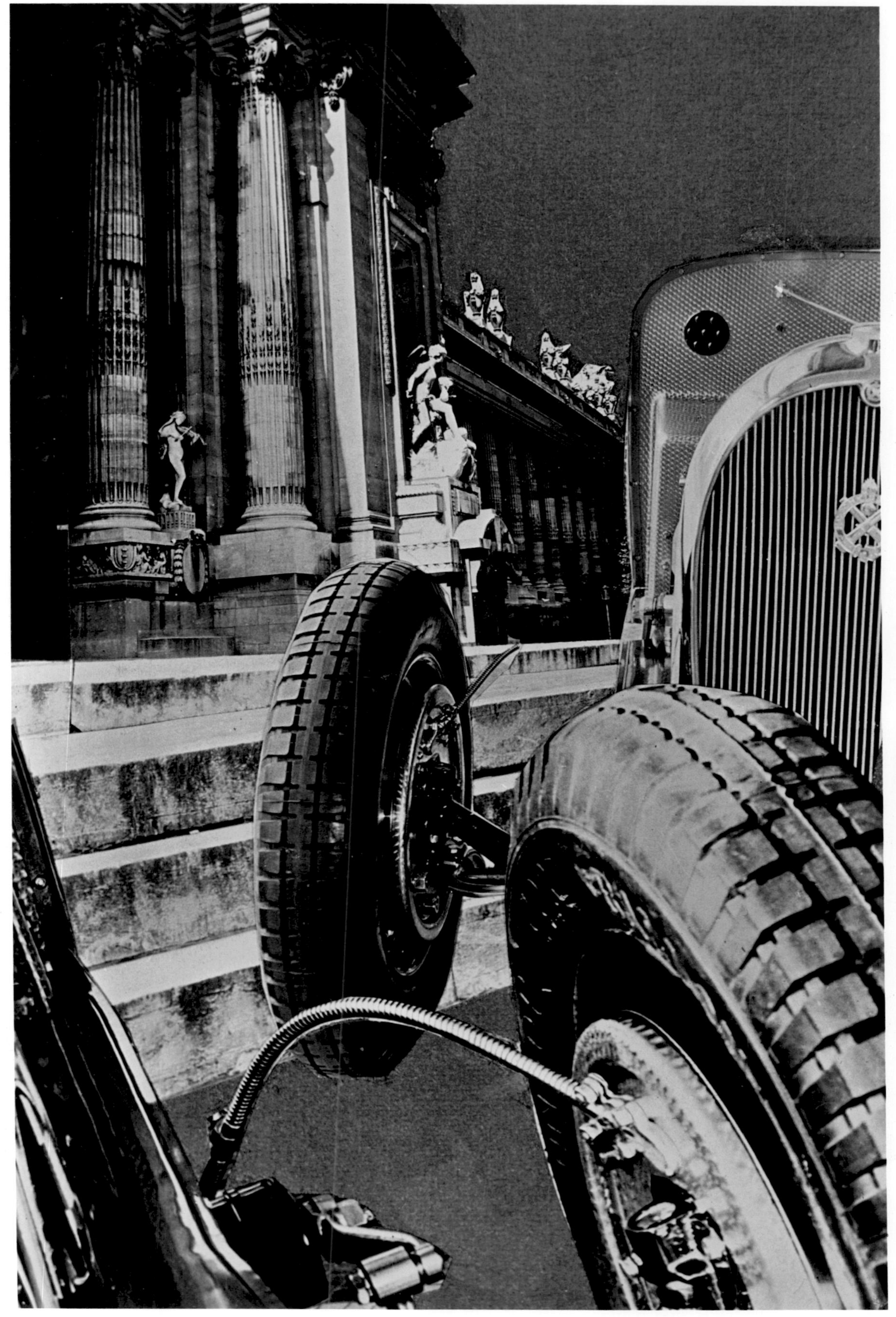

65 · Florence Henri · **Réclame pour Hotchkiss, Paris** · c. 1931

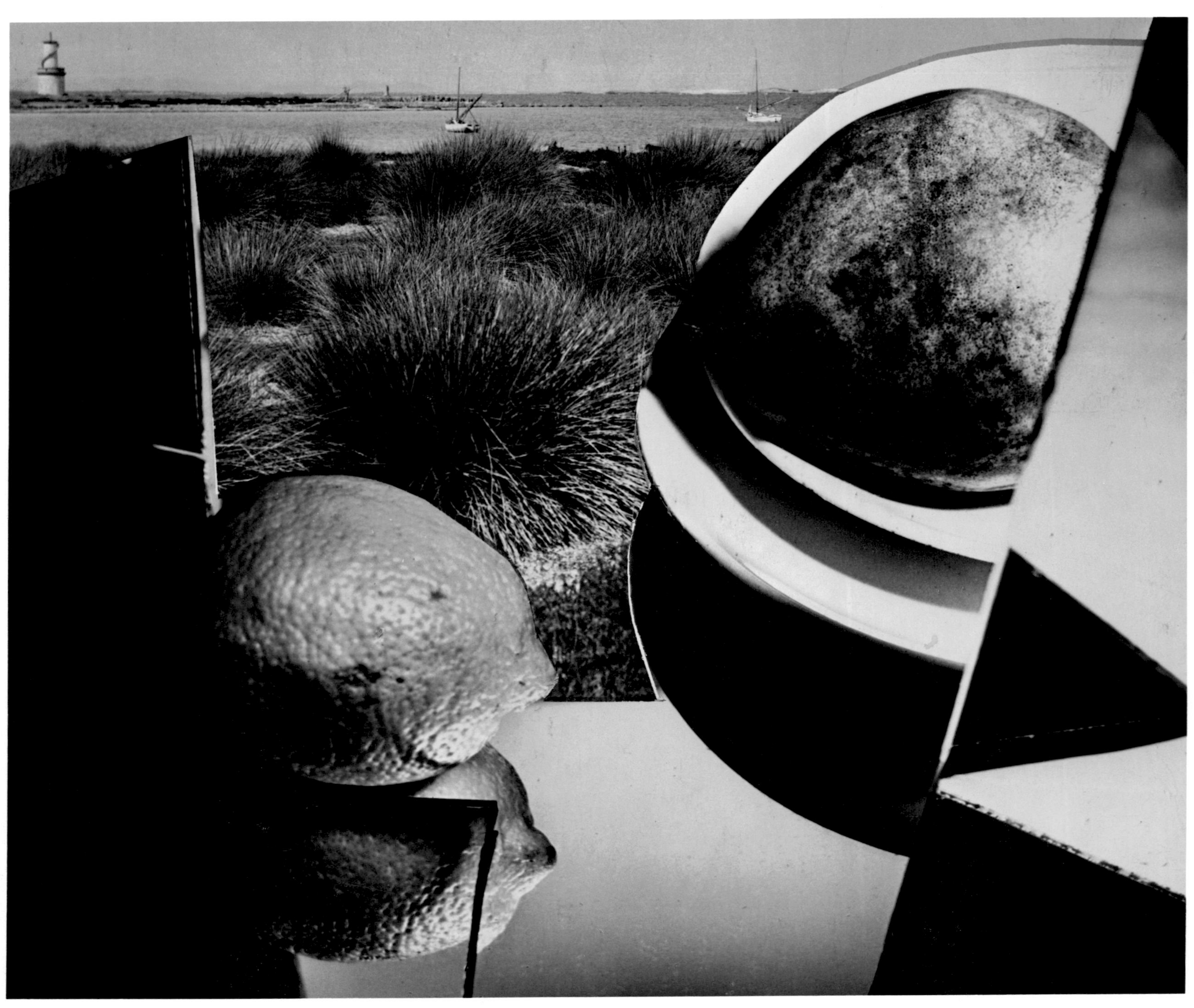

66 · Florence Henri · Photomontage · Brittany, c. 1935

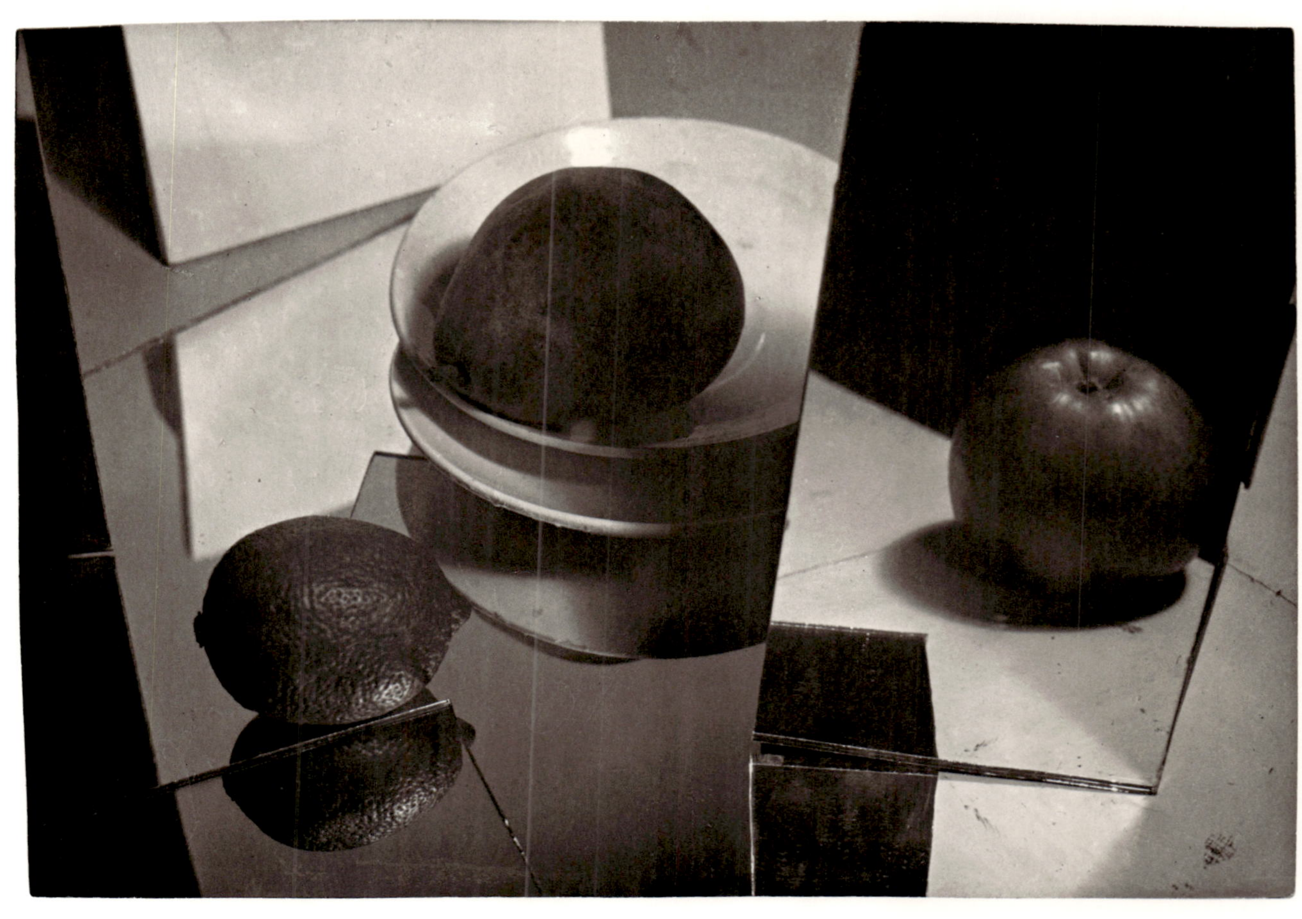

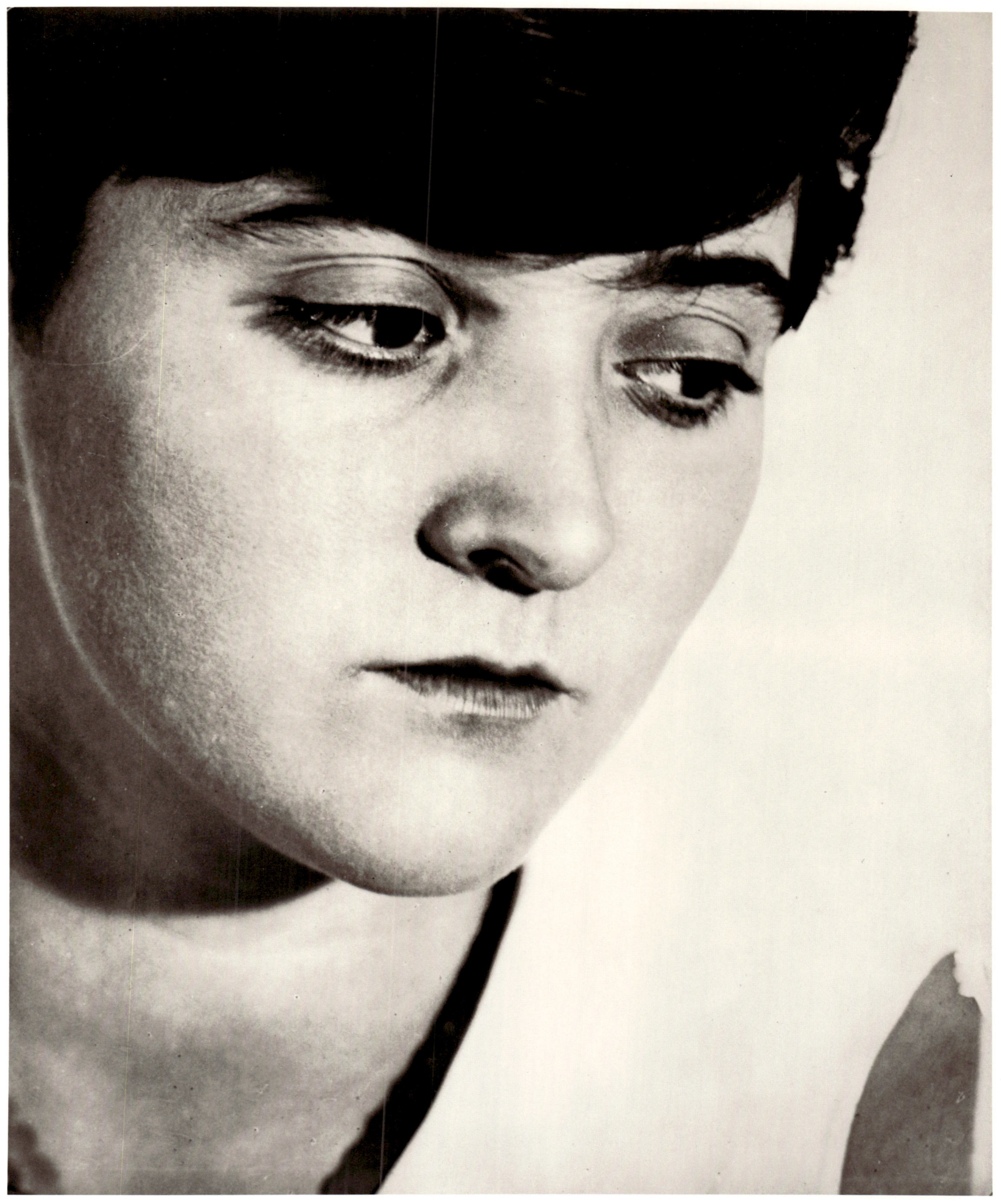

68 · Florence Henri · **Woti Werner** · c. 1929

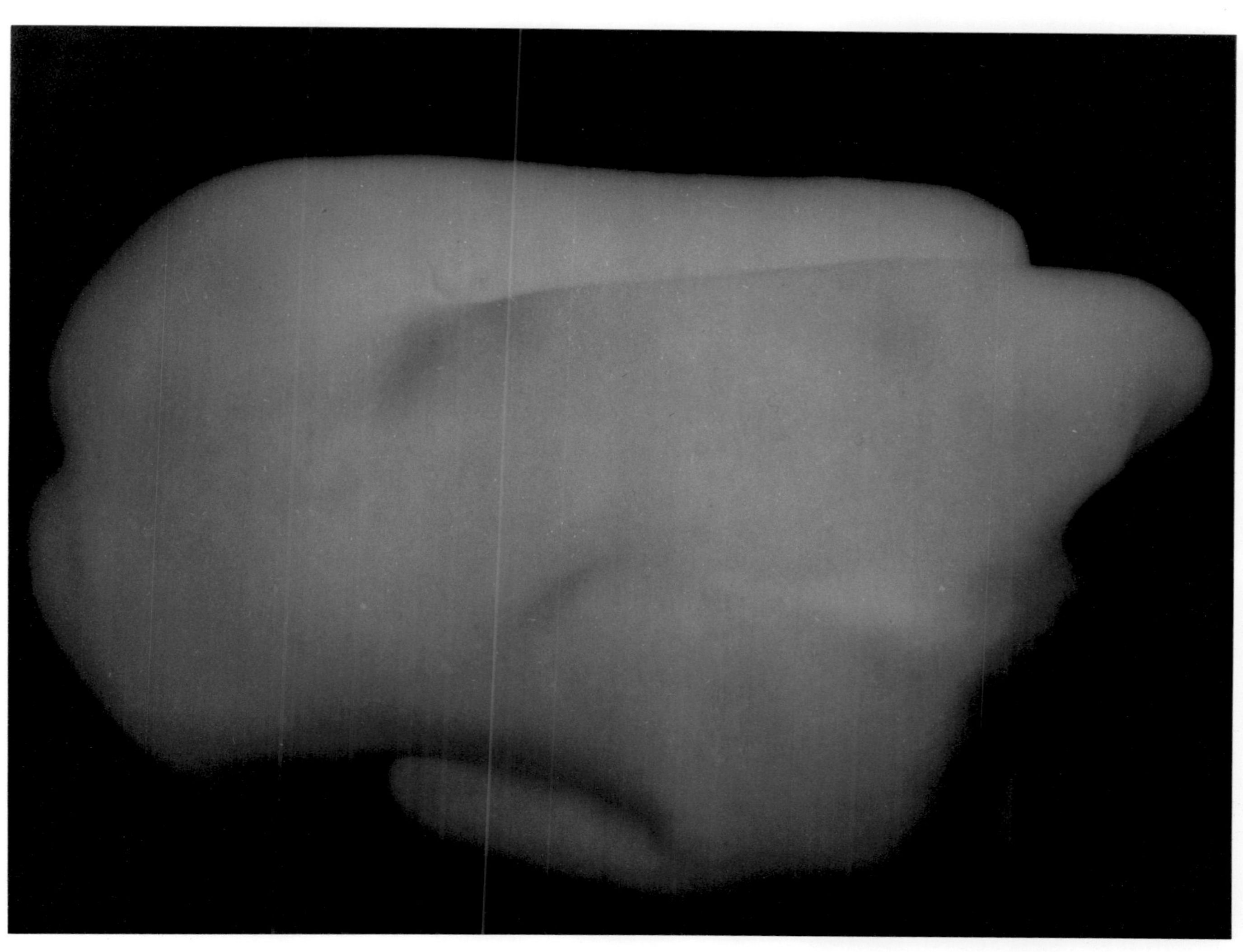

69 · Lee Miller · **Nude** (Self-portrait) · Paris, c. 1931

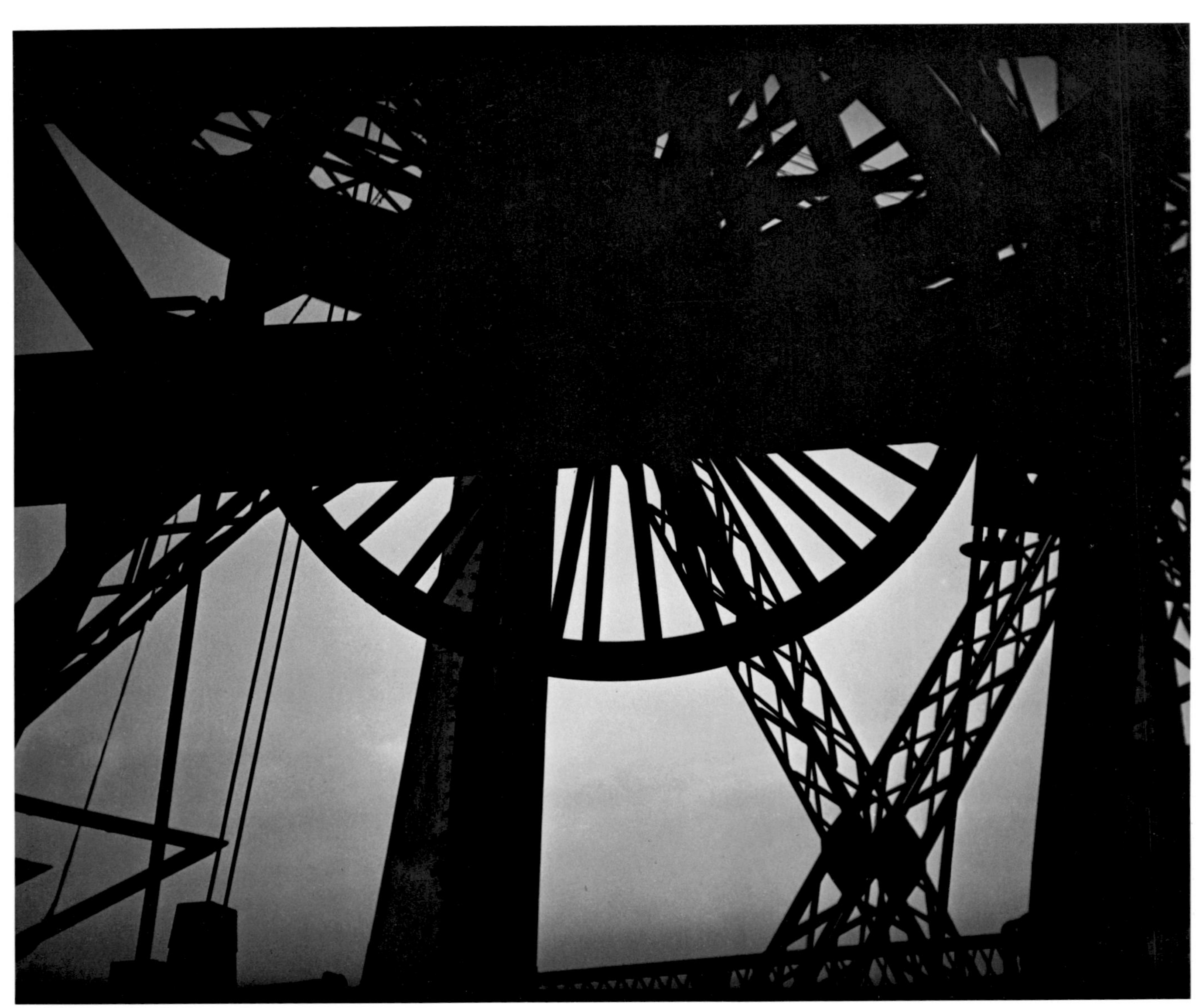

70 · Lee Miller · **Eiffel Tower** · c. 1931

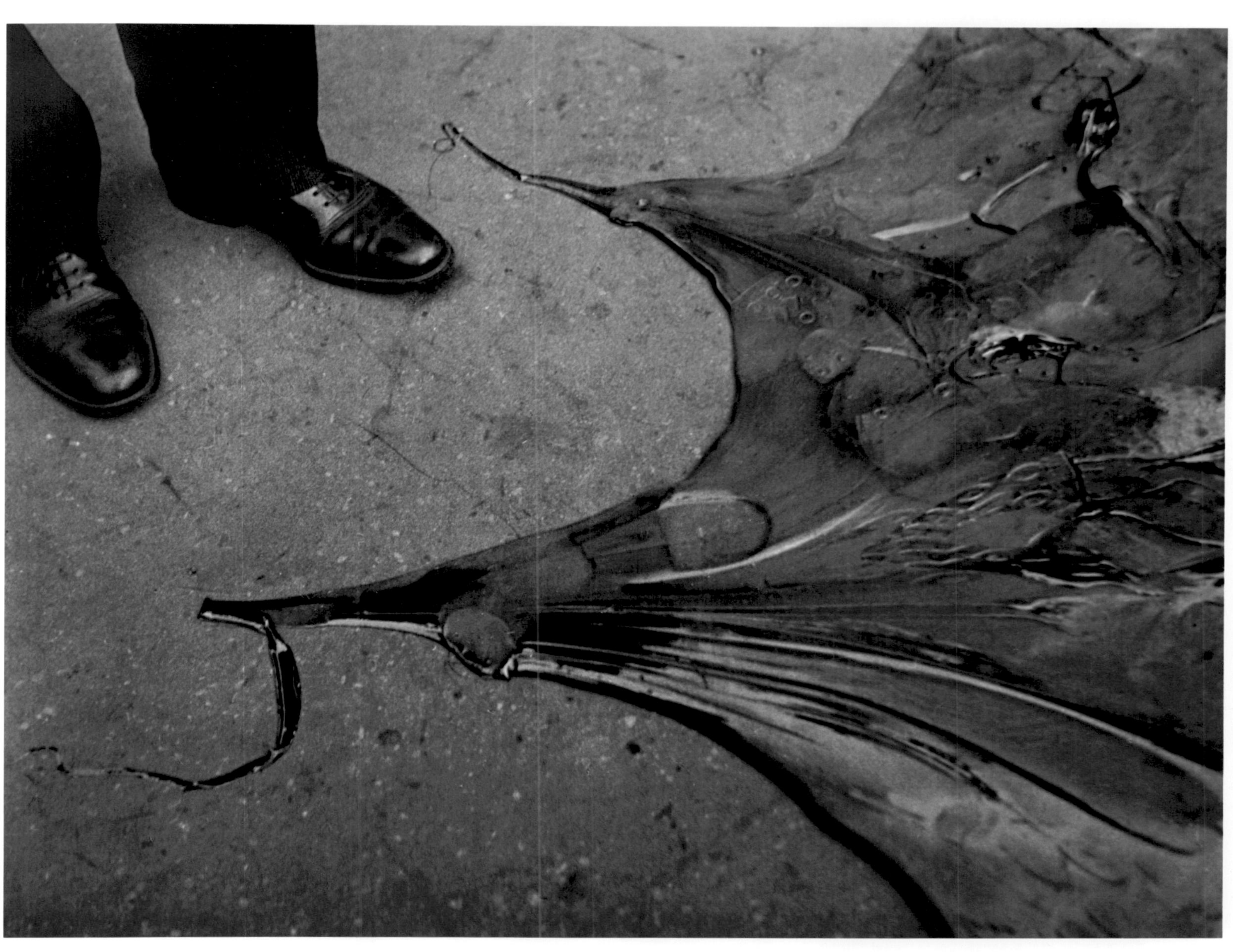

71 · Lee Miller · **Man Standing Near Asphalt** · Paris, c. 1930

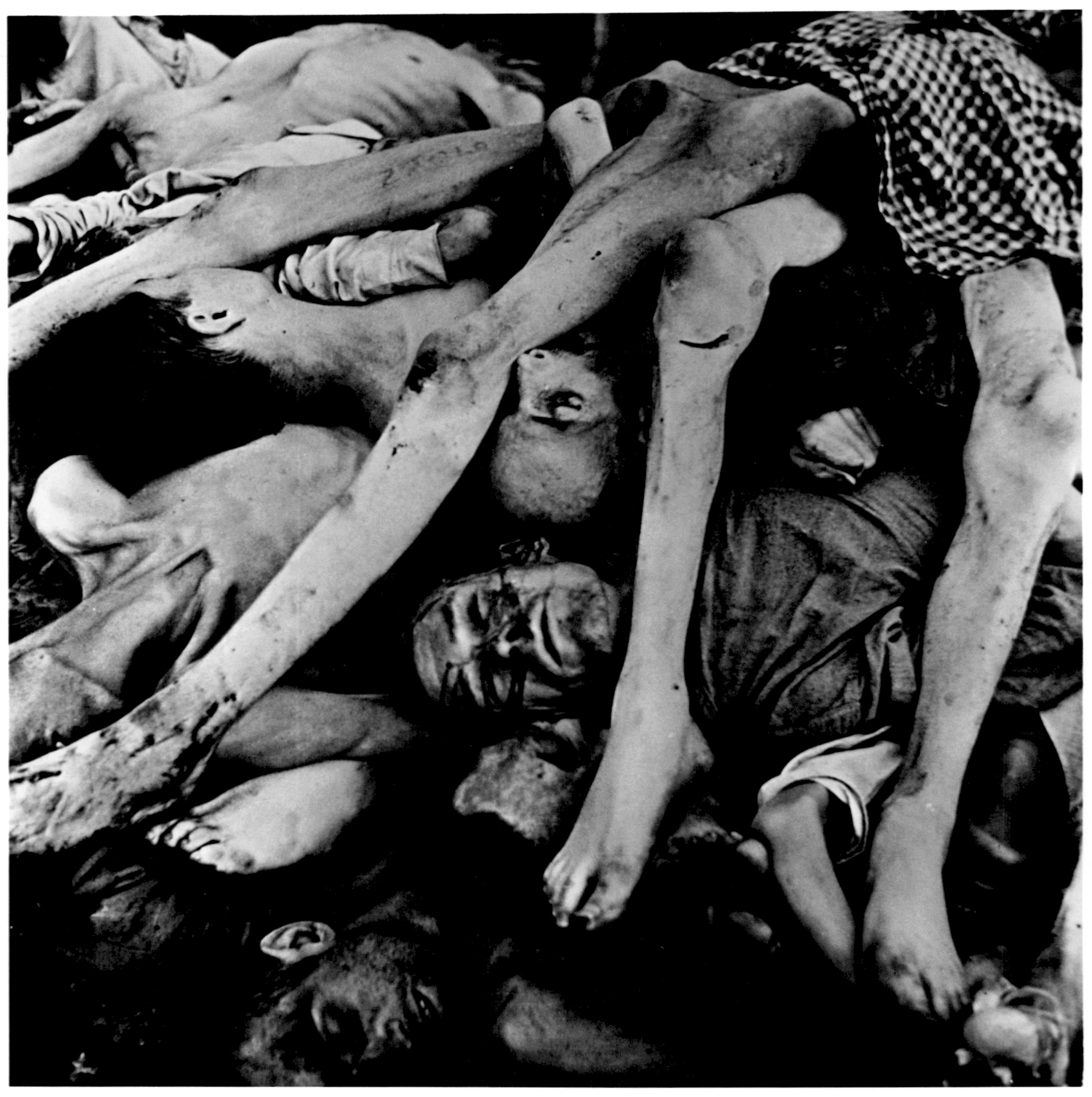

72 · Lee Miller · **Dead Prisoners, Dachau Concentration Camp, Germany** · April 30, 1945

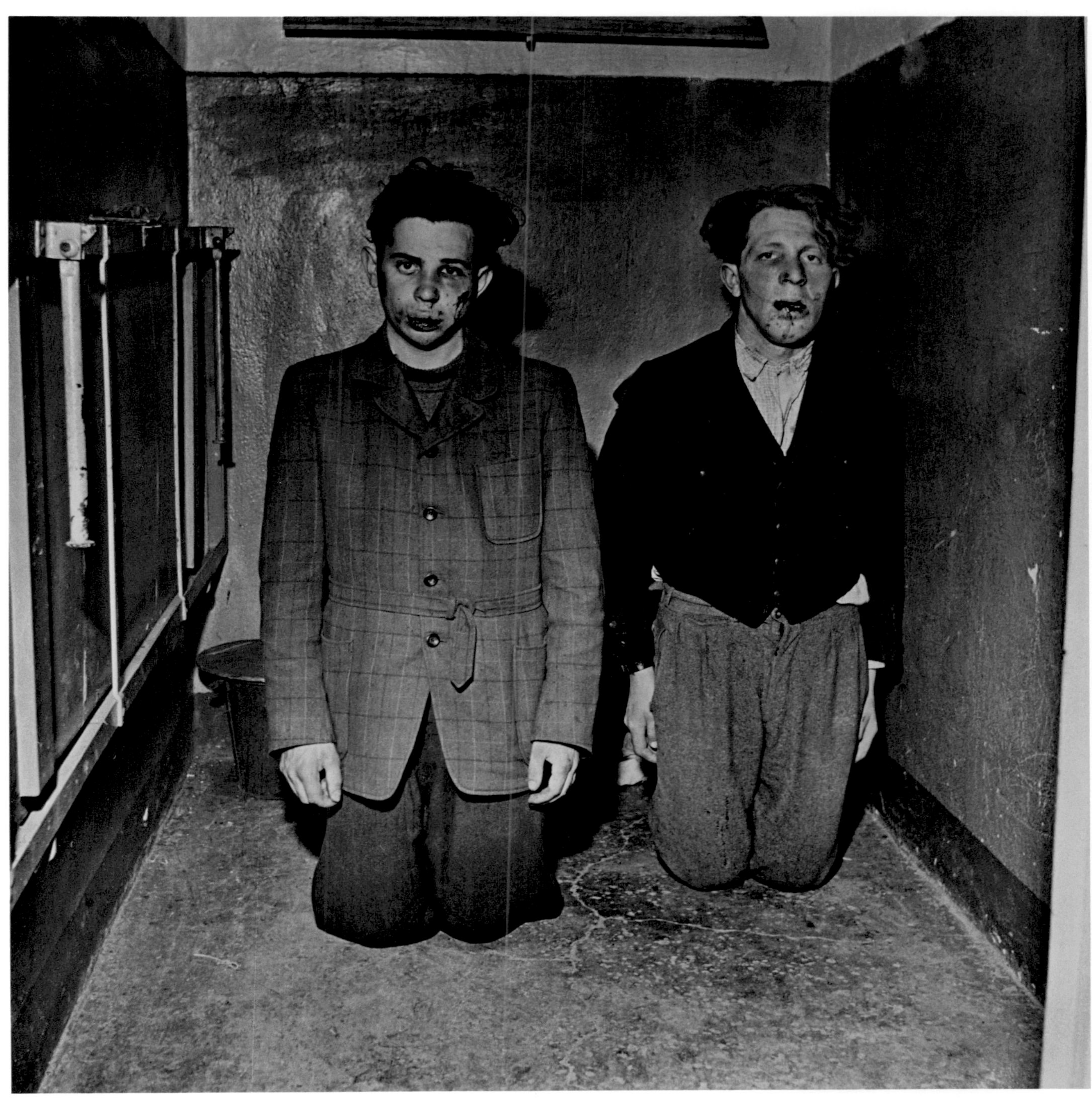

73 · Lee Miller · **Beaten Guards Begging for Mercy, Dachau Concentration Camp, Germany** · April 30, 1945

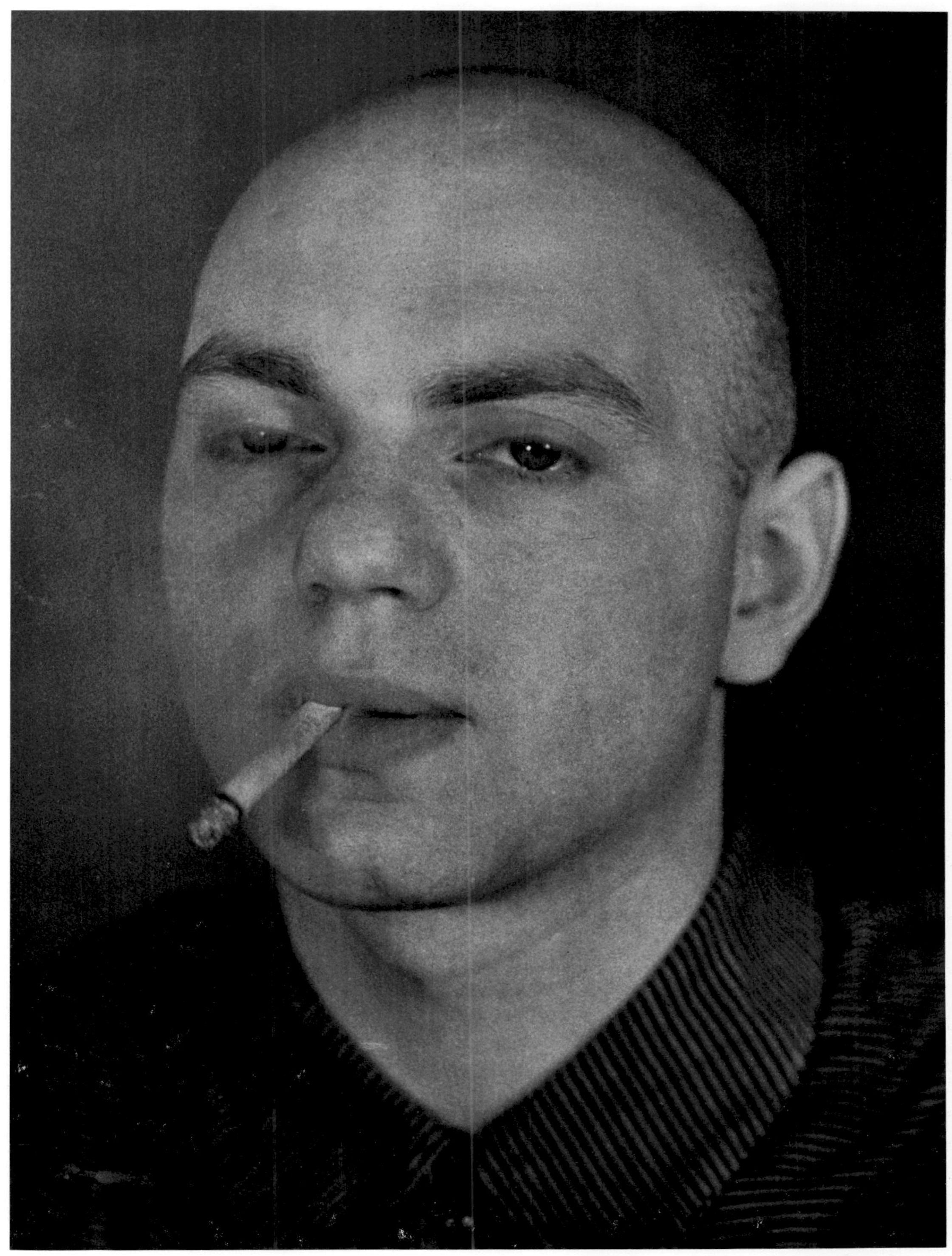

74 · Studio Ringl & Pit · **The Smoker** · 1932

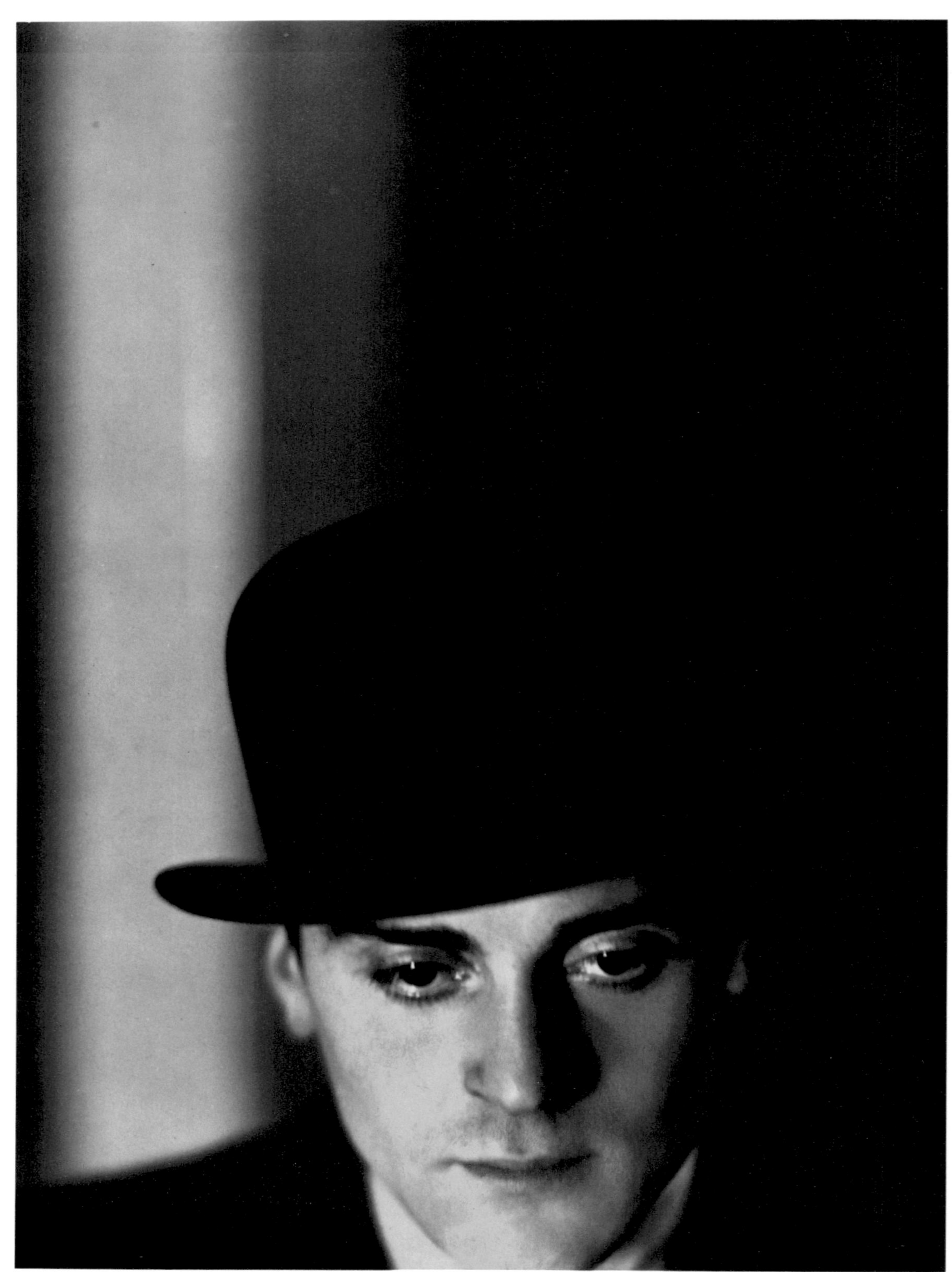

75 · Lotte Jacobi · **Franz Lederer** (Actor) · Berlin, c. 1929

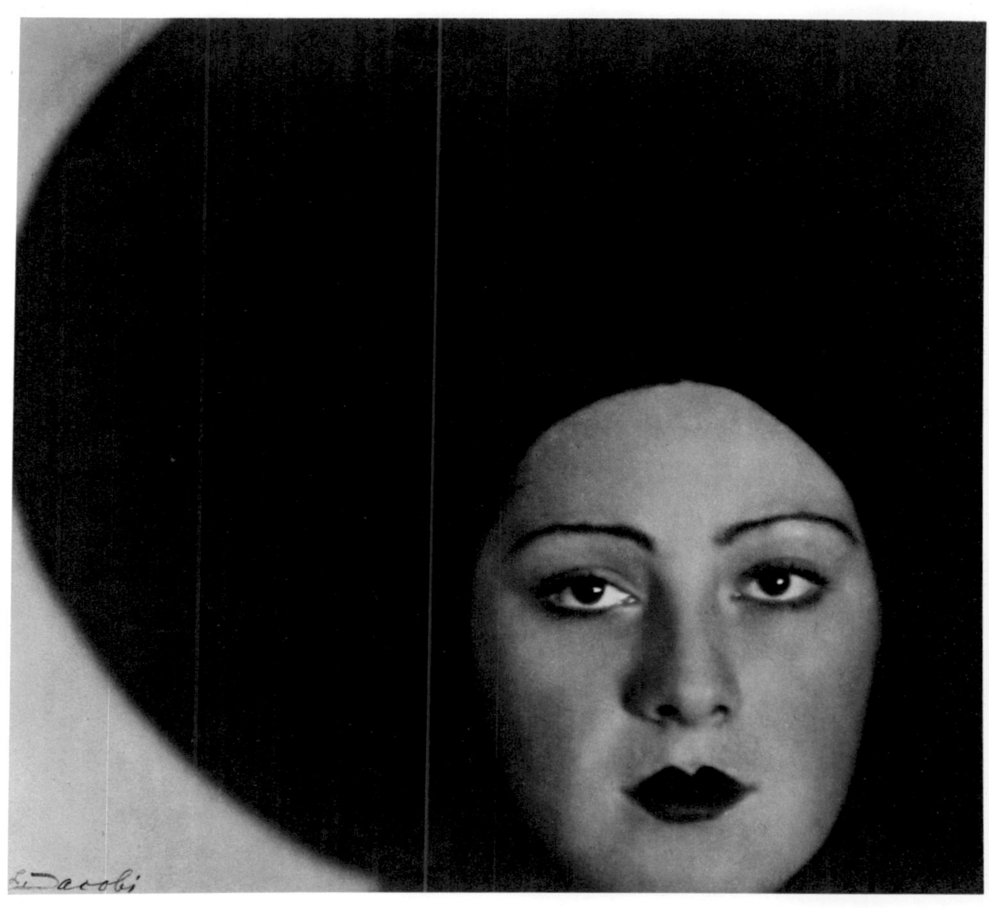

76 · Lotte Jacobi · **Head of a Dancer** (Niura Norskaya) · c. 1929

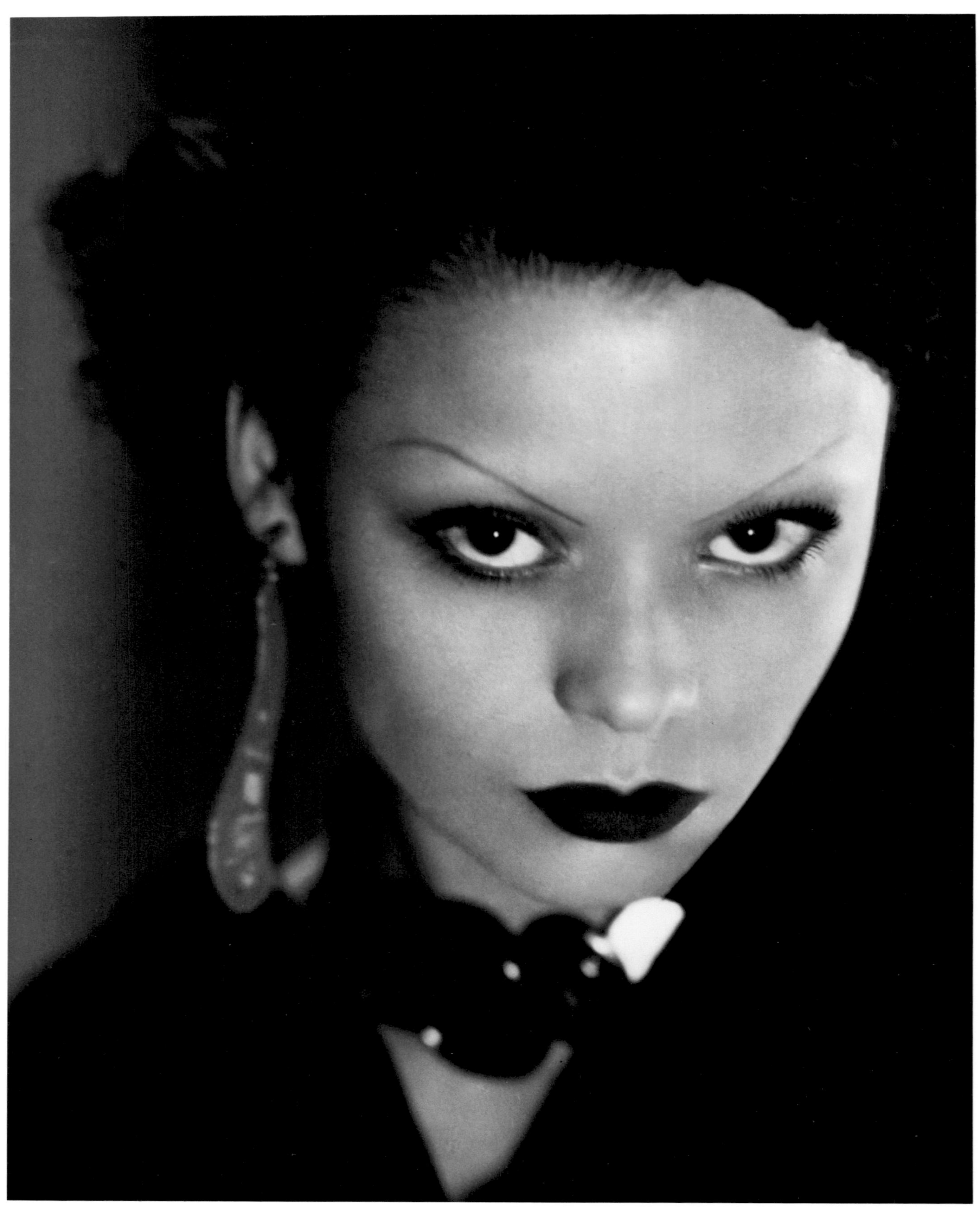

77 · Madame Yevonde · **Florence Lambert (Mrs. Constant Lambert)** · 1933

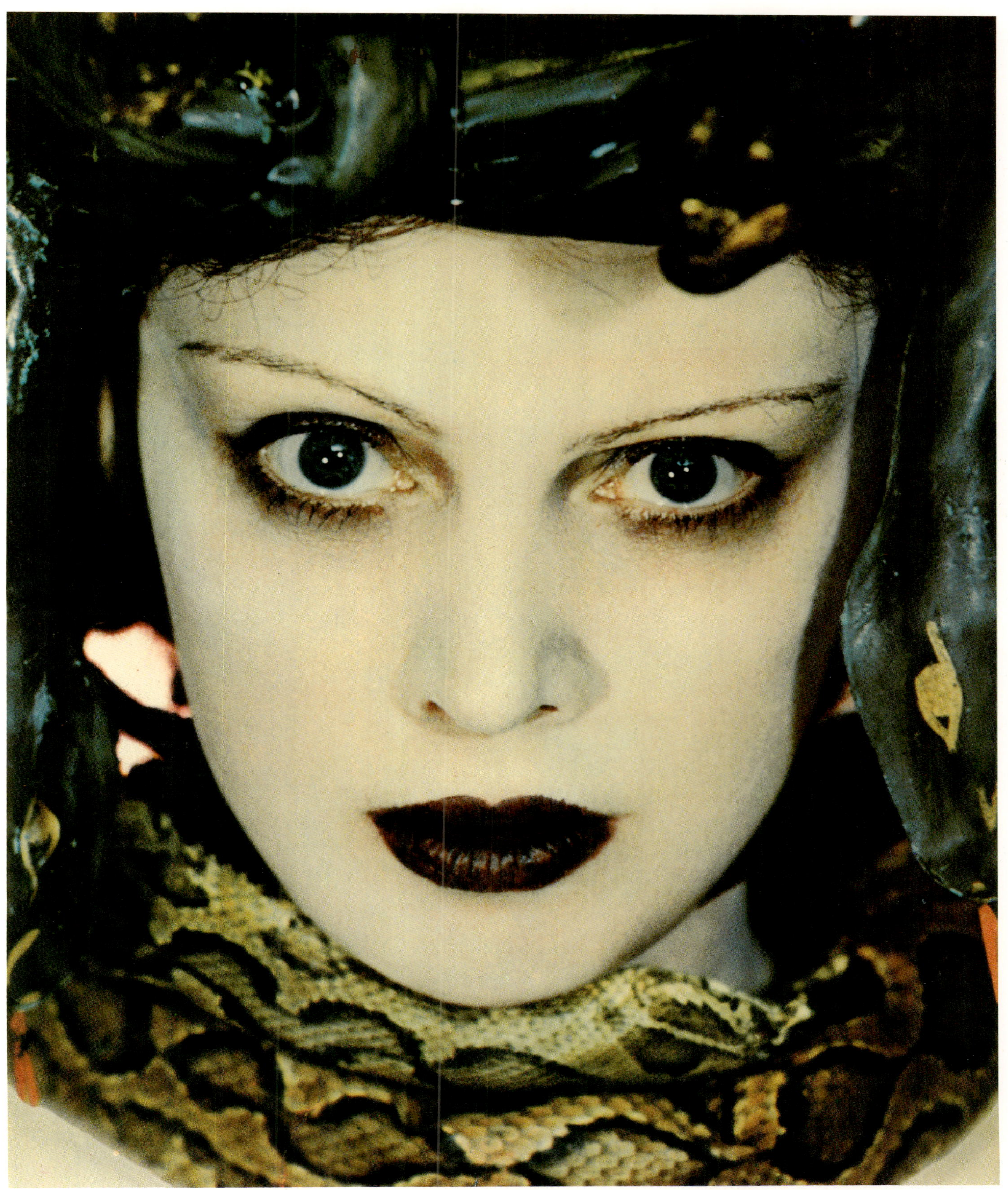

78 · Madame Yevonde · **Medusa** · 1933

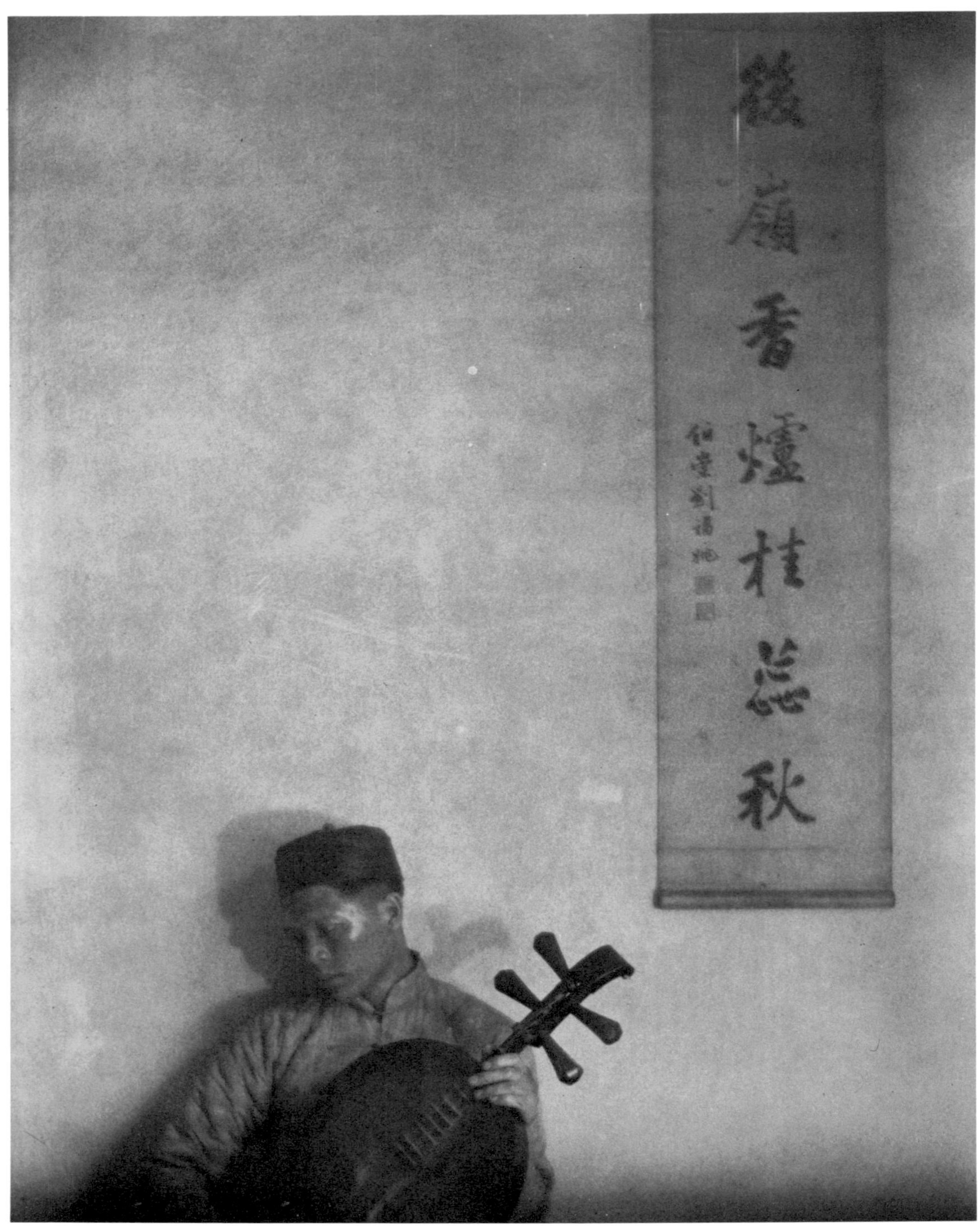

79 · Margrethe Mather · **Moon Kwan with Yib Kirn** · n.d.

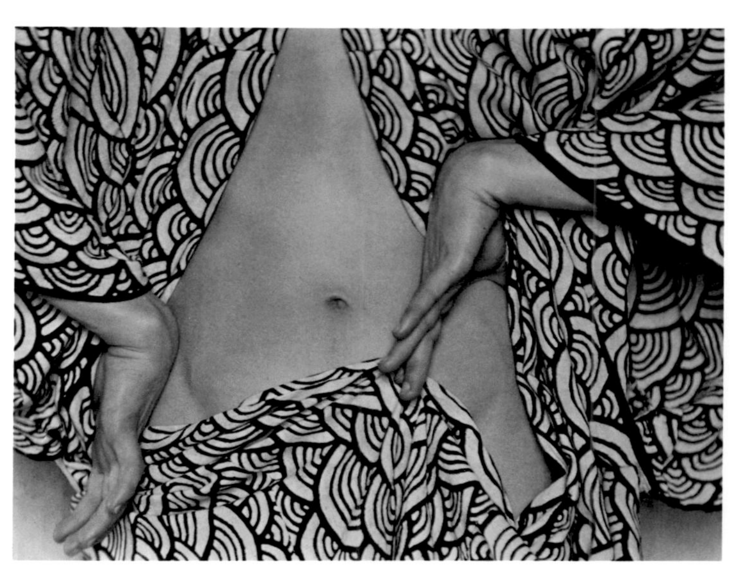 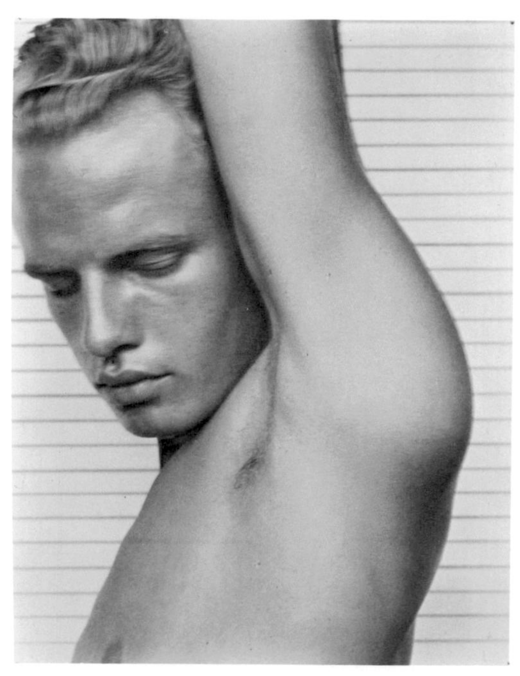

80 · Margrethe Mather · **Semi-Nude** · c. 1923

81 · Margrethe Mather · **Billy Justema, L.A.** · c. 1922

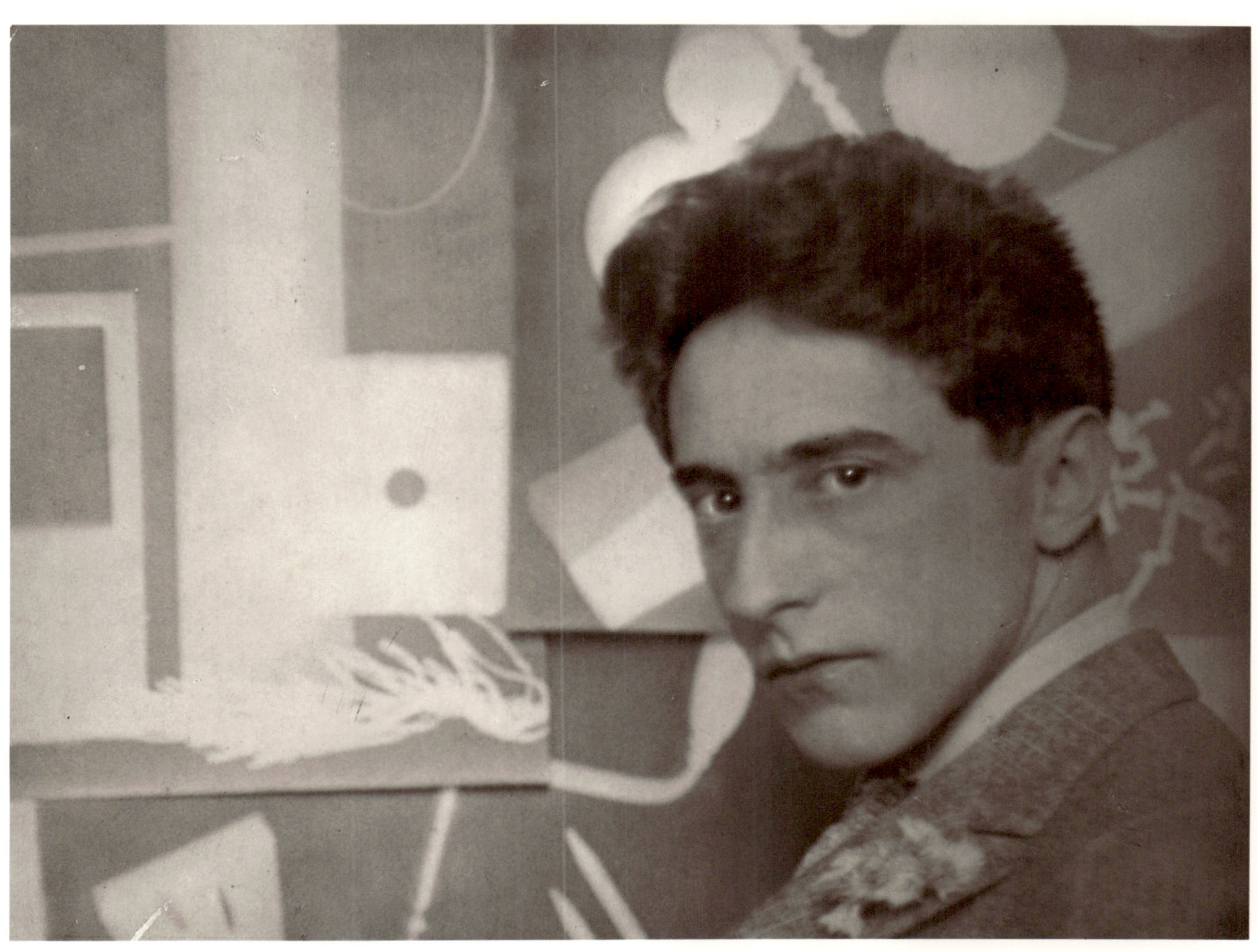

82 · Berenice Abbott · **Jean Cocteau, Paris** · 1926

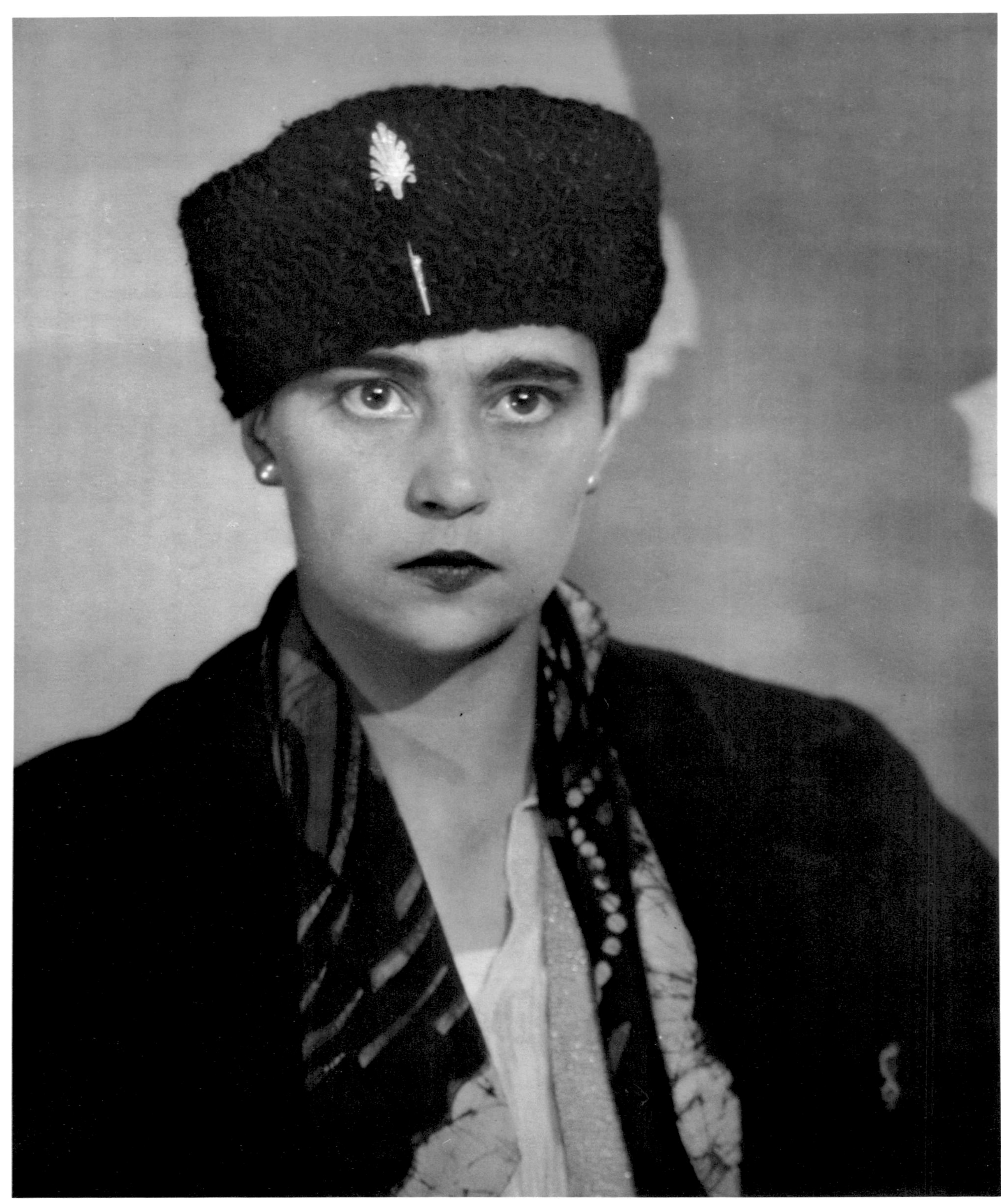

83 · Berenice Abbott · **Gwen Le Gallienne, Paris** · 1927

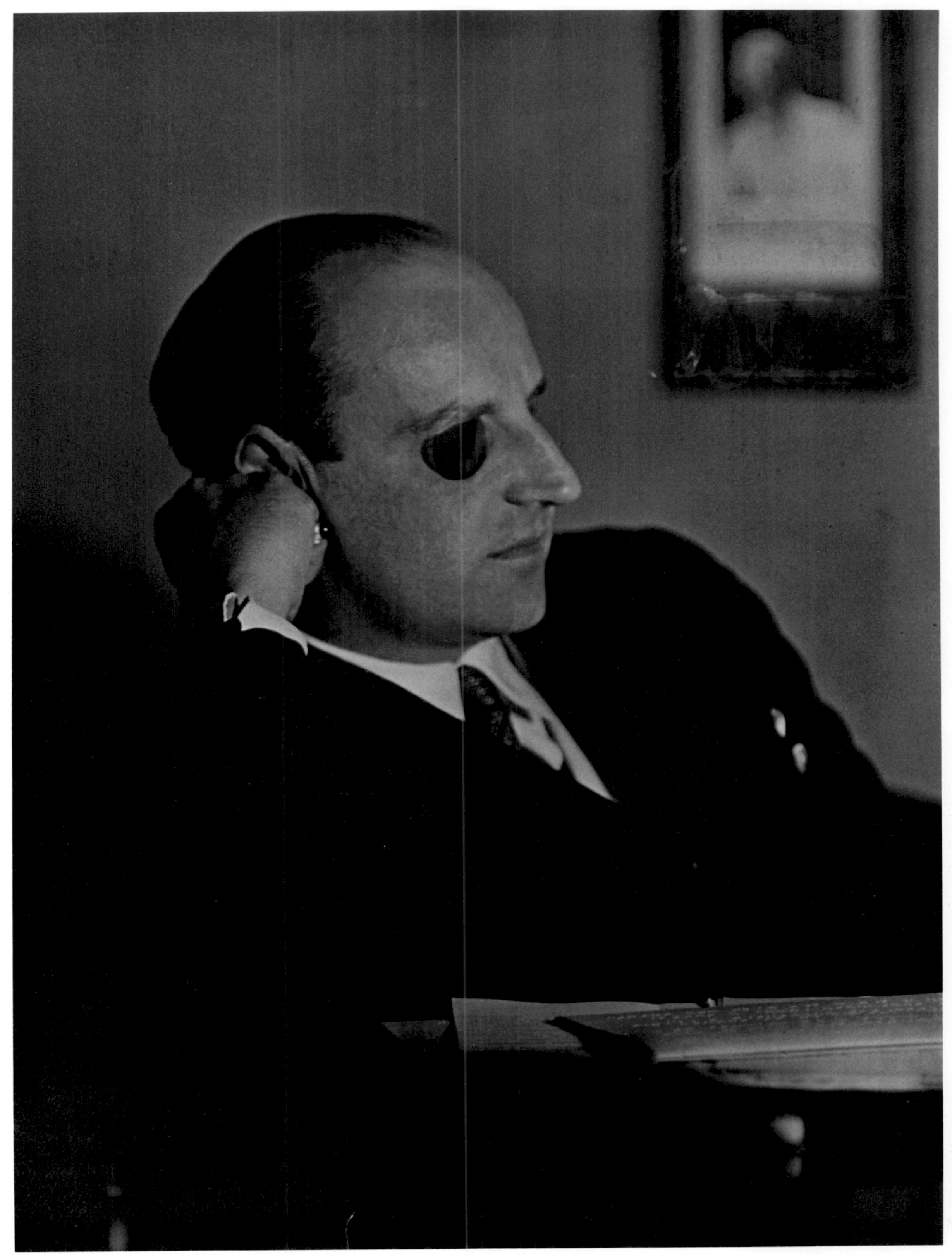

84 · Berenice Abbott · **Deputy M. Scappini, Paris** · 1927

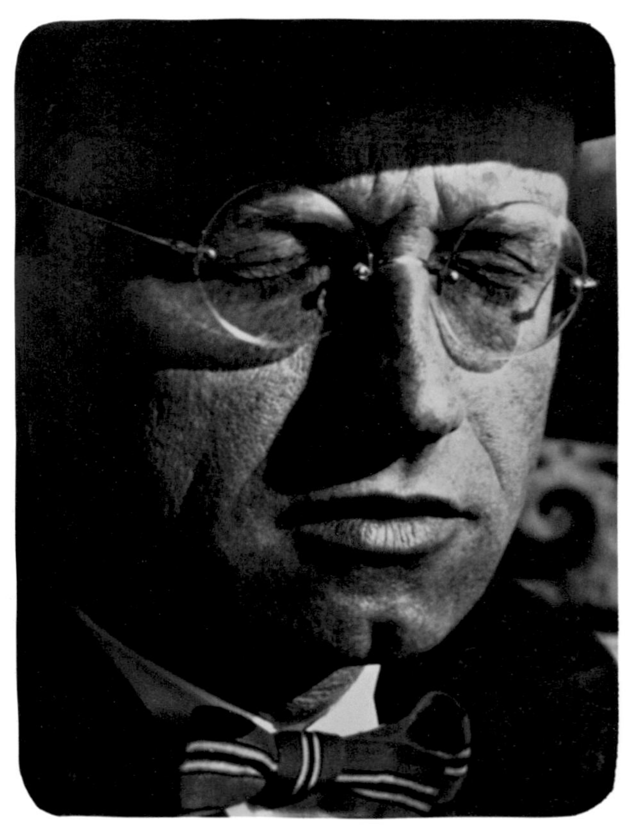

85 · Lucia Moholy · **Portrait of Franz Roh** · 1926

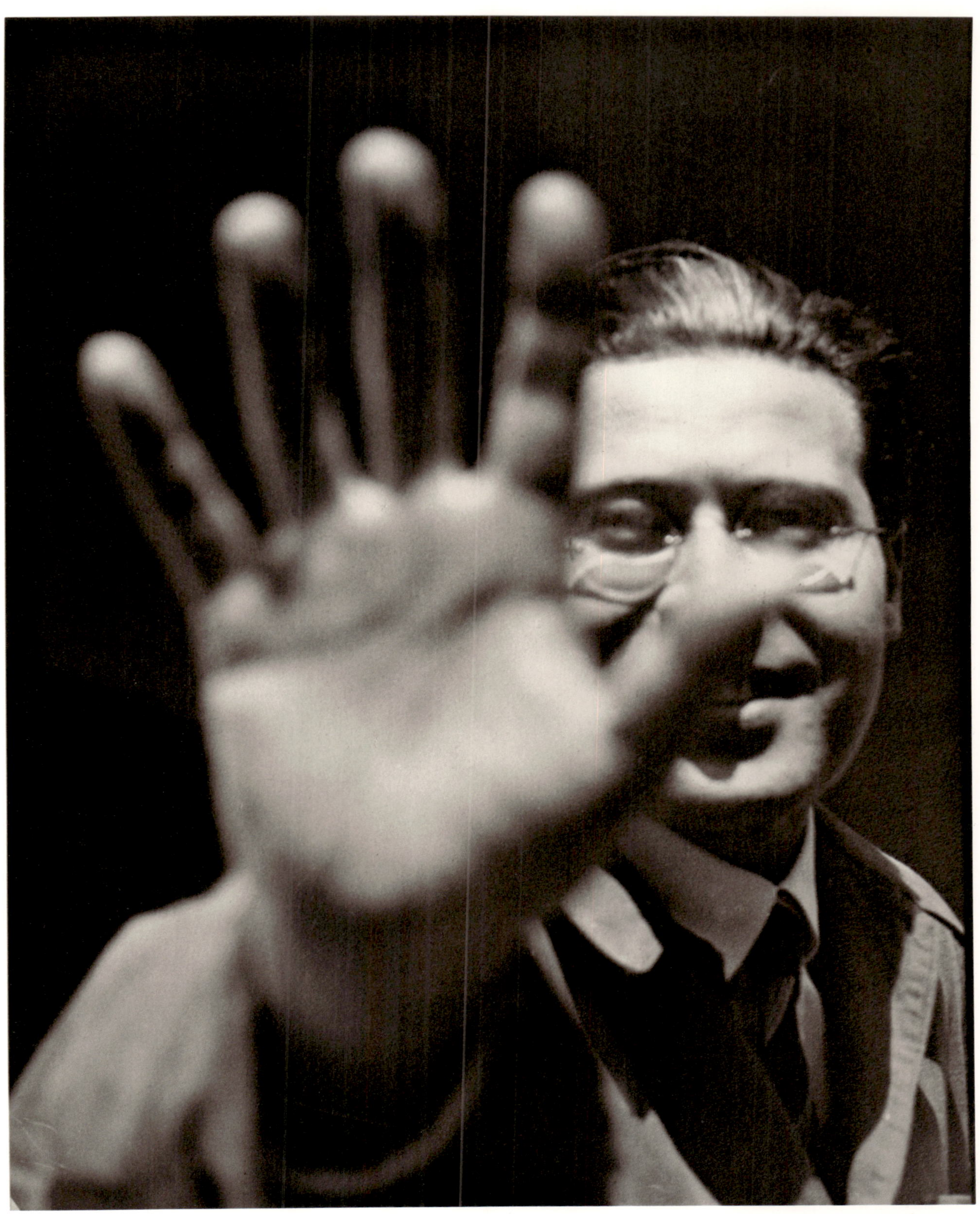

86 · Lucia Moholy · **Portrait of László Moholy-Nagy** · 1925–26

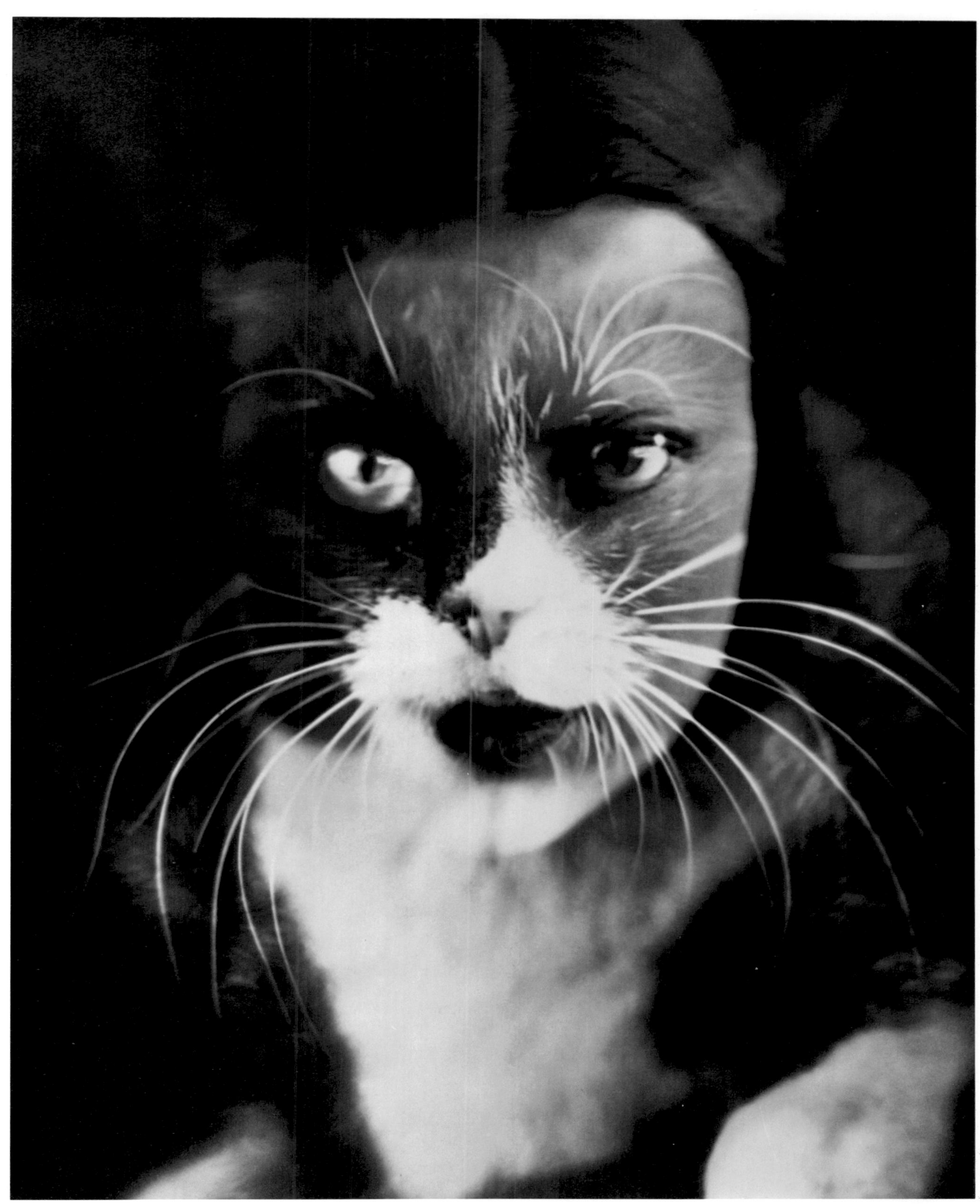

87 · Wanda Wulz · **Lo & Gatto (I and Cat)** · 1932

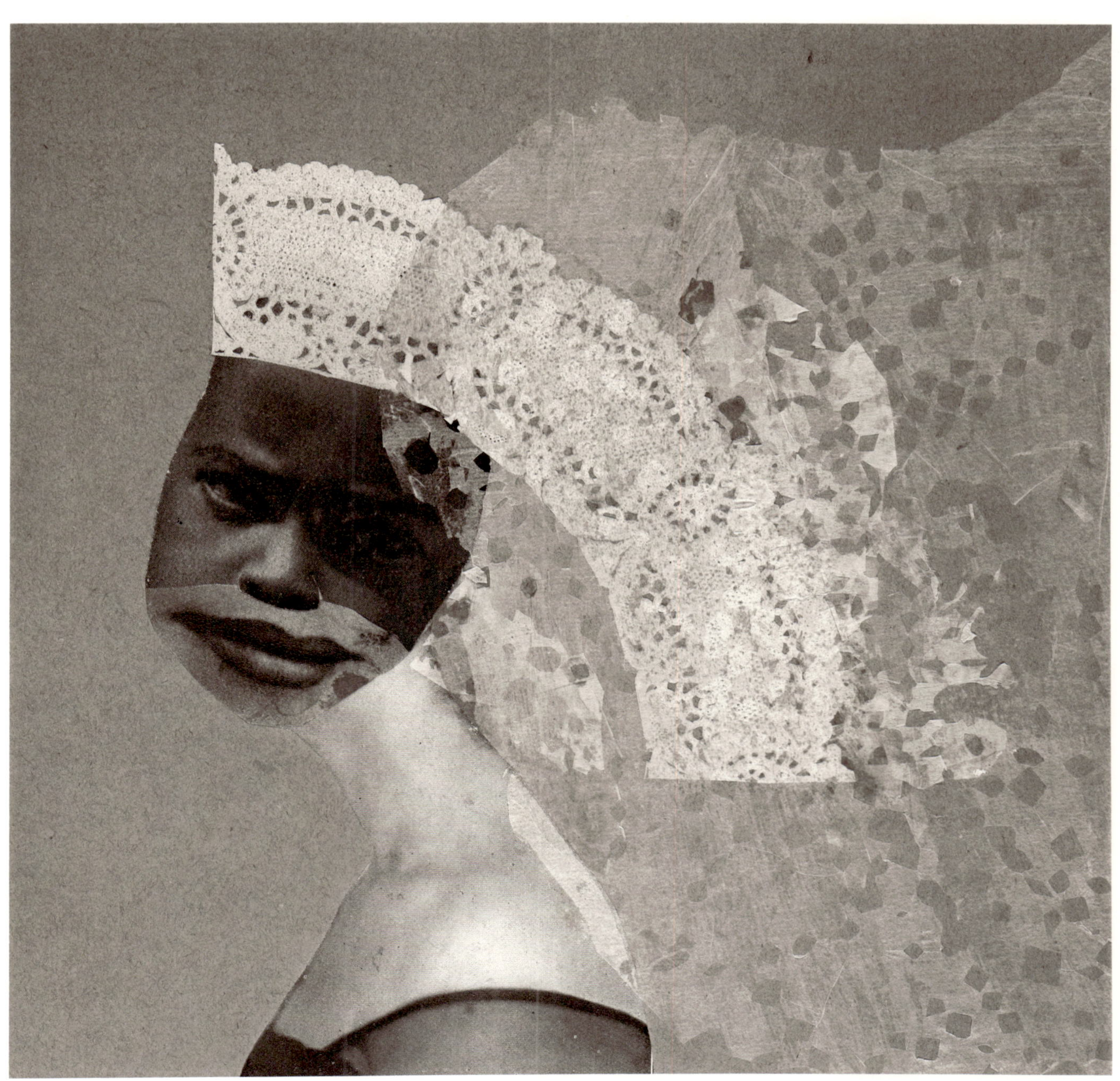

88 · Hannah Höch · **Die Braut** · c. 1928

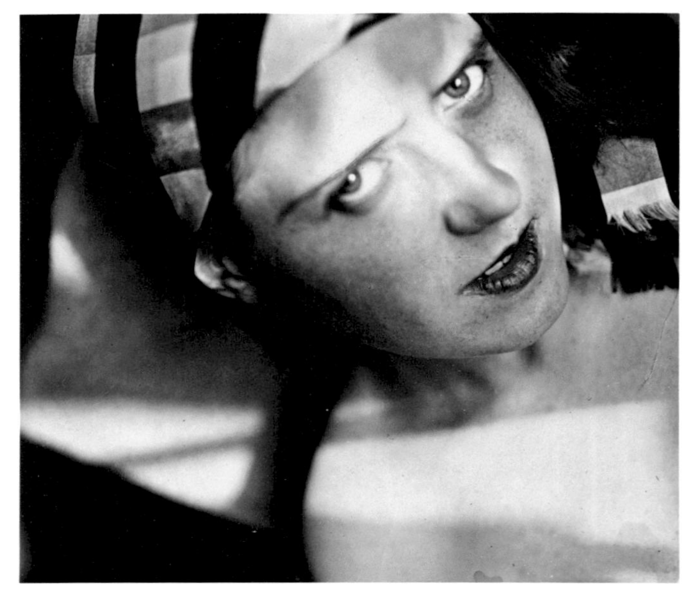

89 · Lotte Beese · **Portrait of Katt Both** · c. 1928

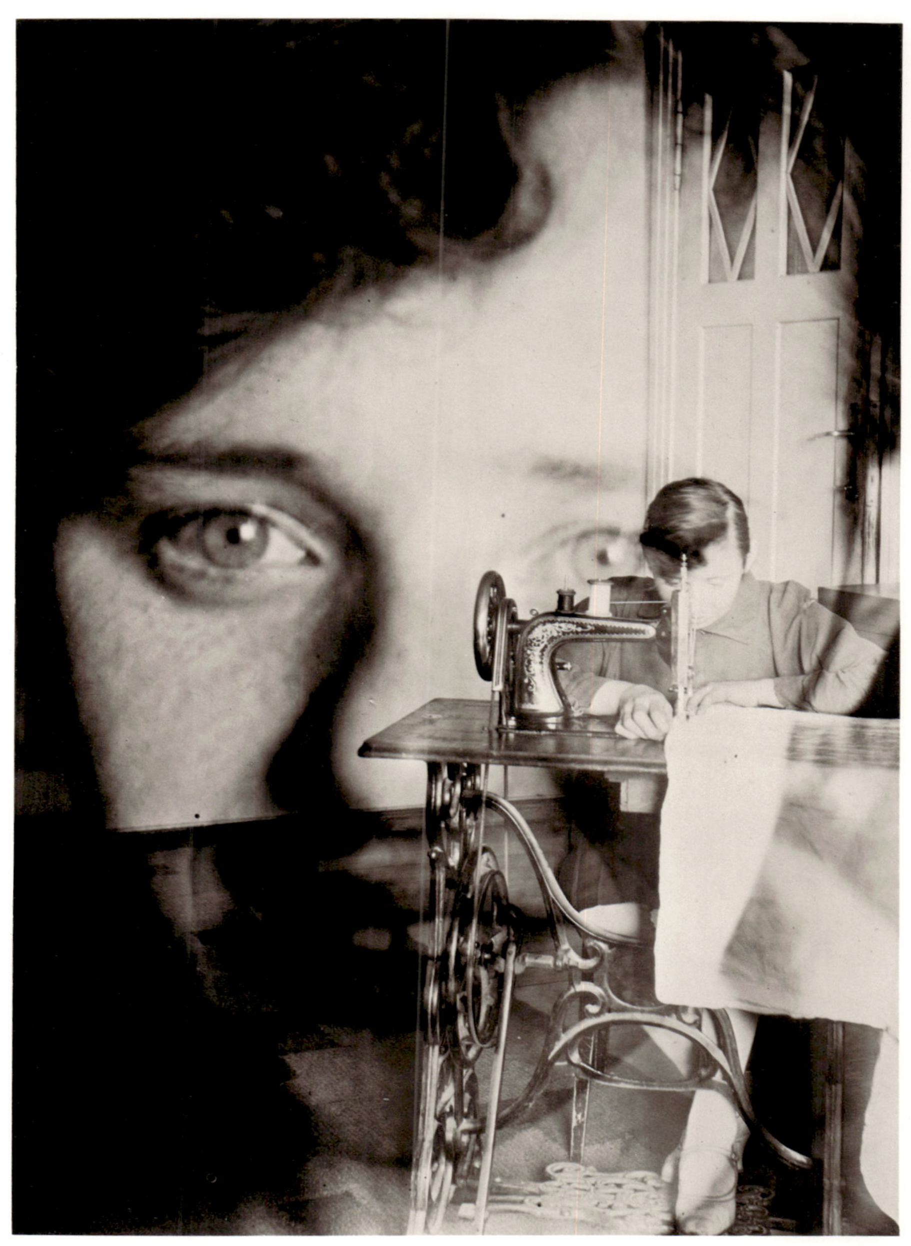

90 · Alice Lex-Nerlinger · **Näherlin** · c. 1930

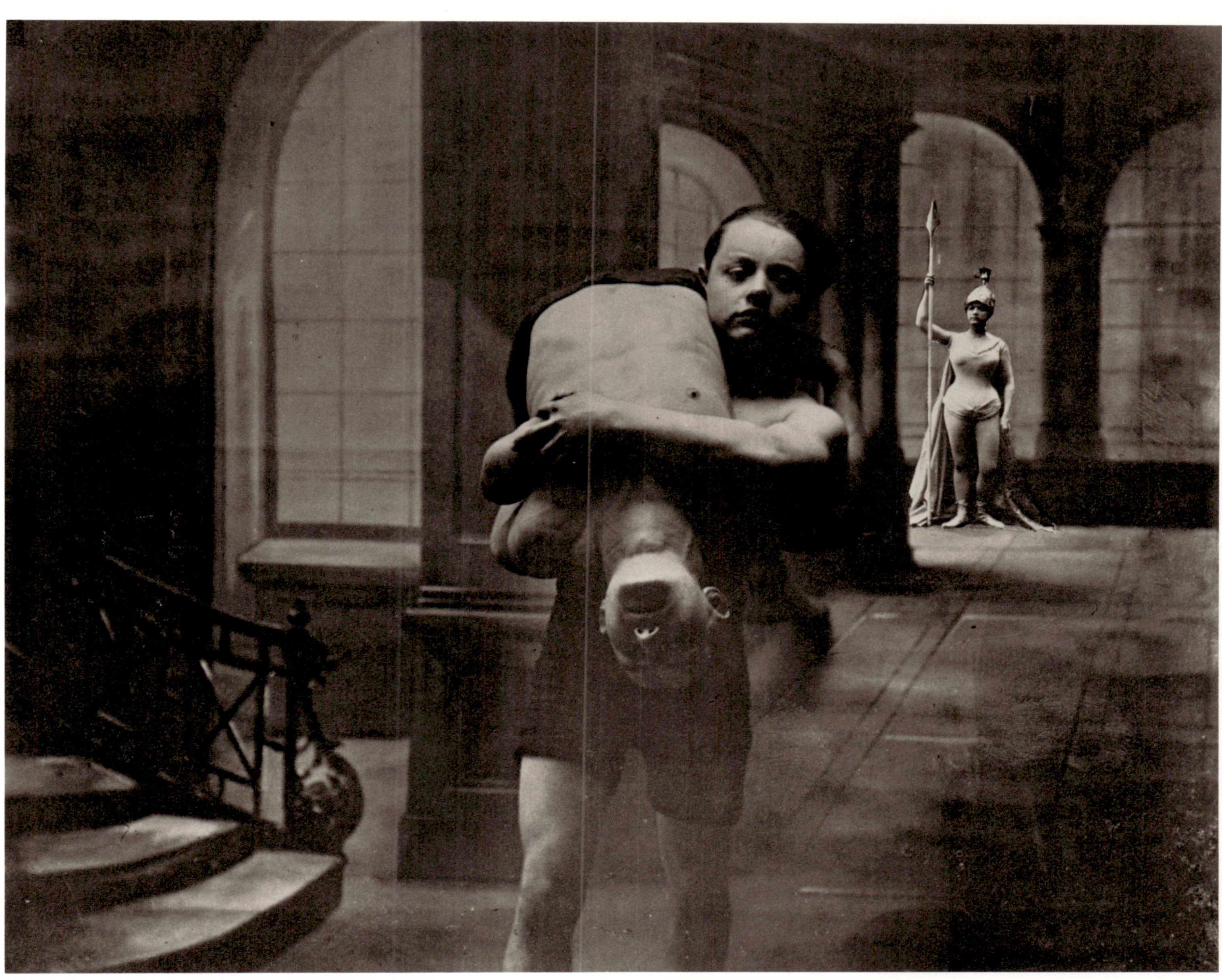

91 · Dora Maar · Untitled · c. 1940

92 · Lotte Beese · **Beese's Studio in the Bauhaus** · c. 1927

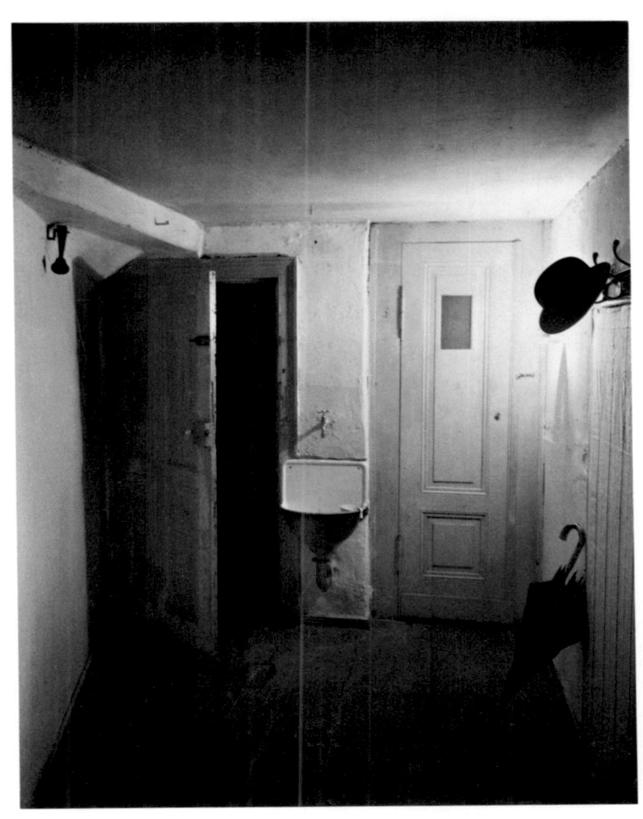

93 · Ellen Auerbach · **Kurfursterstr.** · 1931

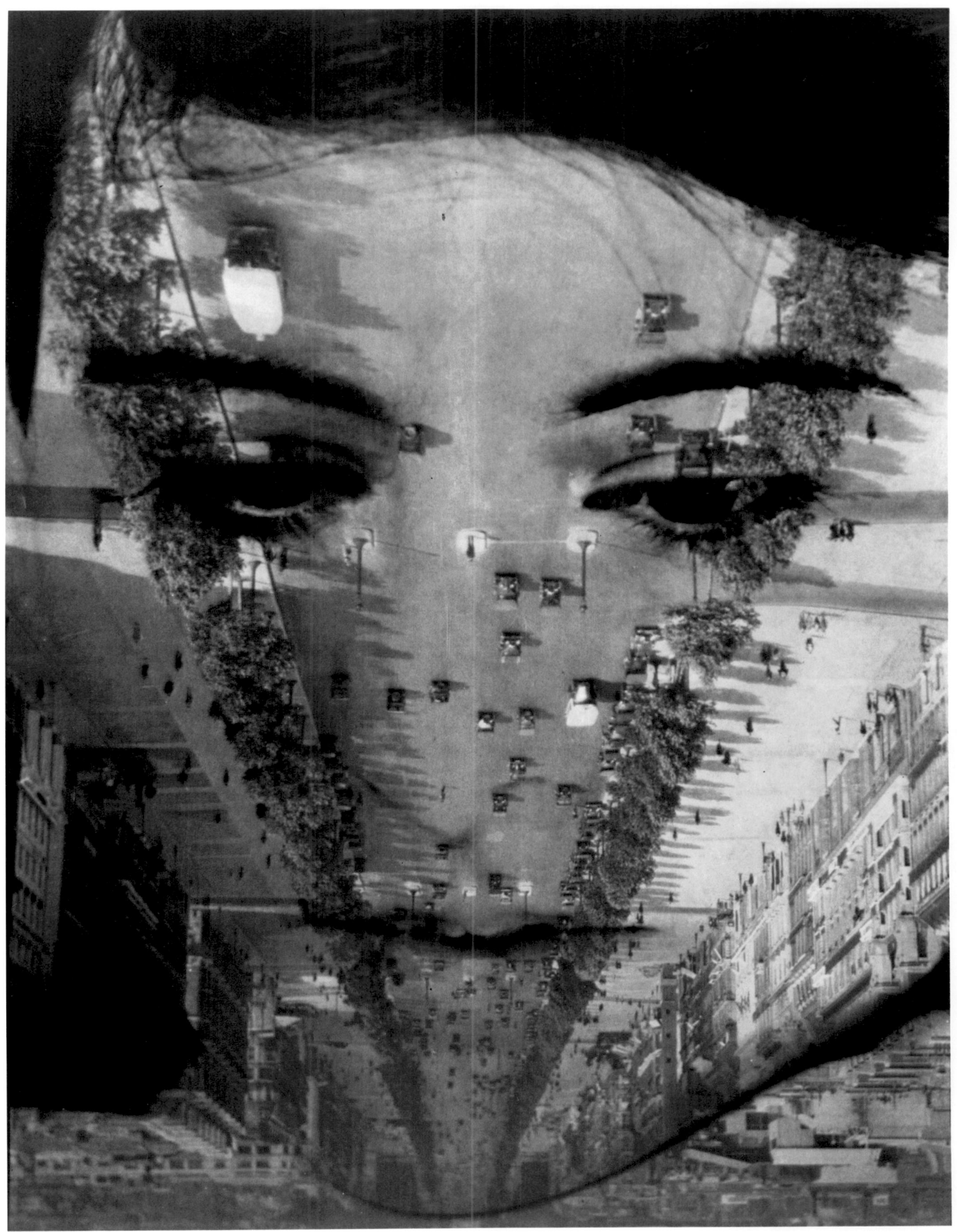

94 · Aenne Biermann · **Portrait mit Champs-Elysées, Paris** · c. 1929

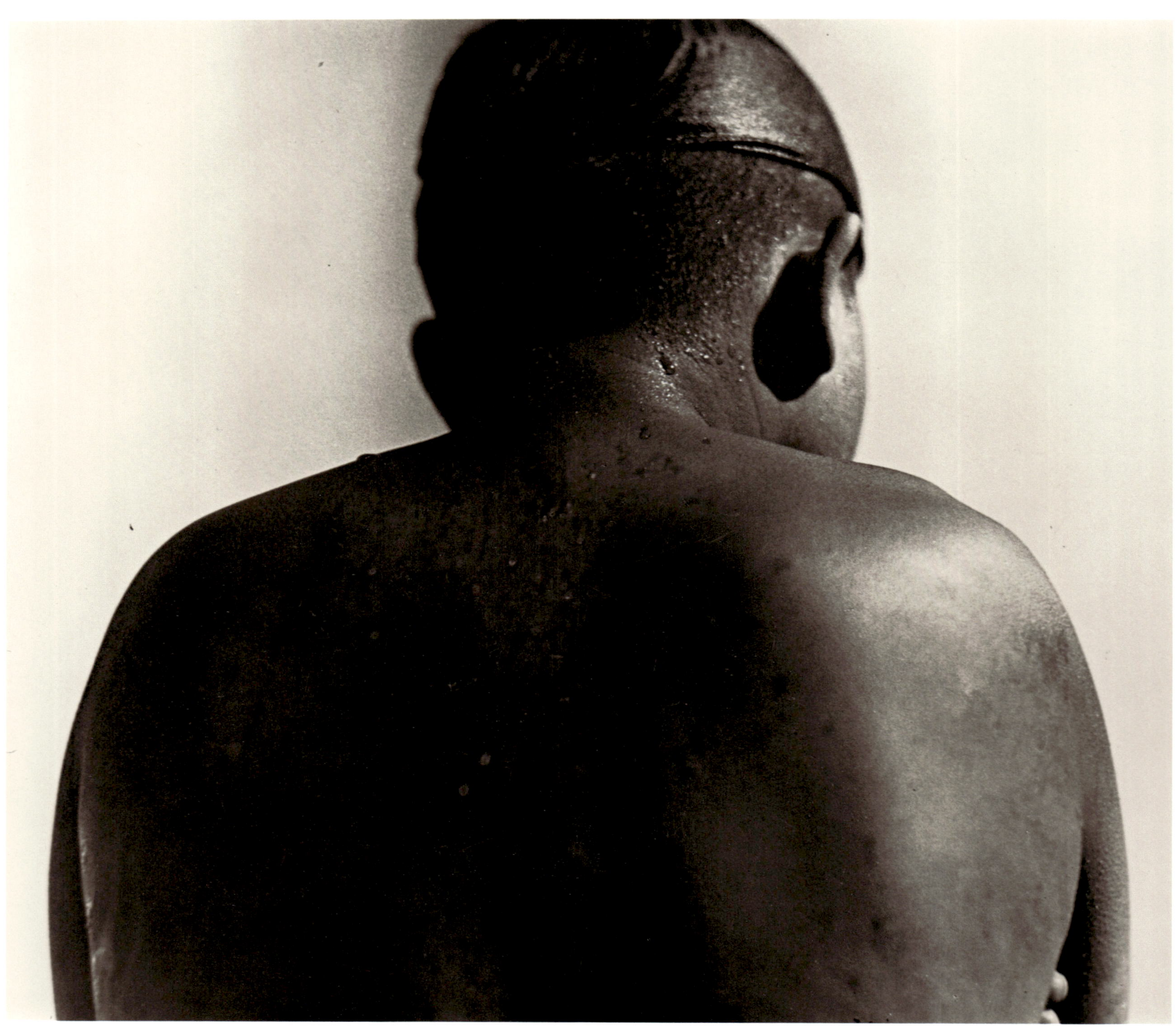

95 · Aenne Biermann · **Sonnenbad** · c. 1929

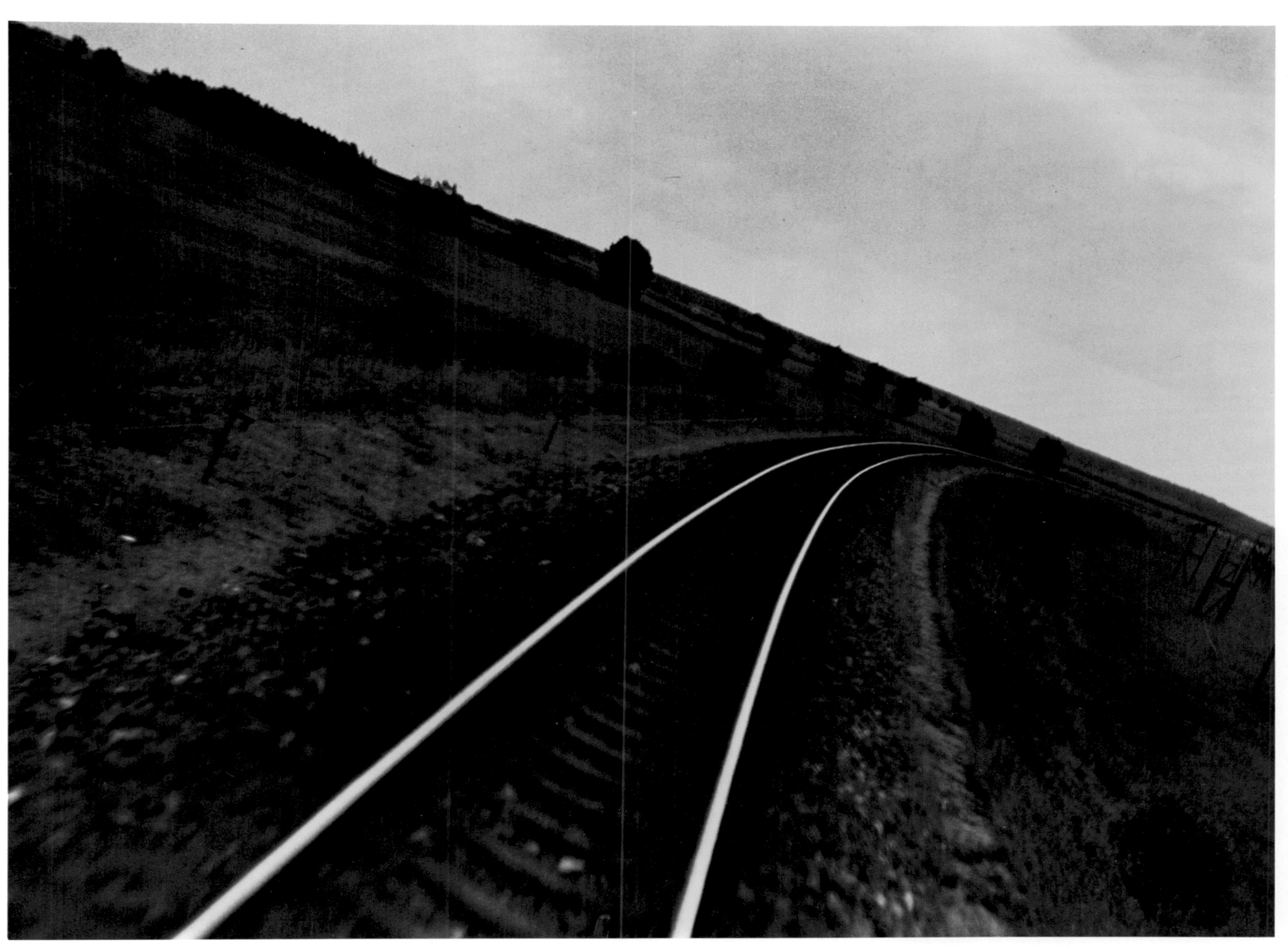

96 · Aenne Biermann · **Aus dem Fahrenden Zug** · c. 1930

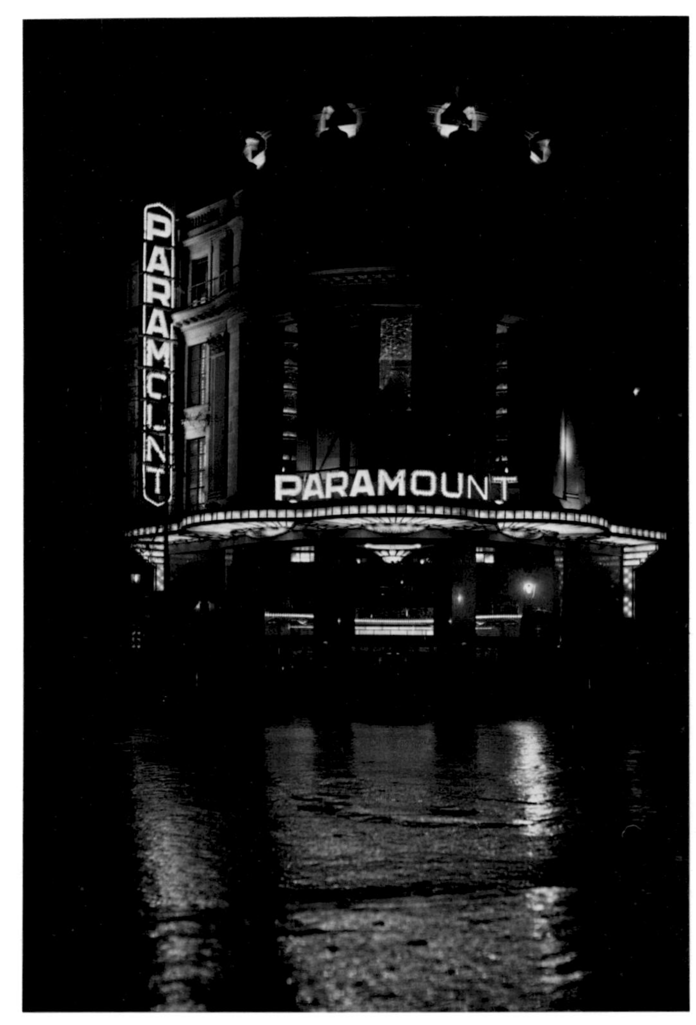

97 · Germaine Krull · **Le Cinéma Paramount** · c. 1935

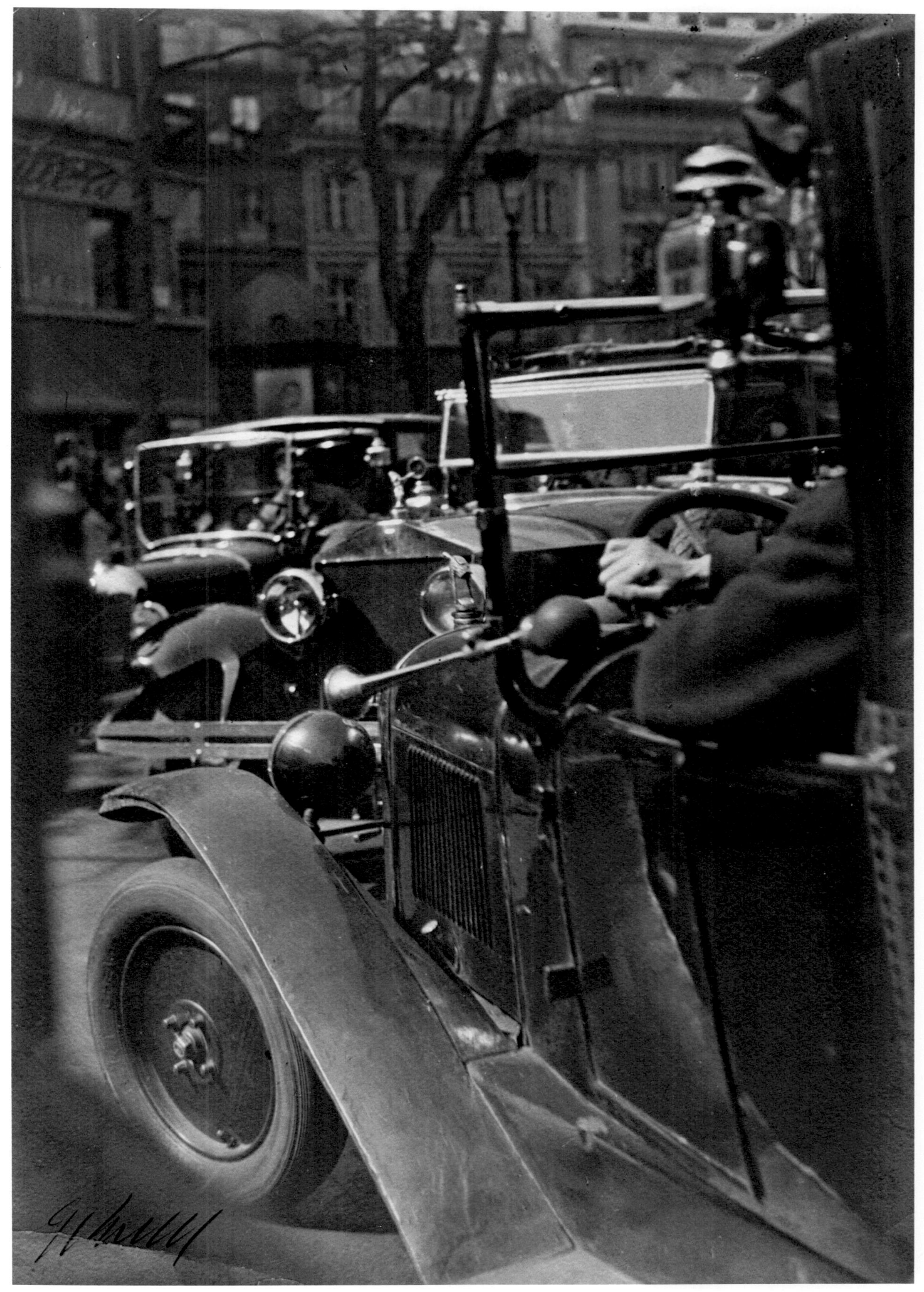

98 · Germa ne Krull · **Traffic in Paris** · 1926

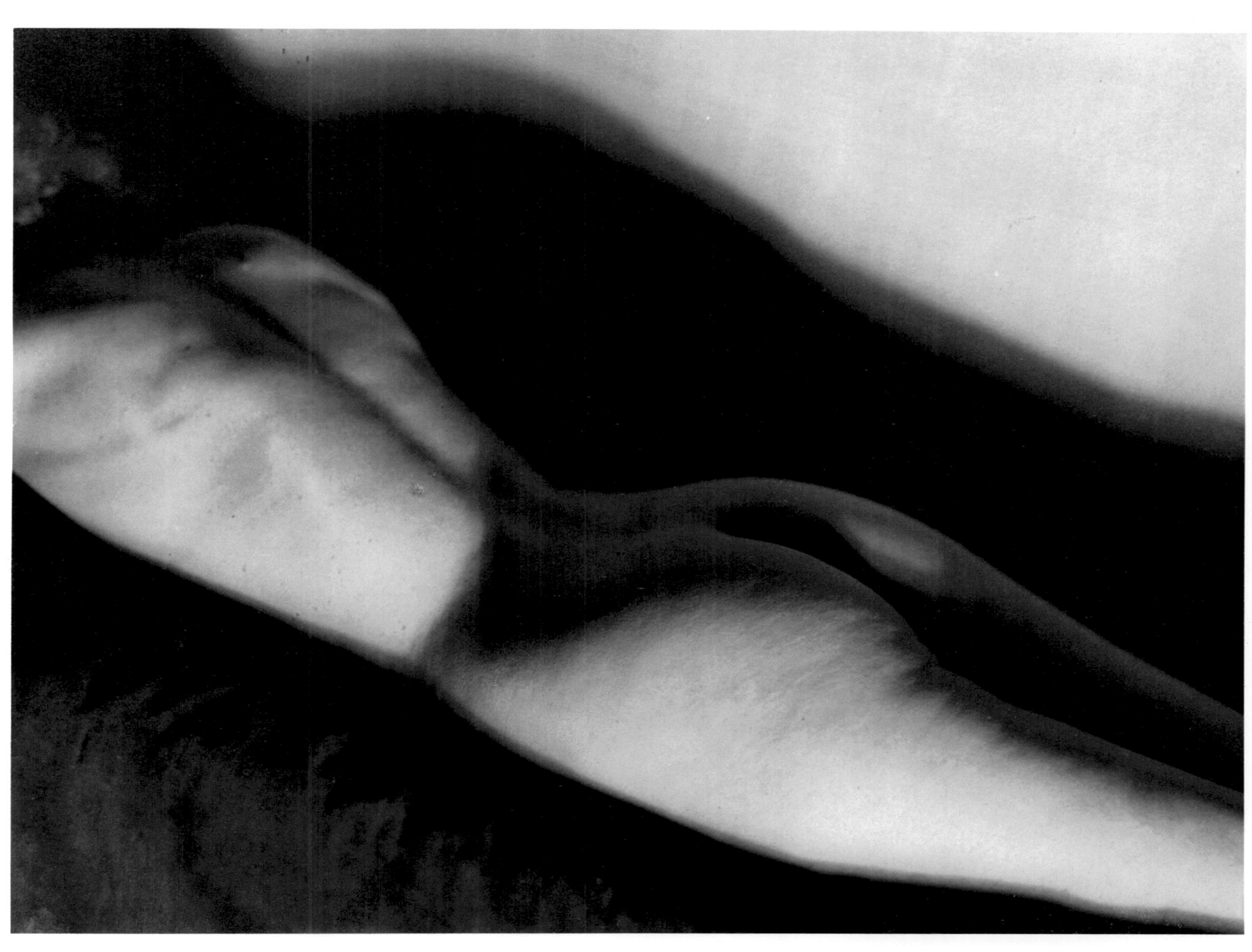

99 · Germaine Krull · **Nude** · Paris, c. 1926

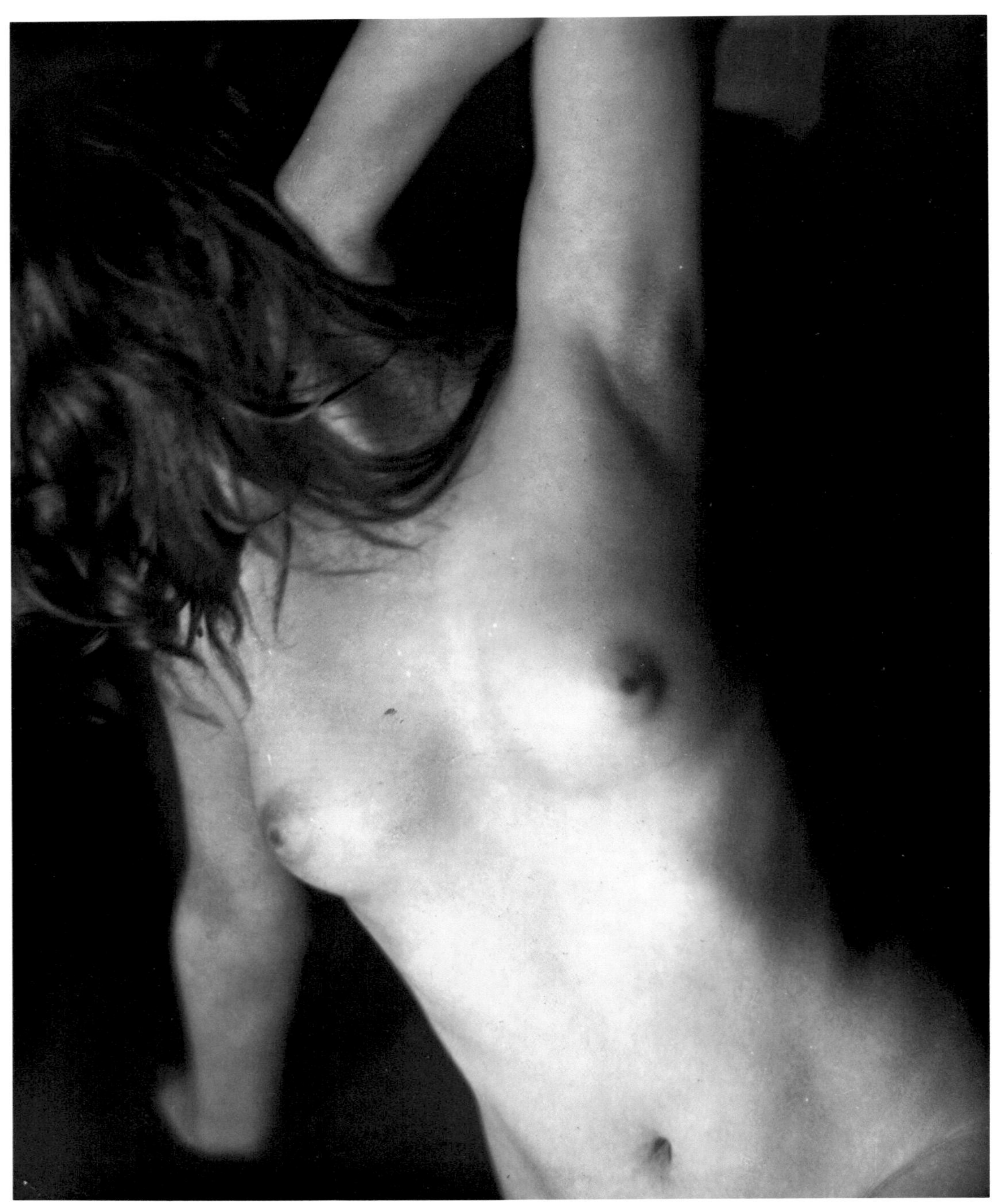

100 · Germaine Krull · Untitled · c. 1929

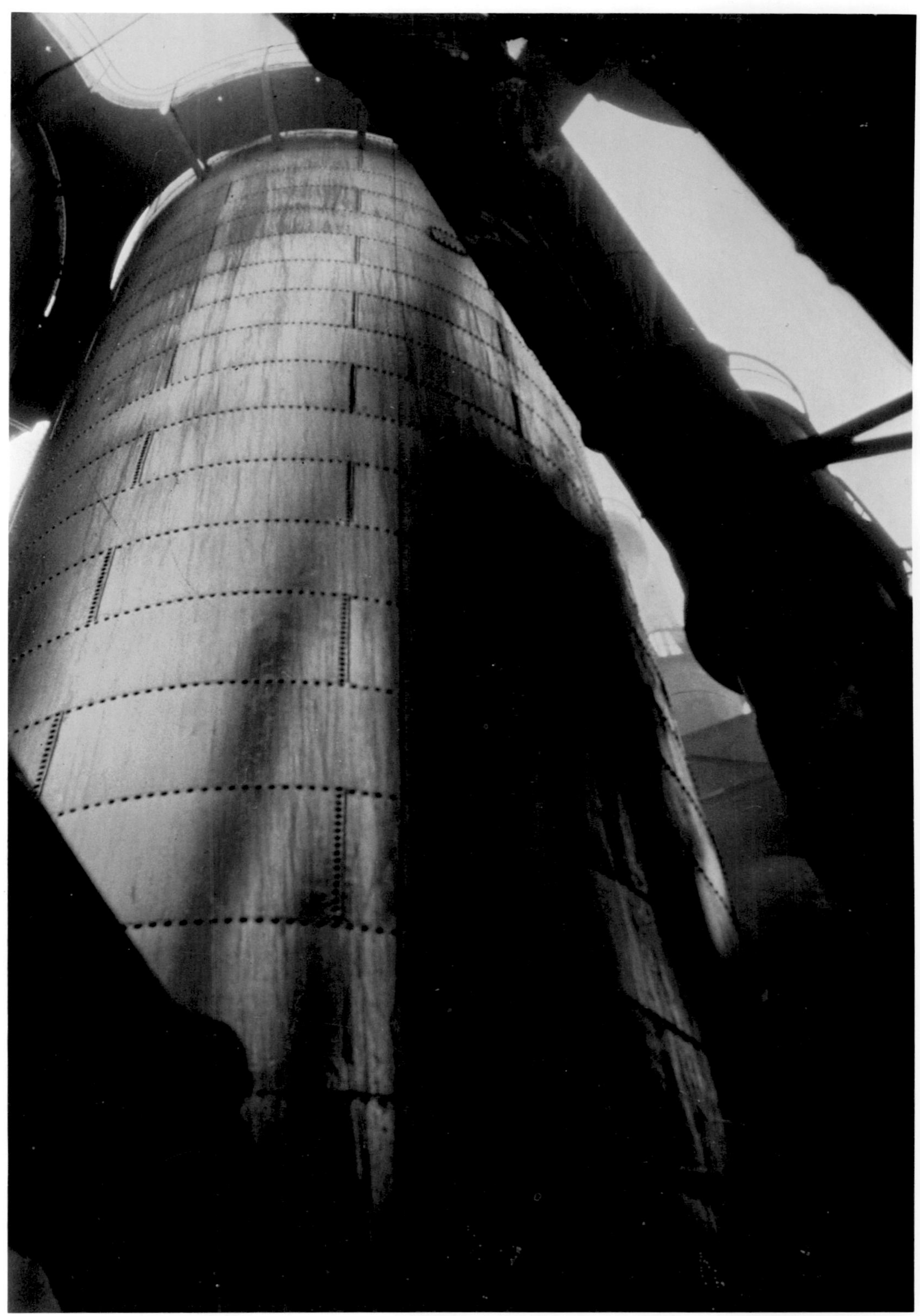

101 · Germaine Krull · **Iron-Work, Pont à Mousson** · 1926

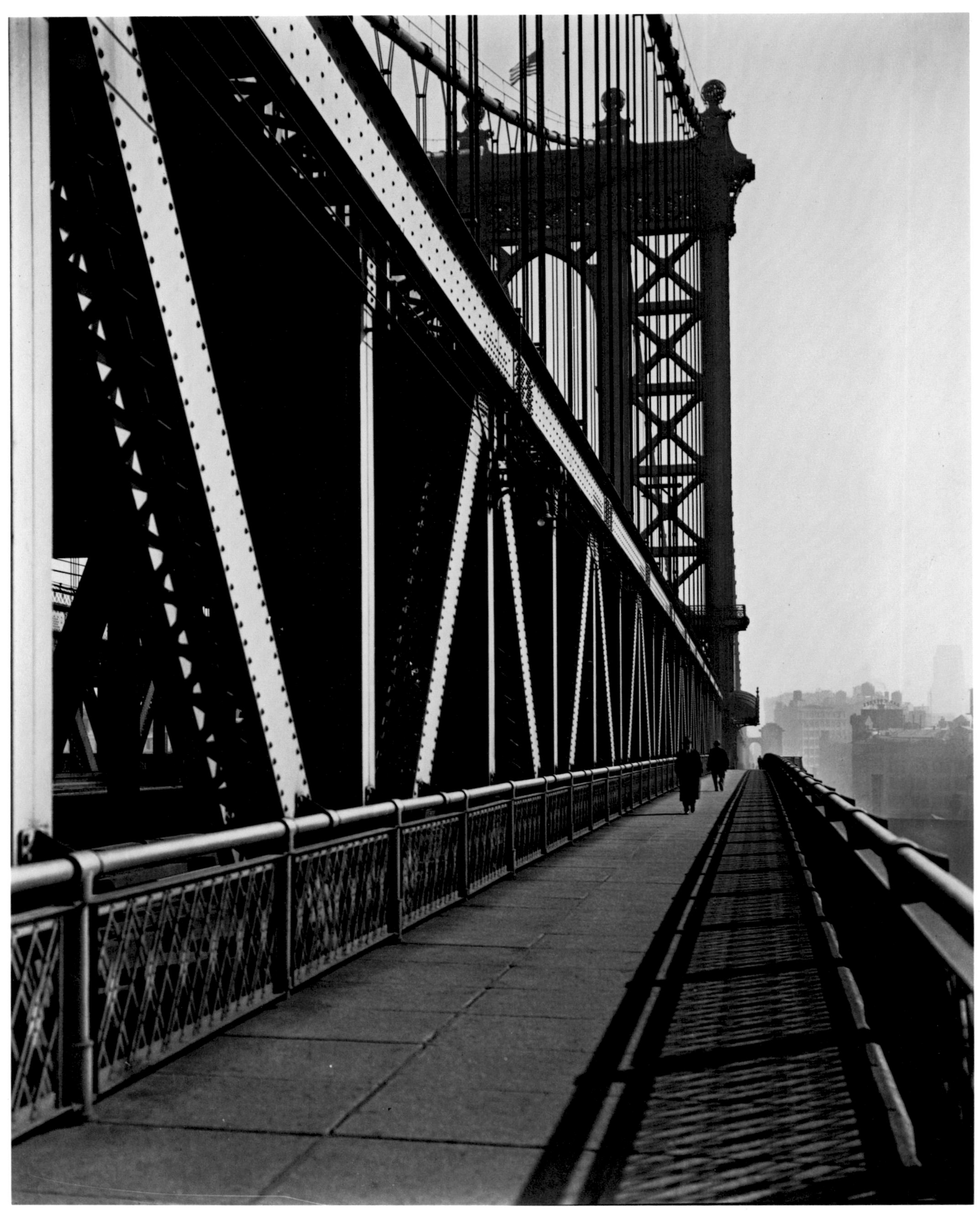

102 · Berenice Abbott · **Walkway, Manhattan Bridge, New York** · 1936

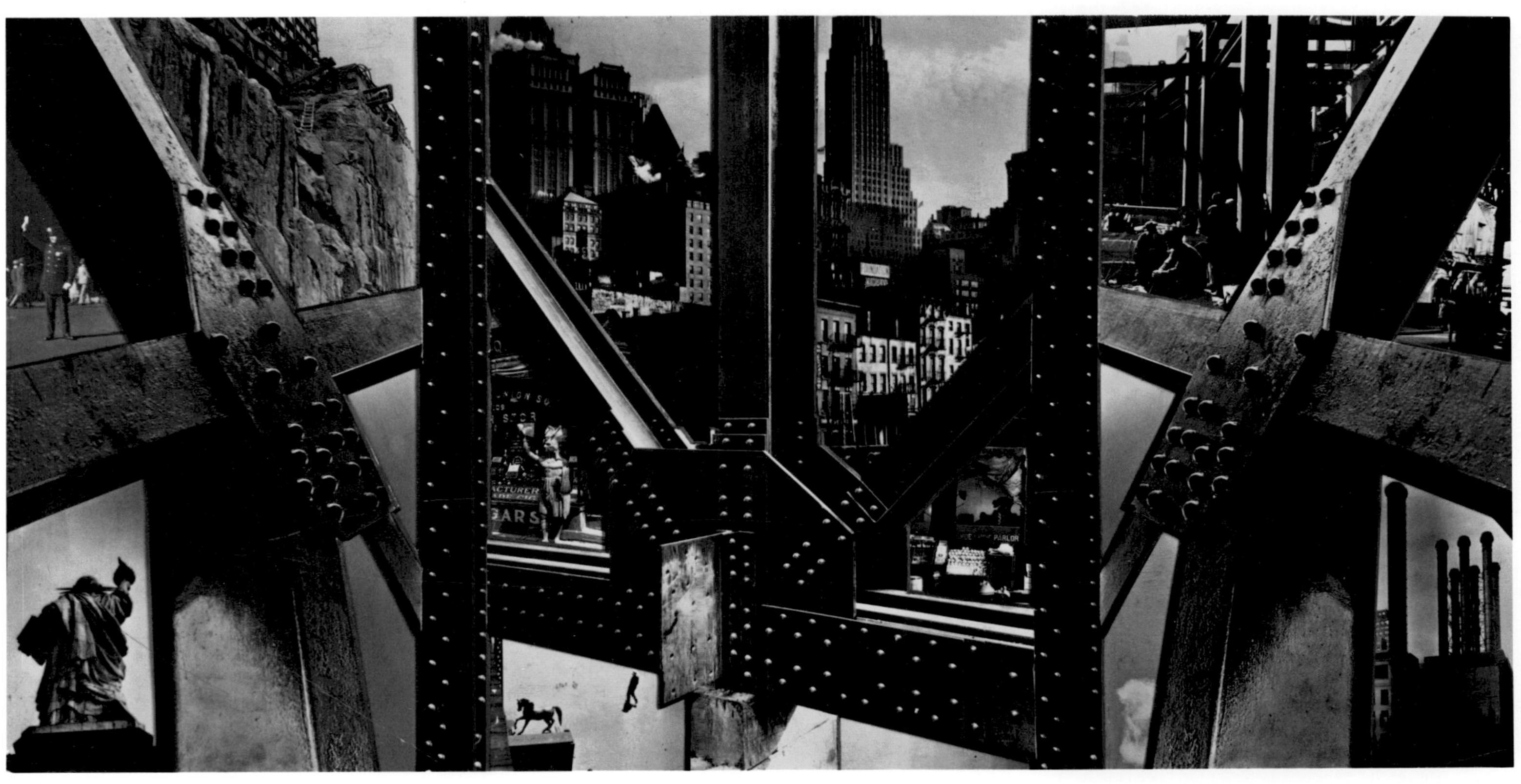

103 · Berenice Abbott · Photomontage · New York, c. 1930

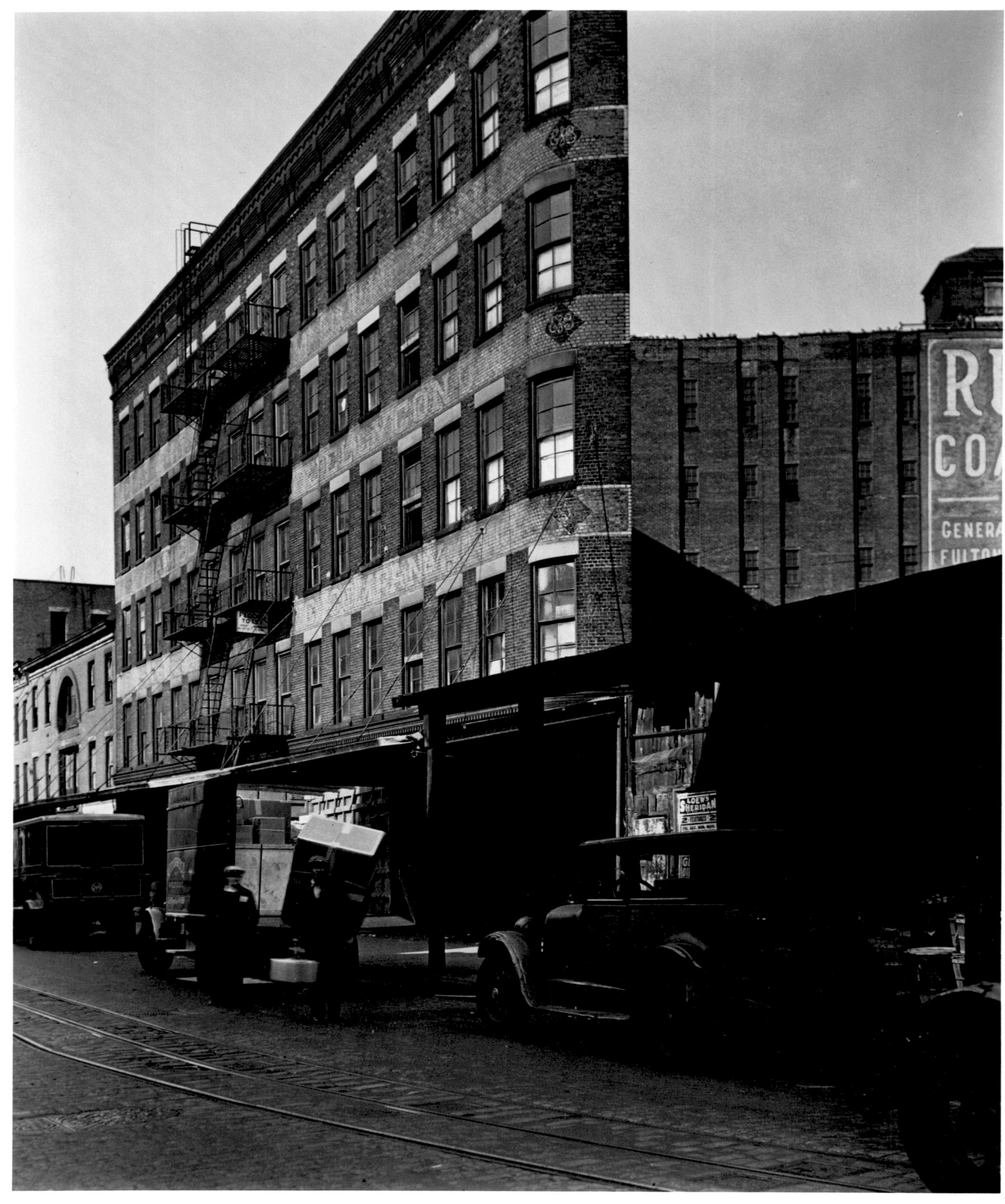

104 · Berenice Abbott · **53 Gannesvoort Street, Brooklyn, New York** · 1936 or later

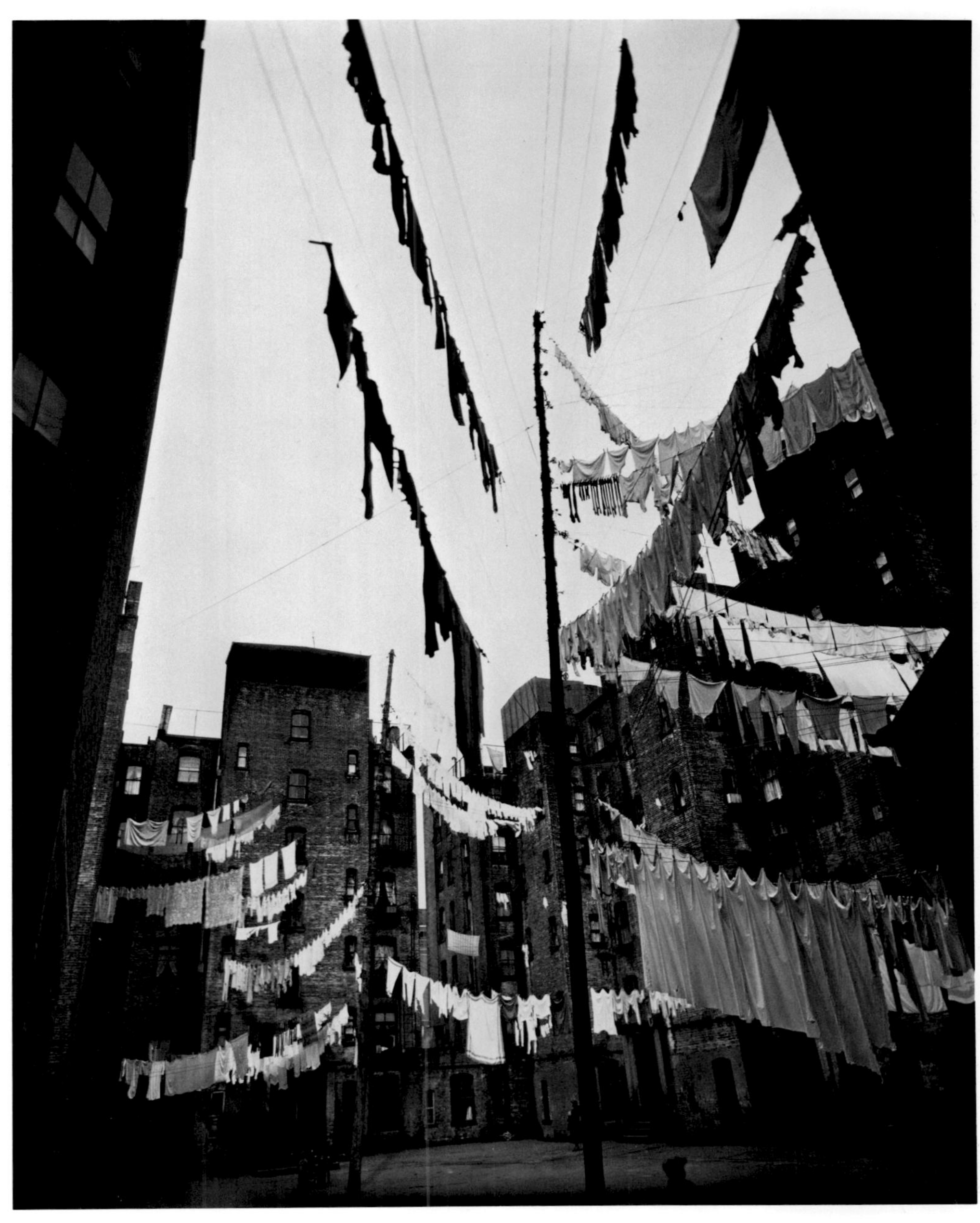

105 · Berenice Abbott · **Court of the First Model Tenements, New York** · 1936

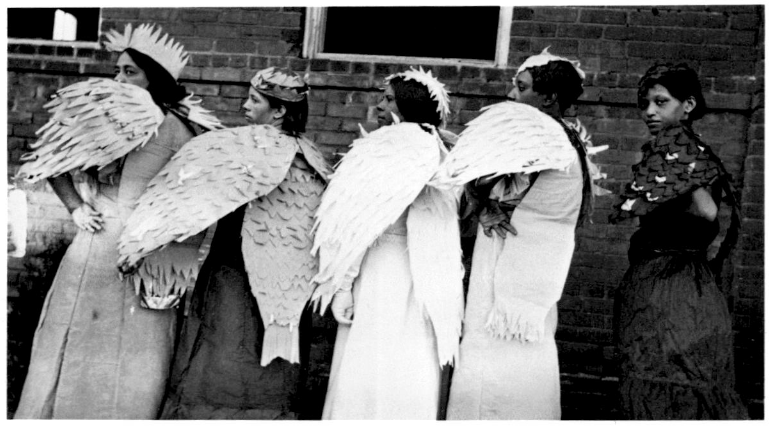

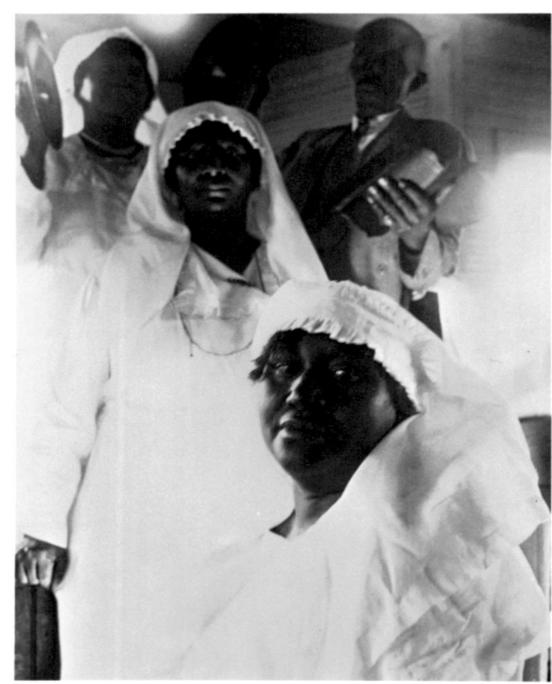

106 · Eudora Welty · **Bird Pageant Costumes** · Before 1935

107 · Eudora Welty · **Preacher and Leaders of the Holiness Church** · c. 1935–36

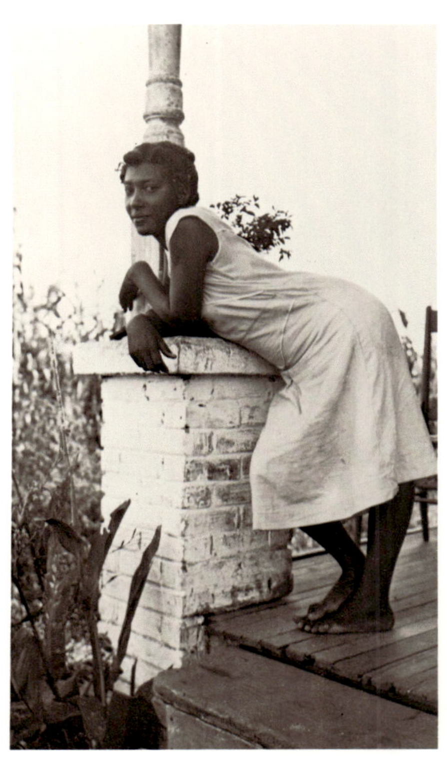

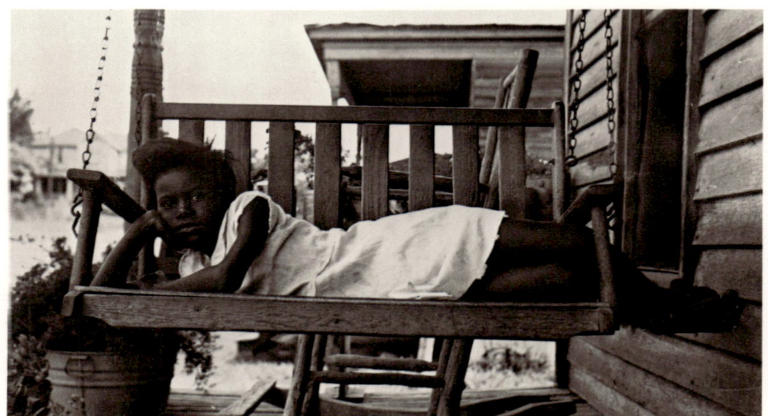

108 · Eudora Welty · **Saturday Off** · Before 1935

109 · Eudora Welty · **Staying Home** · Before 1935

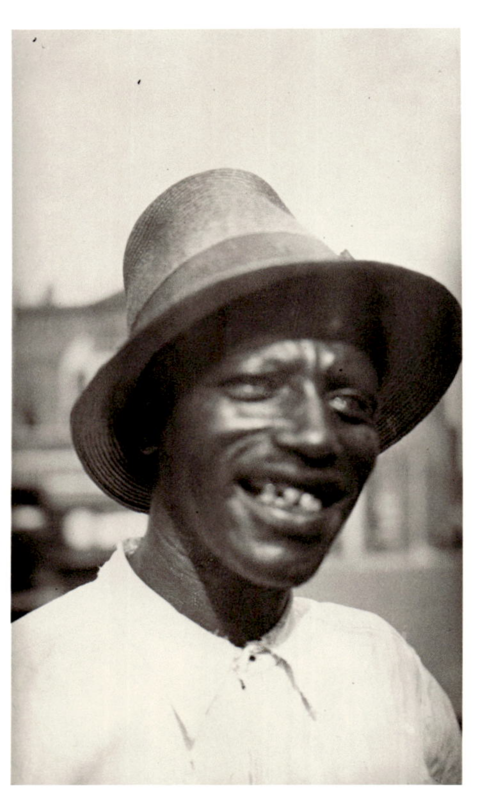 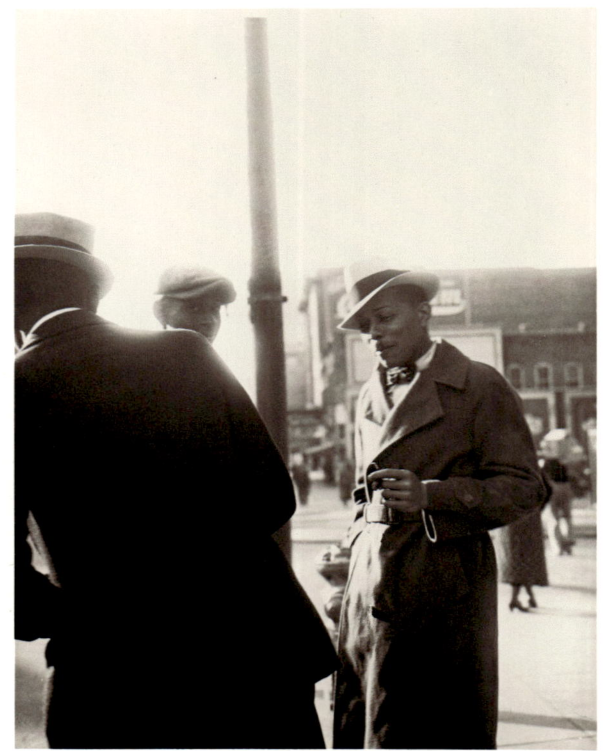

110 · Eudora Welty · Untitled · Before 1935

111 · Eudora Welty · Untitled · c. 1935–36

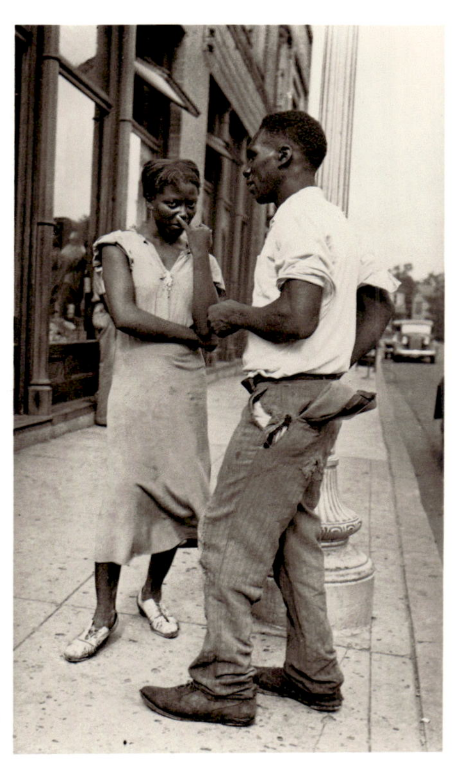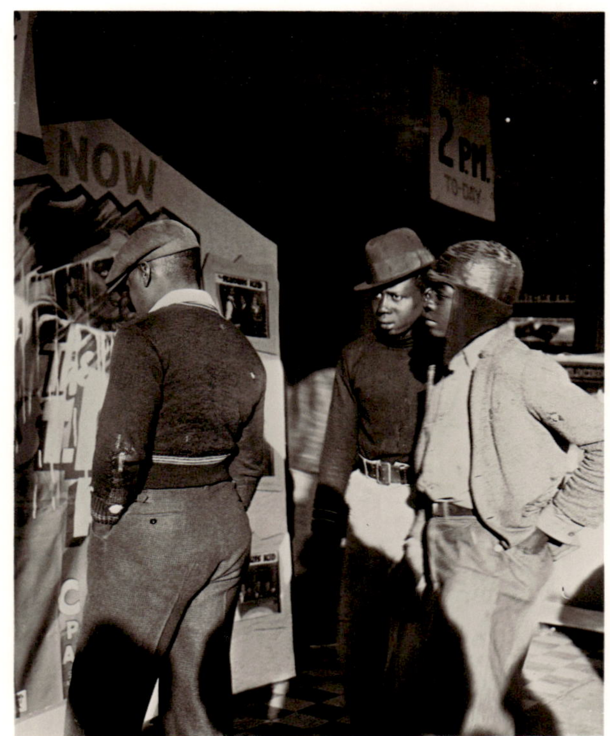

112 · Eudora Welty · **Making a date** · Before 1935

113 · Eudora Welty · Untitled · c. 1935–36

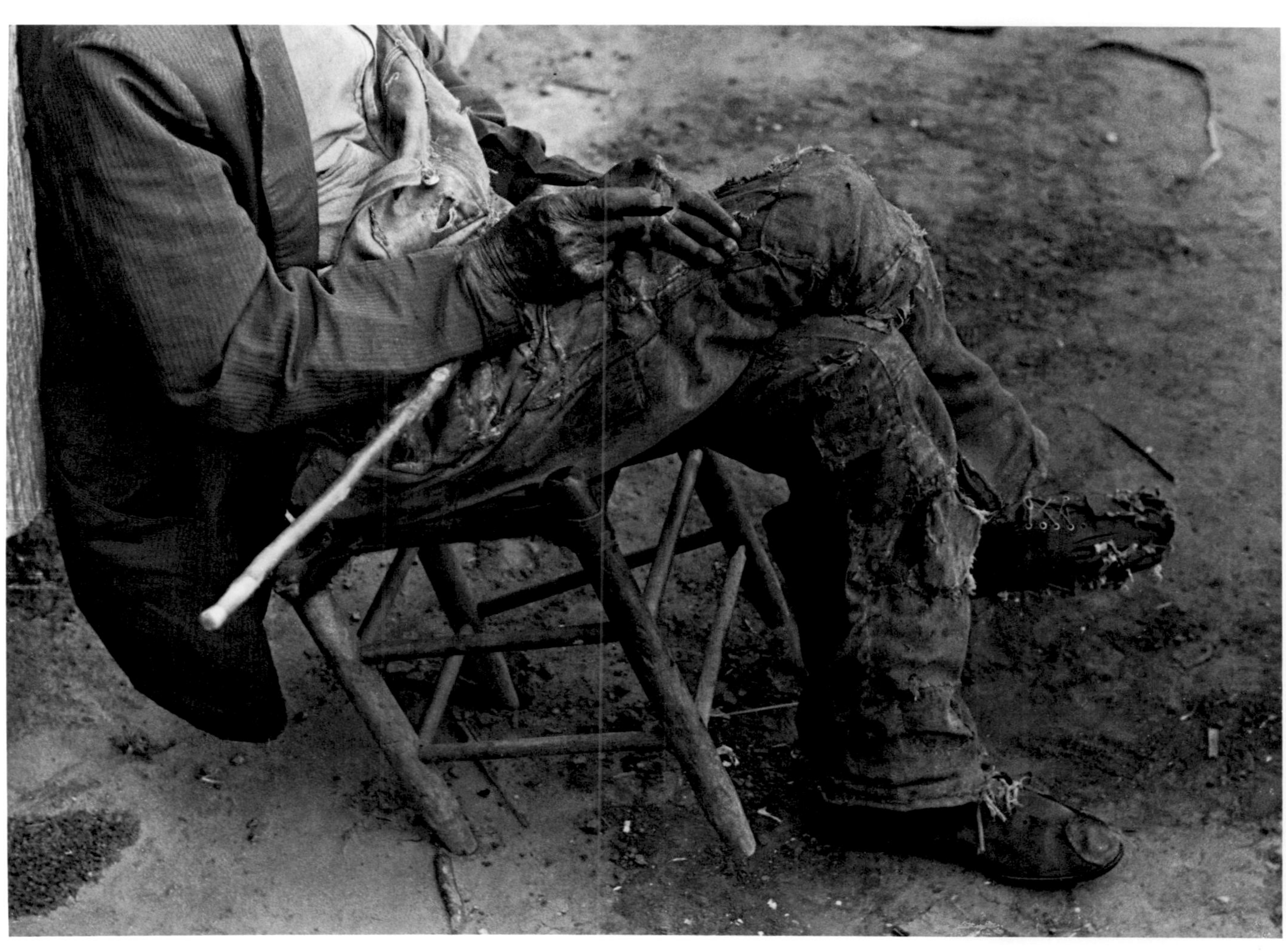

114 · Marion Post Wolcott · **The Whittler** · Camden, Alabama, 1939

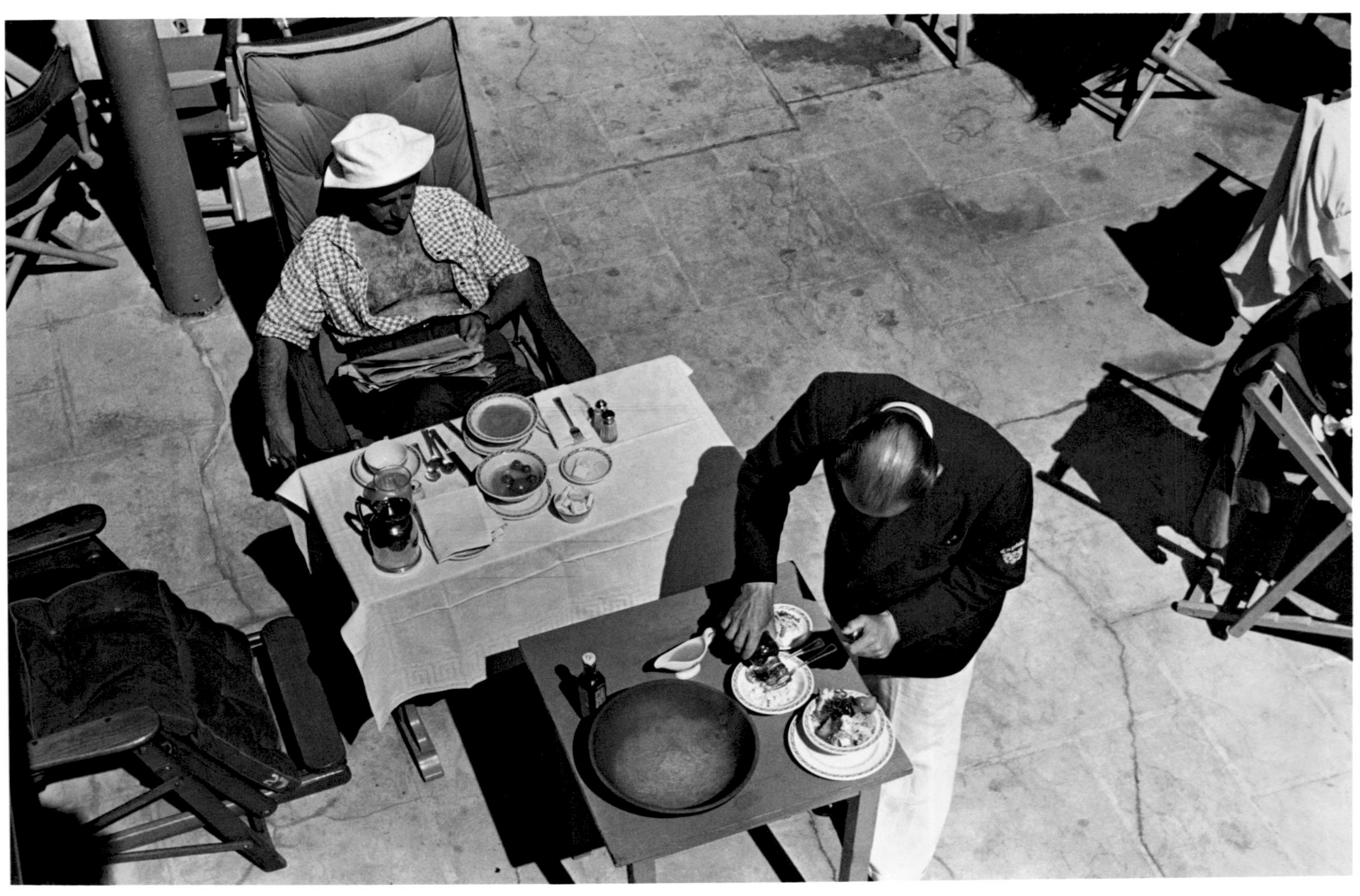

115 · Marion Post Wolcott · Guest being served lunch at private beach club · Palm Beach, Florida, 1939

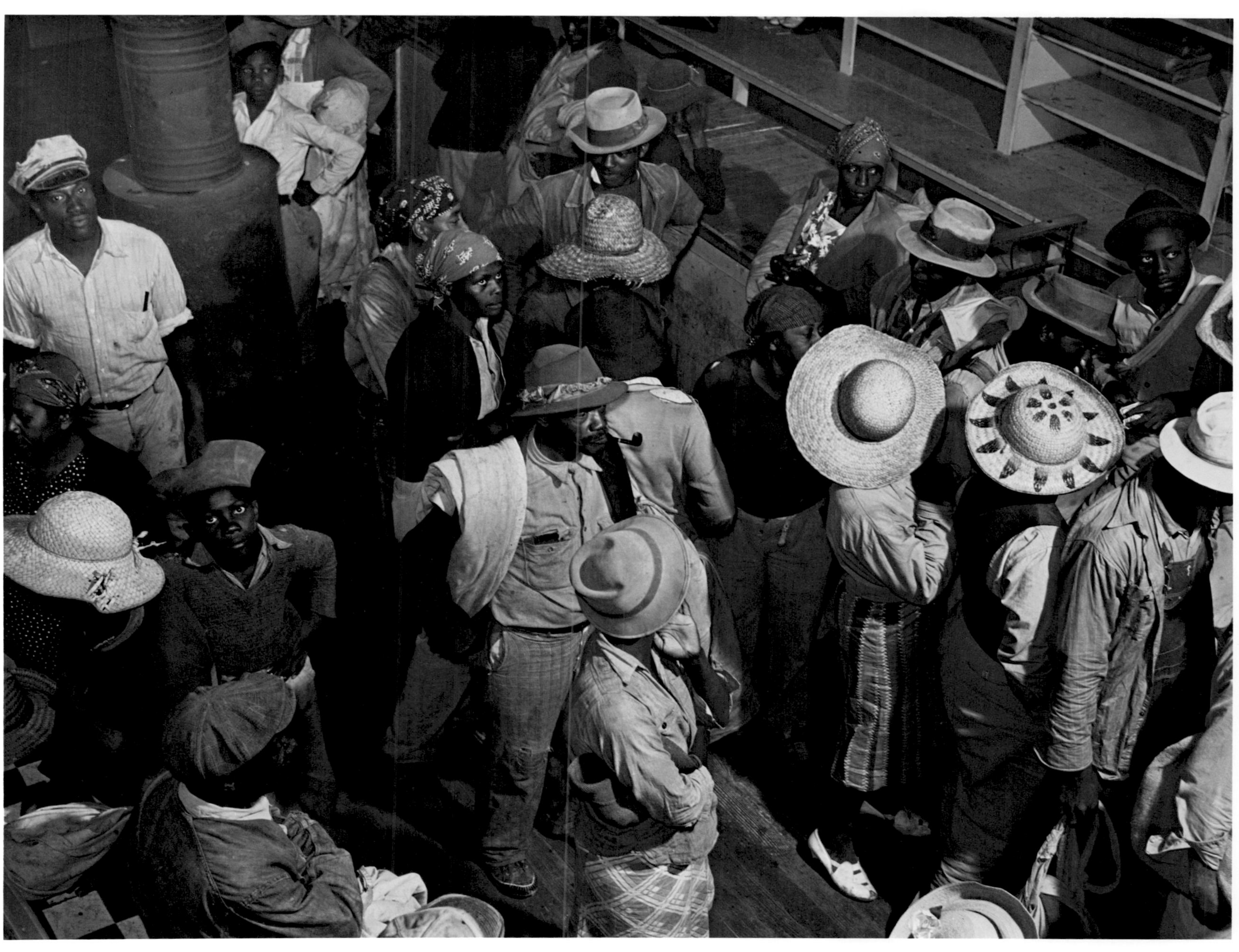

116 · Marion Post Wolcott · Day laborers waiting to be paid, Marcella Plantation · Mileston, Mississippi, 1939

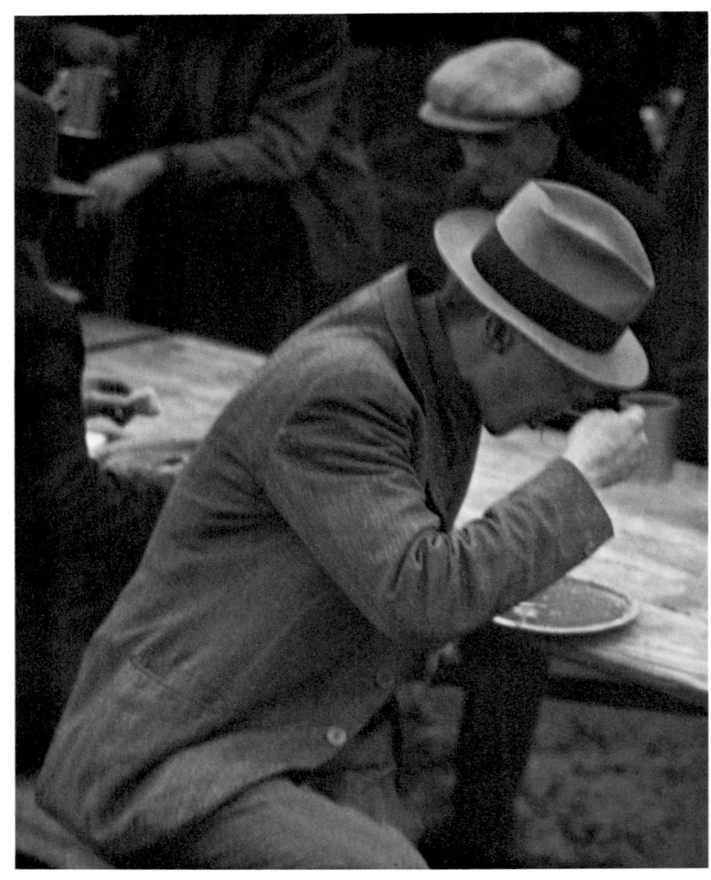

117 · Dorothea Lange · **White Angel Kitchen, San Francisco** · 1933

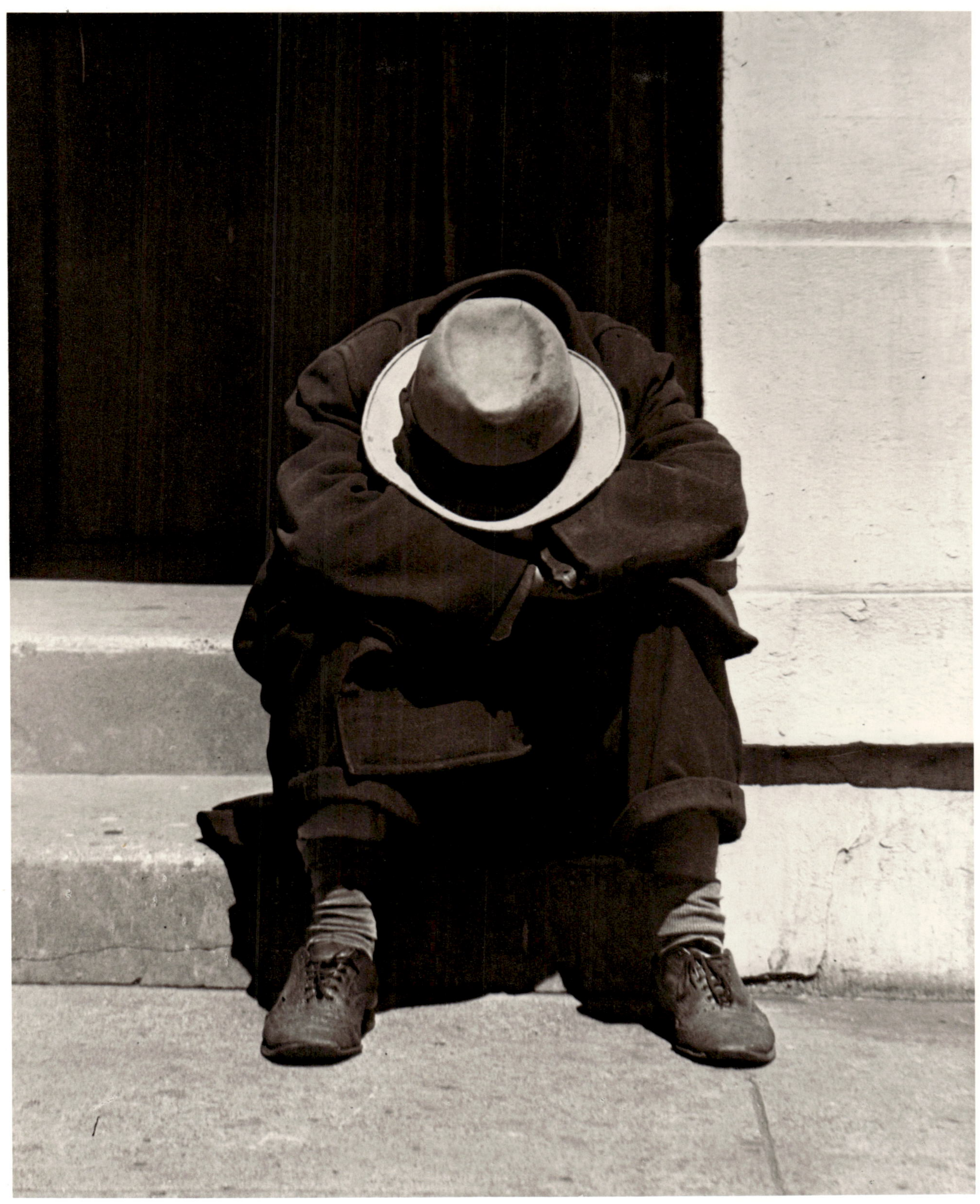

118 · Dorothea Lange · **San Francisco Waterfront** · 1933

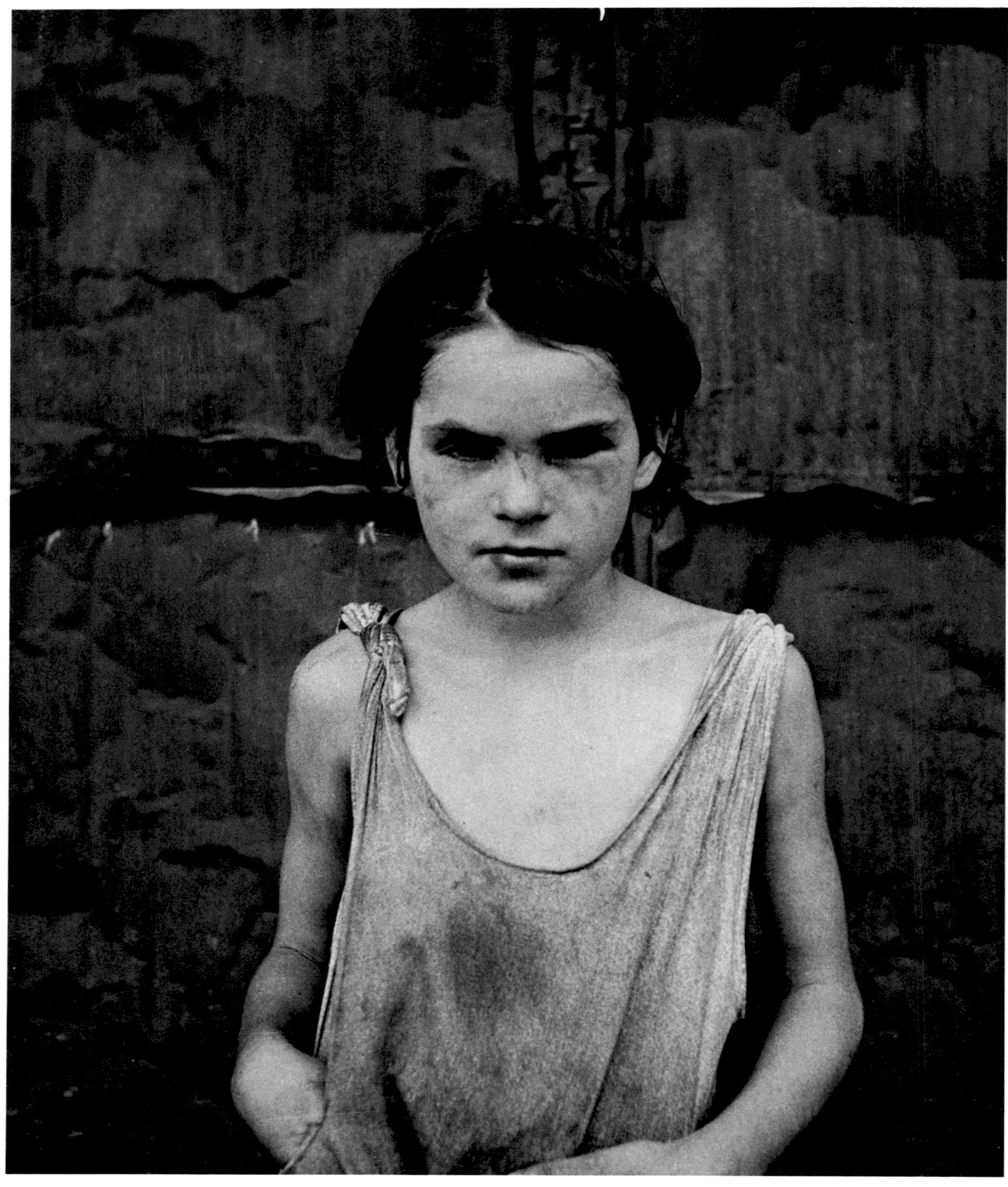

119 · Dorothea Lange · **Damaged Child, Shacktown, Elm Grove, Oklahoma** · 1936

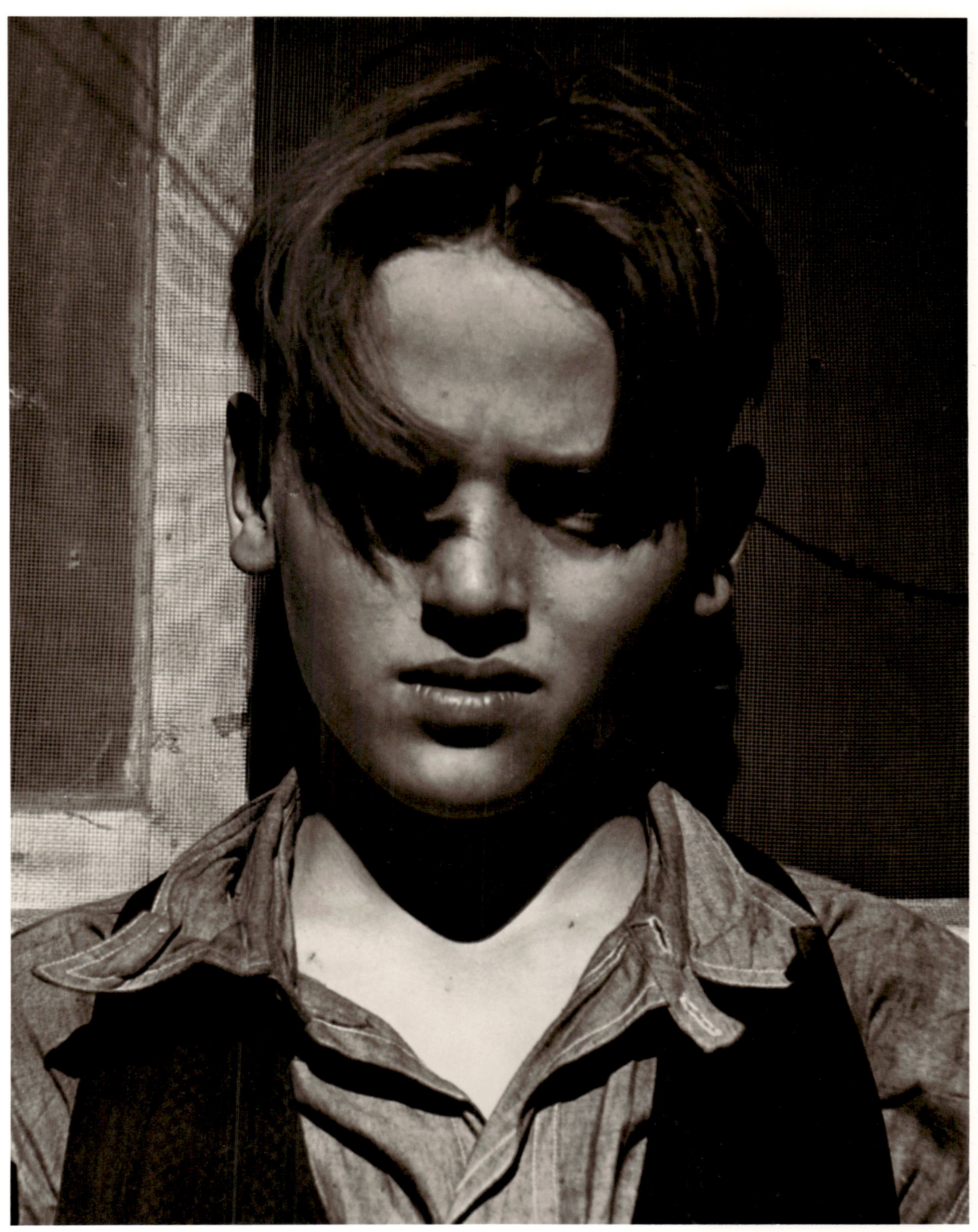

120 · Dorothea Lange · **Homeless Wandering Boy** · 1933

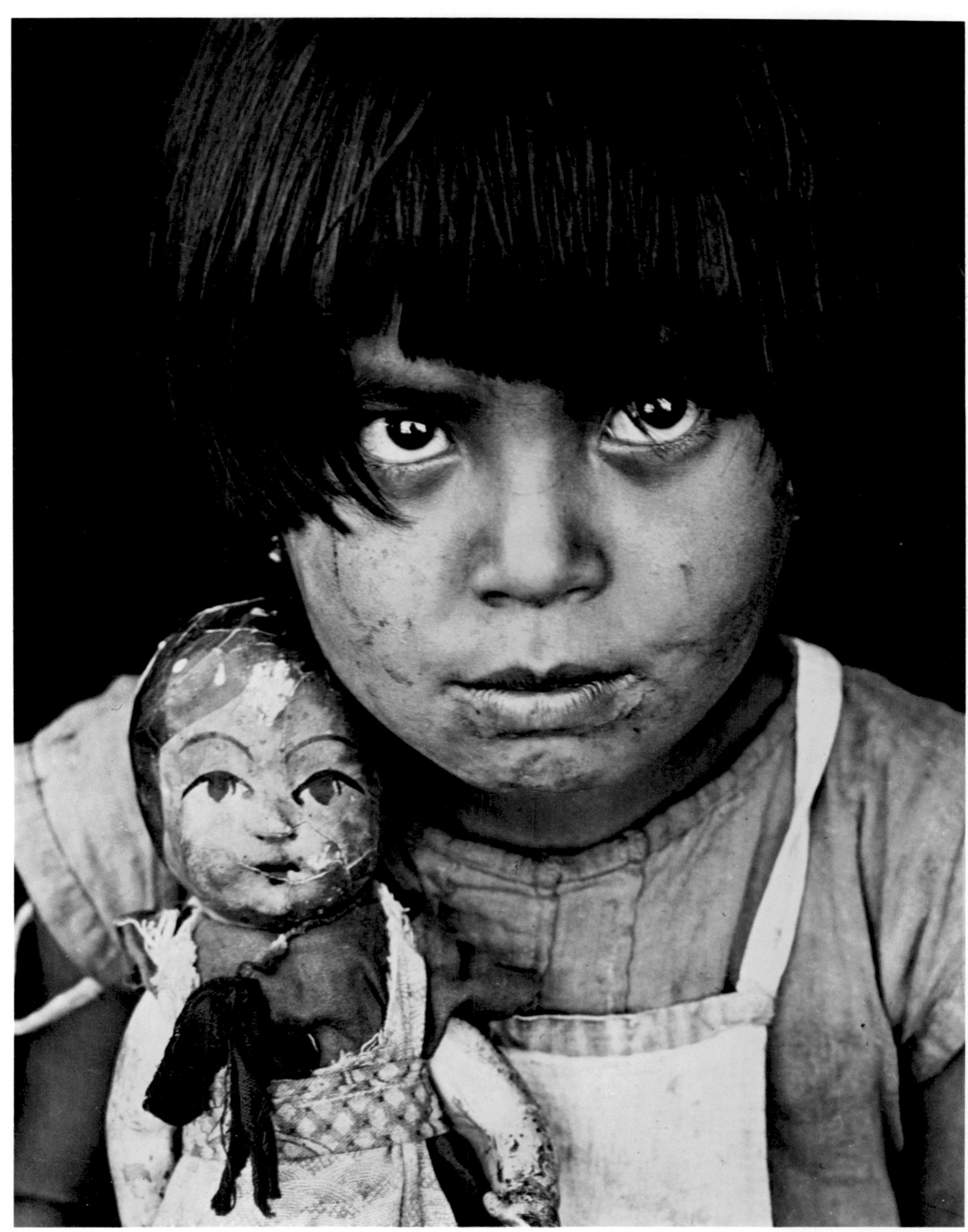

121 · Margaret Bourke-White · **Fazenda Rio des Preda** · 1930s

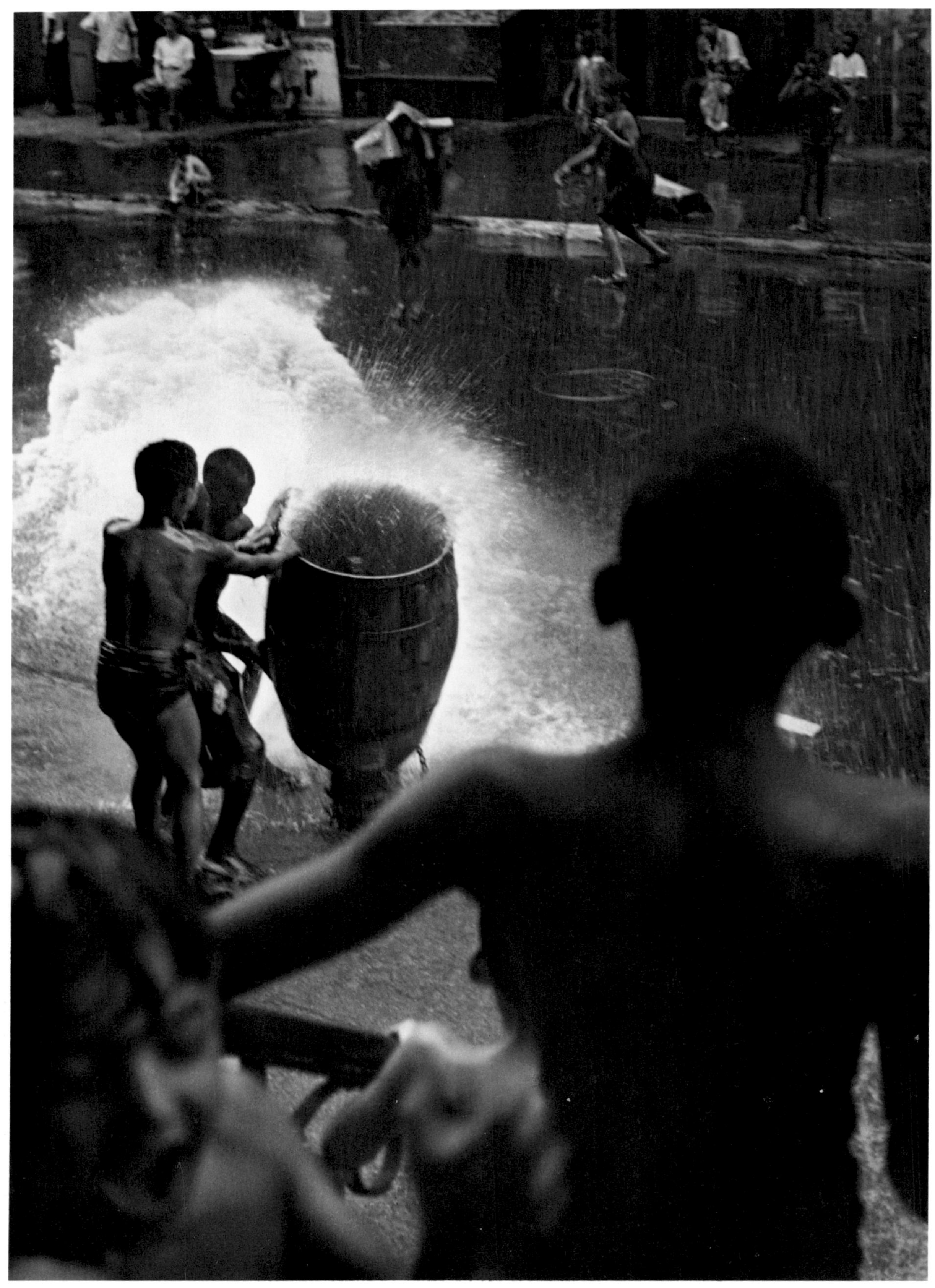

122 · Helen Levitt · **Children and Fire Hydrant** · c. 1945

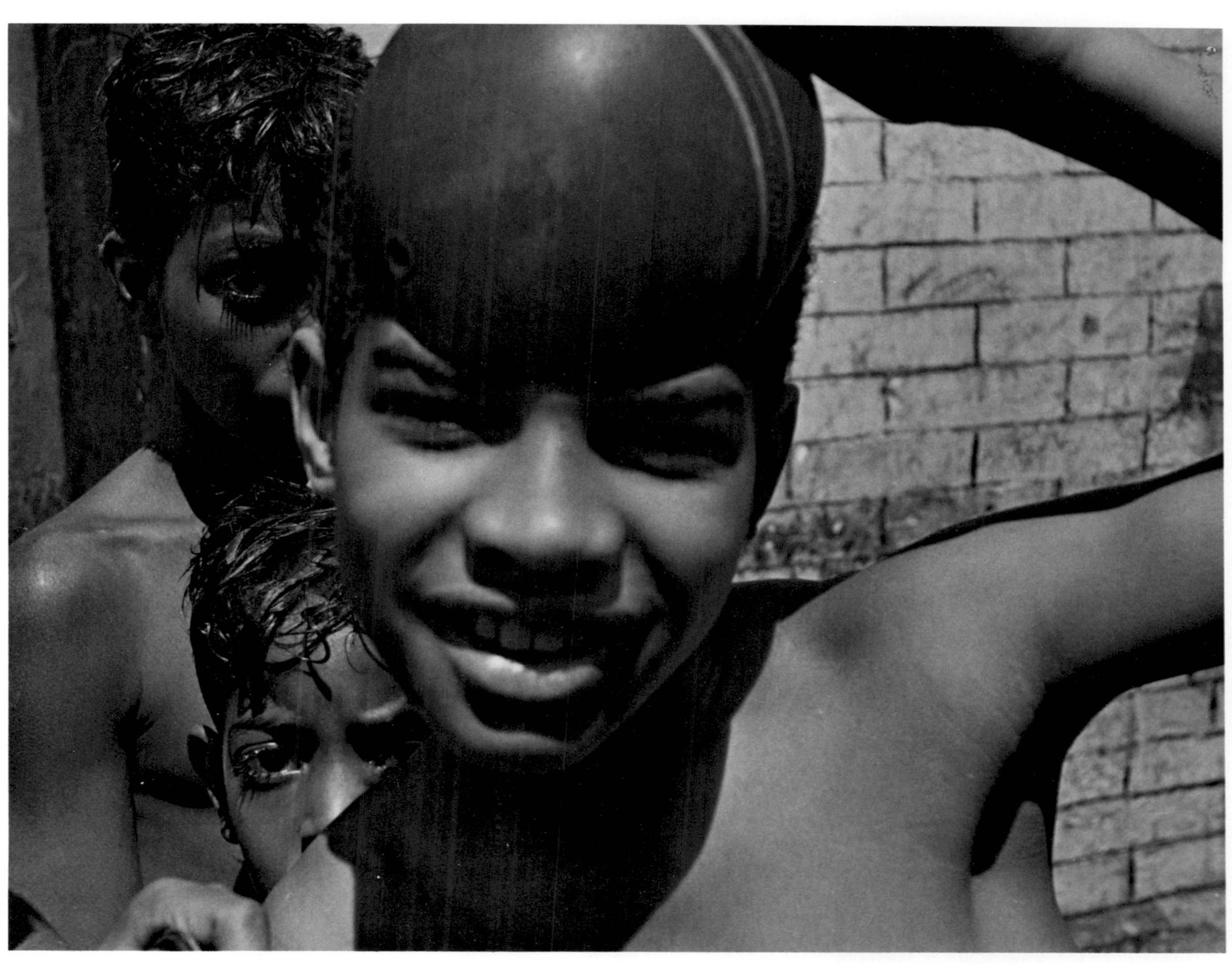

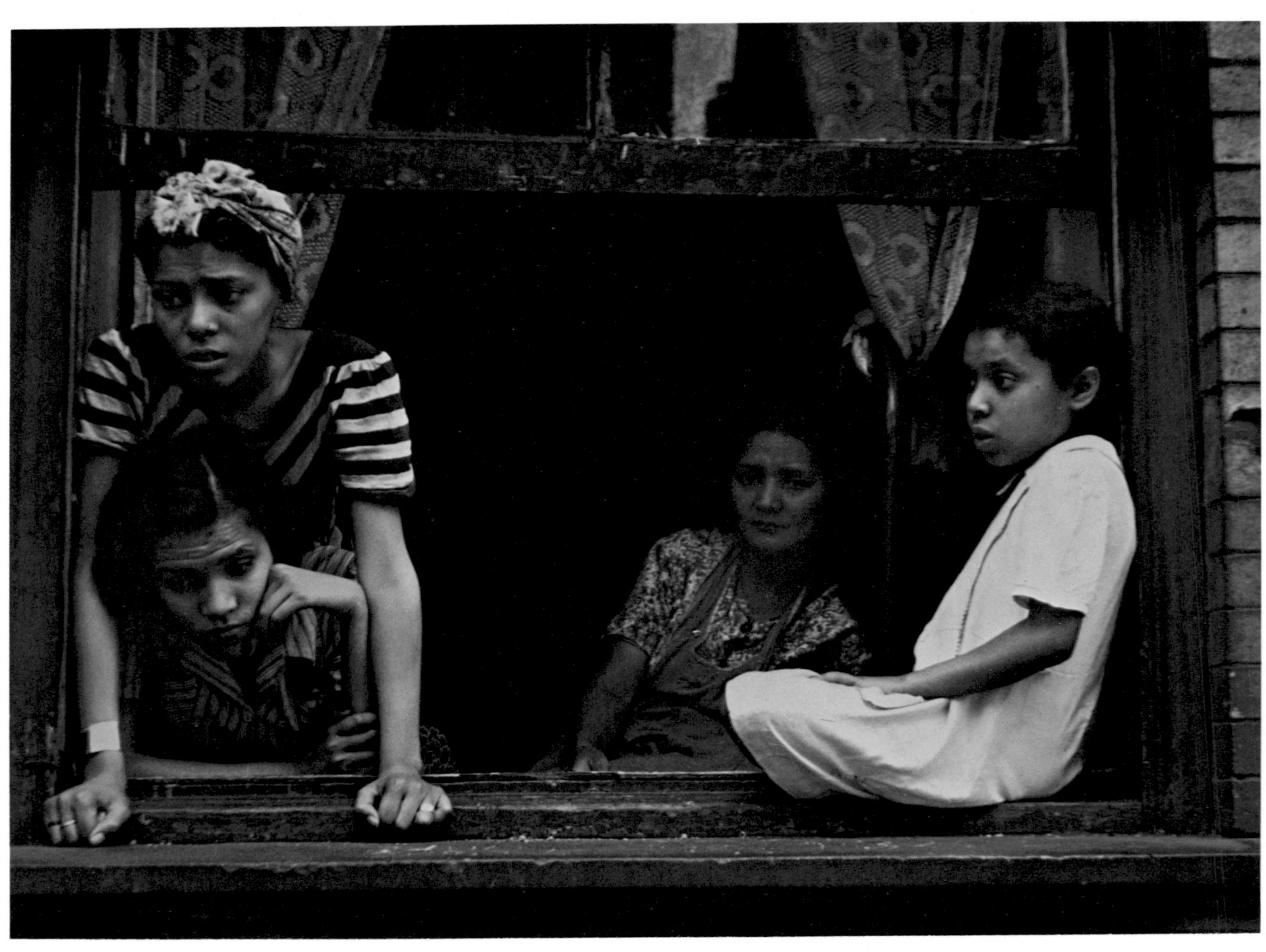

124 · Helen Levitt · **New York** · c. 1942

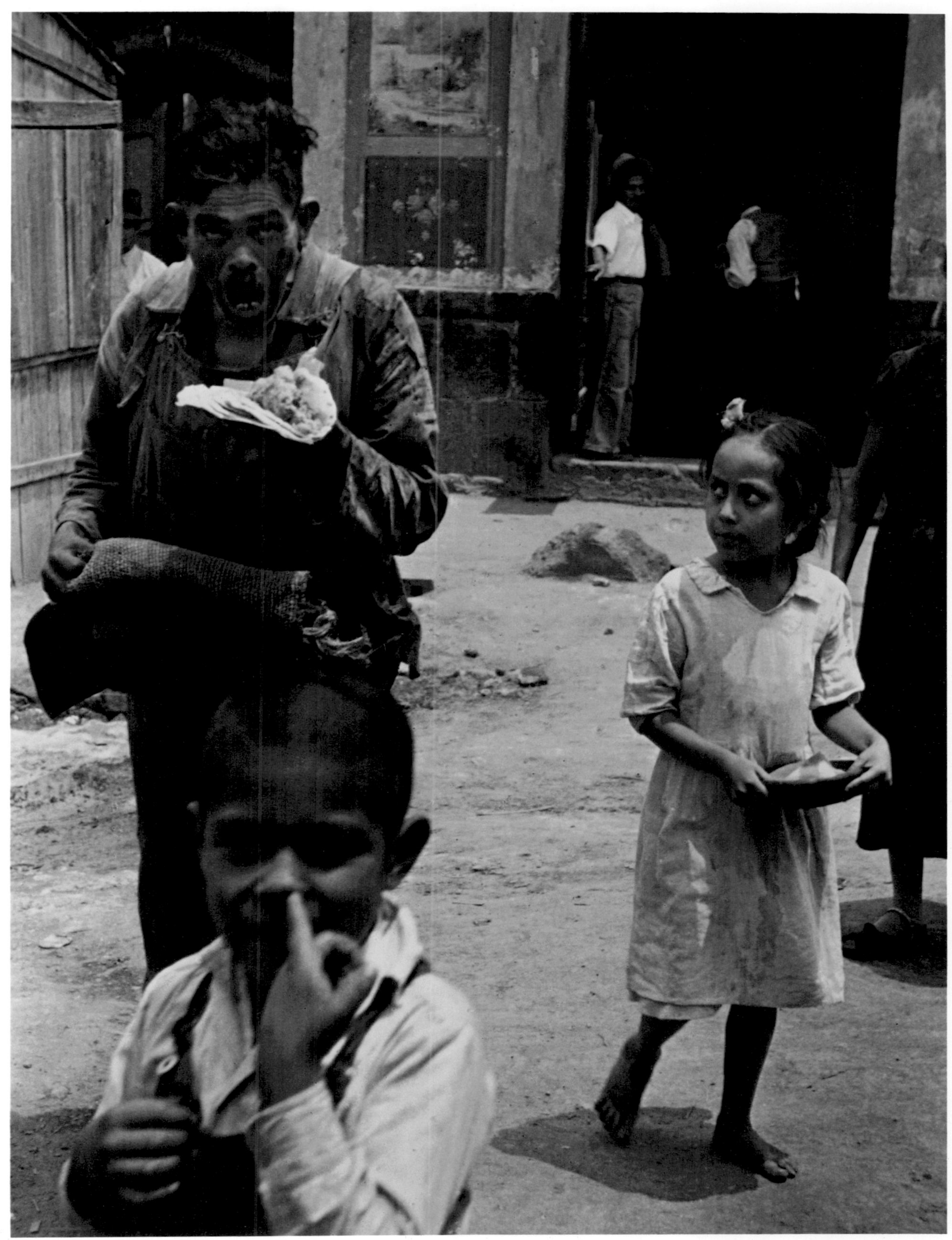

125 · Helen Levitt · **Mexico City** · 1941

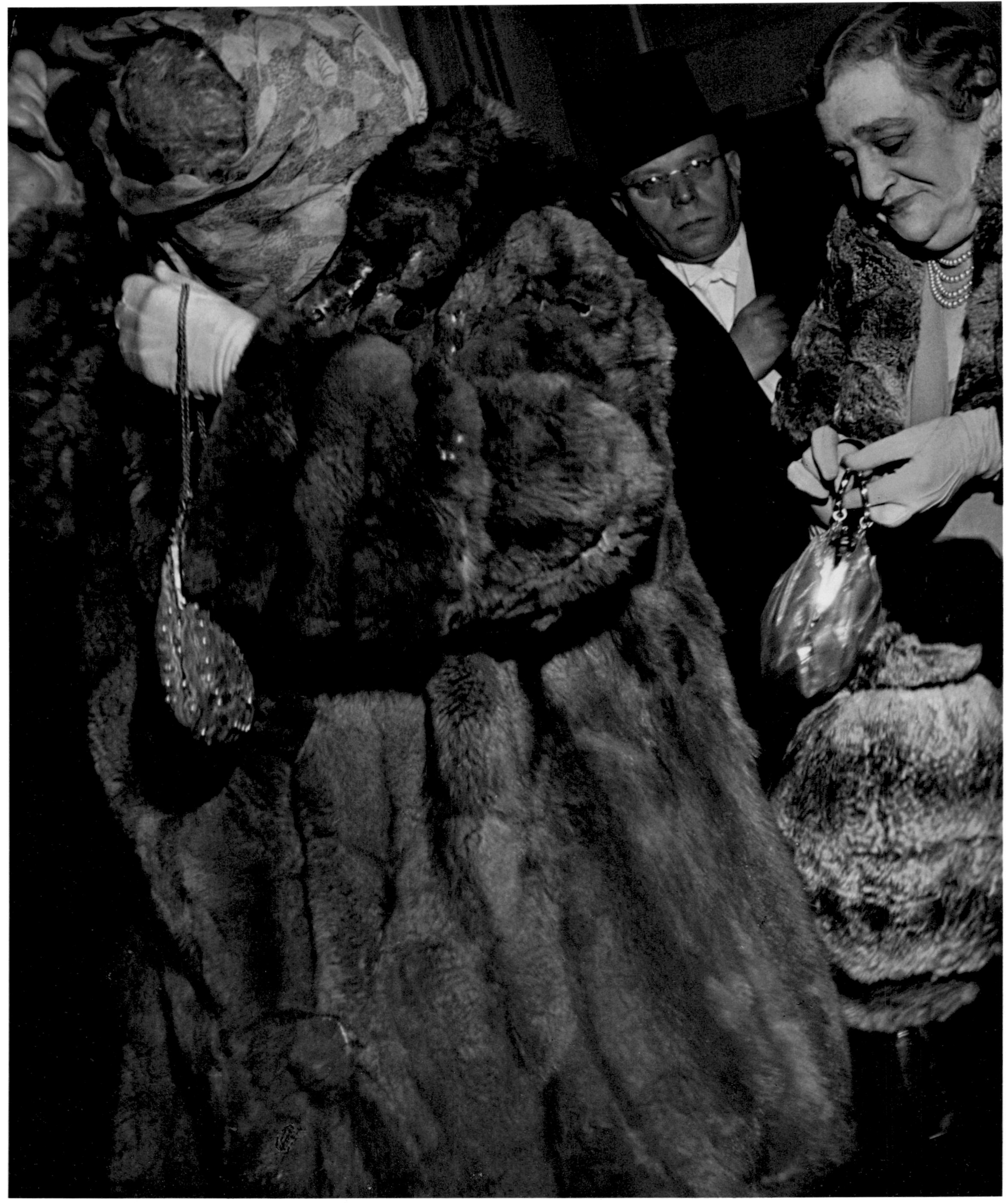

126 · Lisette Model · **Woman at Opera with Face Covered** · c. 1945

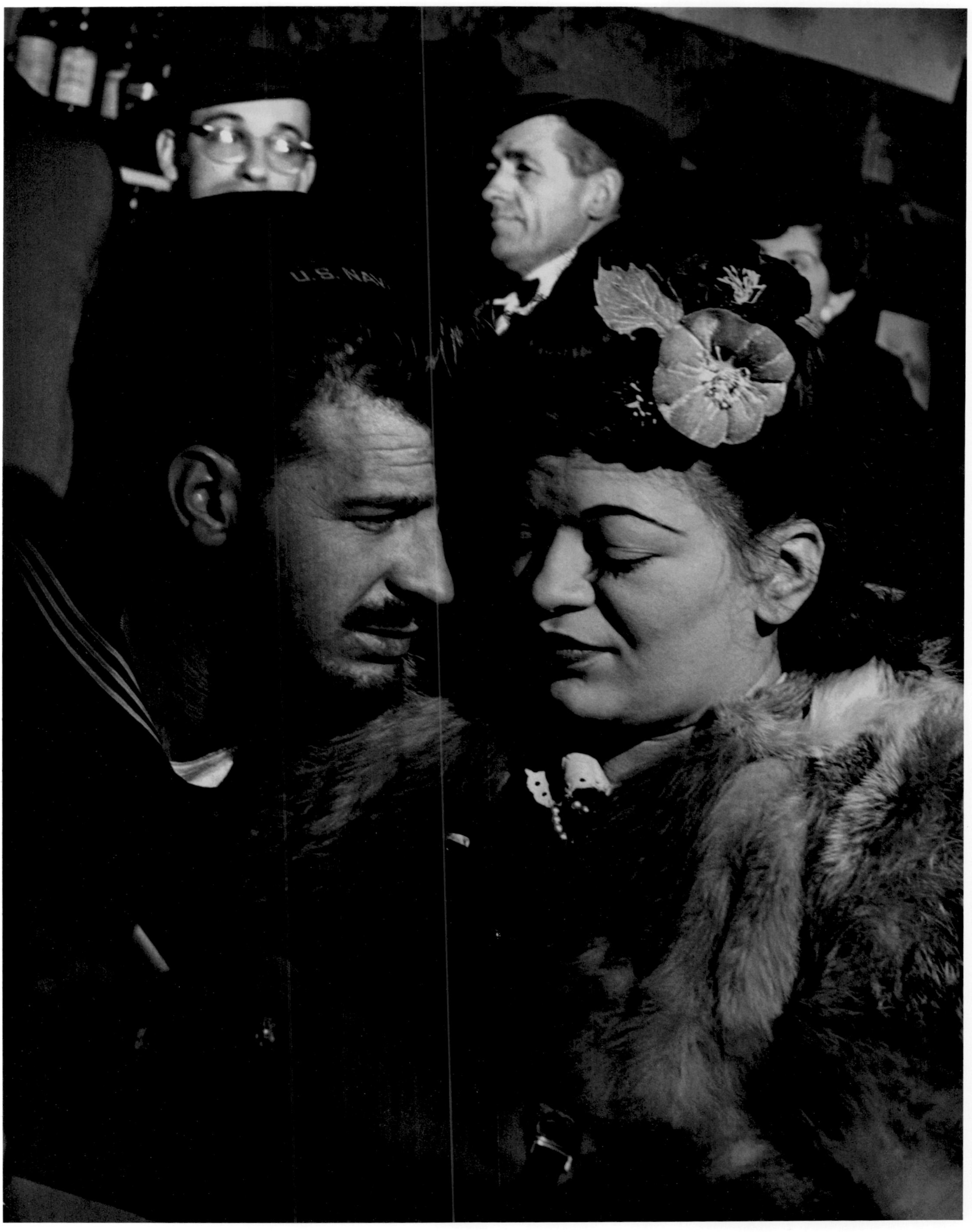

127 · Lisette Model · **Sailor and Girl, Sammy's Bar, New York** · c. 1944 (before 1950)

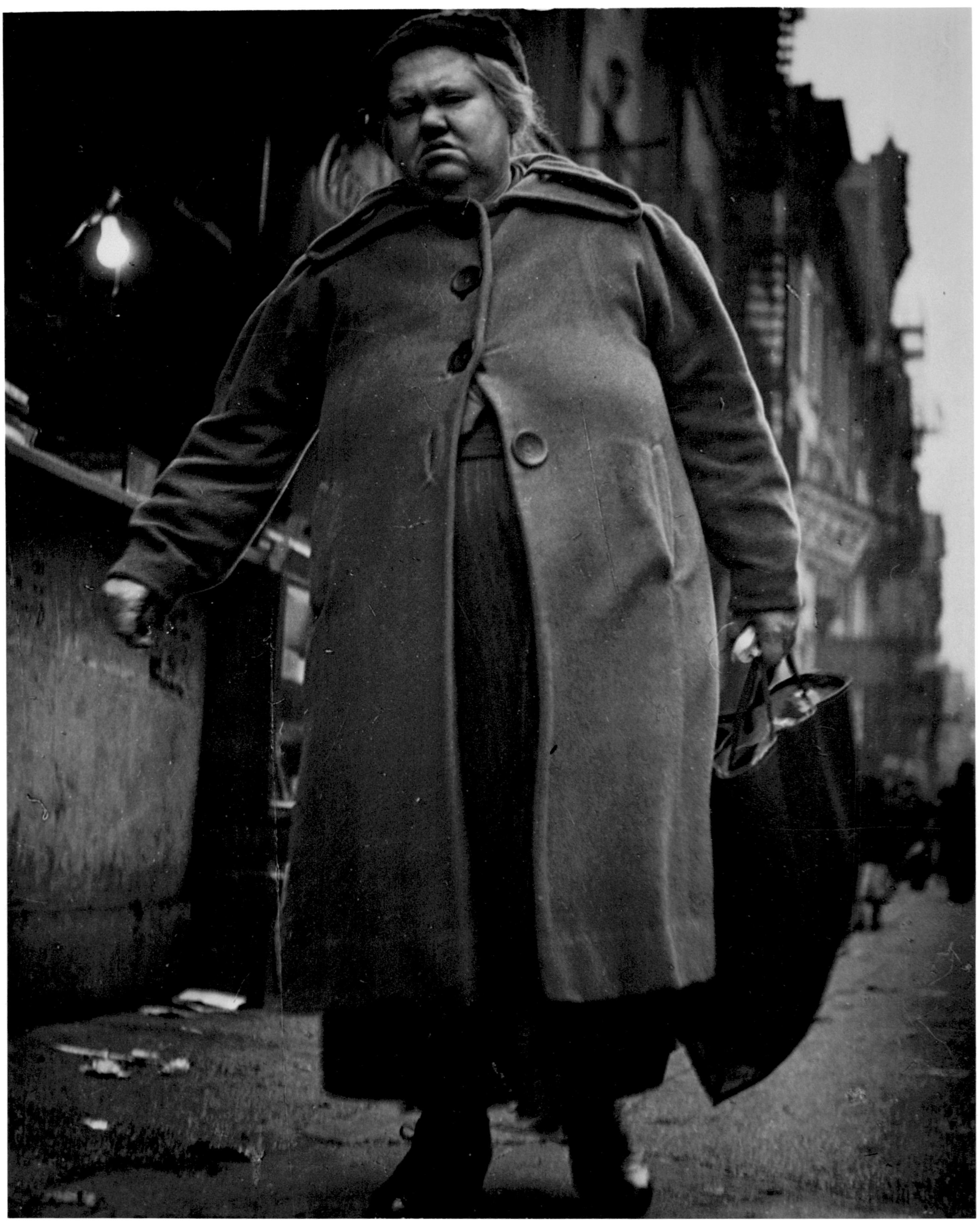

128 · Lisette Model · **Lower East Side** · 1940

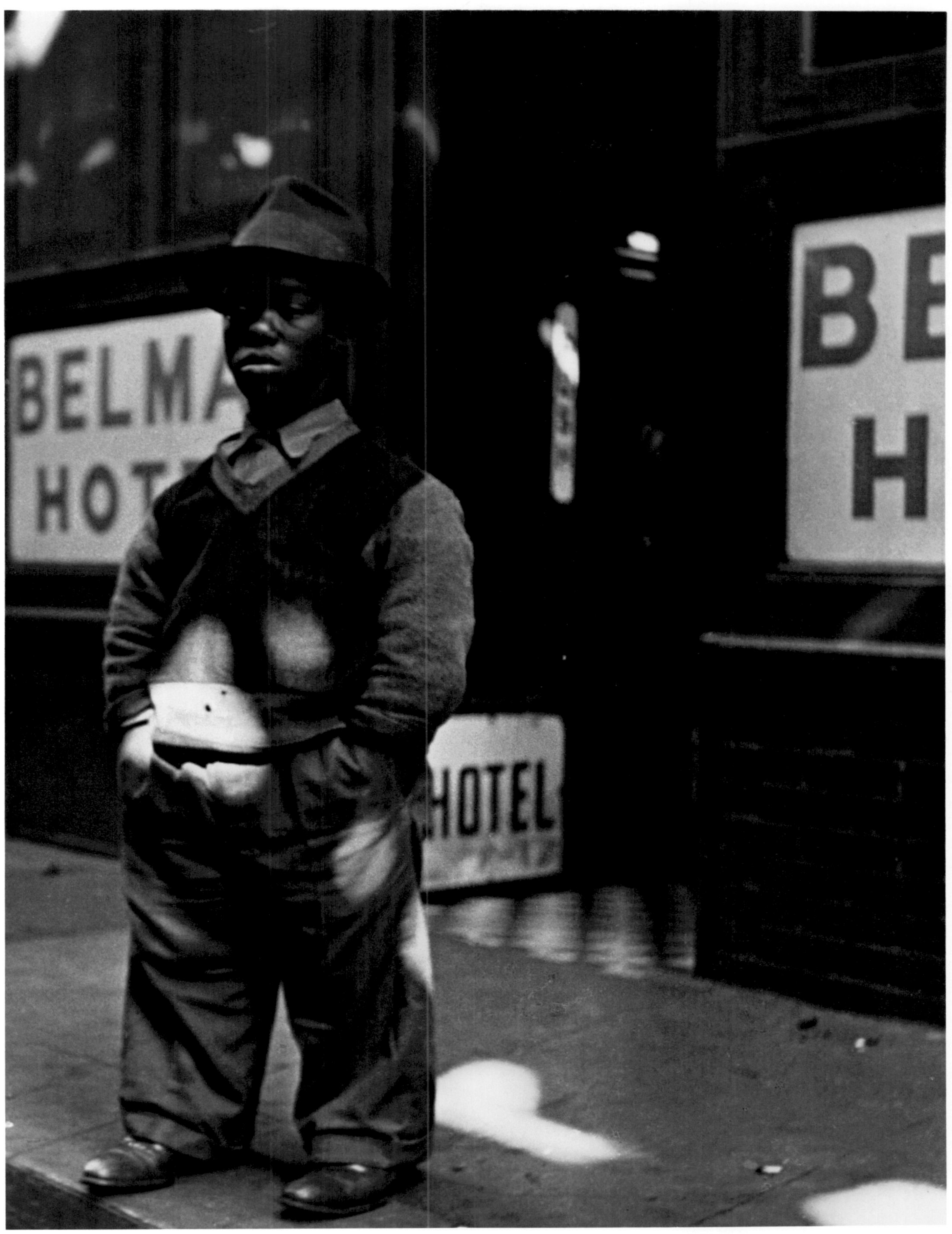

129 · Lisette Model · **Black Dwarf, Lower East Side** · 1950

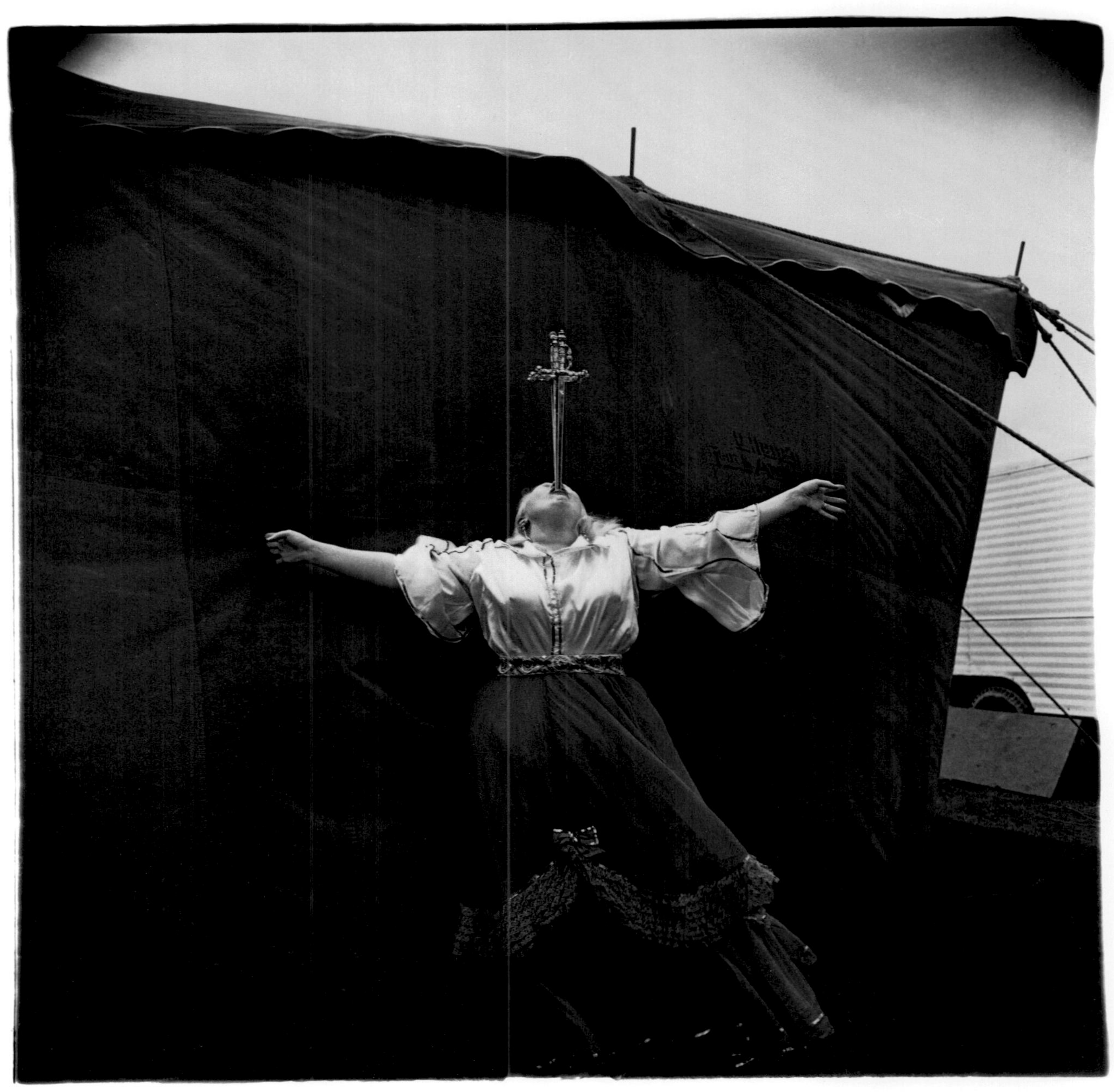

130 · Diane Arbus · **Albino Sword Swallower at a Carnival, MD** · 1970

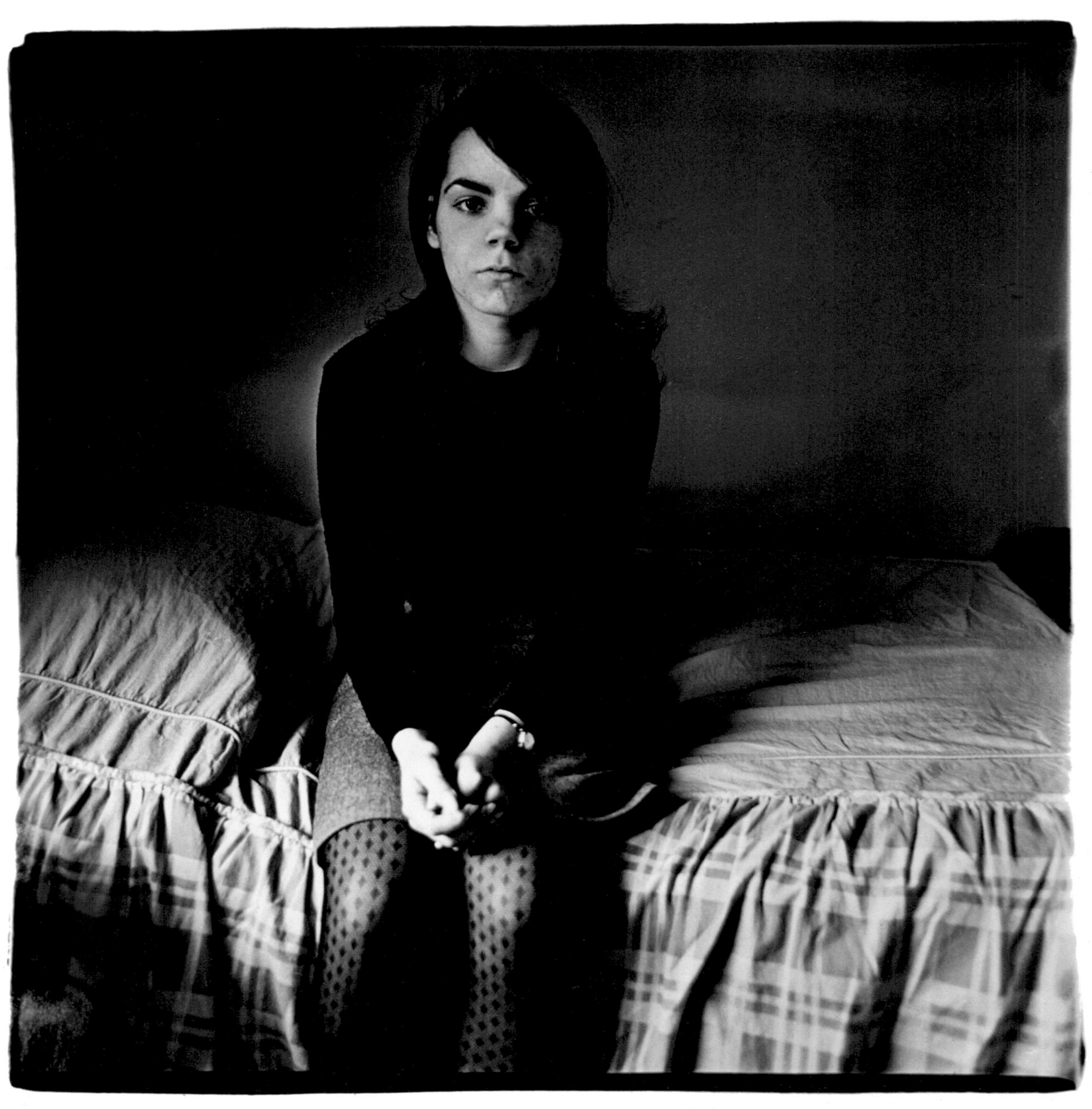

131 · Diane Arbus · **Girl with Patterned Stockings** · c. 1965–69

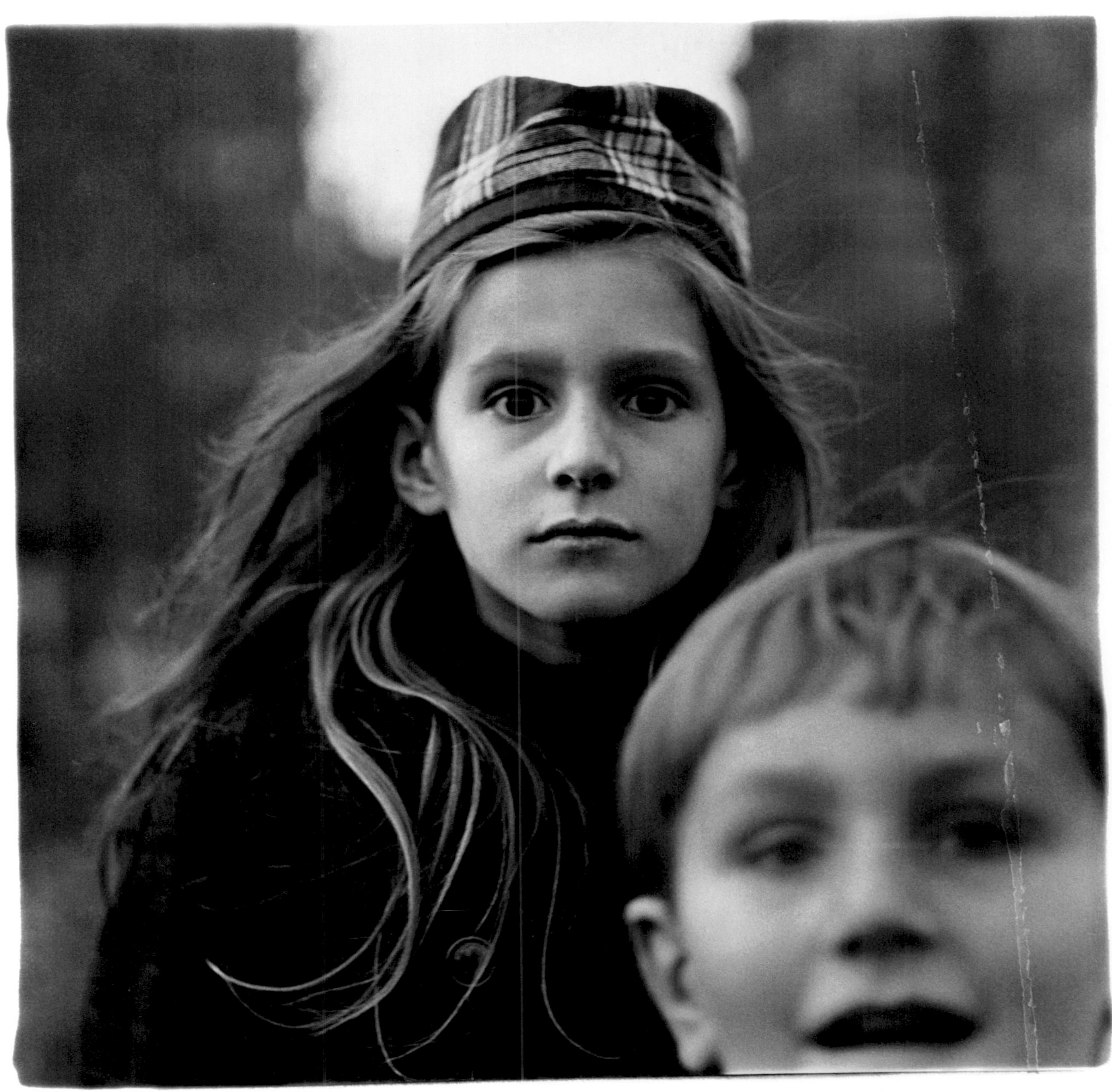

132 · Diane Arbus · **Girl in a Watch Cap, New York City** · 1965

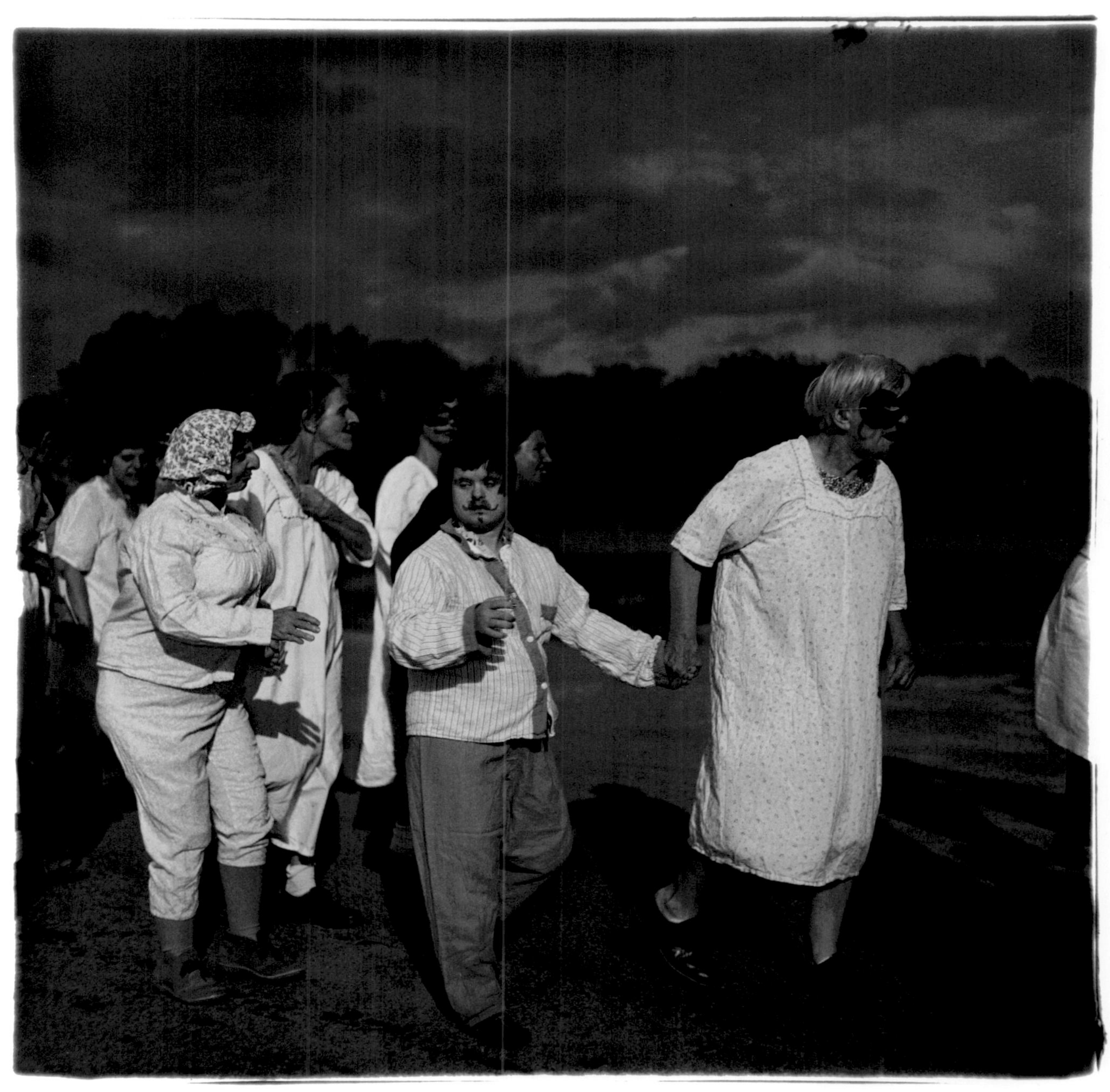

133 · Diane Arbus · Untitled (7) · 1970–71

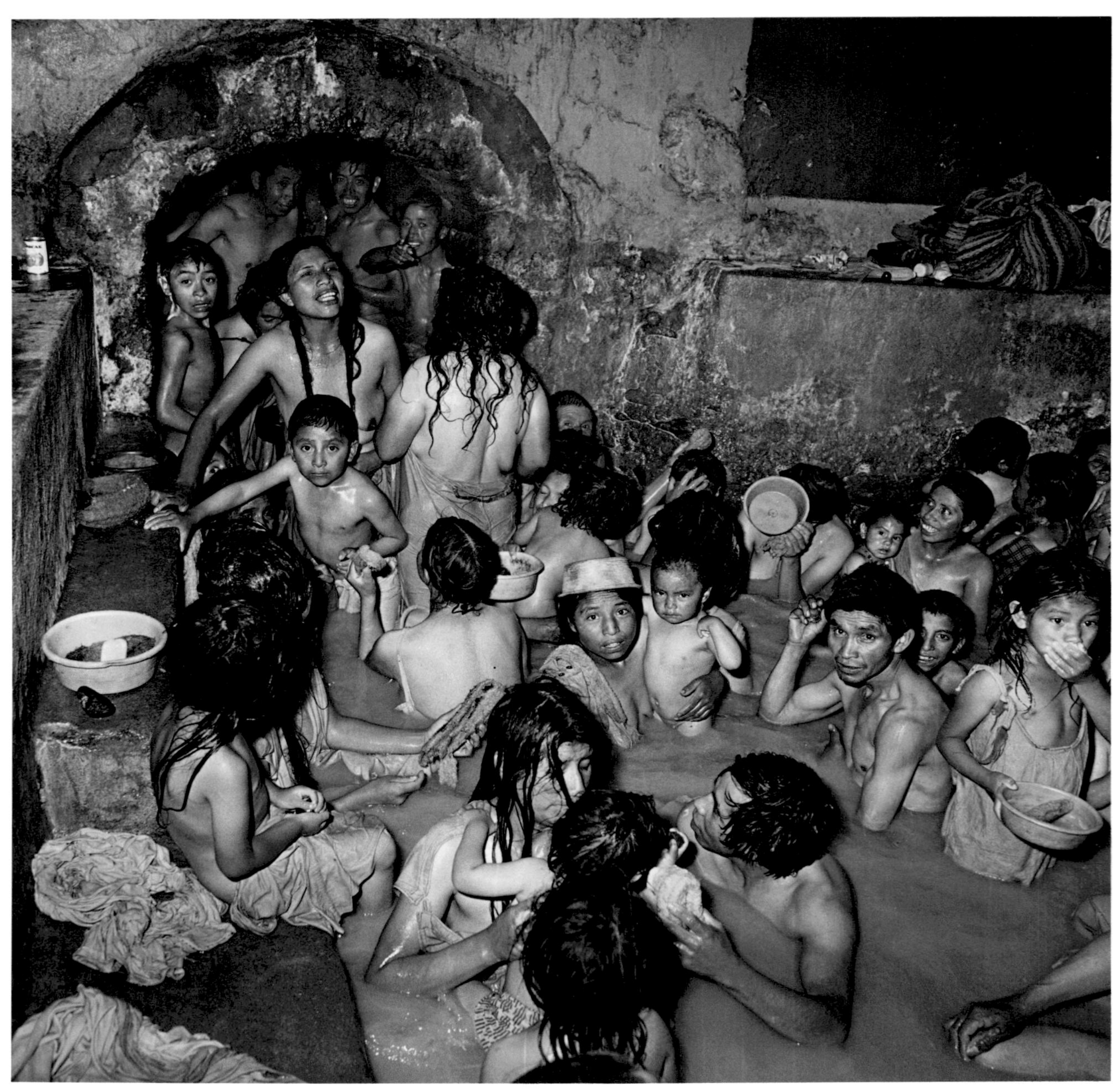

134 · Rosalind Solomon · **Bathers, Guatemala** · 1979

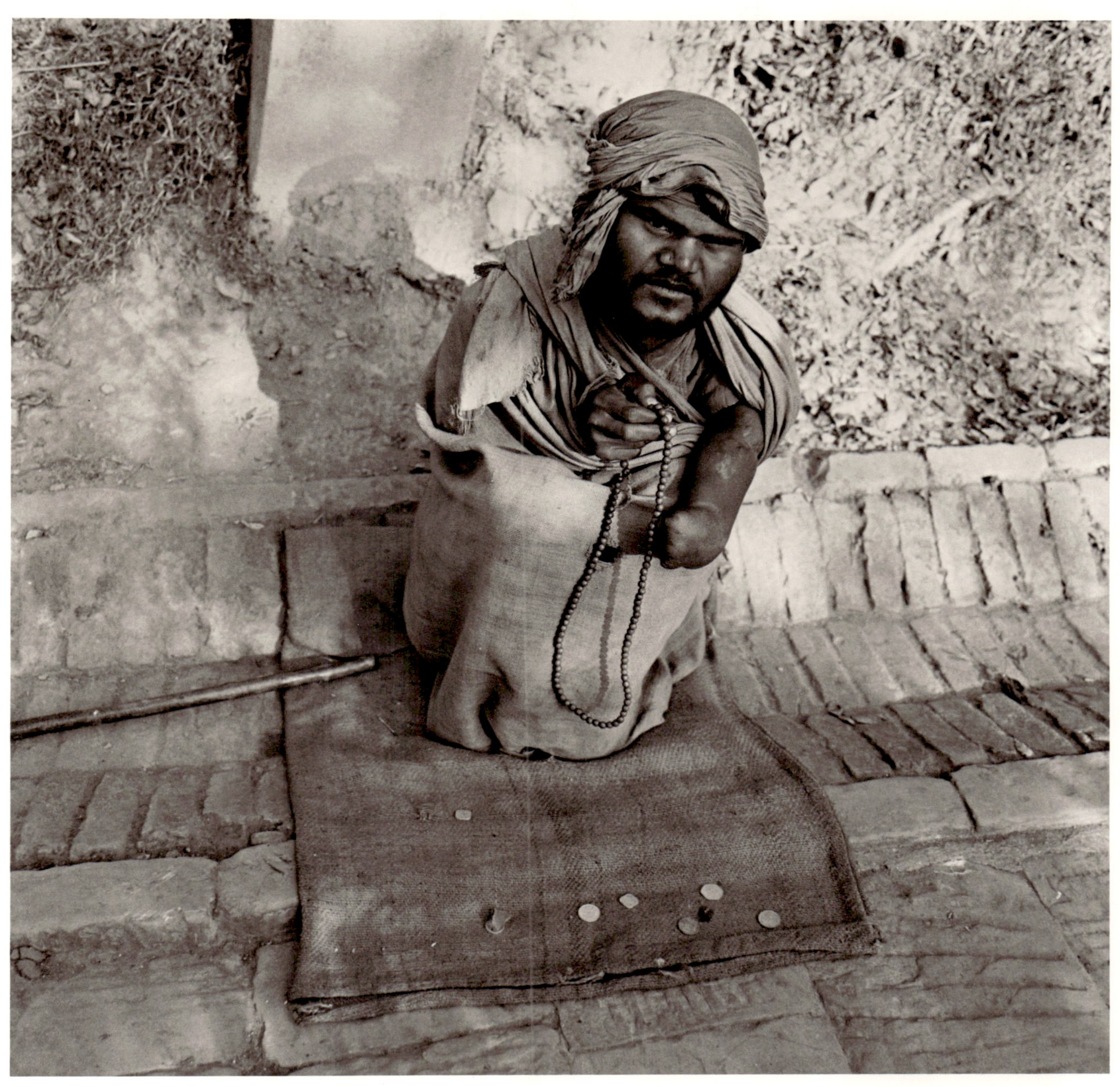

135 · Rosalind Solomon · **Man at Swayamanboth Temple, Kathmandu, Nepal** · 1985

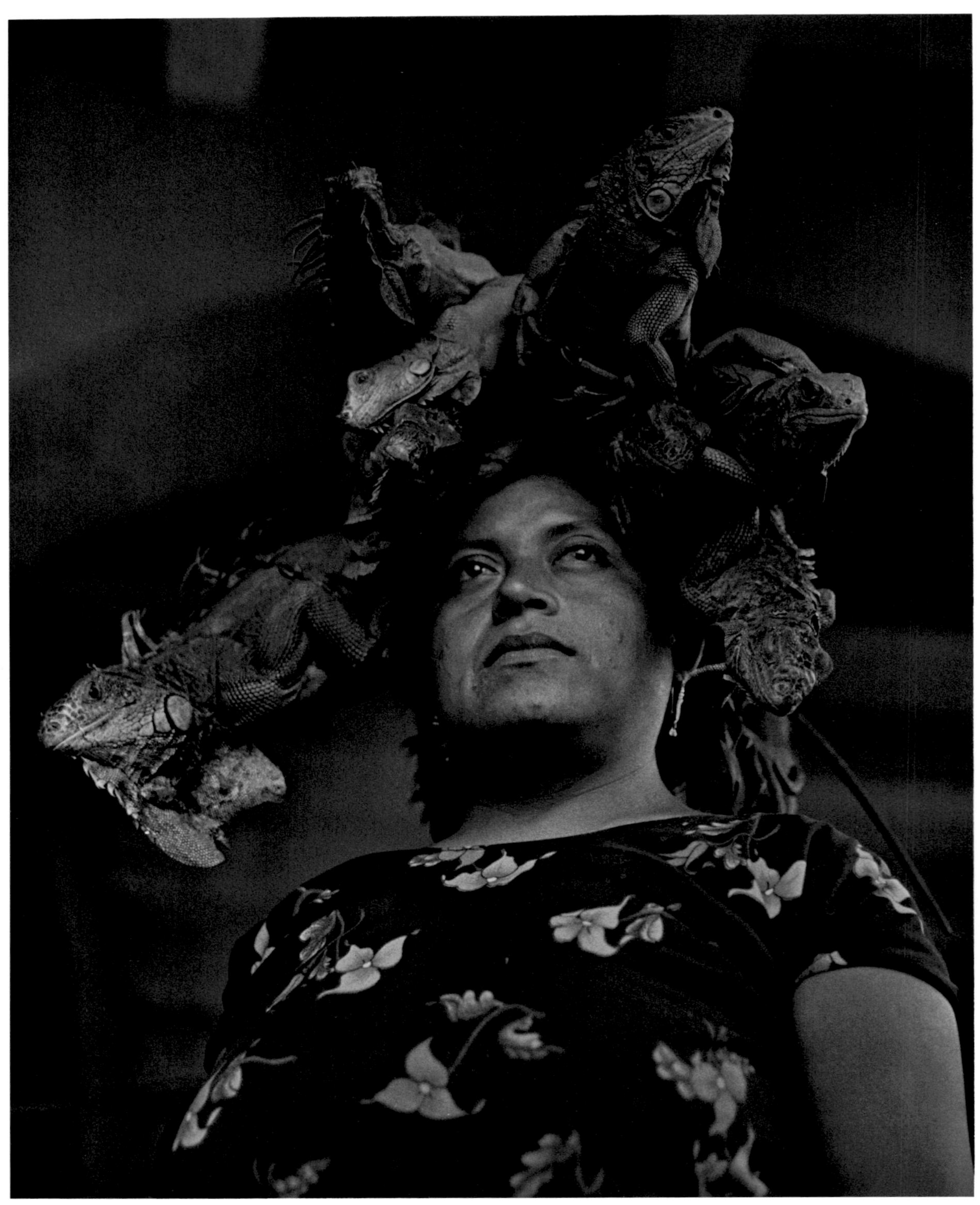

136 · Graciela Iturbide · **Nuestra Señora de las Iguanas, Juchitán** · 1980

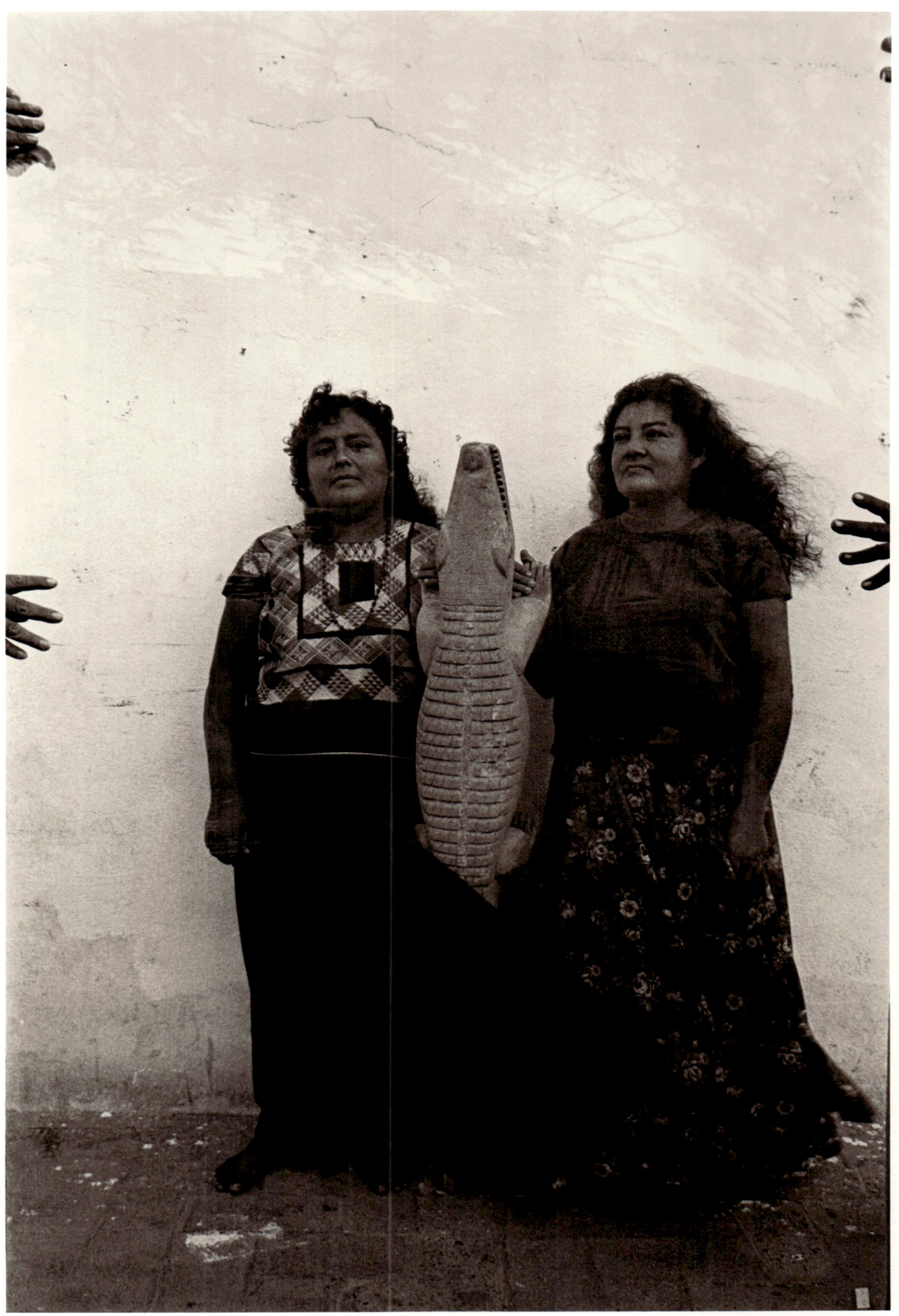

137 · Graciela Iturbide · **Laganto, Juchitán** · 1988

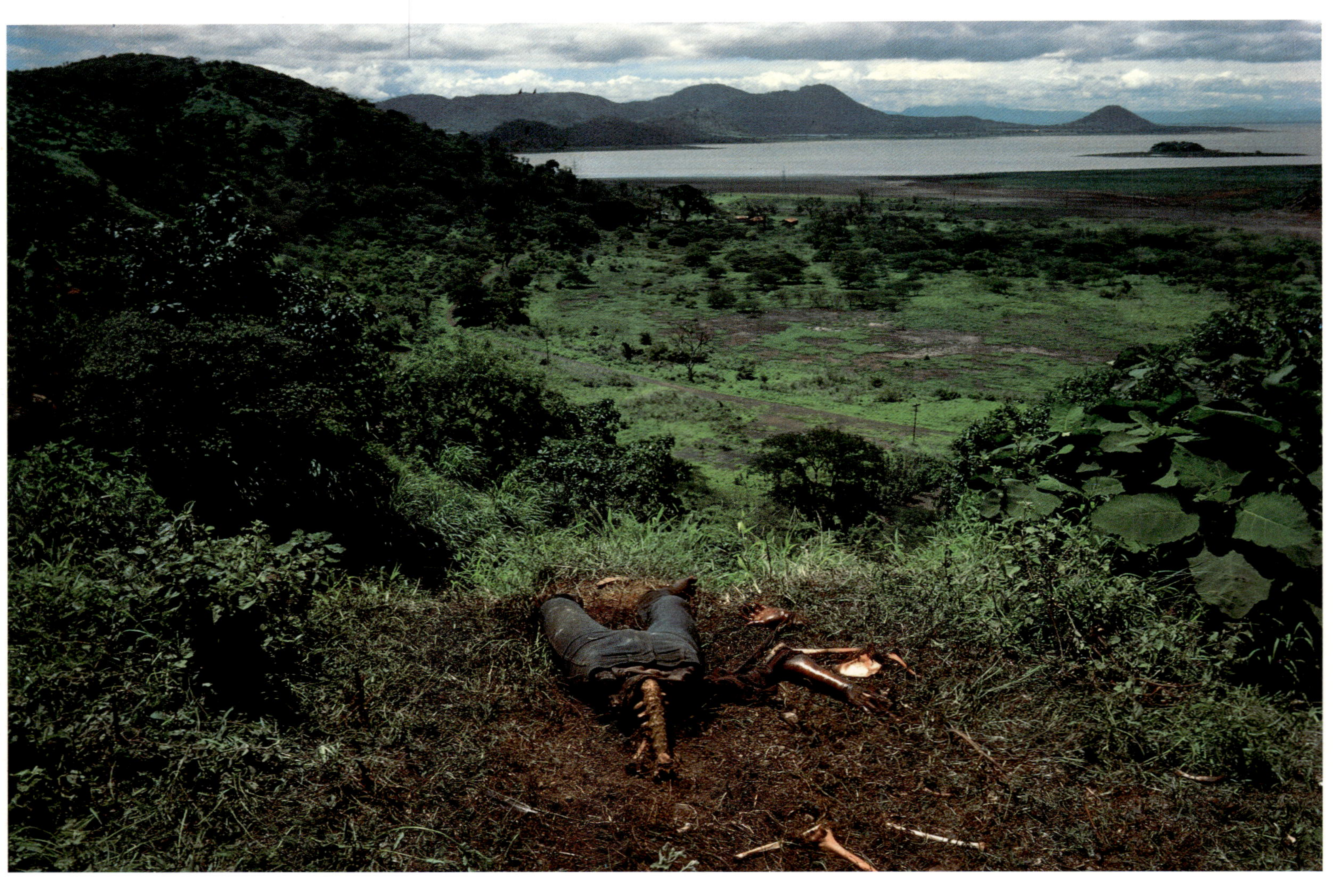

138 · Susan Meiselas · **Cuesta del Plomo. Hillside outside Managua,
a well-known site of many assassinations carried out by the National Guard.
People searched here daily for missing persons** · 1978–79

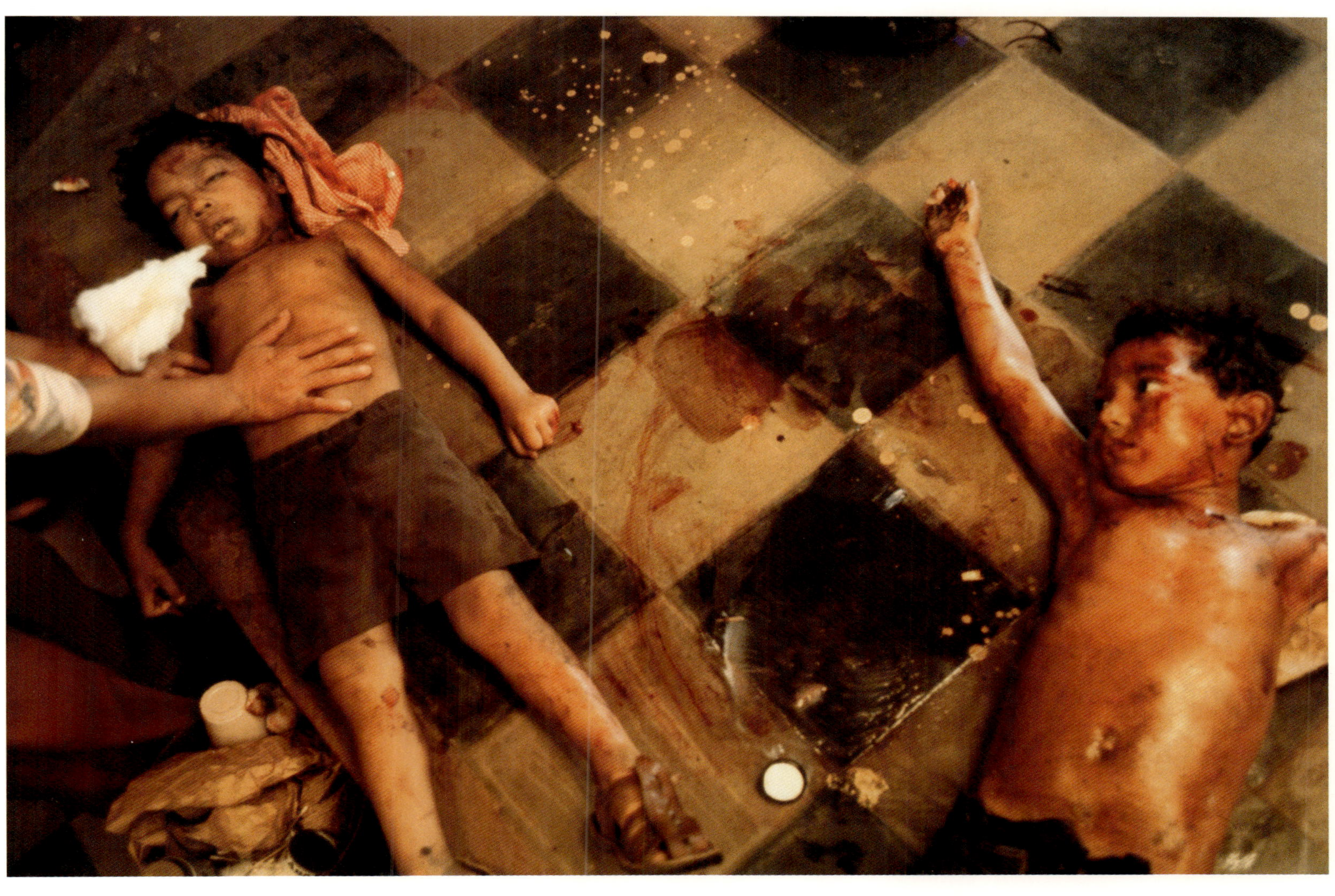

139 · Susan Meiselas · **Children rescued from a house destroyed by a 1000-pound bomb dropped in Managua. They died shortly thereafter** · 1978–79

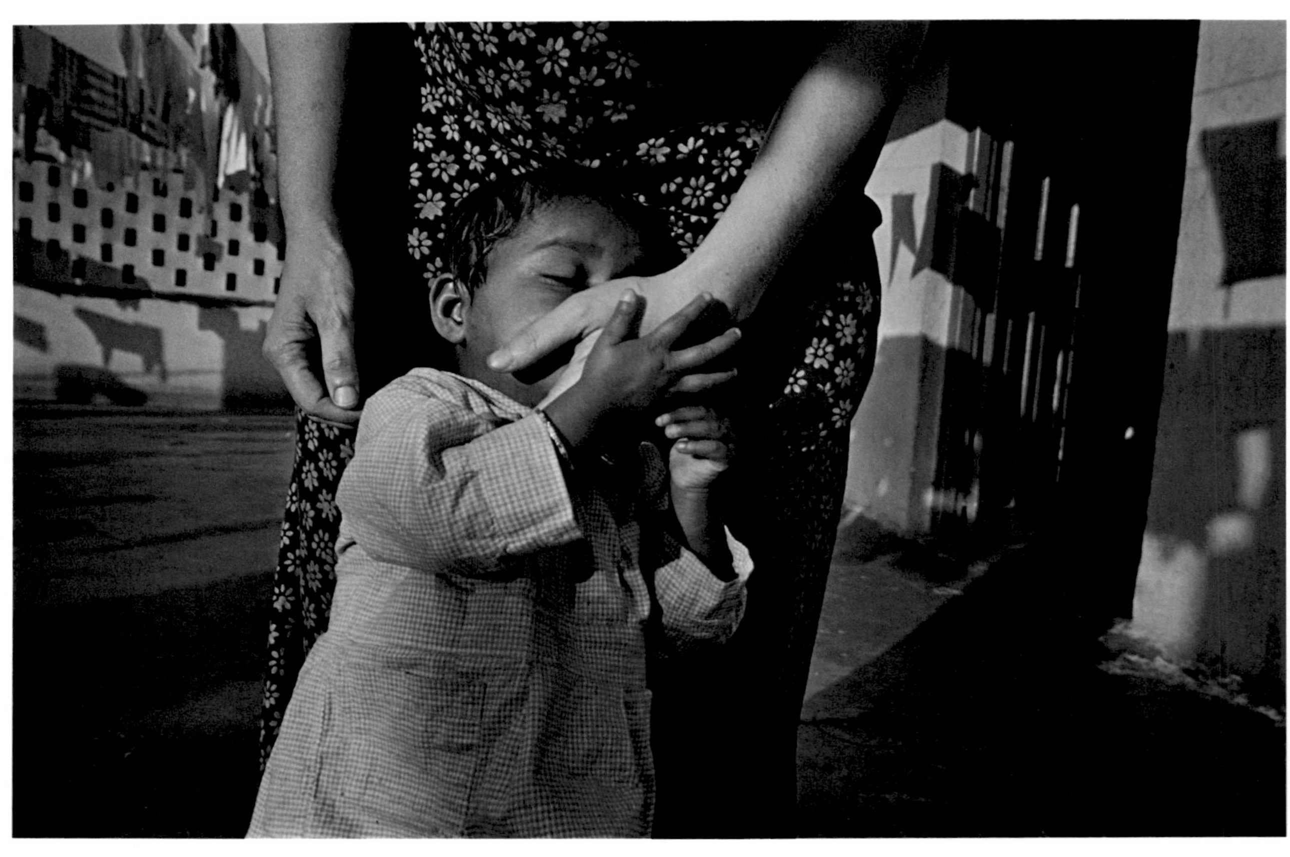

140 · Mary Ellen Mark · **Blind Orphan at Shishu Bhawan, Calcutta, India** · 1980

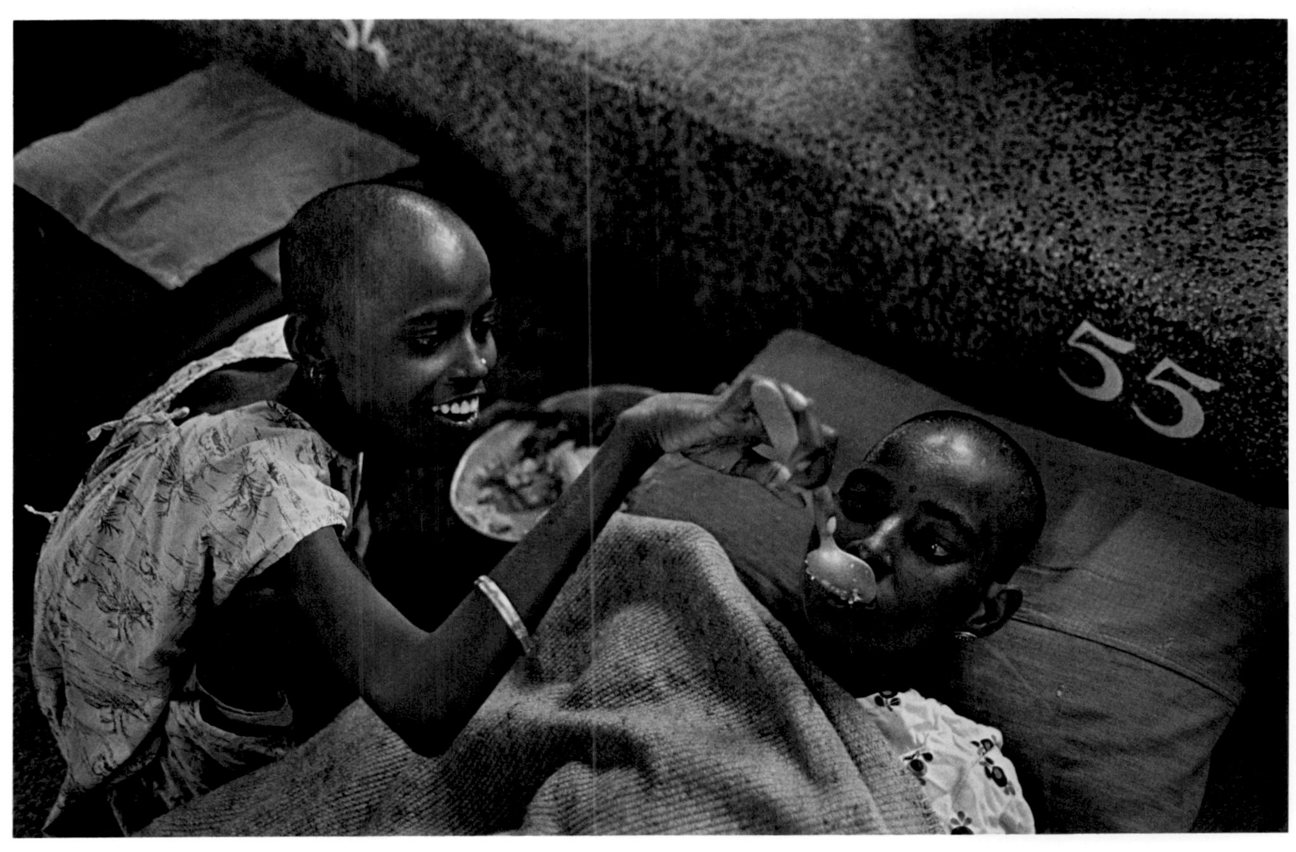

141 · Mary Ellen Mark · **Home for the Dying, Calcutta, India** · 1981

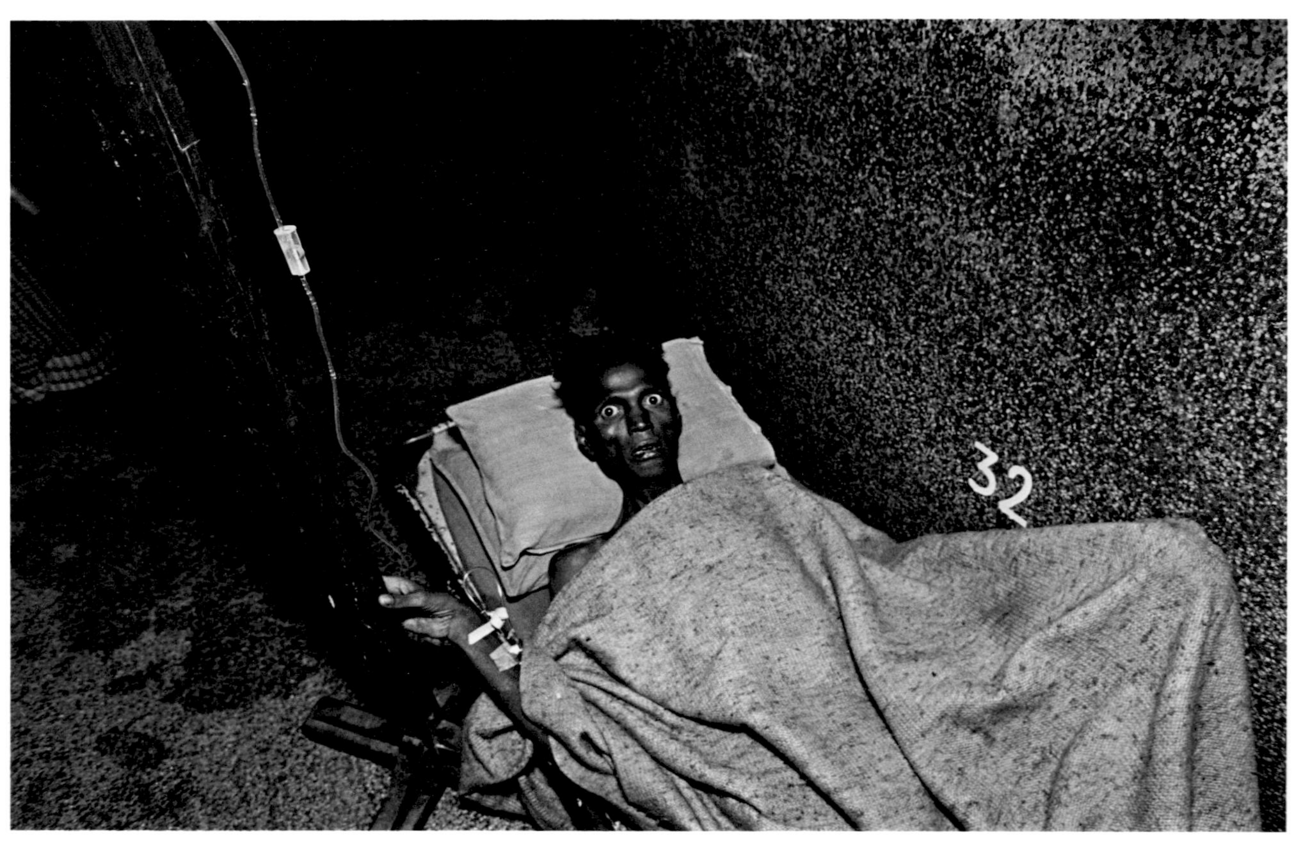

142 · Mary Ellen Mark · **Home for the Dying, Calcutta, India** · 1980

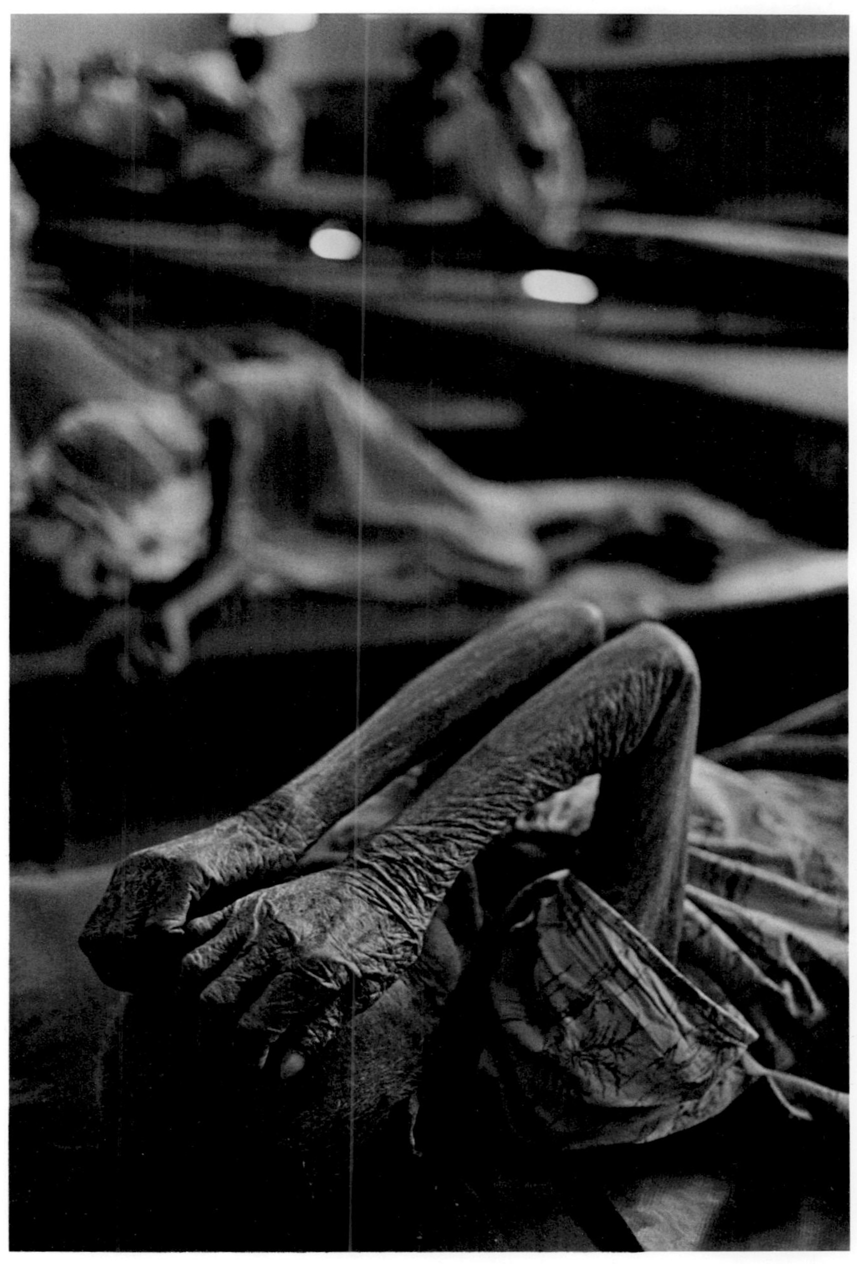

143 · Mary Ellen Mark · **Home for the Dying, Calcutta, India** · 1980

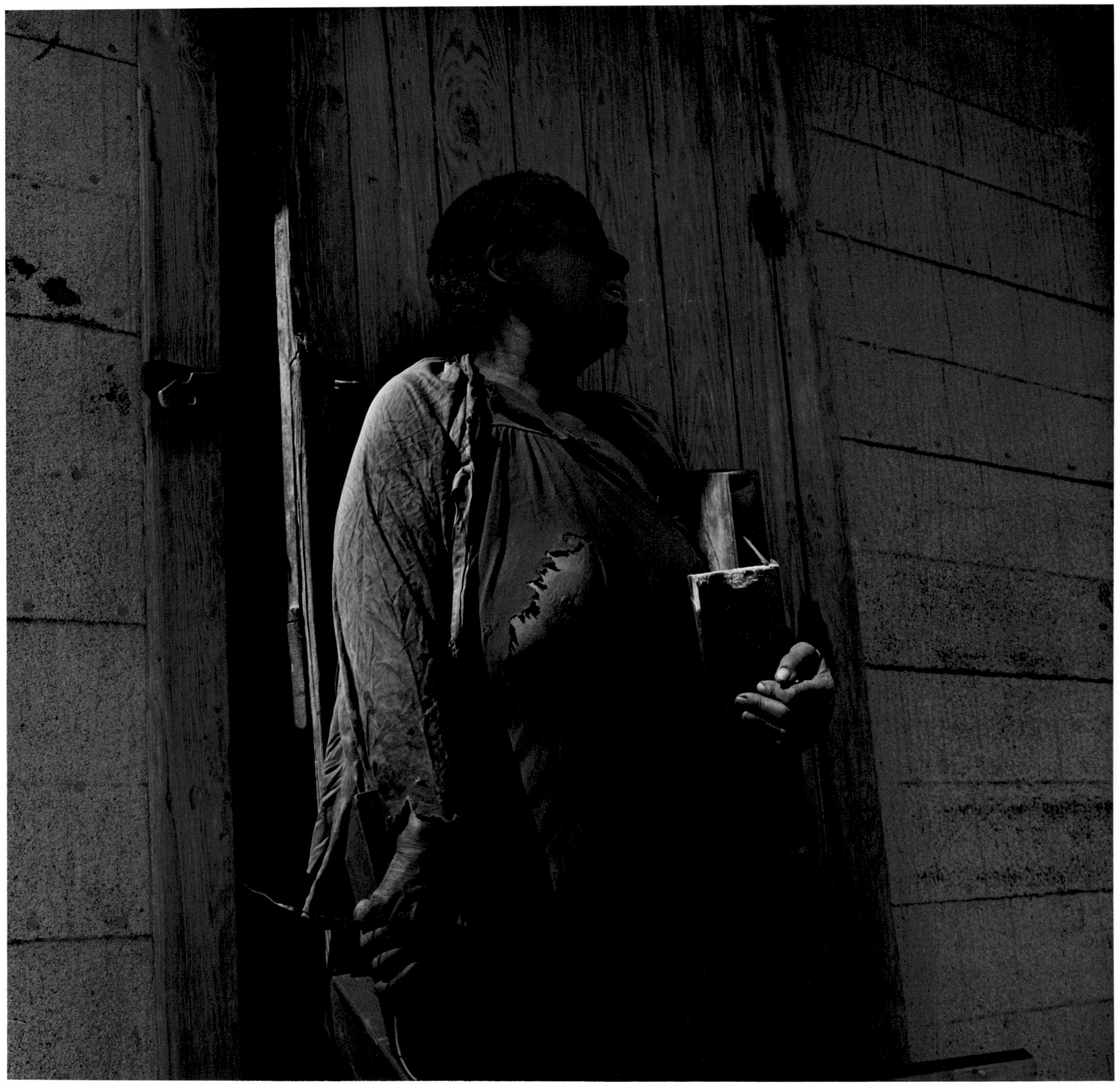

144 · Debbie Fleming Caffery · Untitled · 1984

145 · Debbie Fleming Caffery · **Enterprise Sugar Mill** · 1987

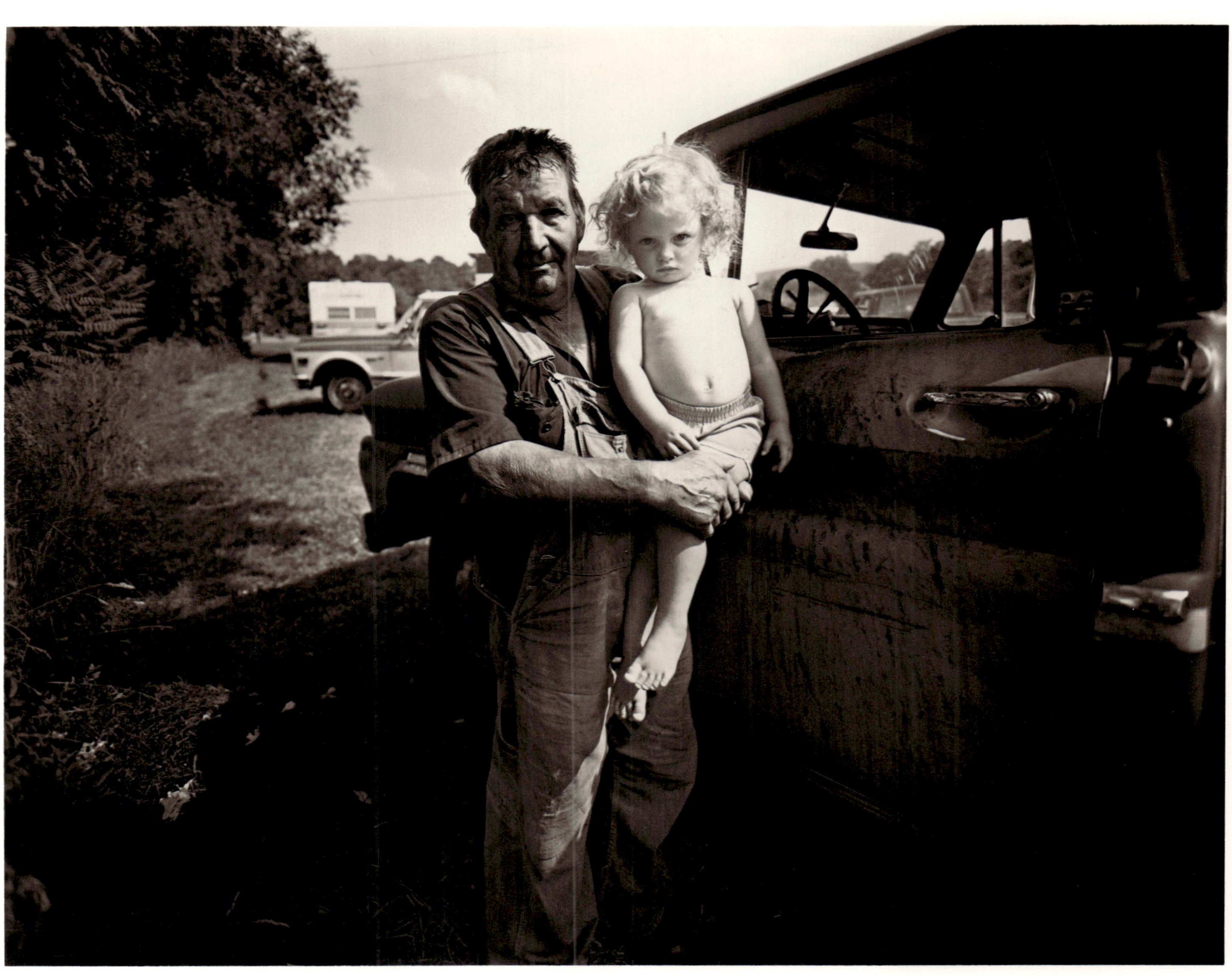

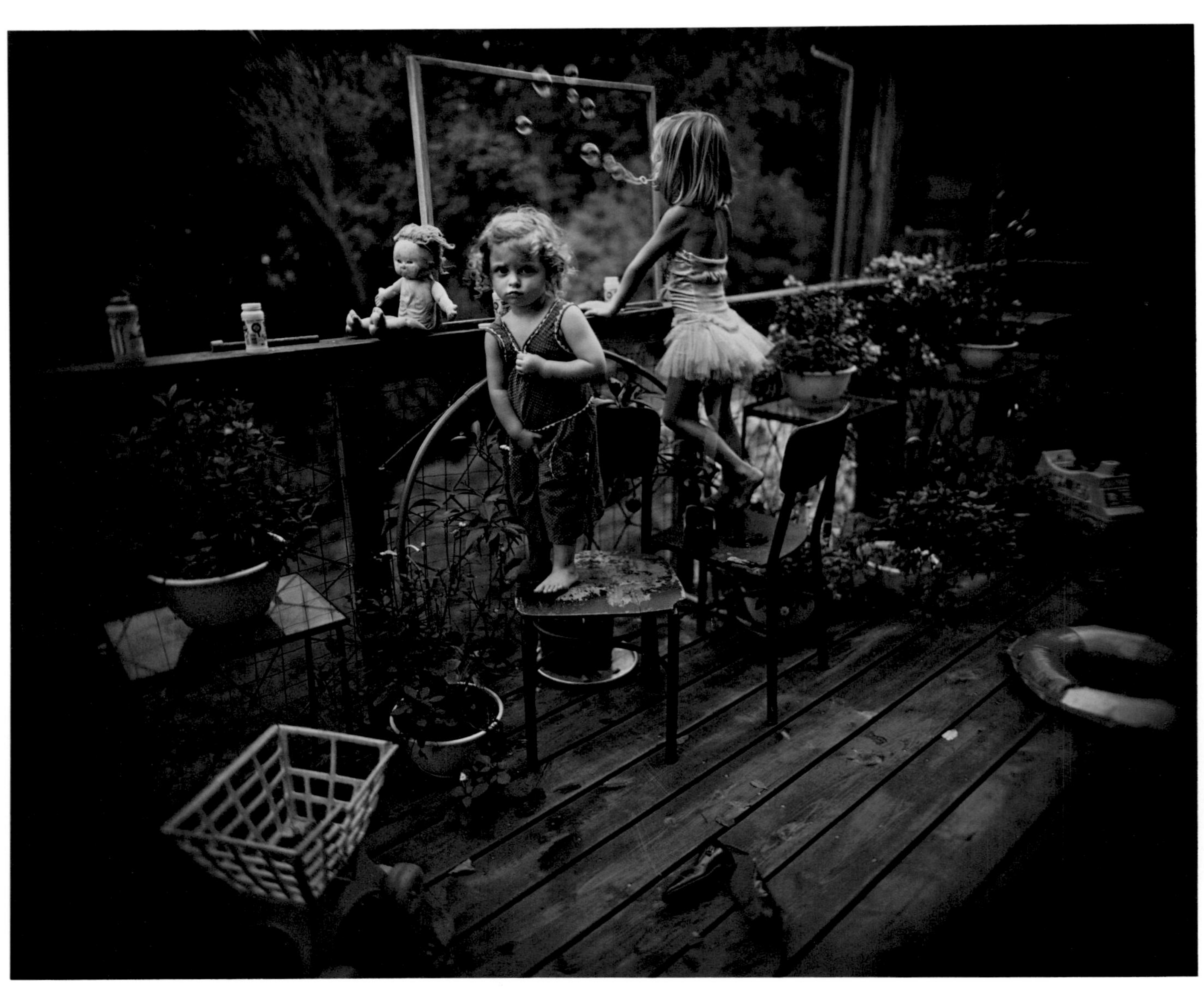

147 · Sally Mann · **Blowing Bubbles** · 1987

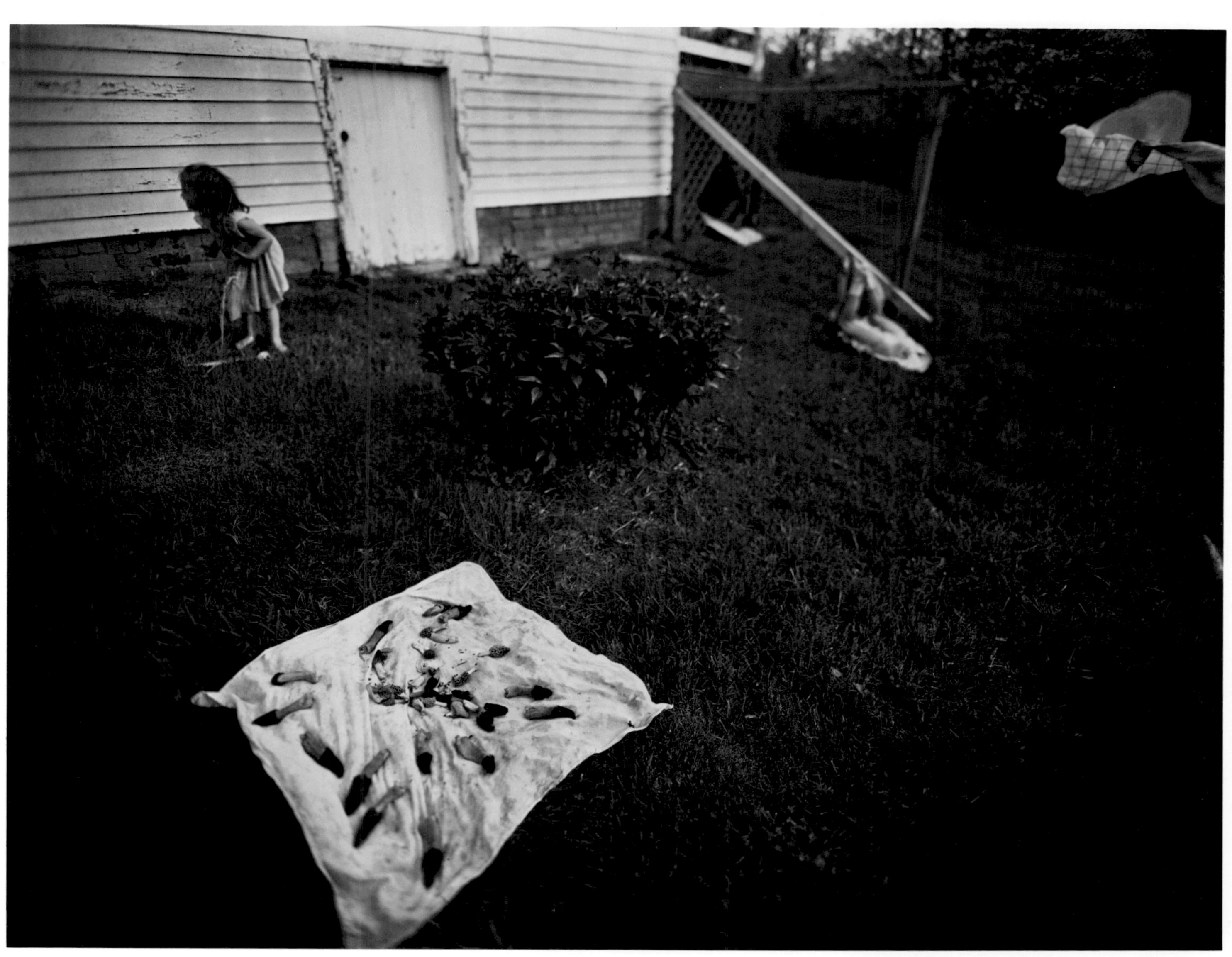

148 · Sally Mann · **Drying Morels** · 1988

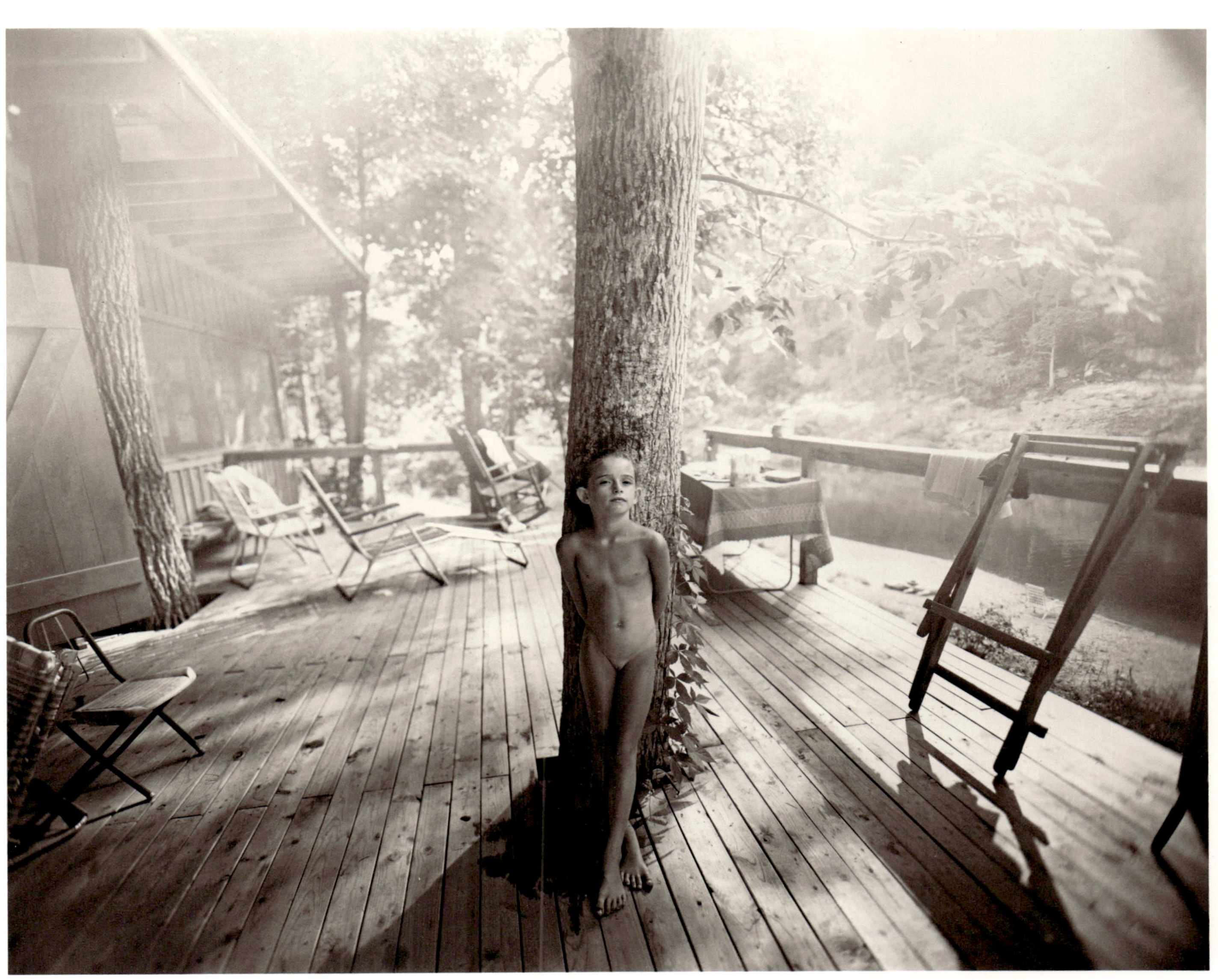

149 · Sally Mann · **Jessie at Six** · 1988

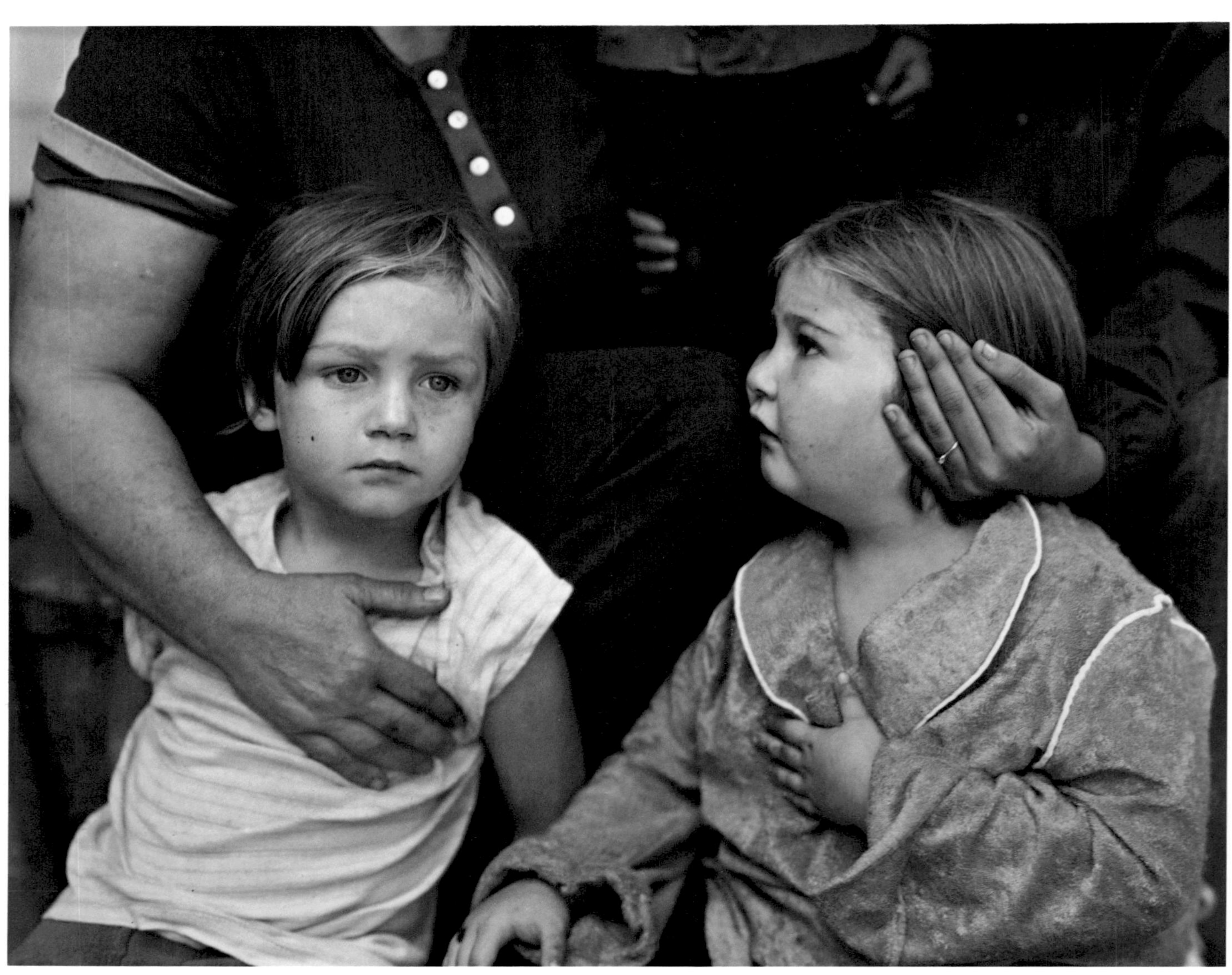

150 · Andrea Modica · **Treadwell, New York** · 1986

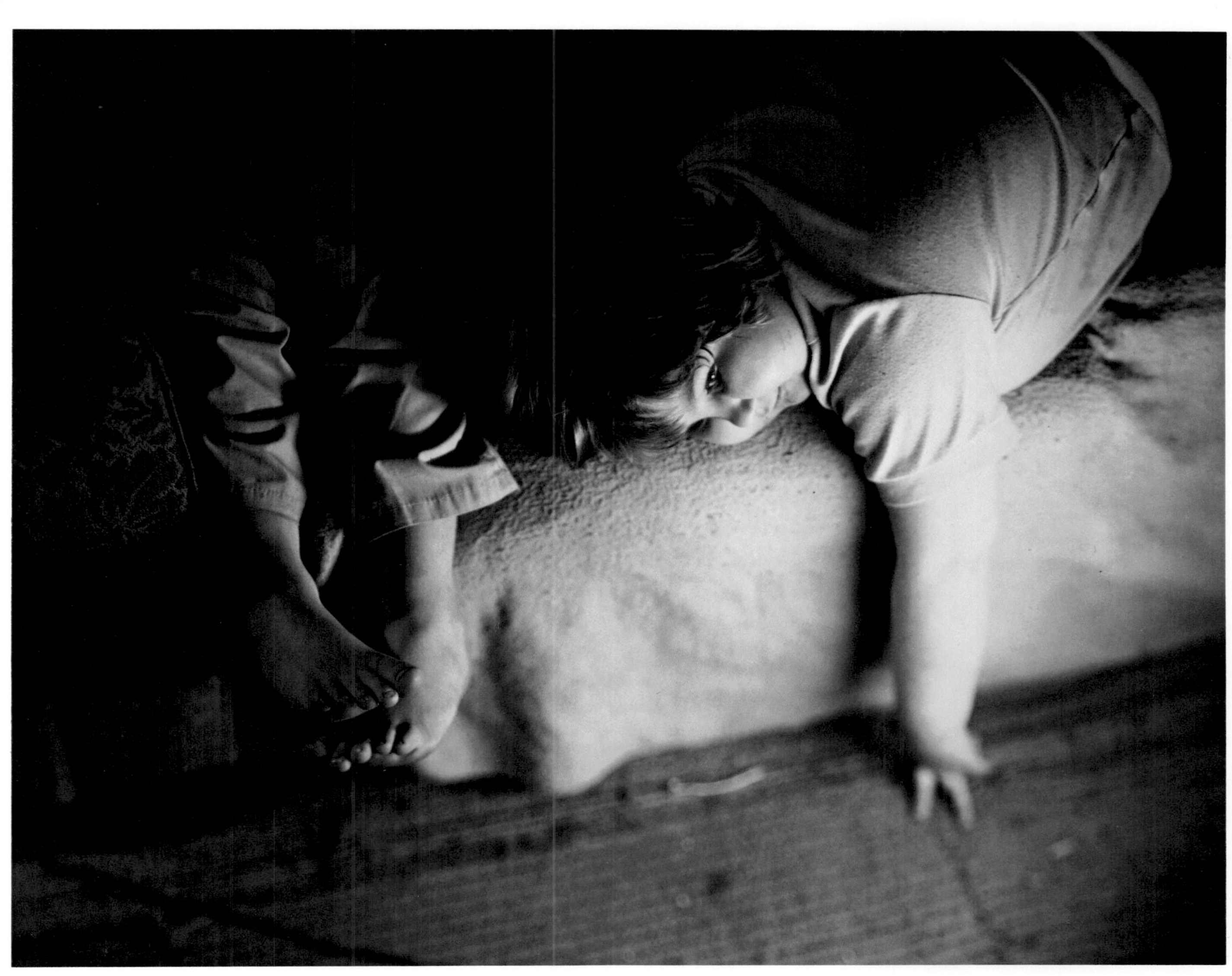

151 · Andrea Modica · **Treadwell, New York** · 1987

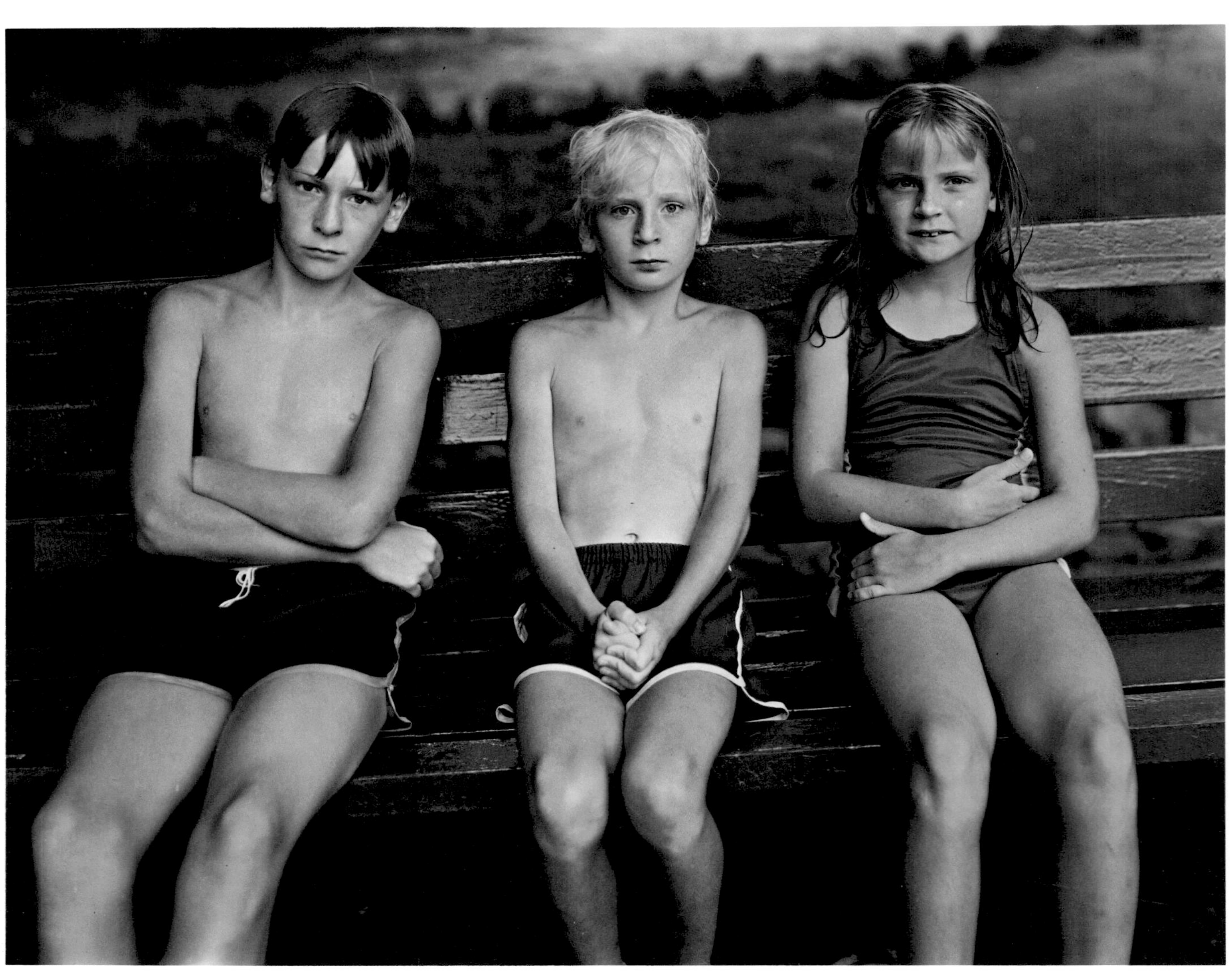

152 · Judith Joy Ross · Untitled from **Eurana Park, Weatherly, PA** · 1982

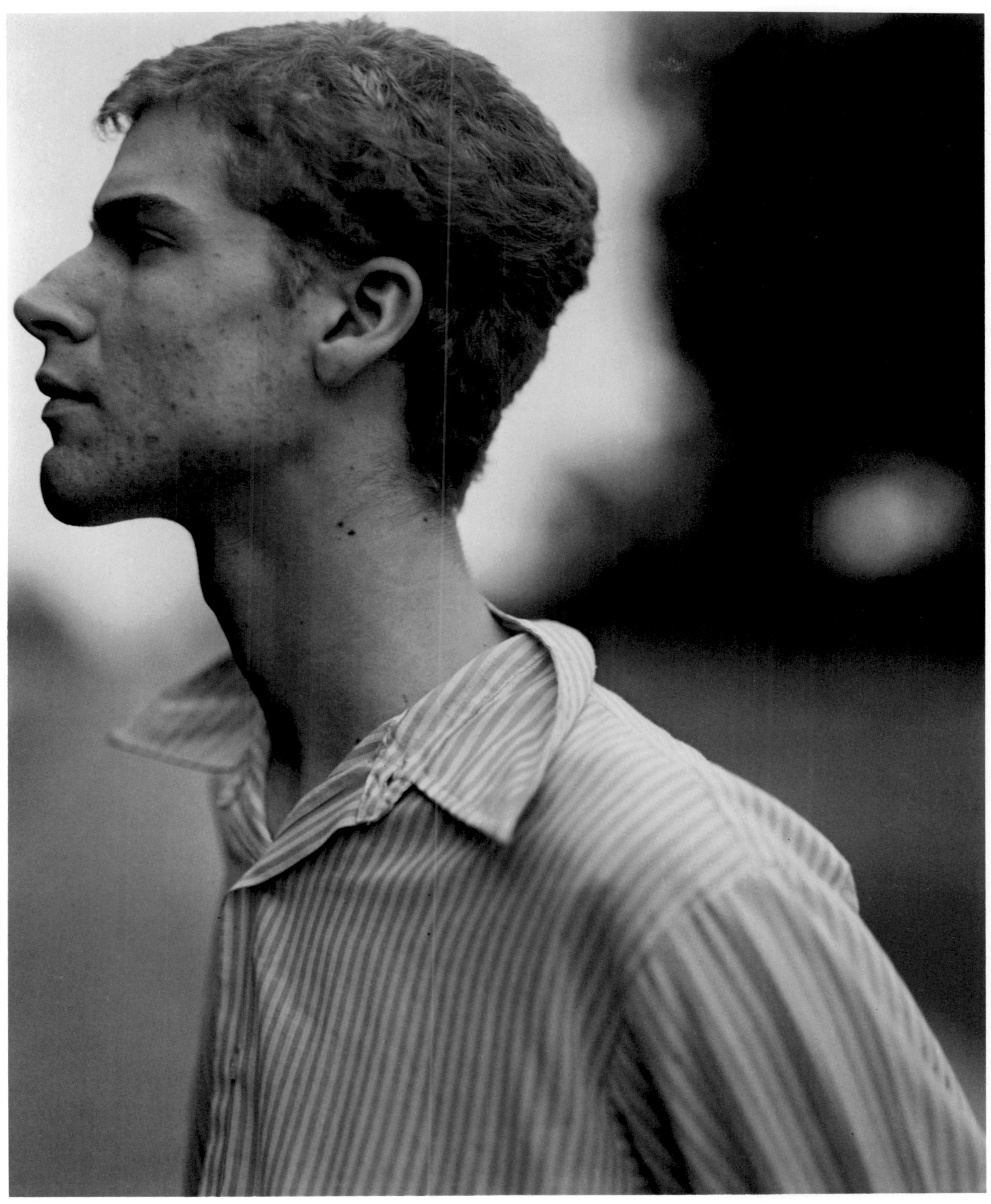

153 · Judith Joy Ross · Untitled from **Portraits at the Vietnam Veterans Memorial, Washington, DC** · 1983–84

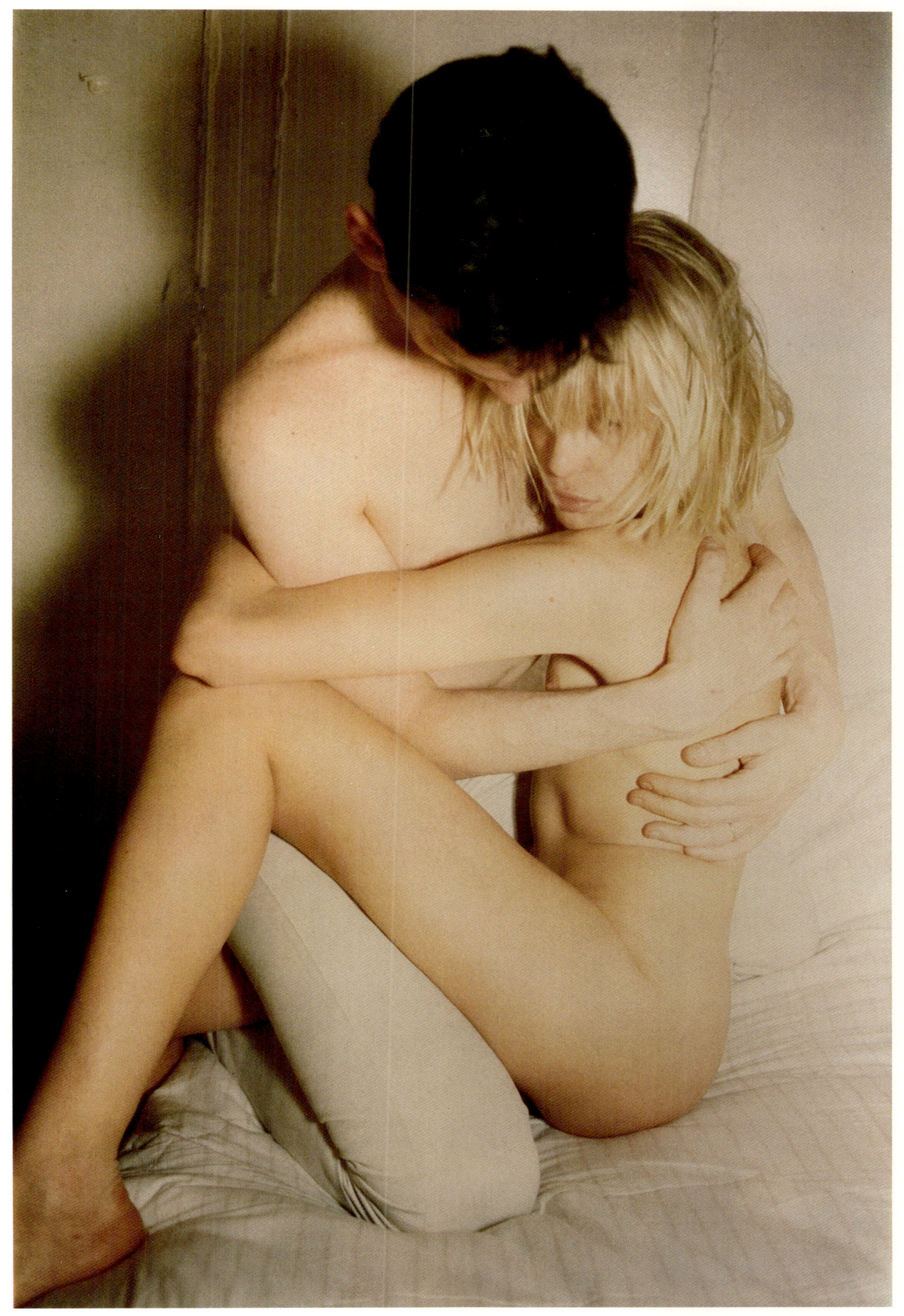

154 · Nan Goldin · **Patrick Fox and Teri Toye on their Wedding Night, New York City** · 1987

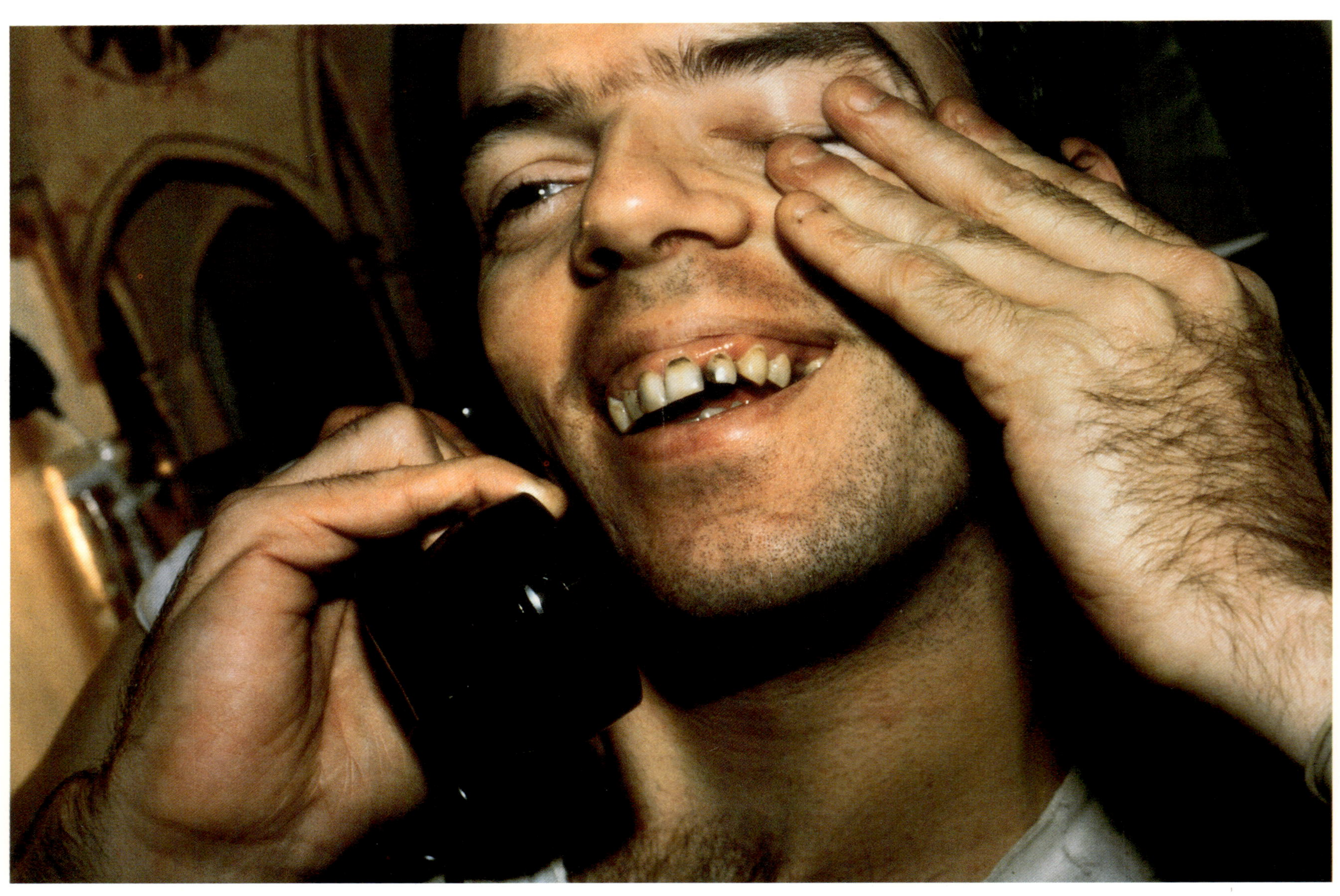

155 · Nan Goldin · **Brian on the Phone, New York City** · 1981

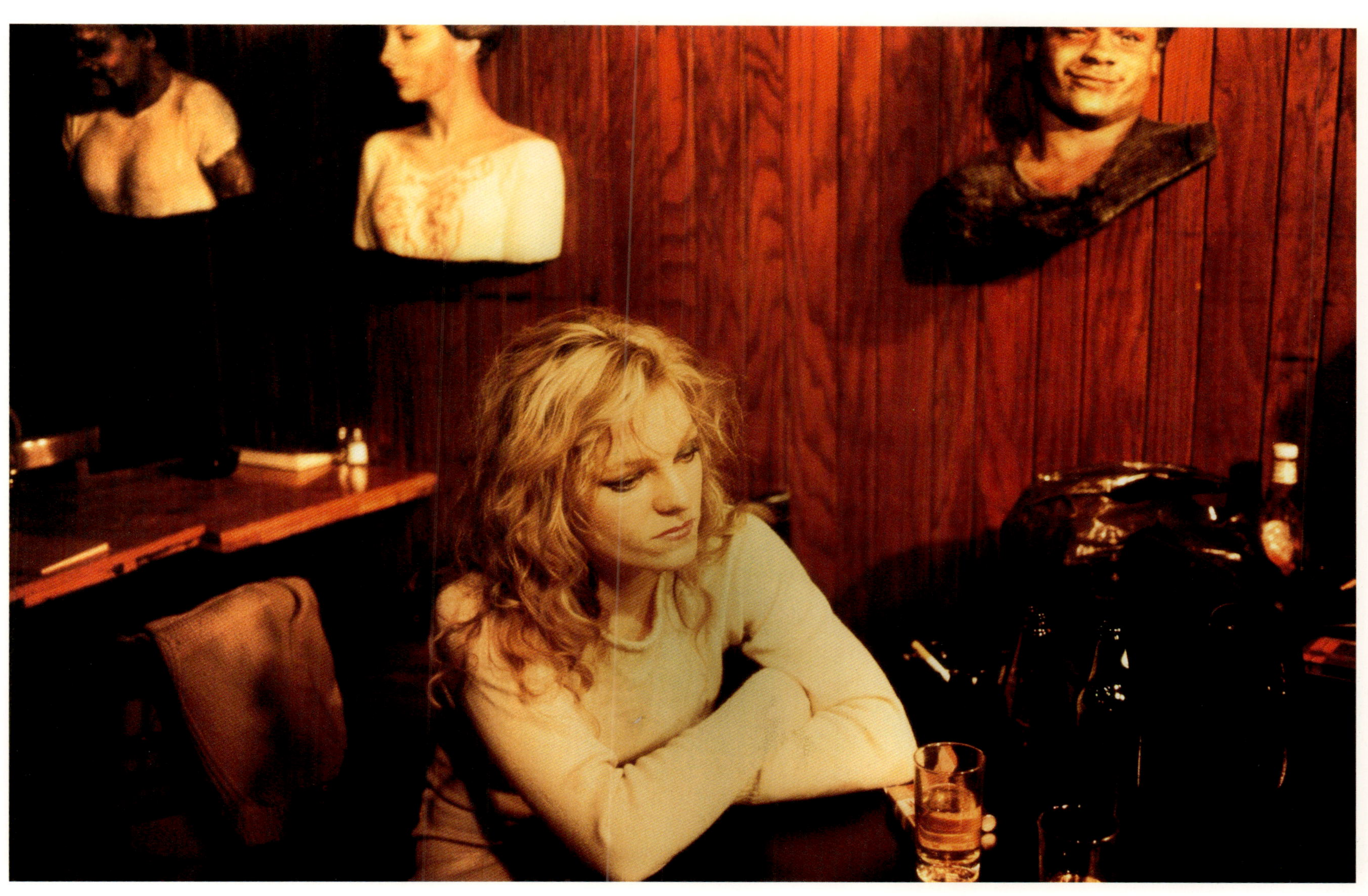

156 · Nan Goldin · **Cookie at Tin Pan Alley, New York City** · 1983

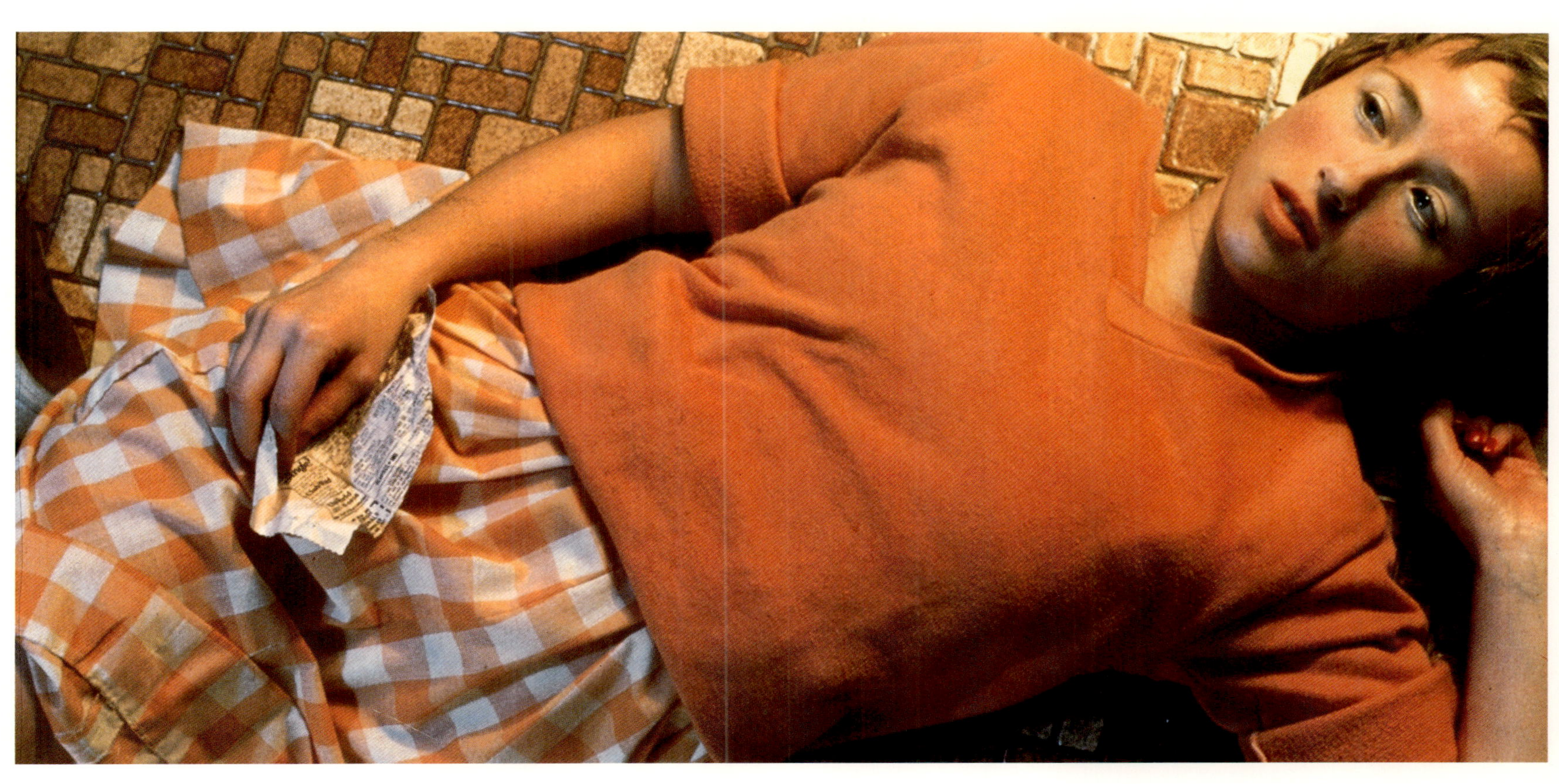

157 · Cindy Sherman · Untitled #96 · 1981

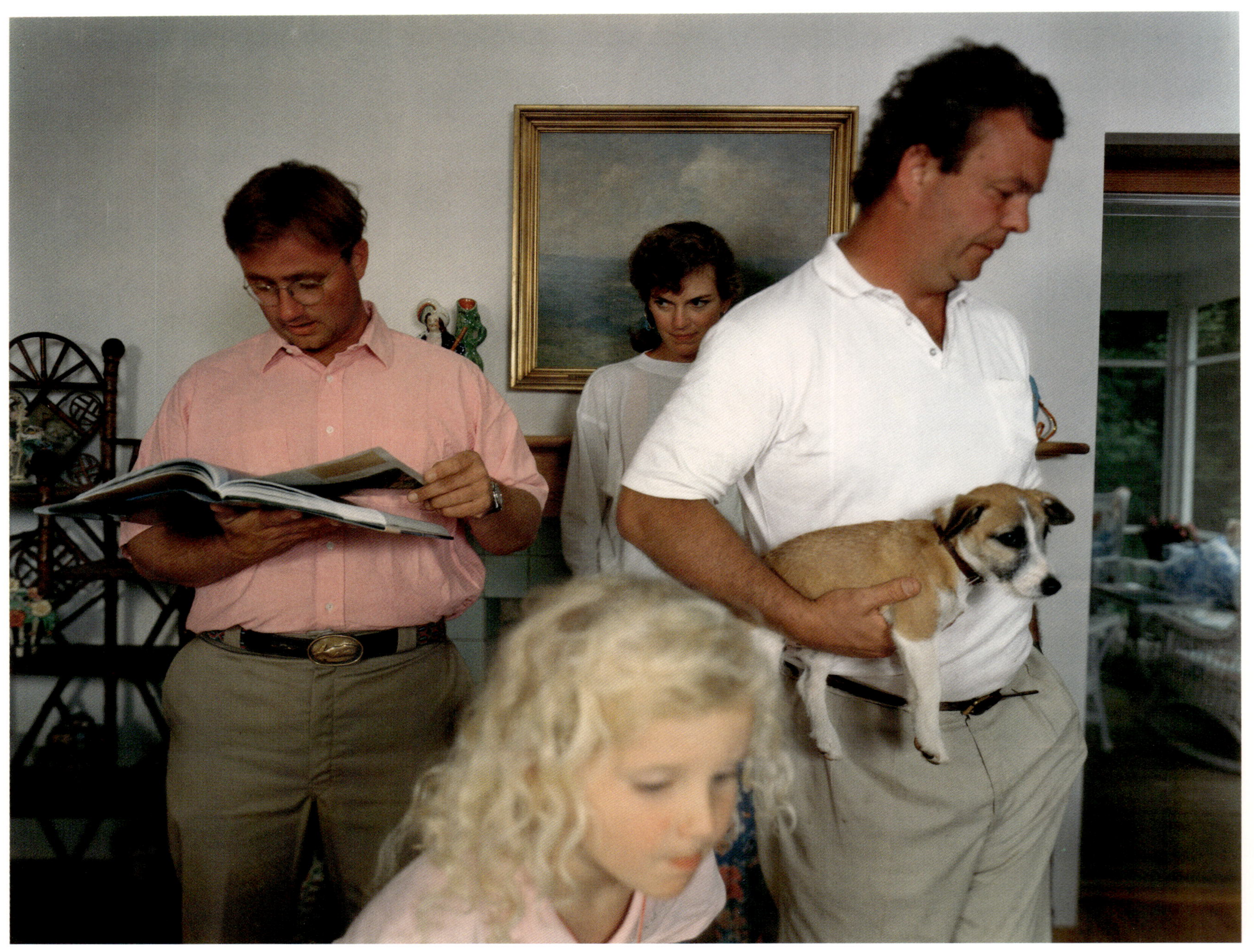

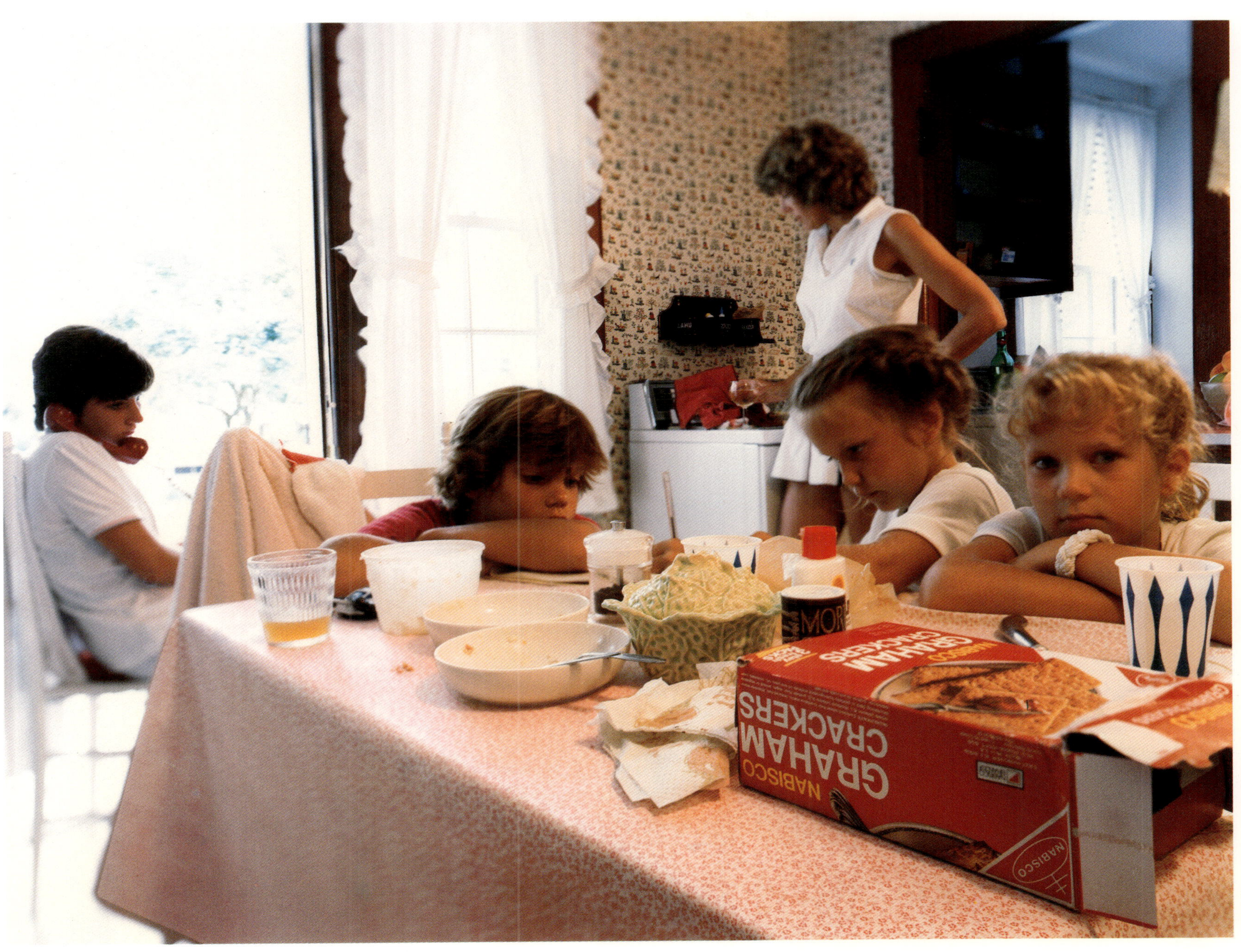

159 · Tina Barney · **The Graham Cracker Box** · 1983

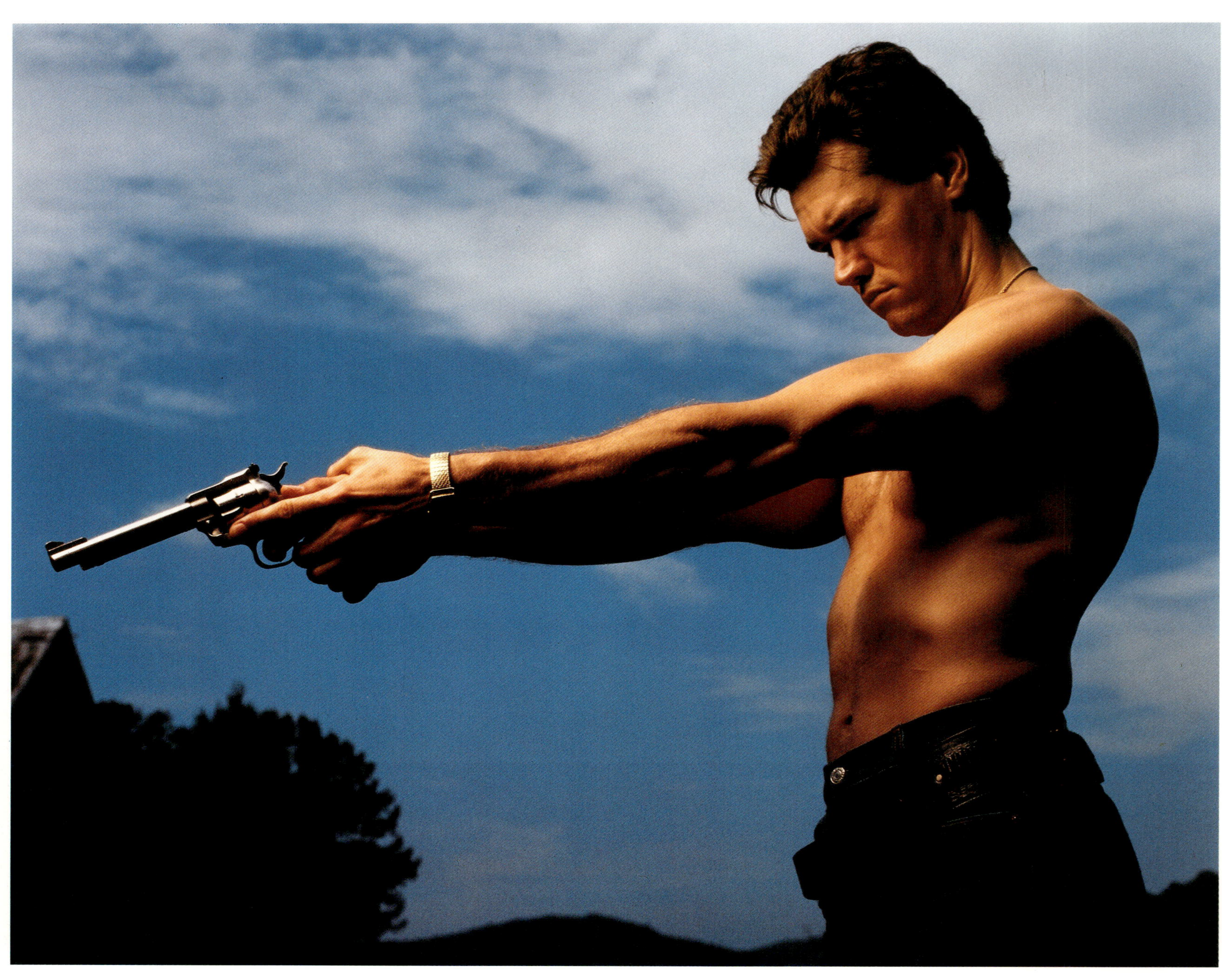

160 · Annie Leibovitz · **Randy Travis, Nashville** · 1987

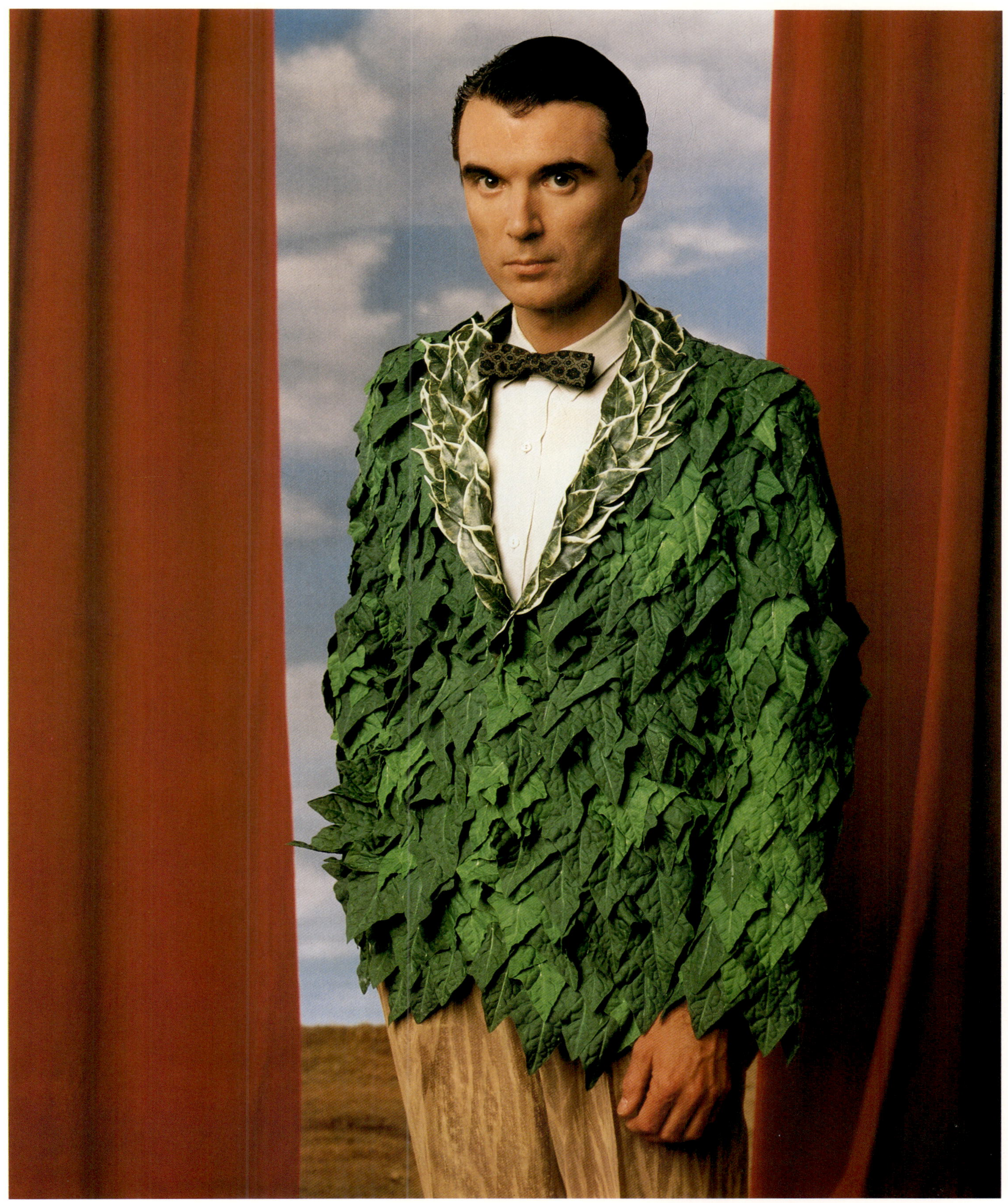

161 · Annie Leibovitz · **David Byrne, Los Angeles** · 1989

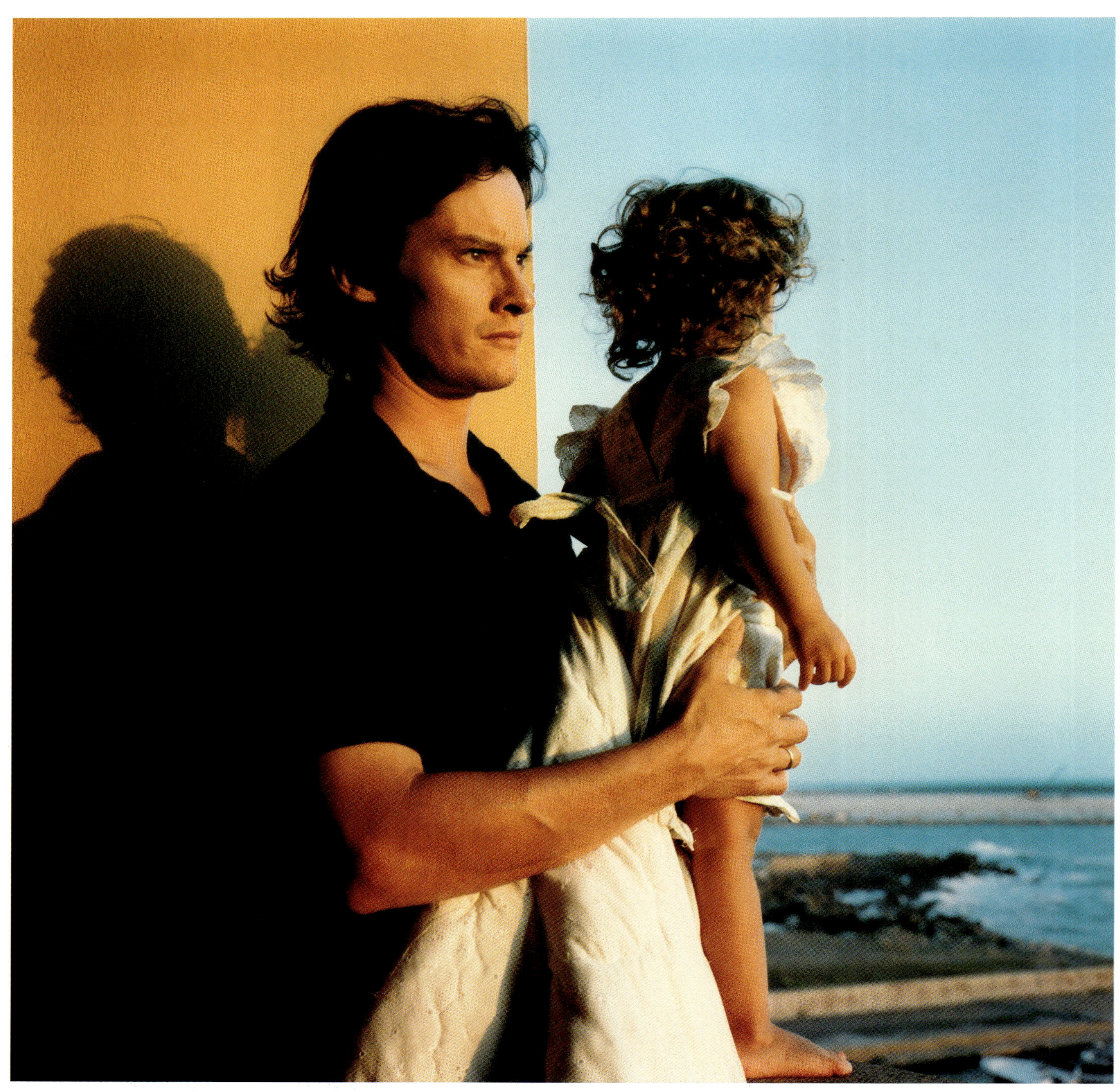

162 · Maude Schuyler Clay · **Langdon and Anna Clay, near Rome, 1988**

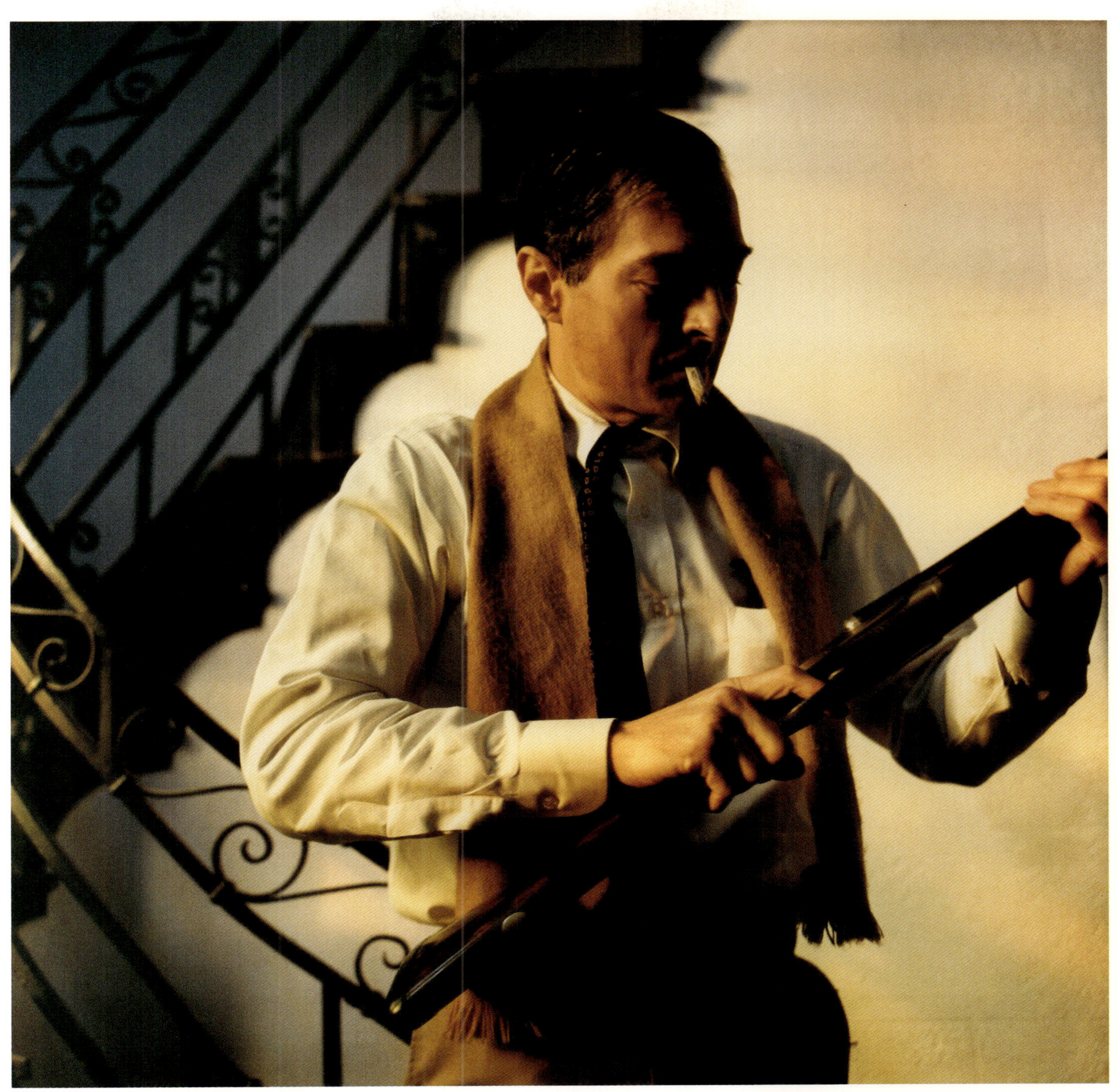

163 · Maude Schuyler Clay · **William Eggleston, Memphis, 1988**

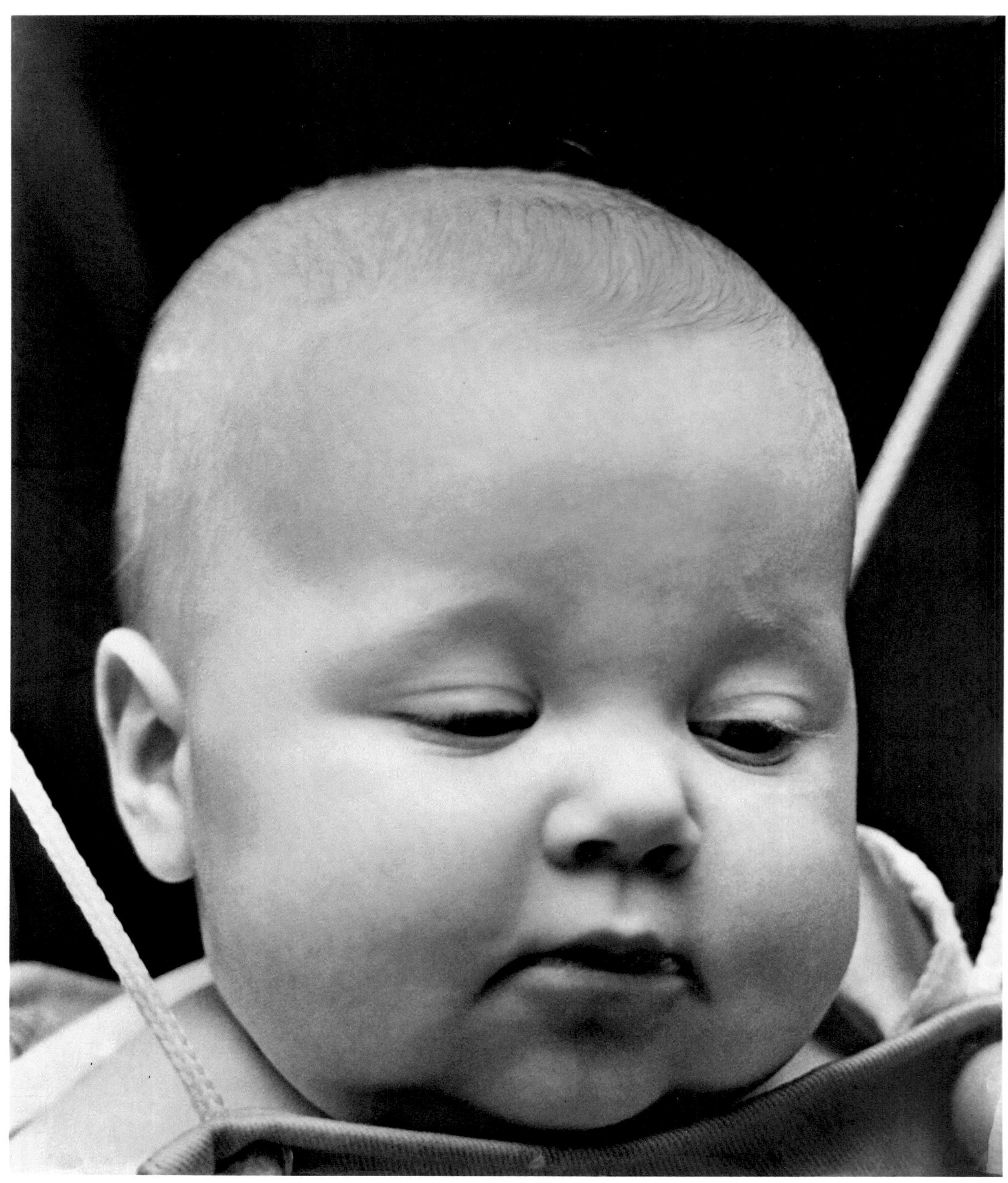

164 · W. Snyder MacNeil · **Jazimina** · 1985–87

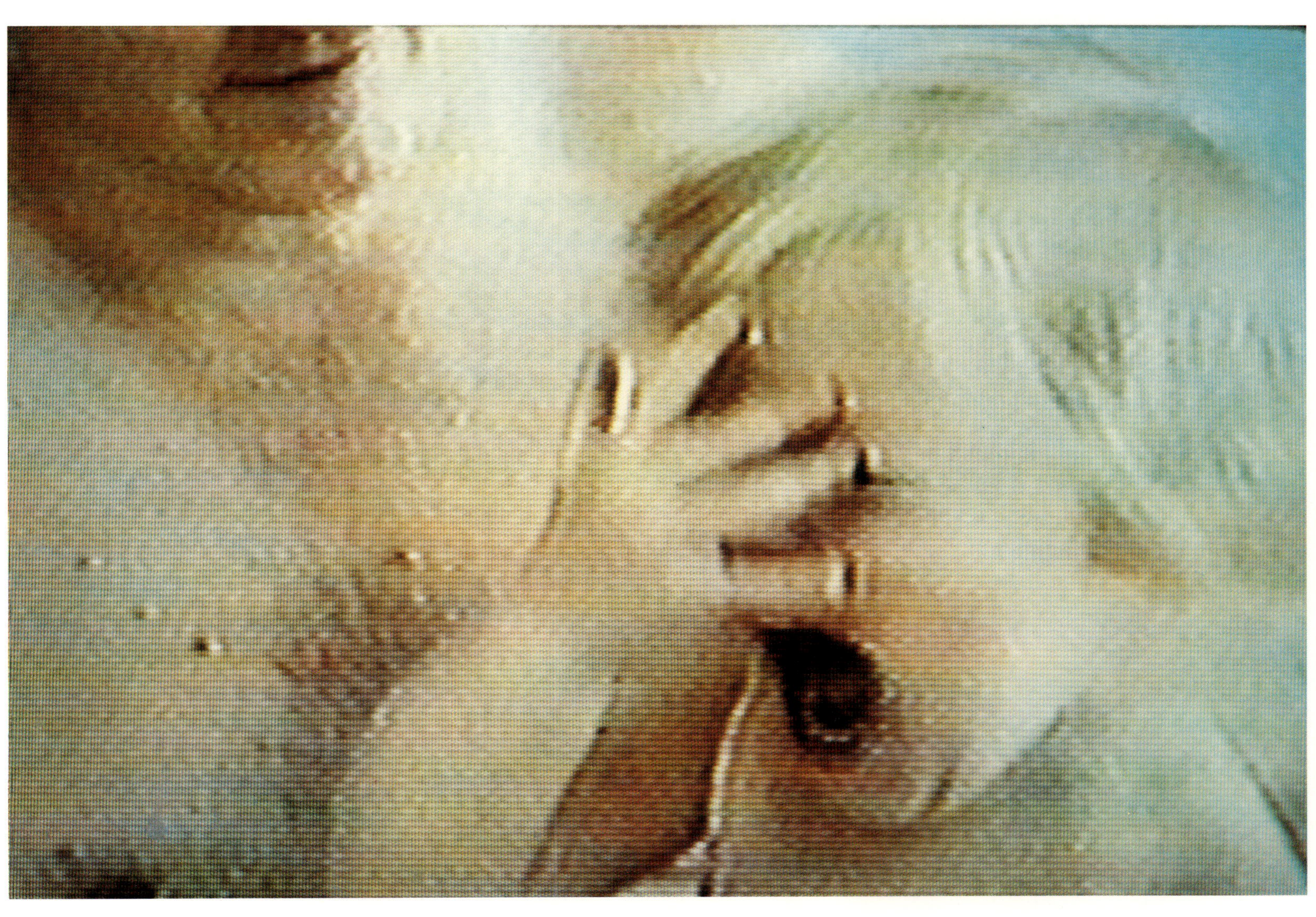

165 · W. Snyder MacNeil · **Jazimina and Ronald,** from the **Nuclear Portrait** series · 1987–89

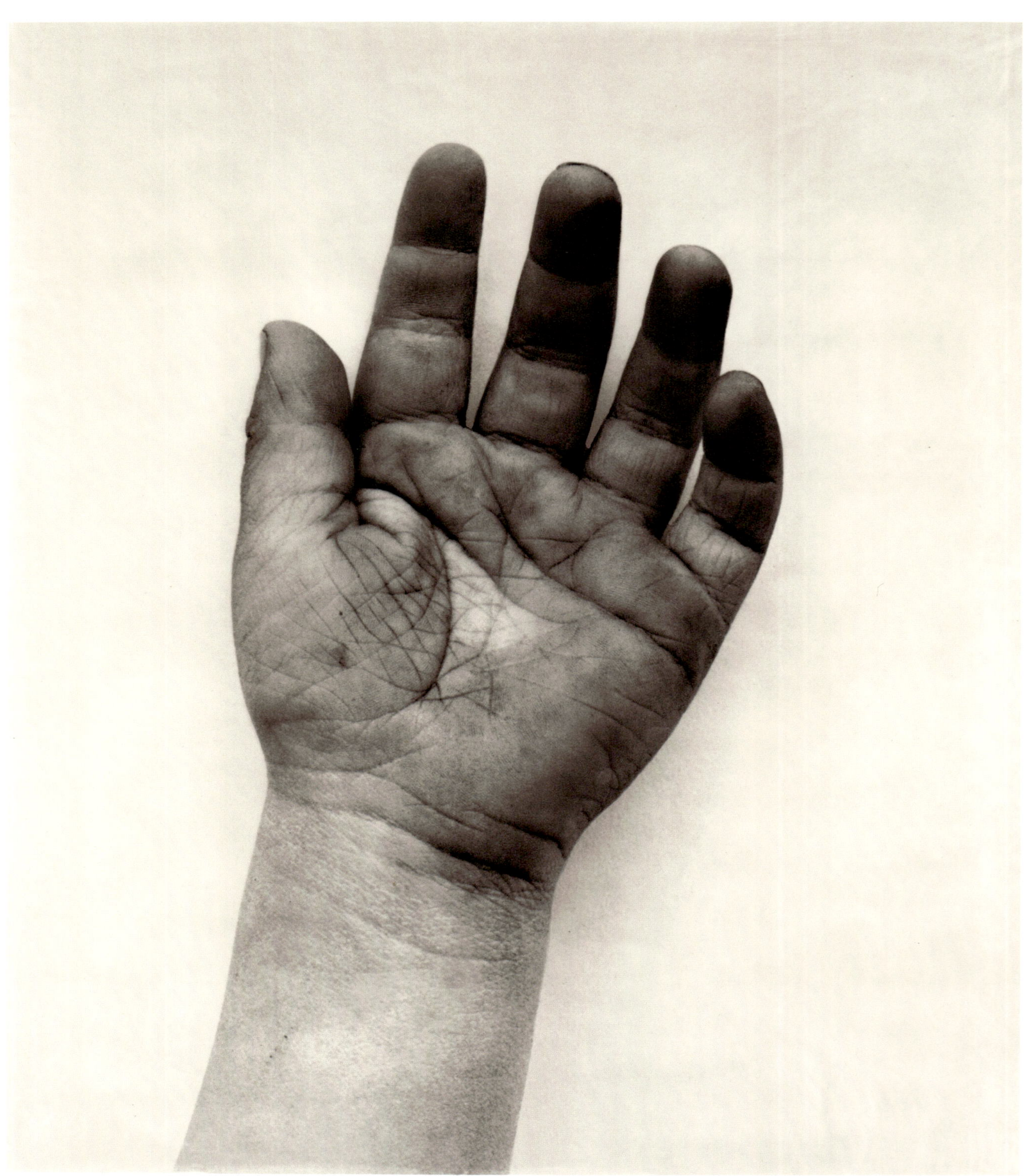

166 · W. Snyder MacNeil · **Ezra Sesto** · 1977–88

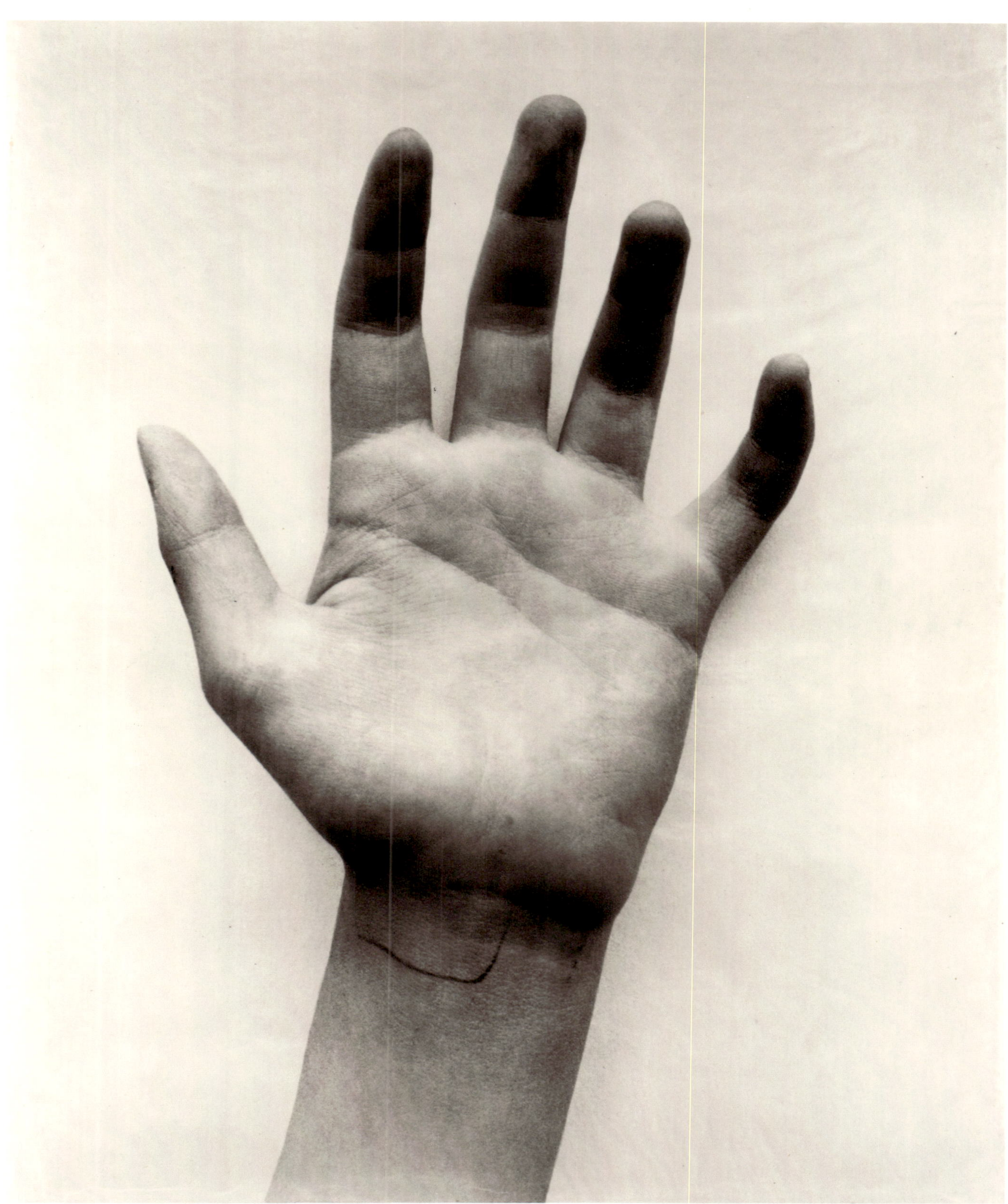

167 · W. Snyder MacNeil · **Adrian Sesto** · 1977–88

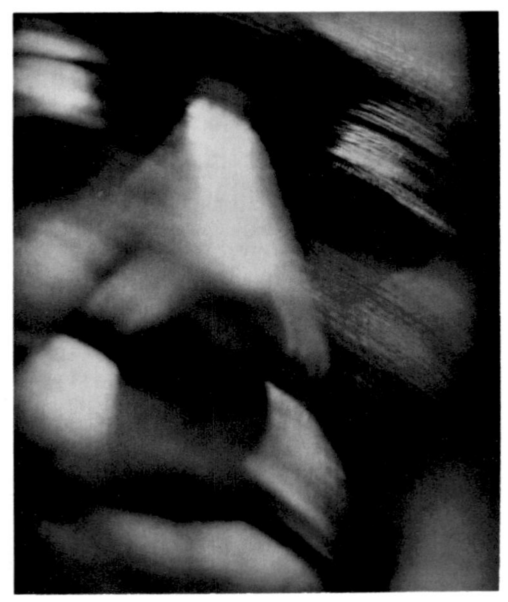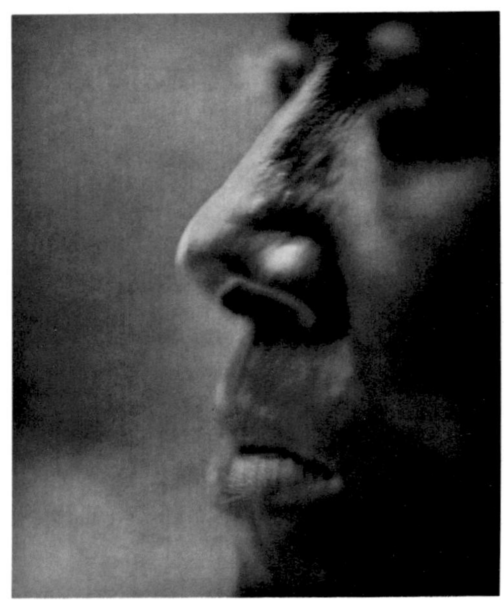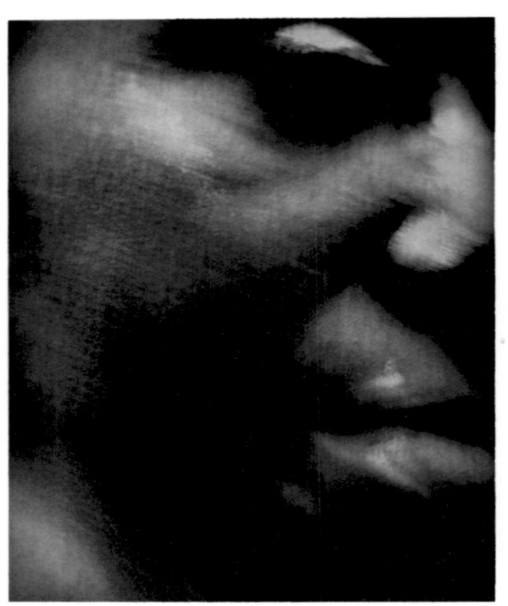

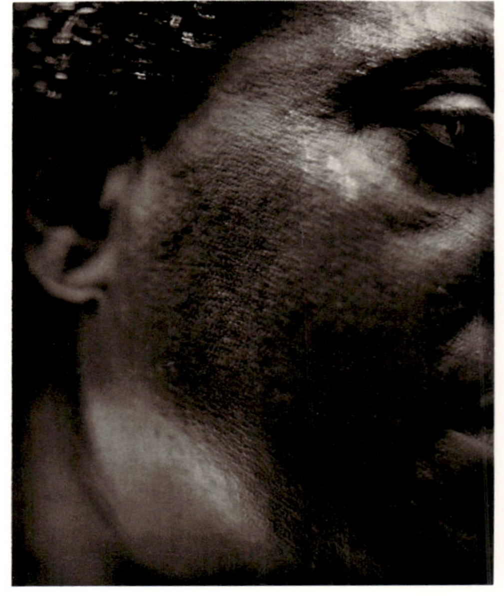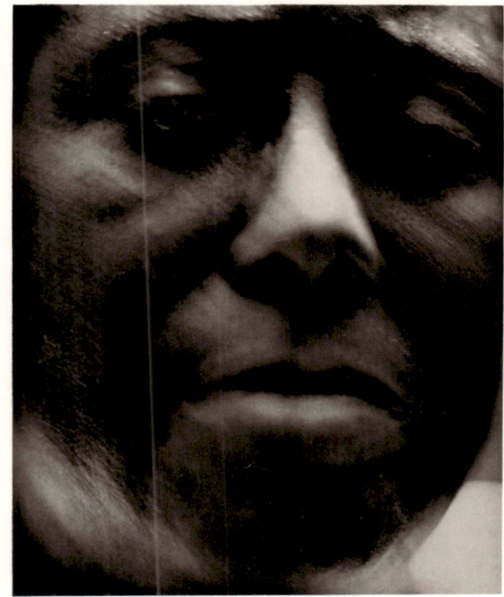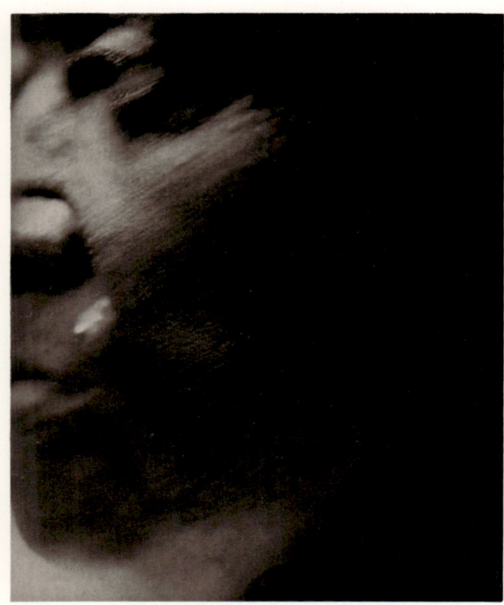

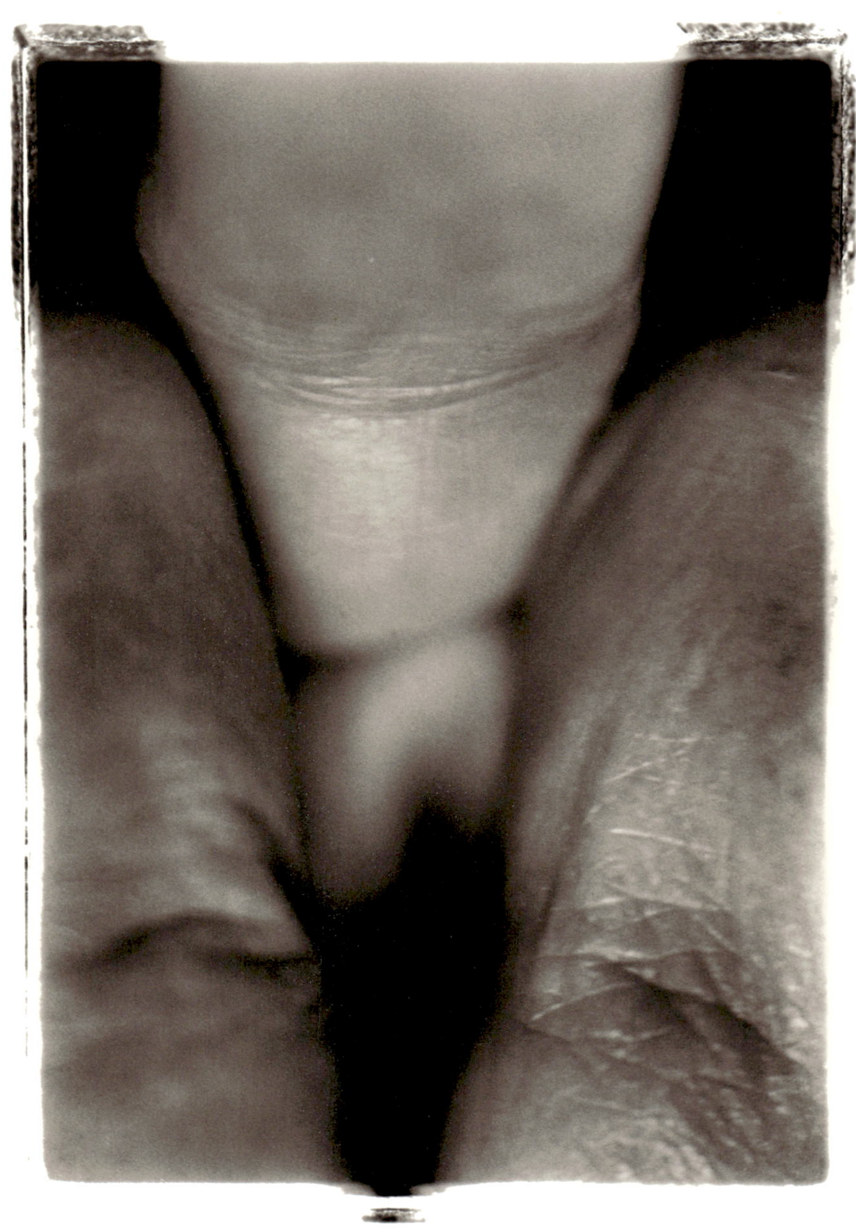

169 · Holly Wright · Untitled, from the **Vanity** series · 1988

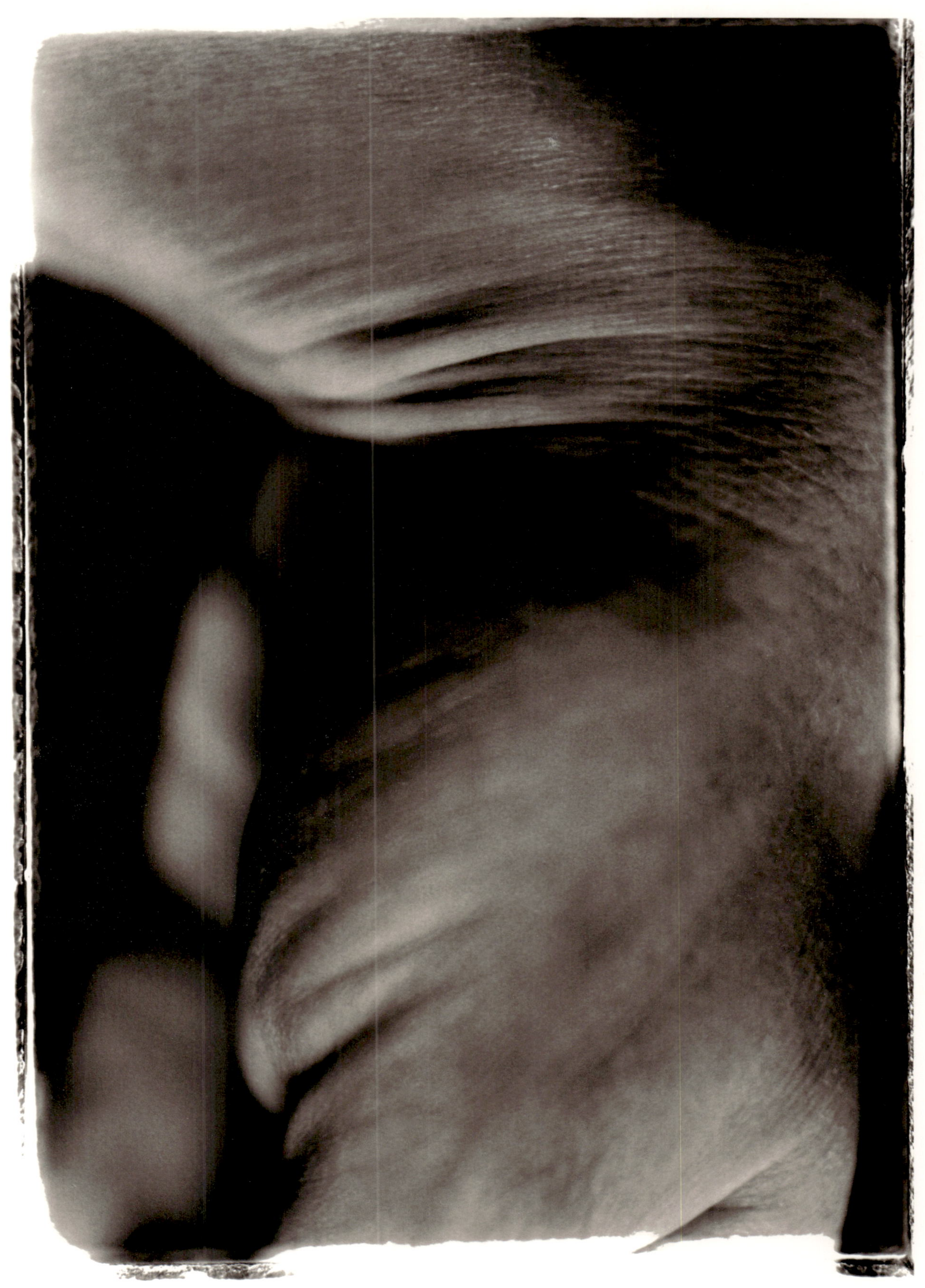

170 · Holly Wright · Untitled, from the **Vanity** series · 1986

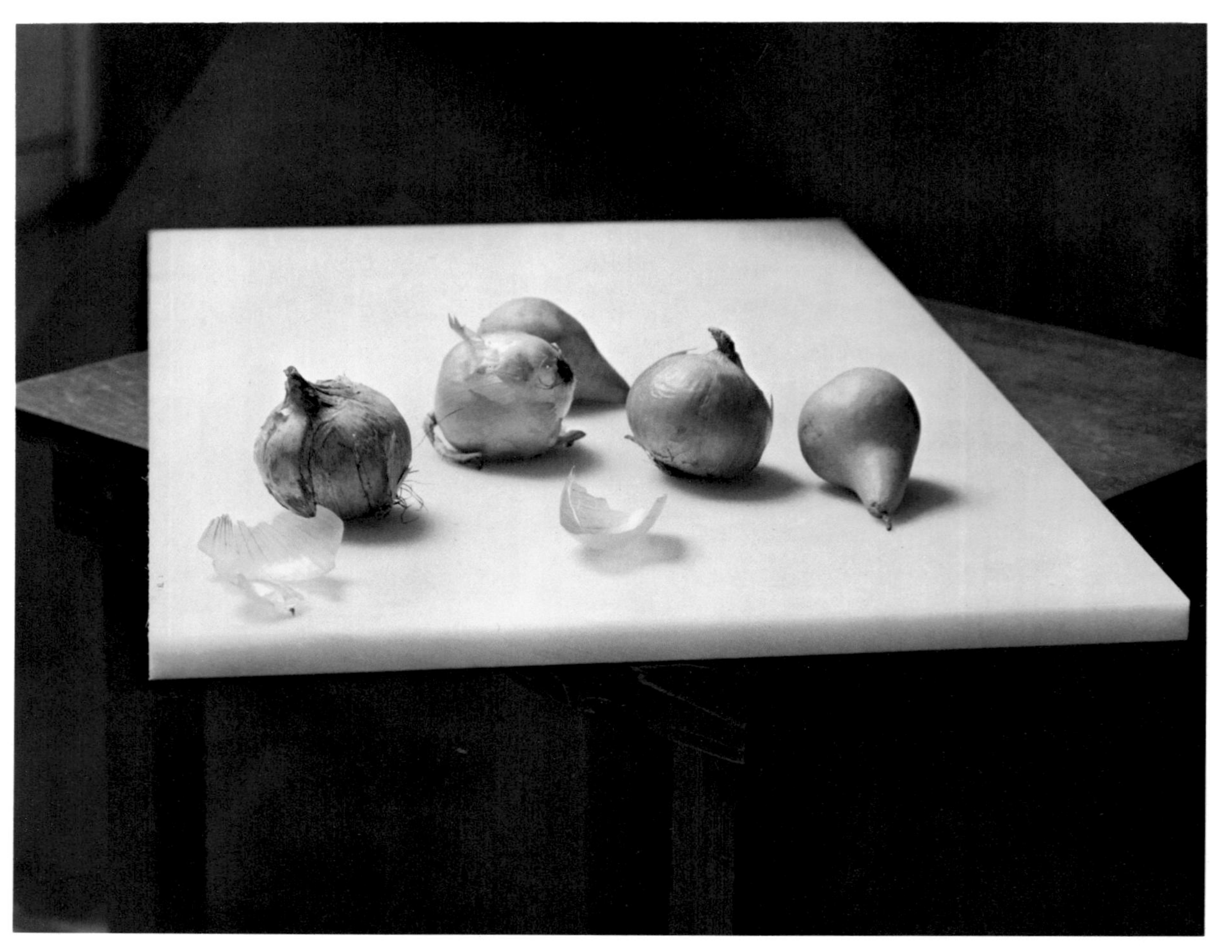

171 · Jan Groover · Untitled · 1983

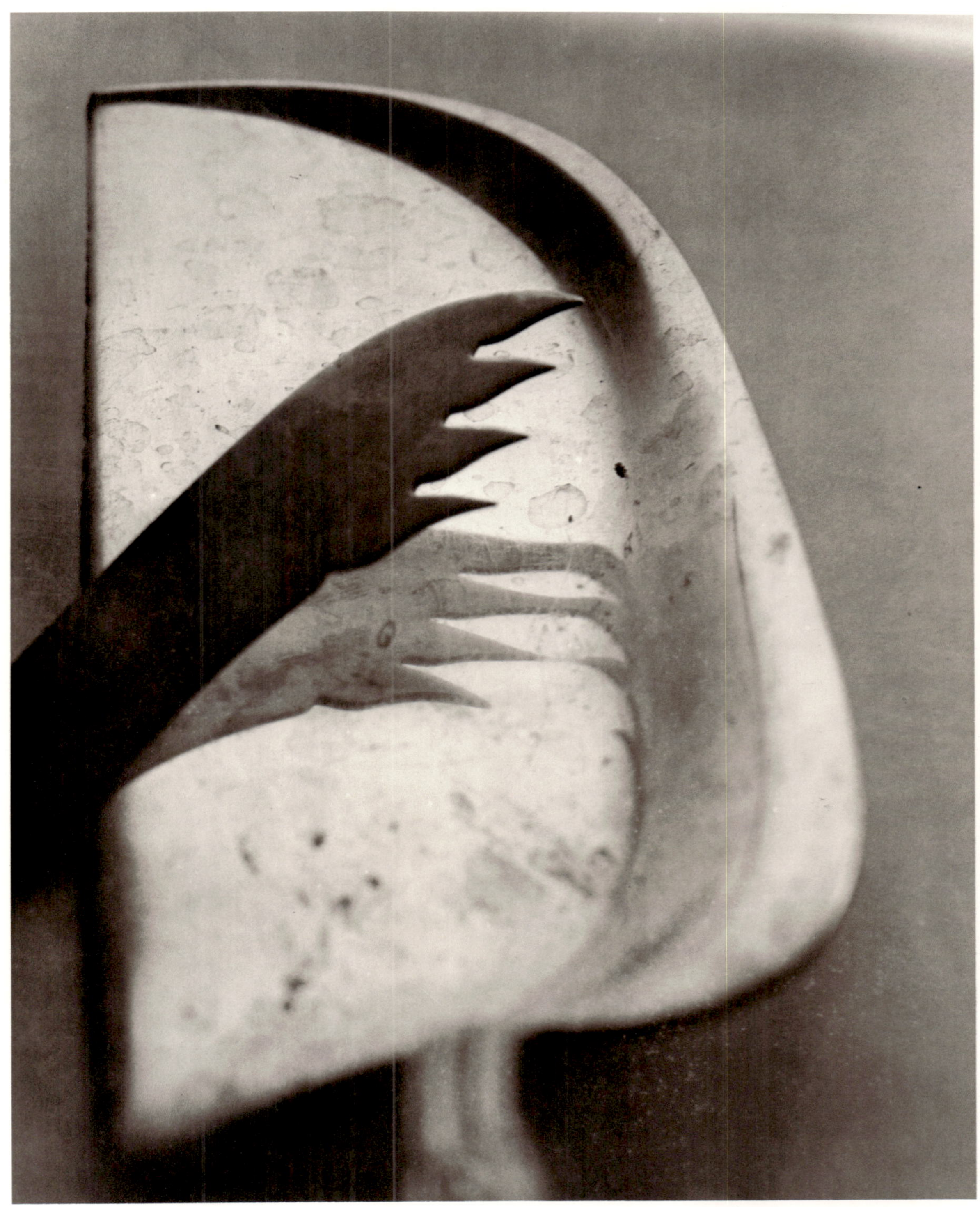

172 · Jan Groover · Untitled · 1983

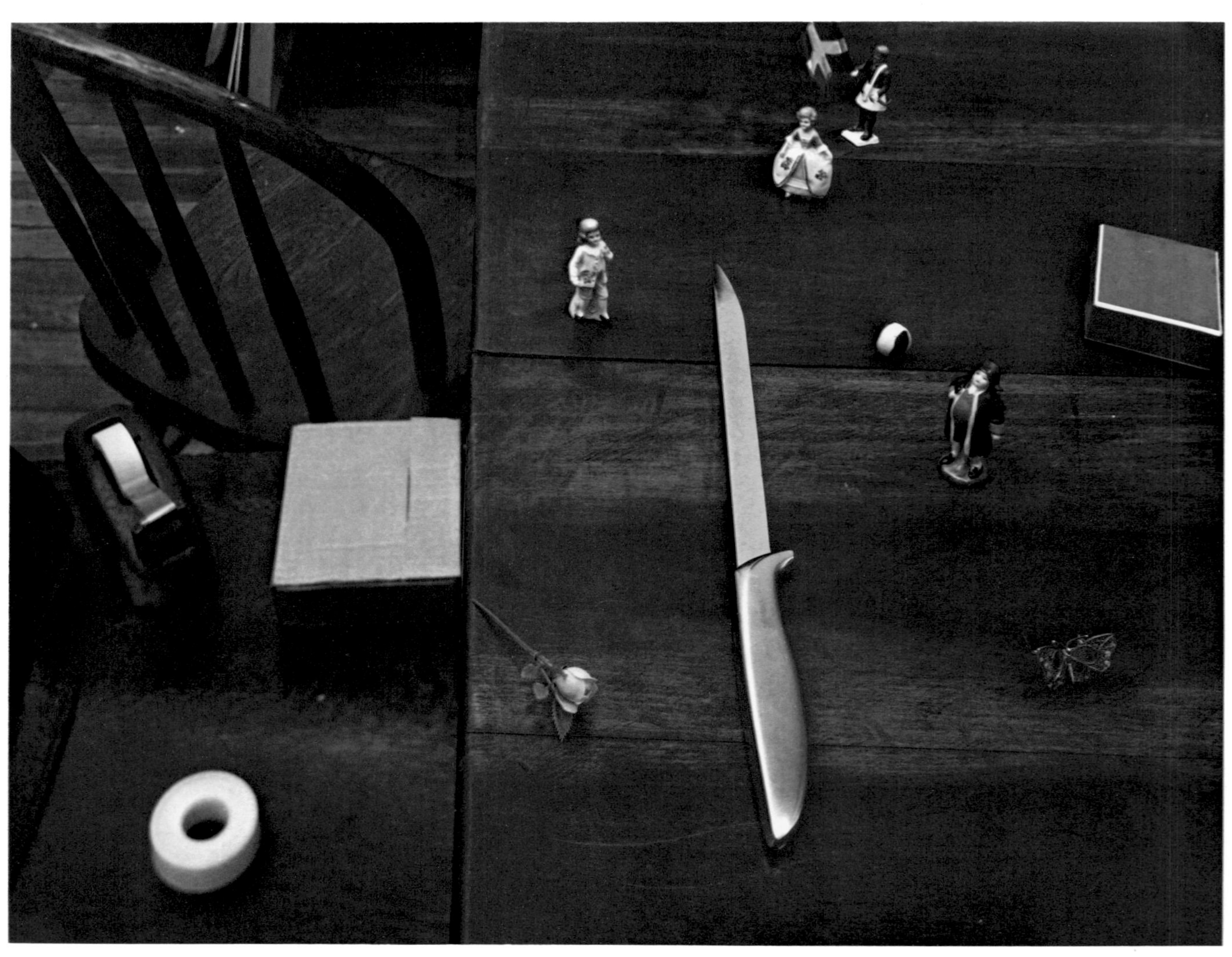

173 · Jan Groover · Untitled · 1984

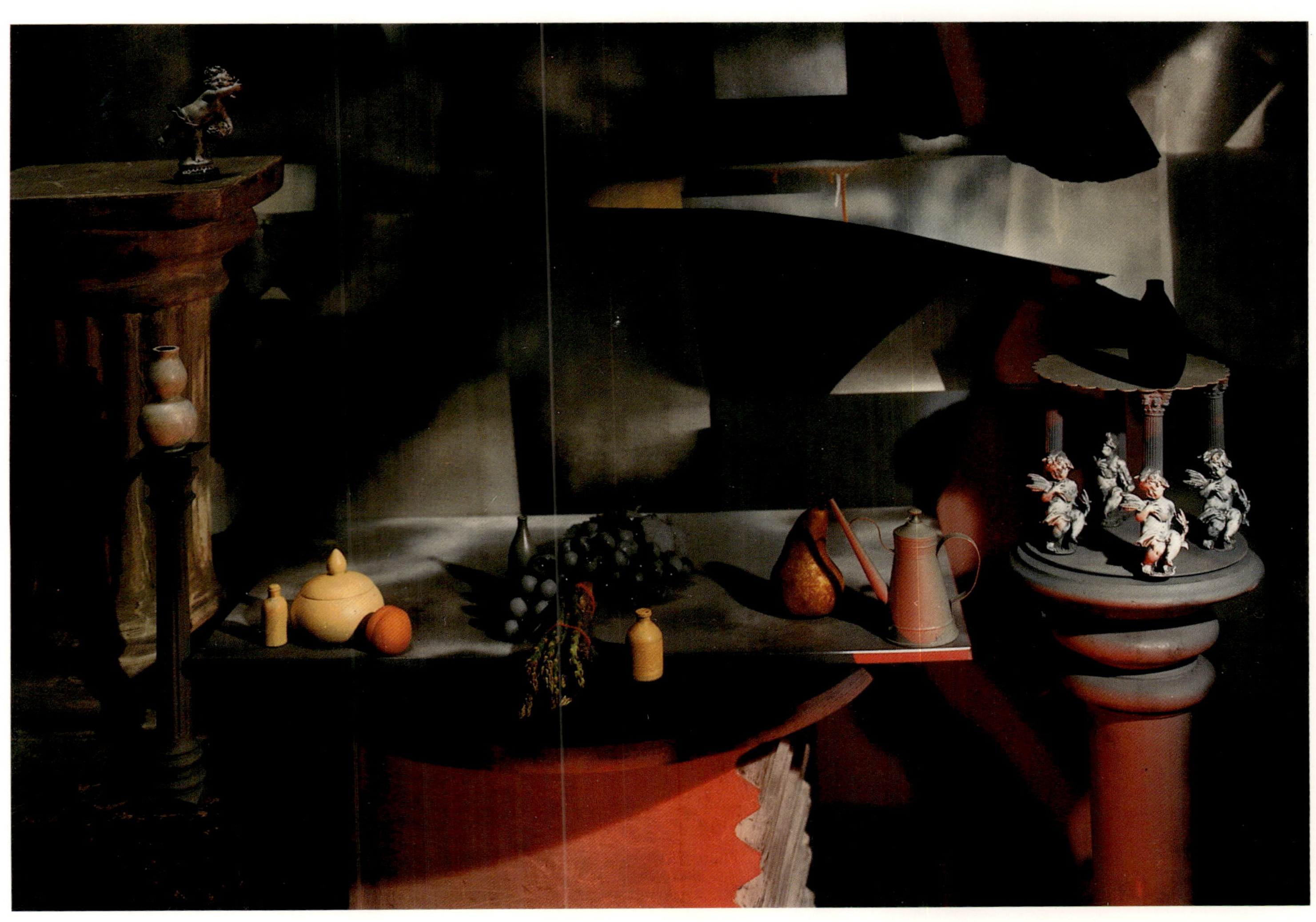

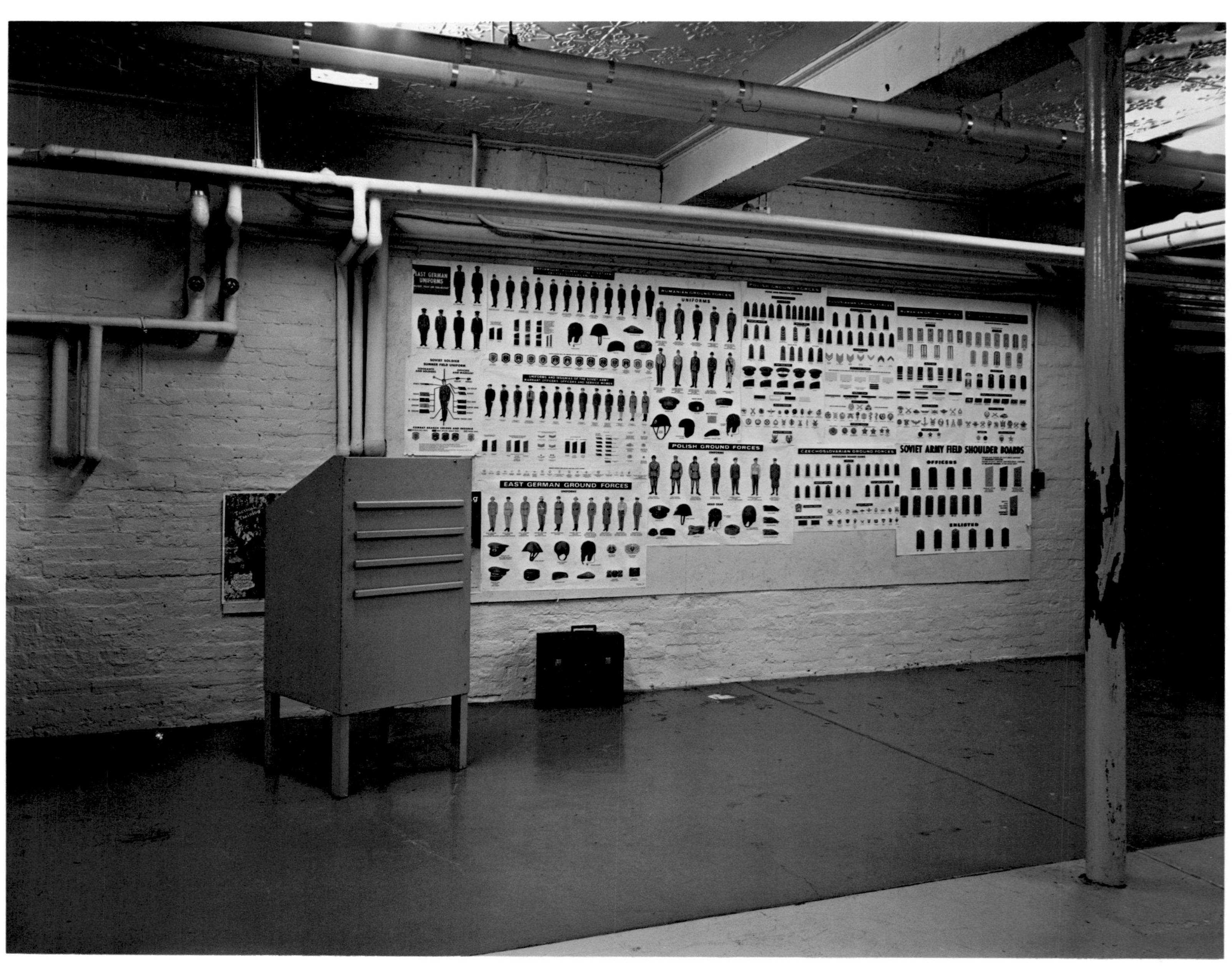

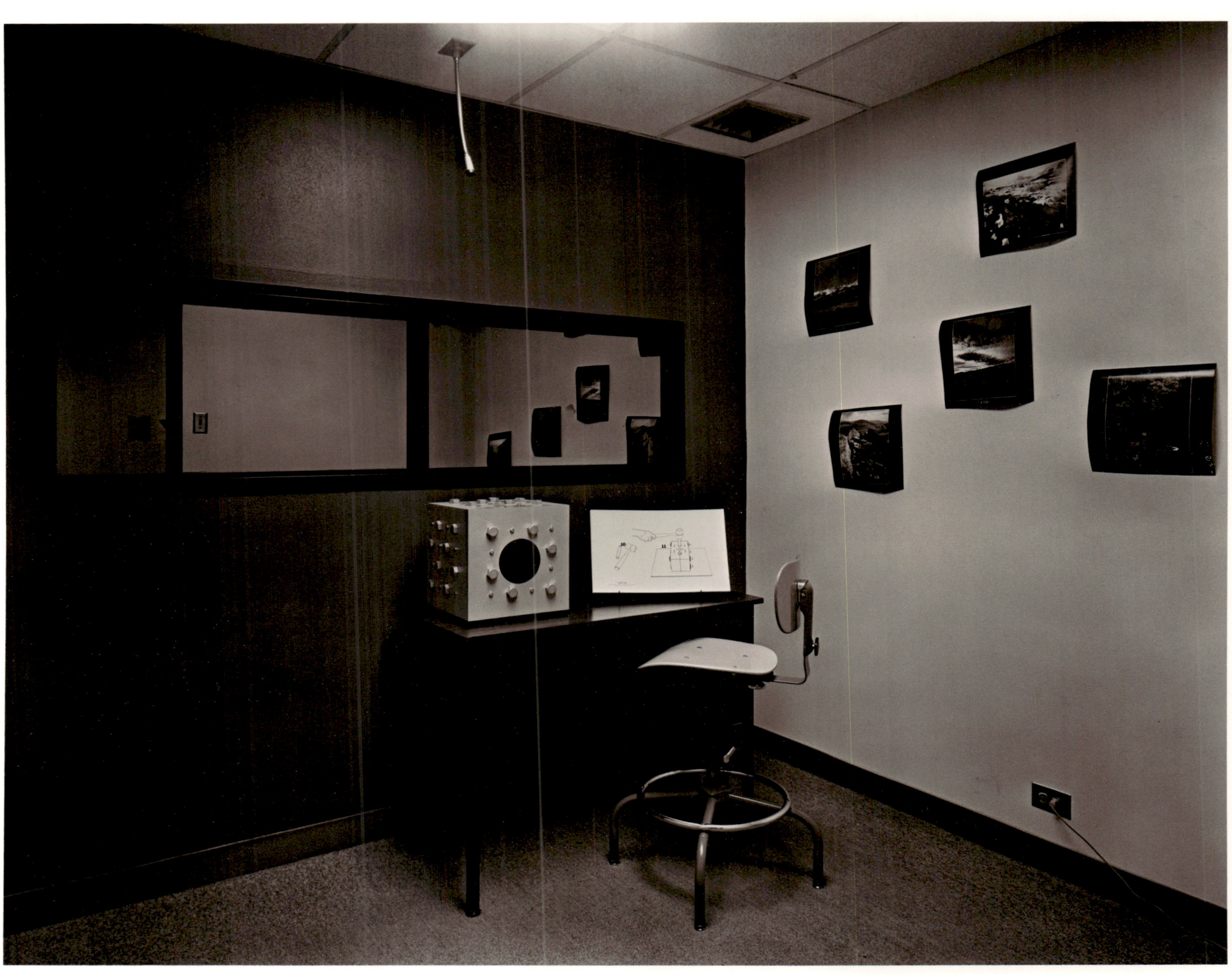

176 · Lynne Cohen · **Observation Room** · n.d.

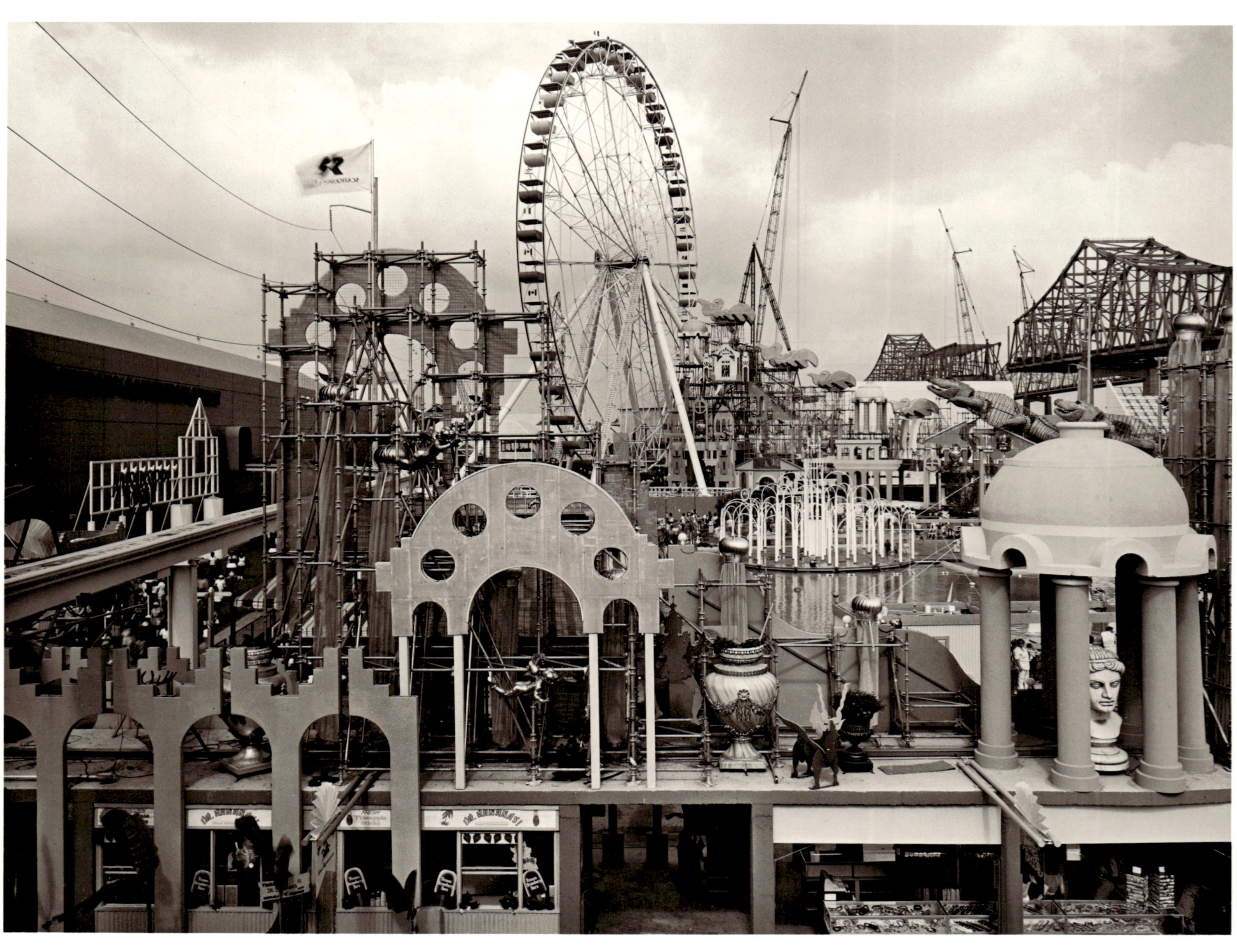

177 · Catherine Wagner · **Vista from Monorail, Wonderwall, Louisiana World Exposition,
New Orleans, Louisiana** · 1984

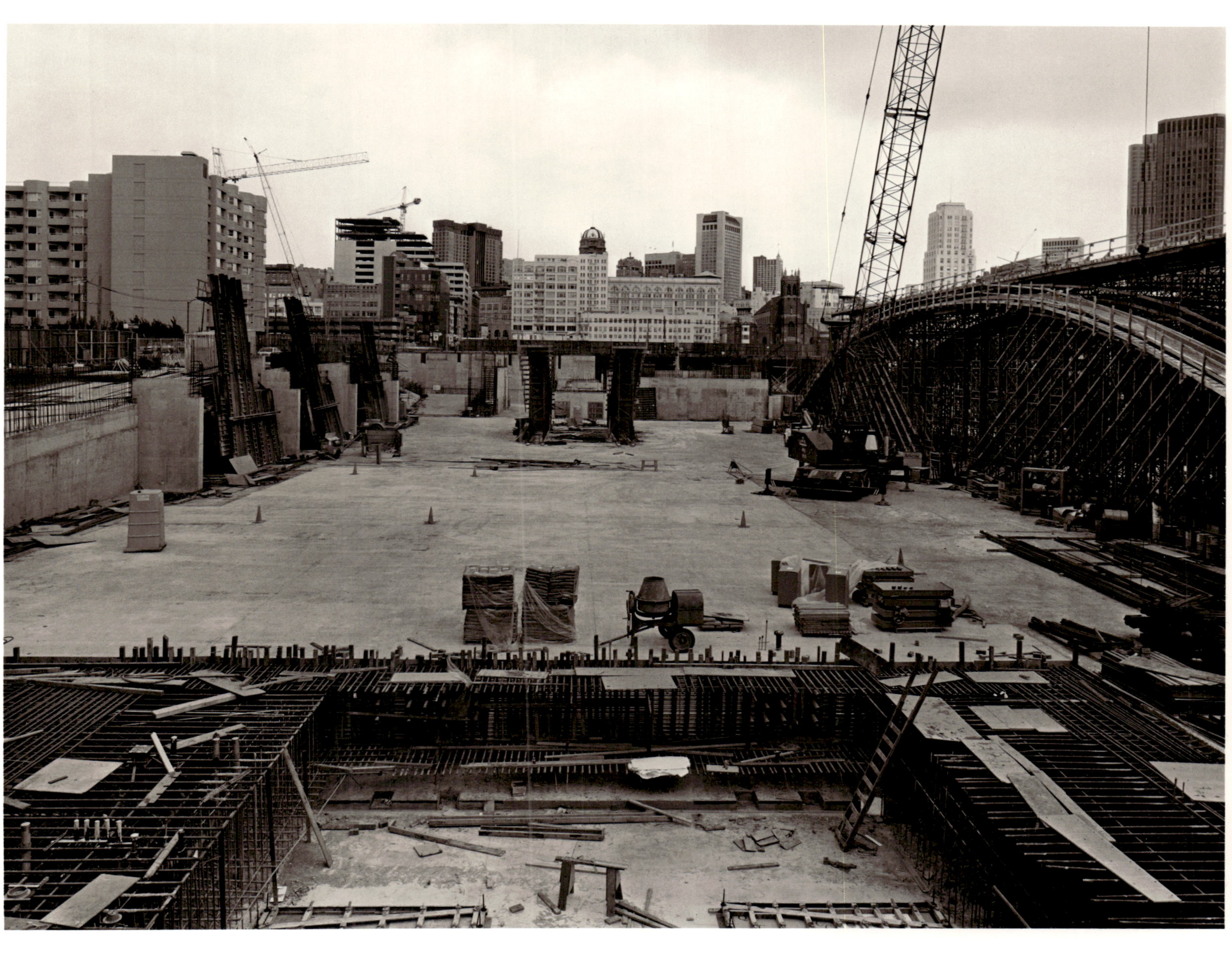

178 · Catherine Wagner · **Northwestern Corner with Sawhorse and Cement Mixer,
George Moscone Site, San Francisco, California** · 1981

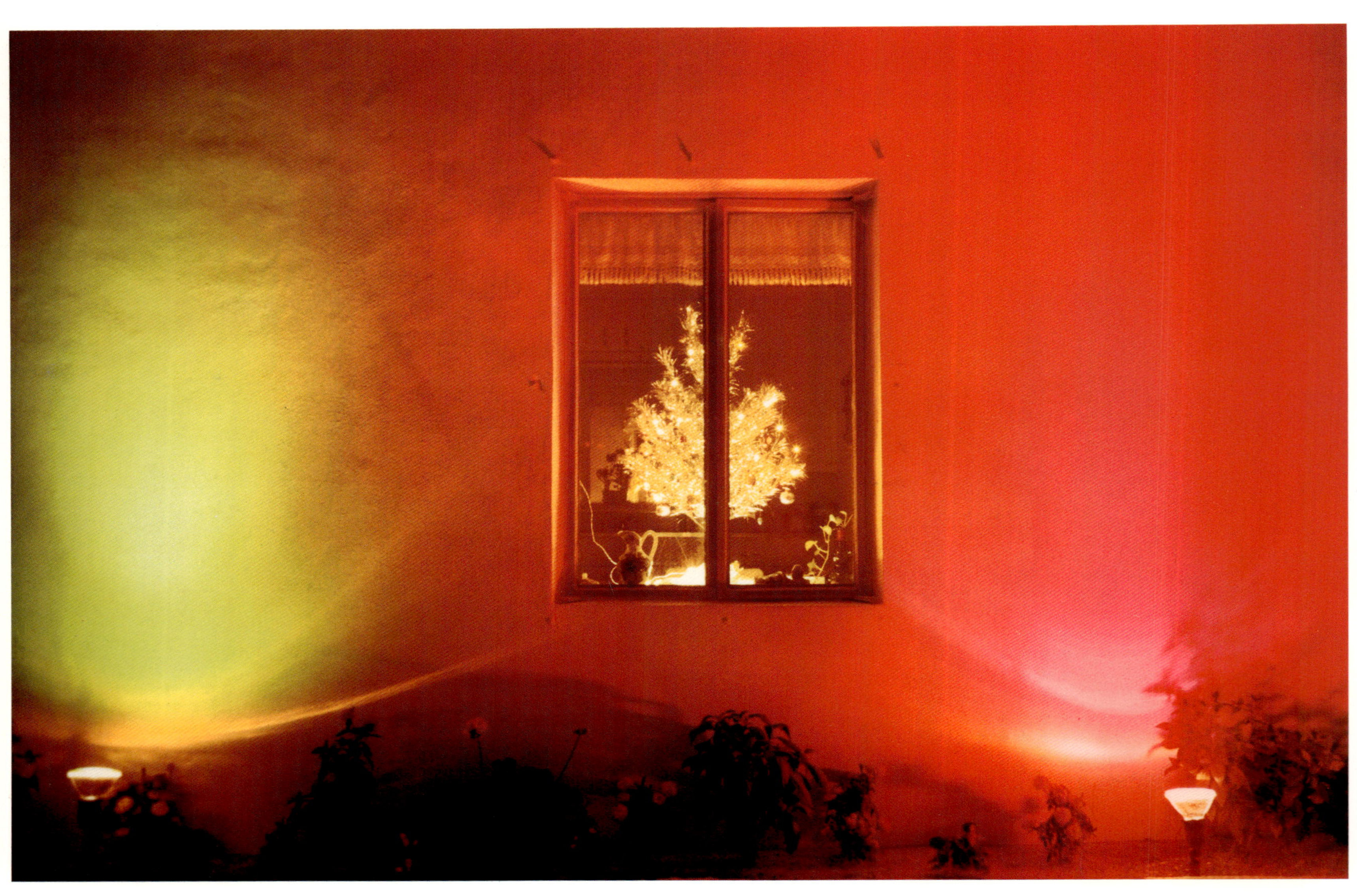

179 · Patty Carroll · **Xmas Tree in Window**, Pompano Beach, Florida · 1976

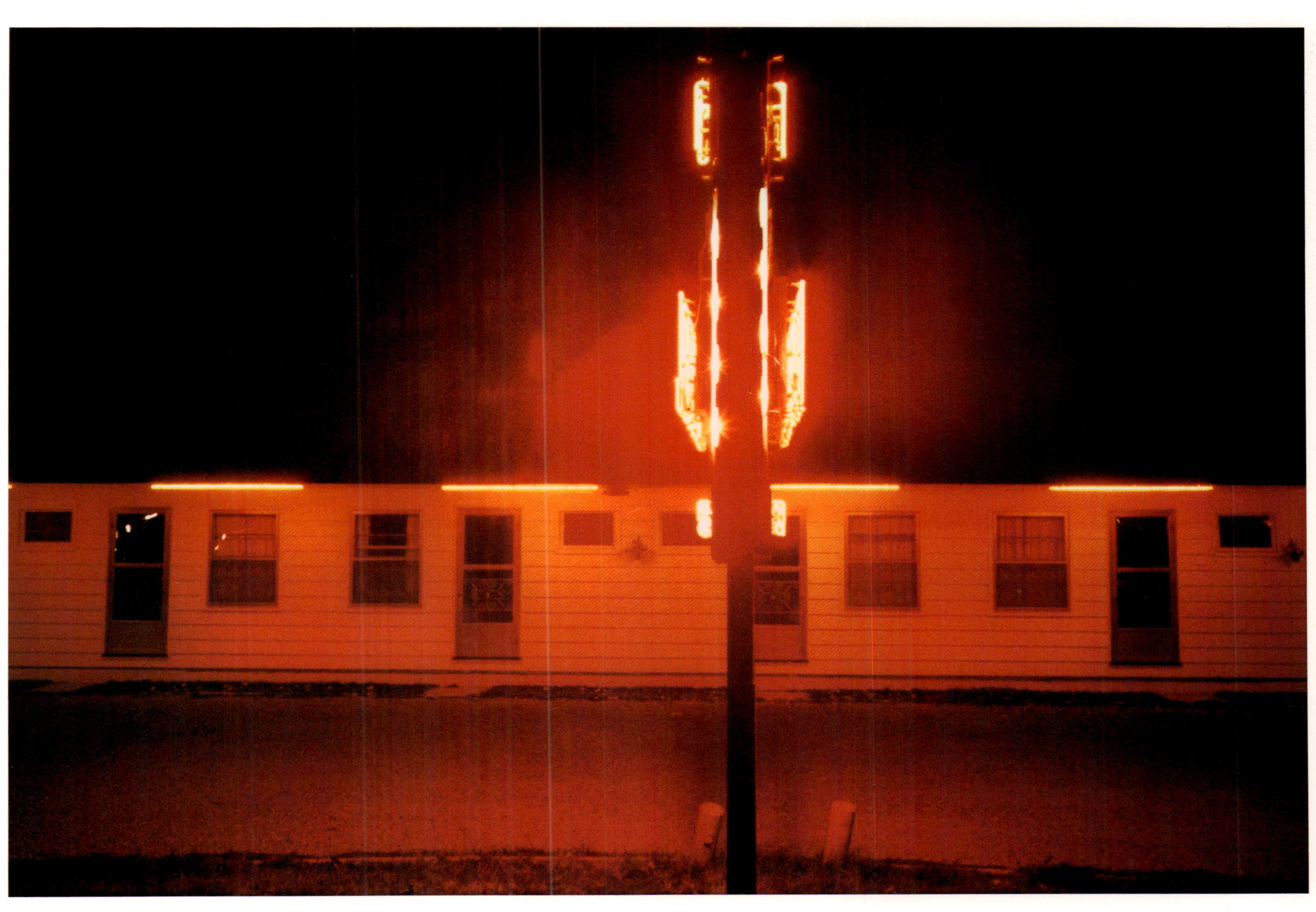

180 · Patty Carroll · **Motel in Hell**, Michigan · 1975

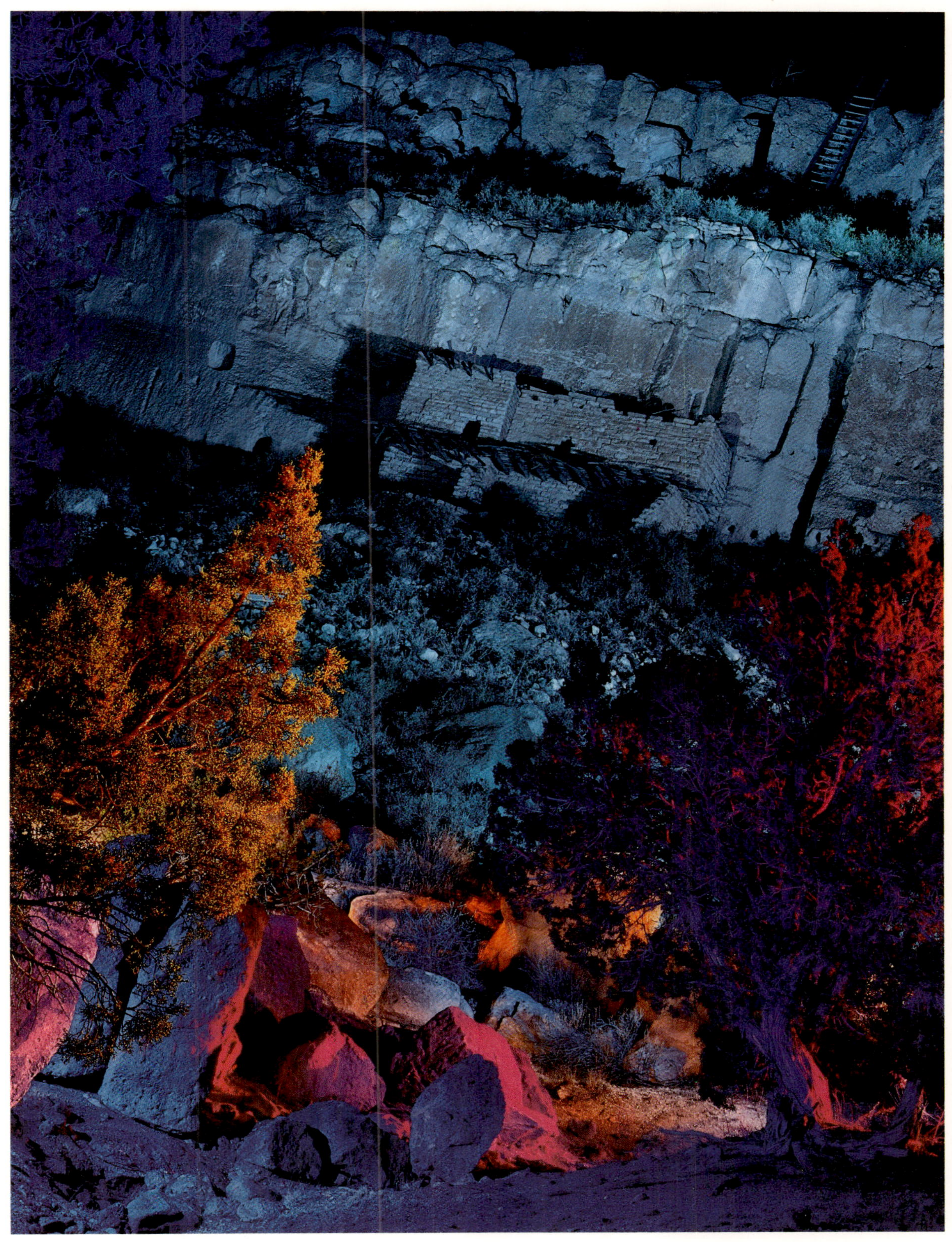

181 · Barbara Kasten · **Puye Cliff Dwelling** · 1990

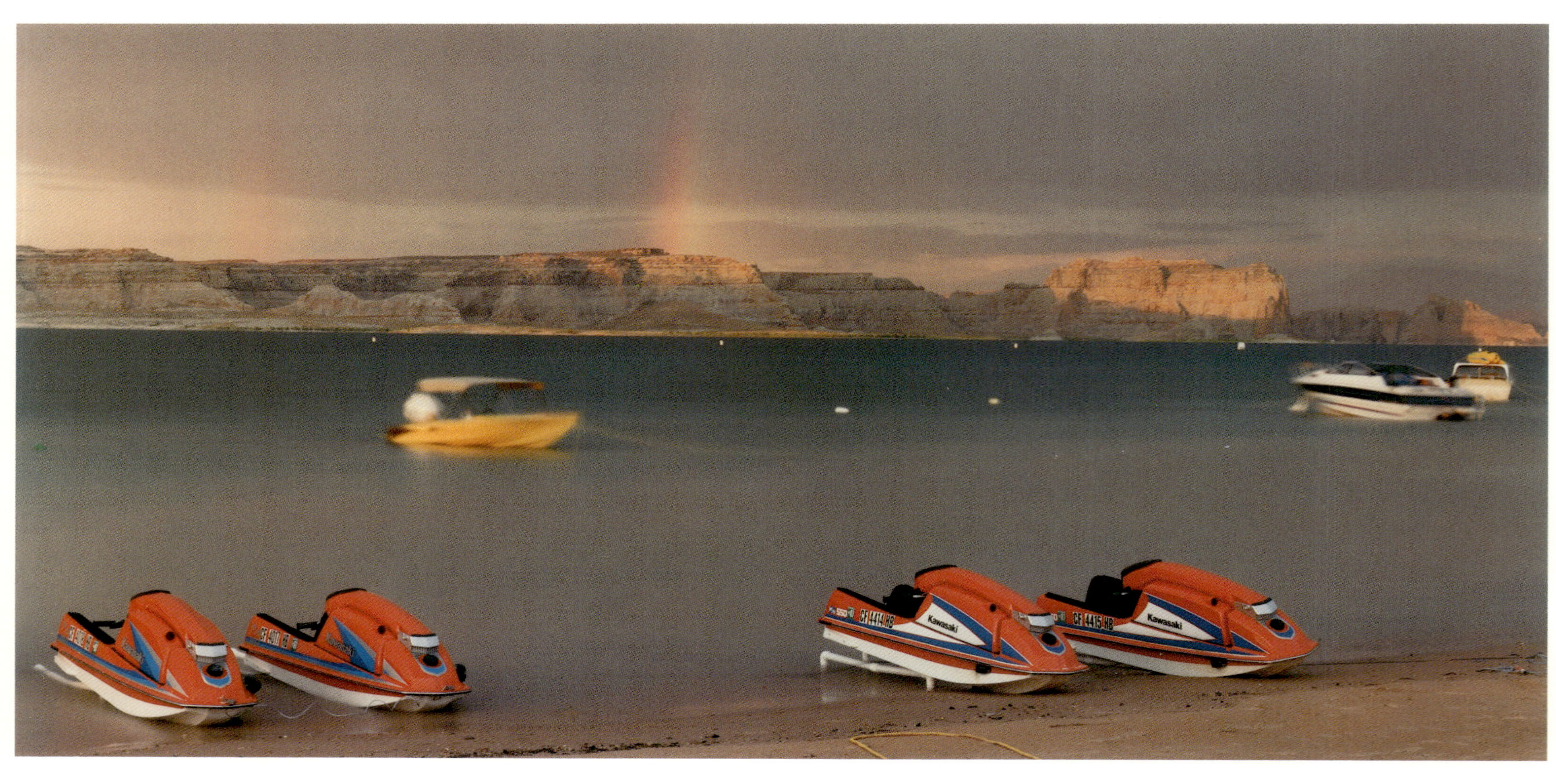

182 · Karen Halverson · **Lake Powell, near Wahweap Marina, Utah, 1987**

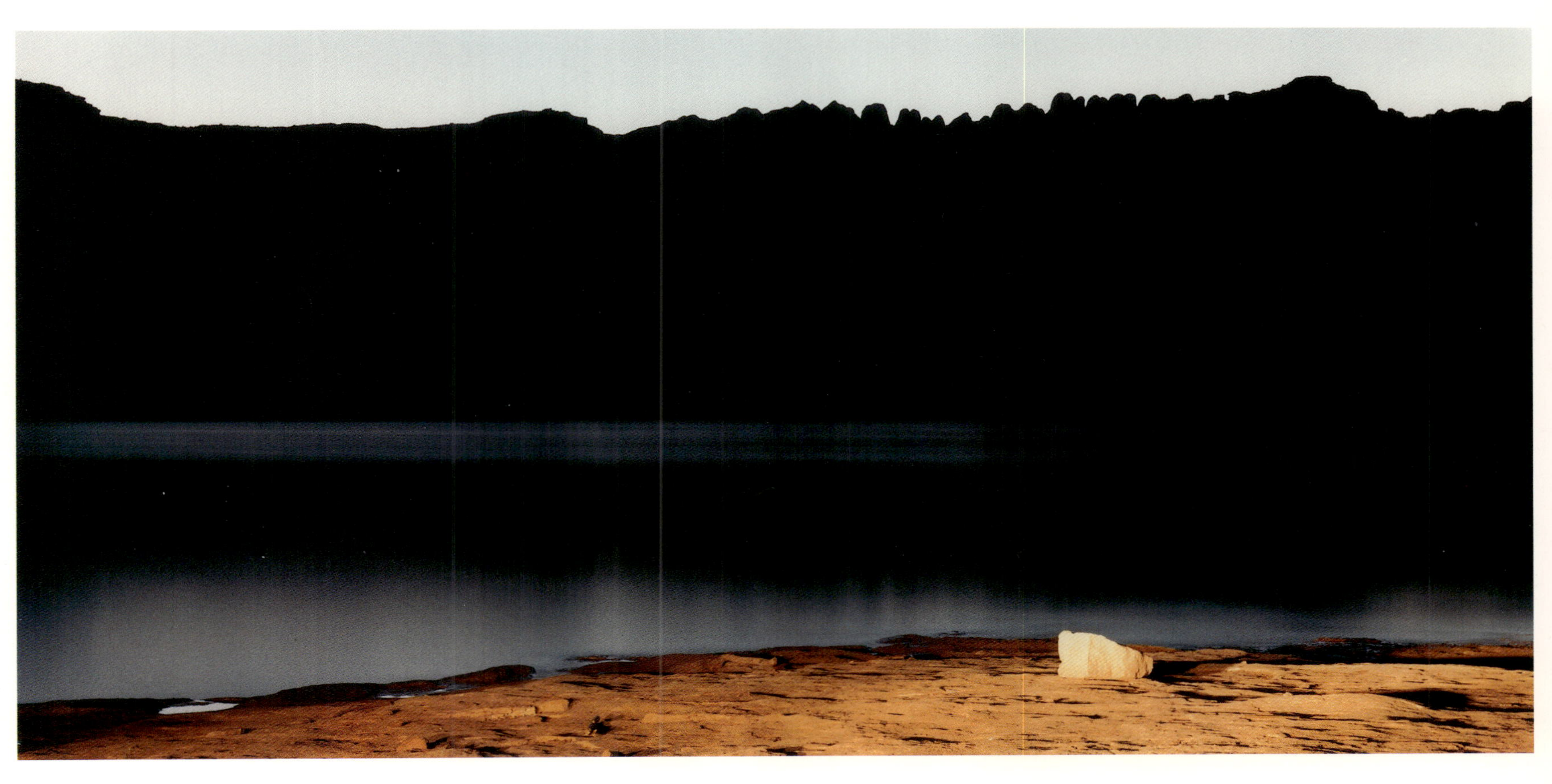

183 · Karen Halverson · **Hite Crossing, Lake Powell, Utah, 1988**

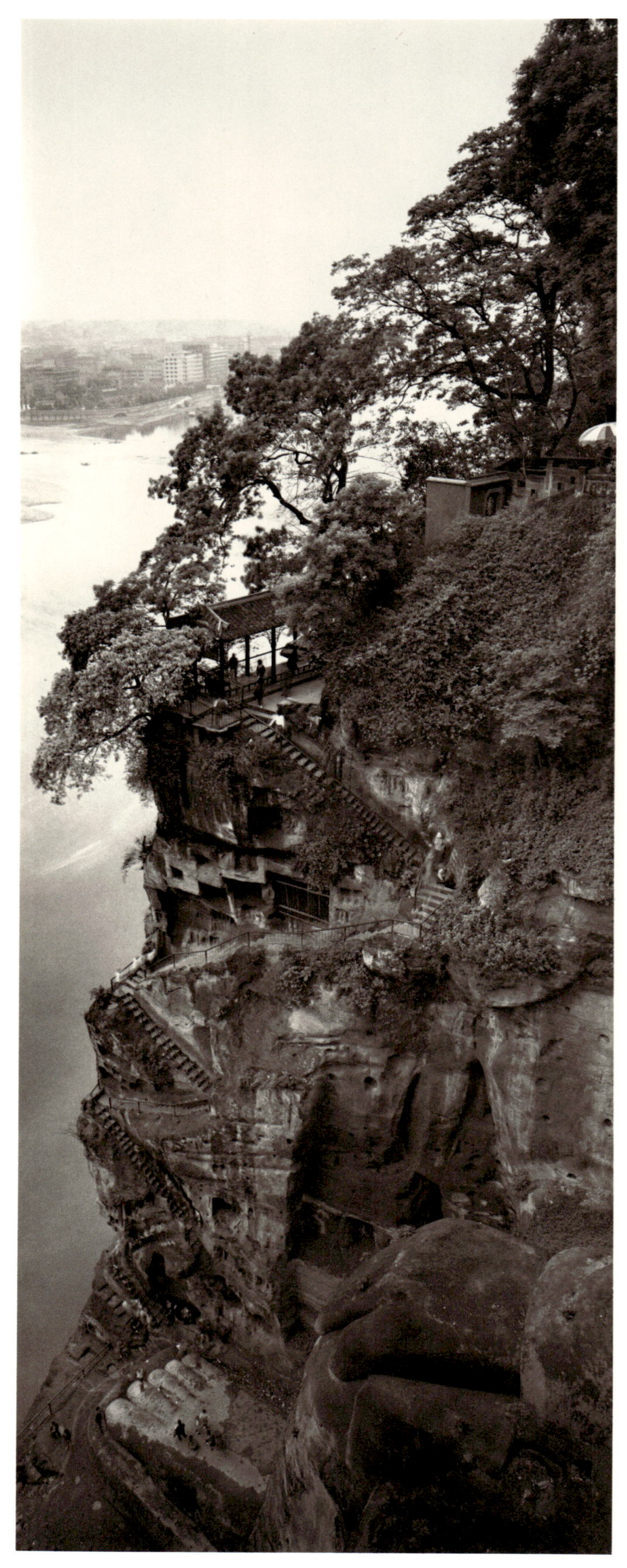

184 · Lois Conner · **Beijing, China** · 1988

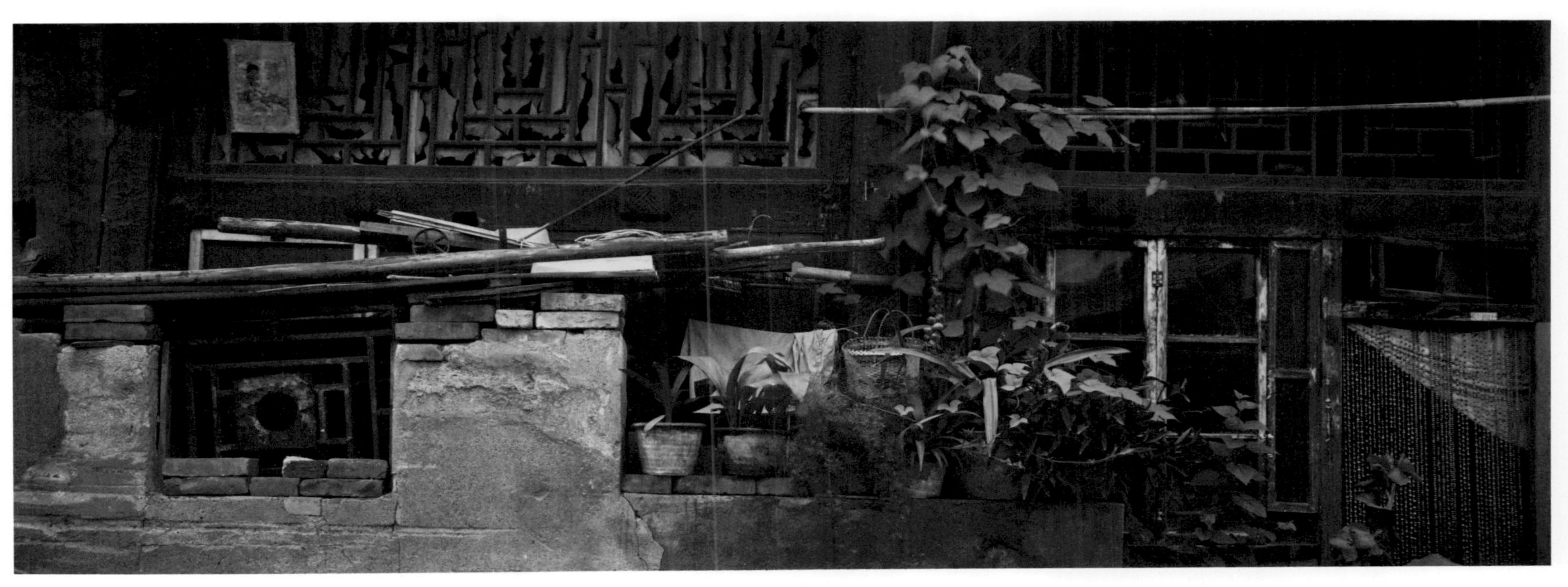

185 · Lois Conner · **Buddha, Le Shan, Szechuan, China** · 1986

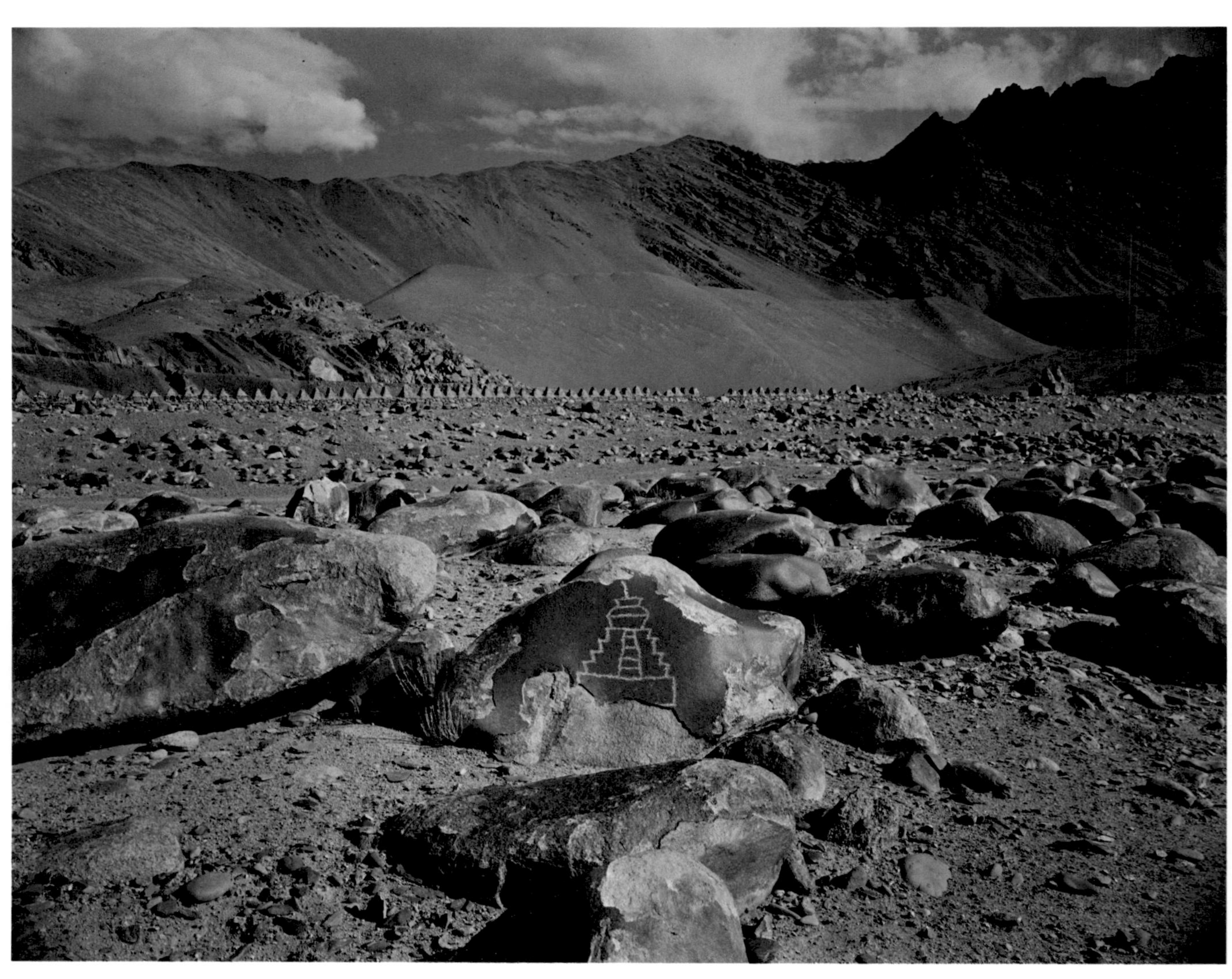

186 · Linda Connor · **Chörten, Ladakh, India** · 1985

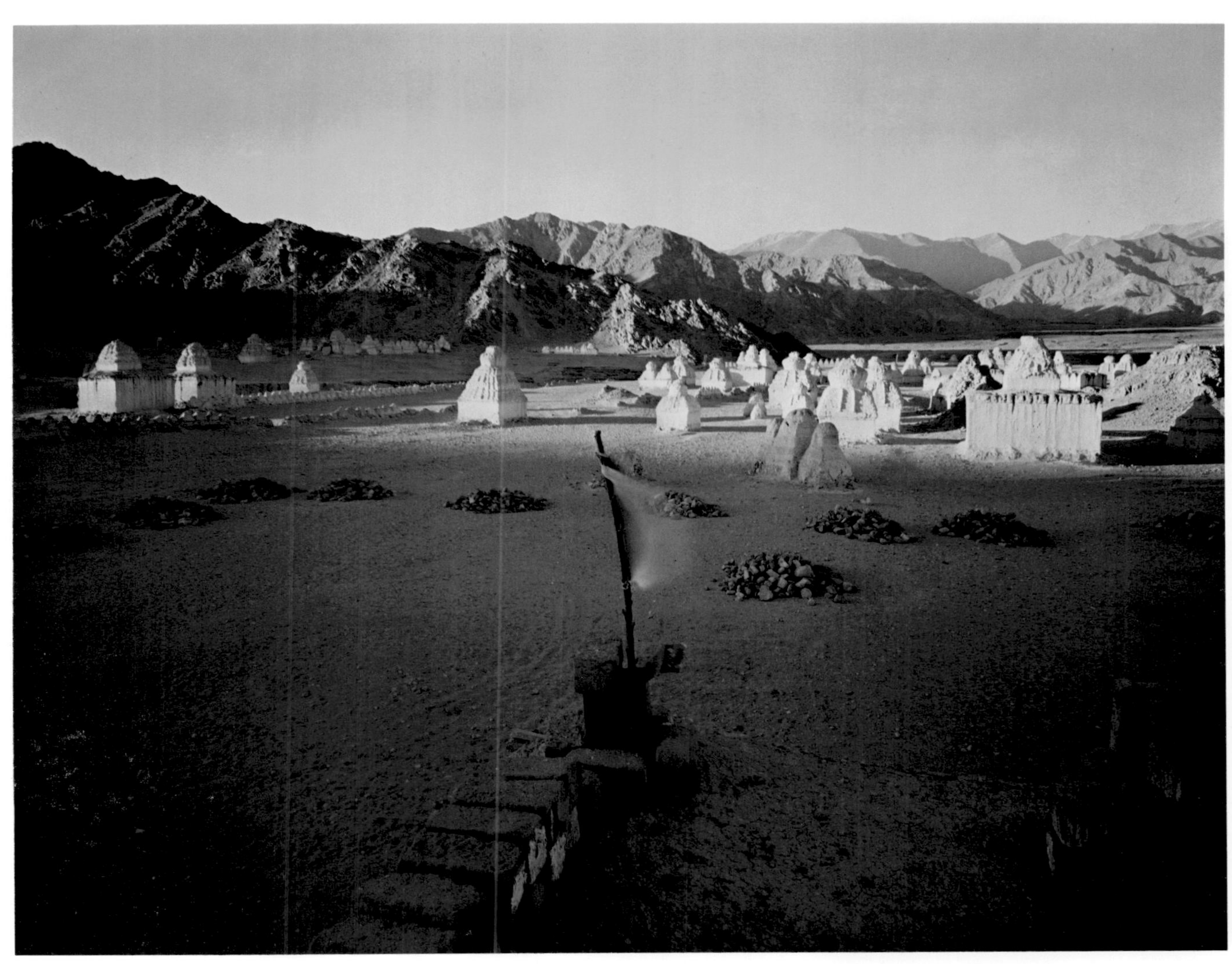

187 · Linda Connor · **Prayer Flag with Chörtens, Ladakh, India** · 1988

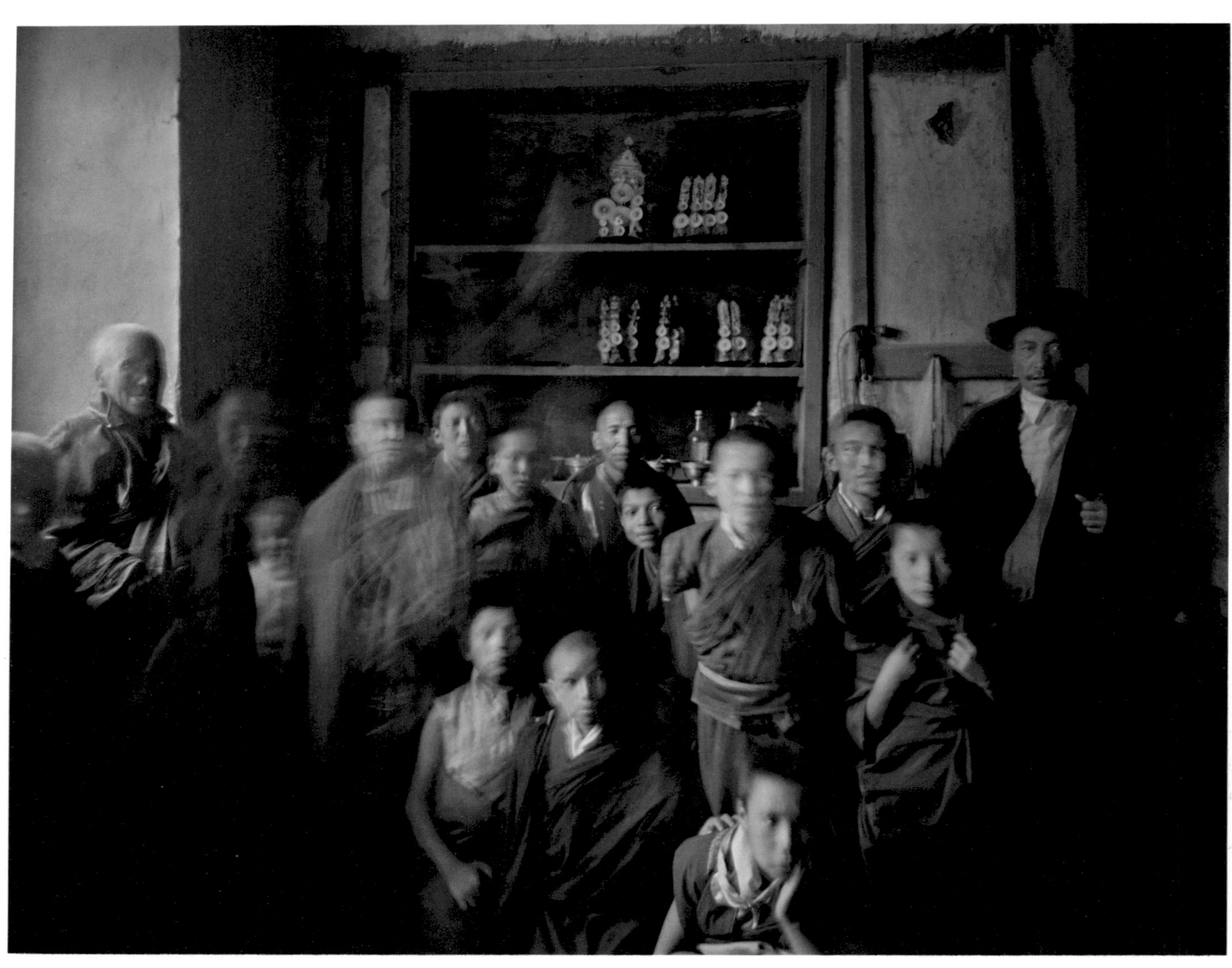

188 · Linda Connor · **Monks, Phiyang Monastery, Ladakh, India** · 1985

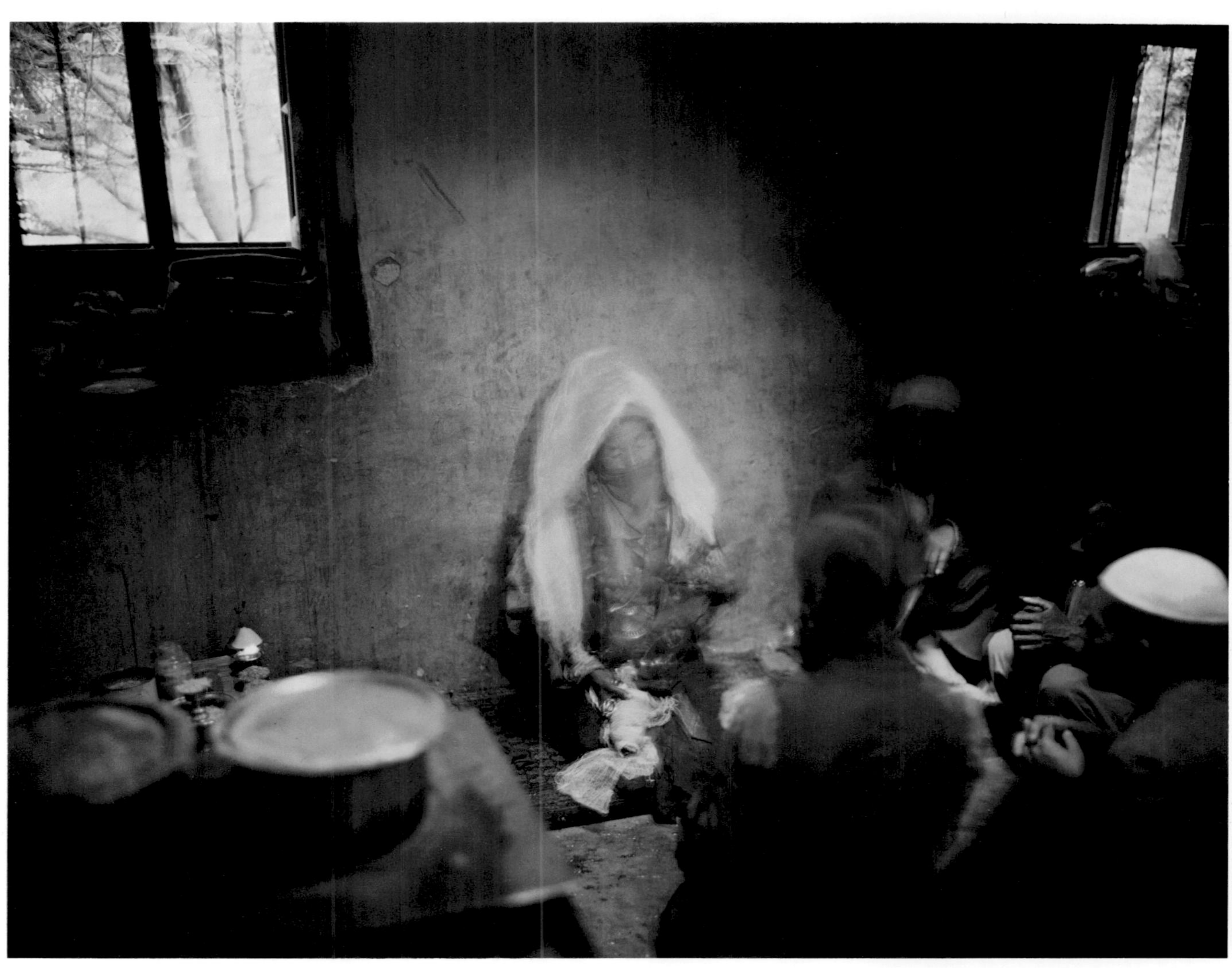

189 · Linda Connor · **The Oracle of Sabu in Trance, Ladakh, India** · 1988

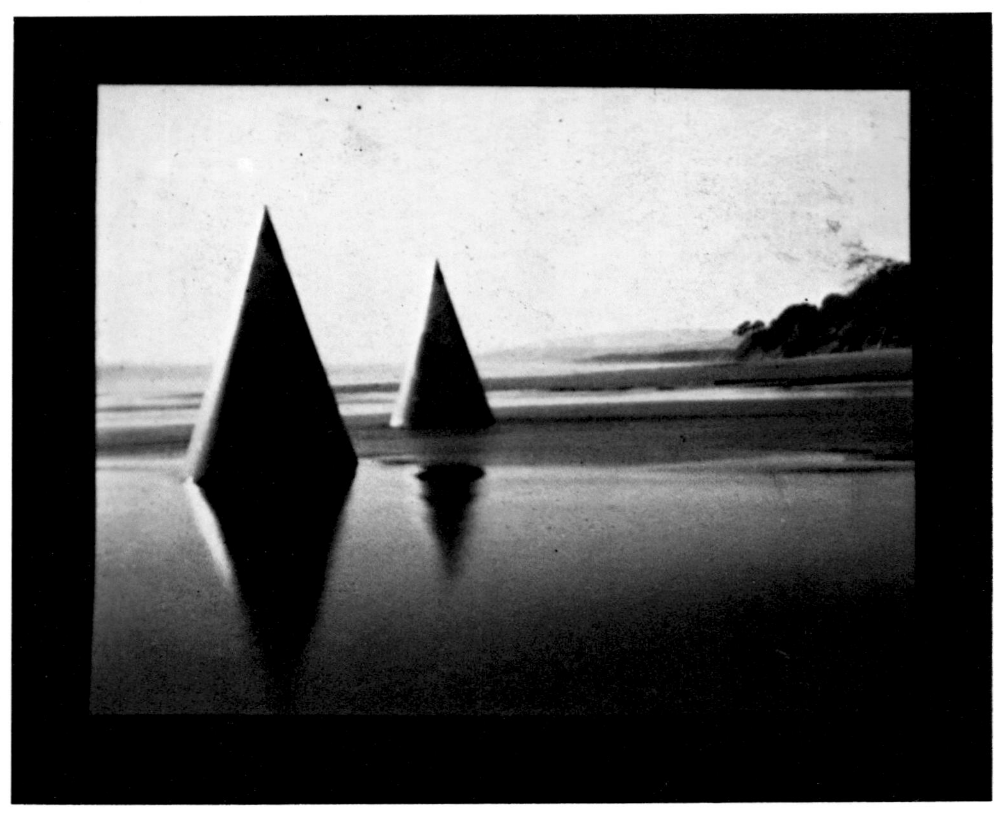

190 · Ruth Thorne Thomsen · **Cones,** from the **Expedition** series · c. 1982

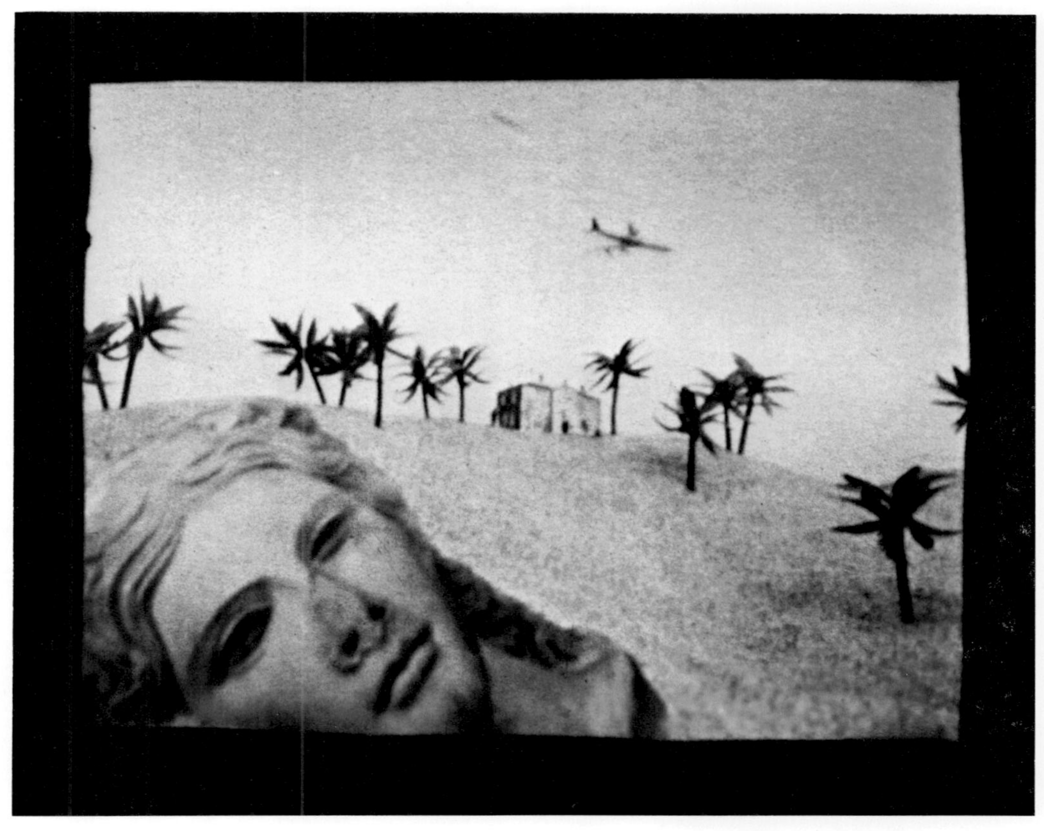

191 · Ruth Thorne Thomsen · **Head with Plane,** from the **Expedition** series · Illinois, 1979

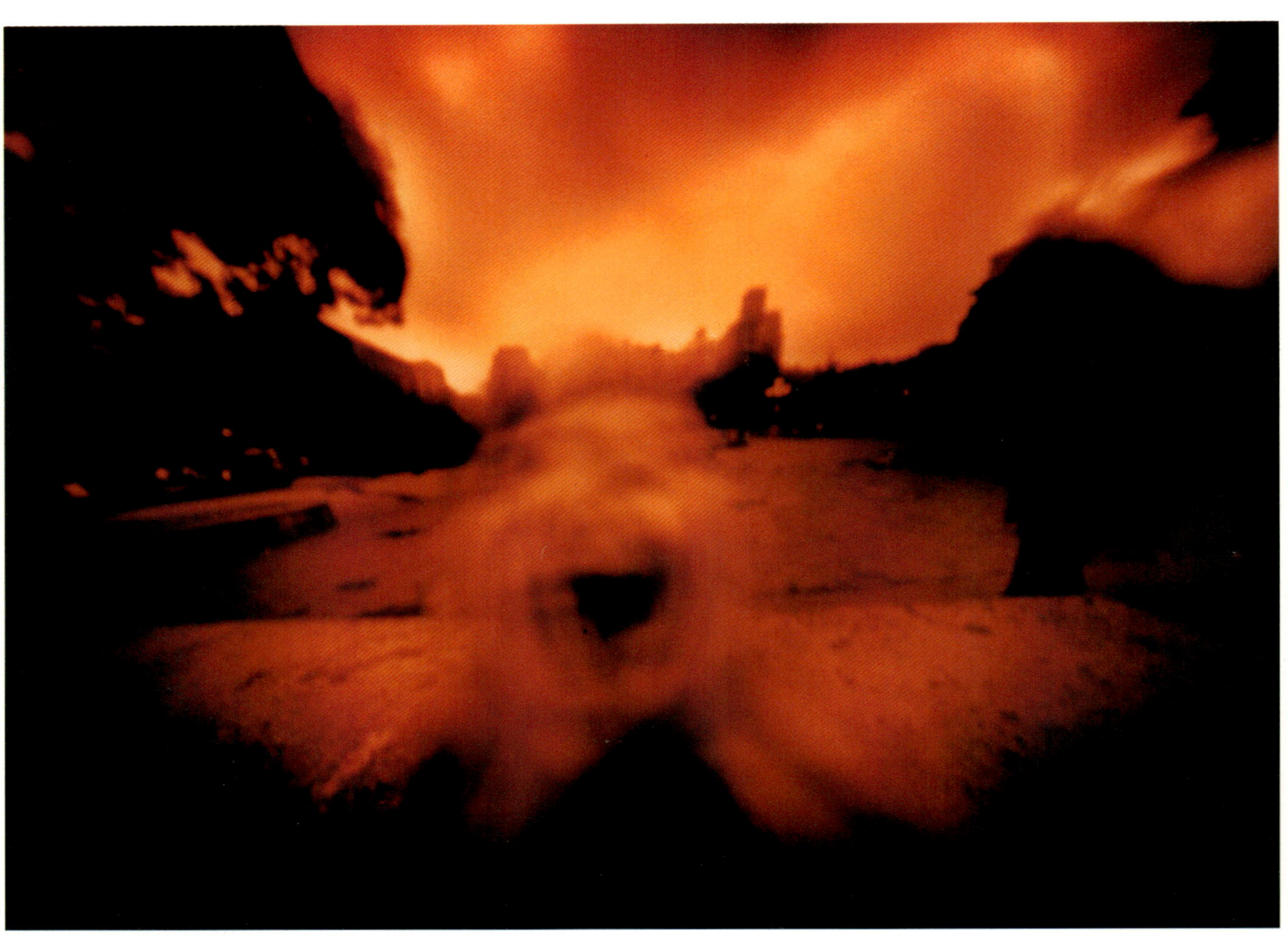

192 · Barbara Ess · Untitled, from the **Food for the Moon** series · 1986

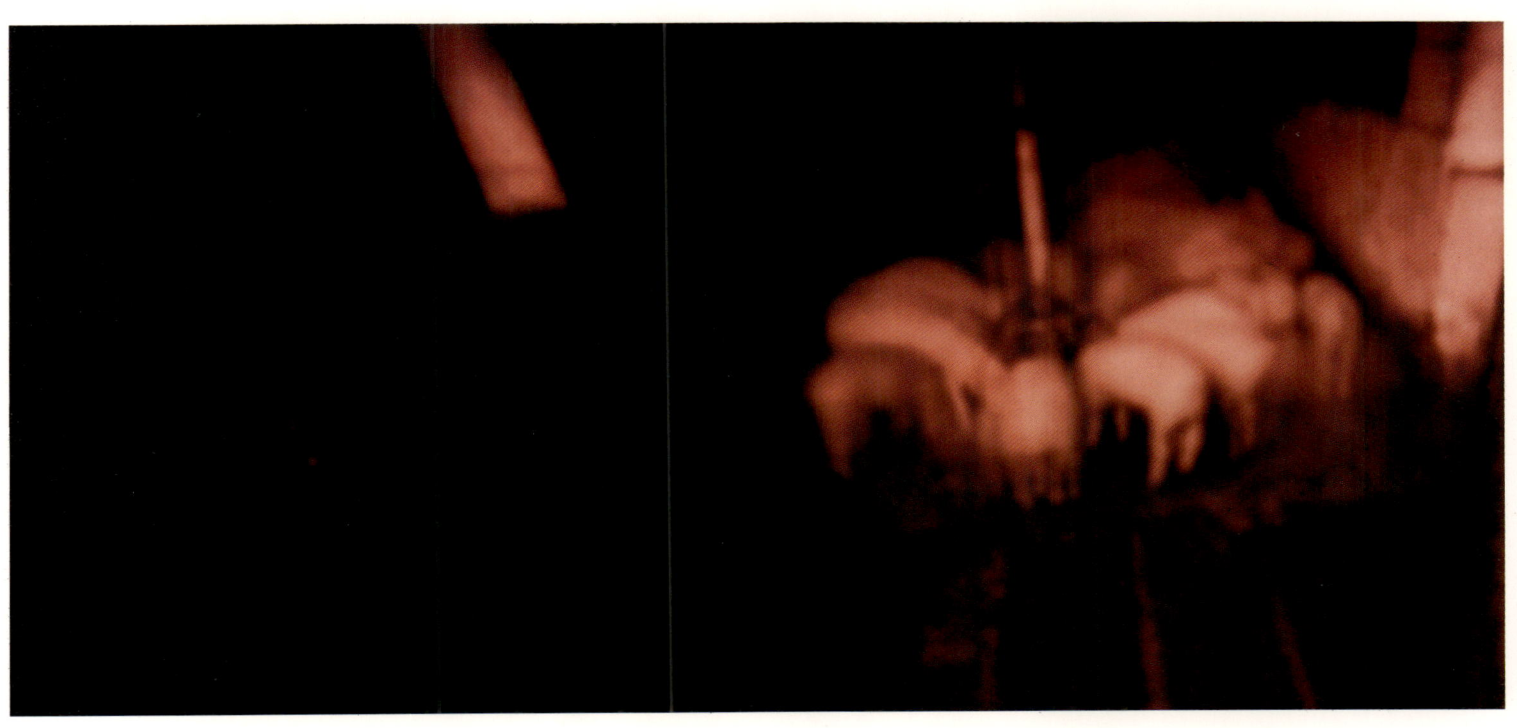

193 · Barbara Ess · Untitled · 1988

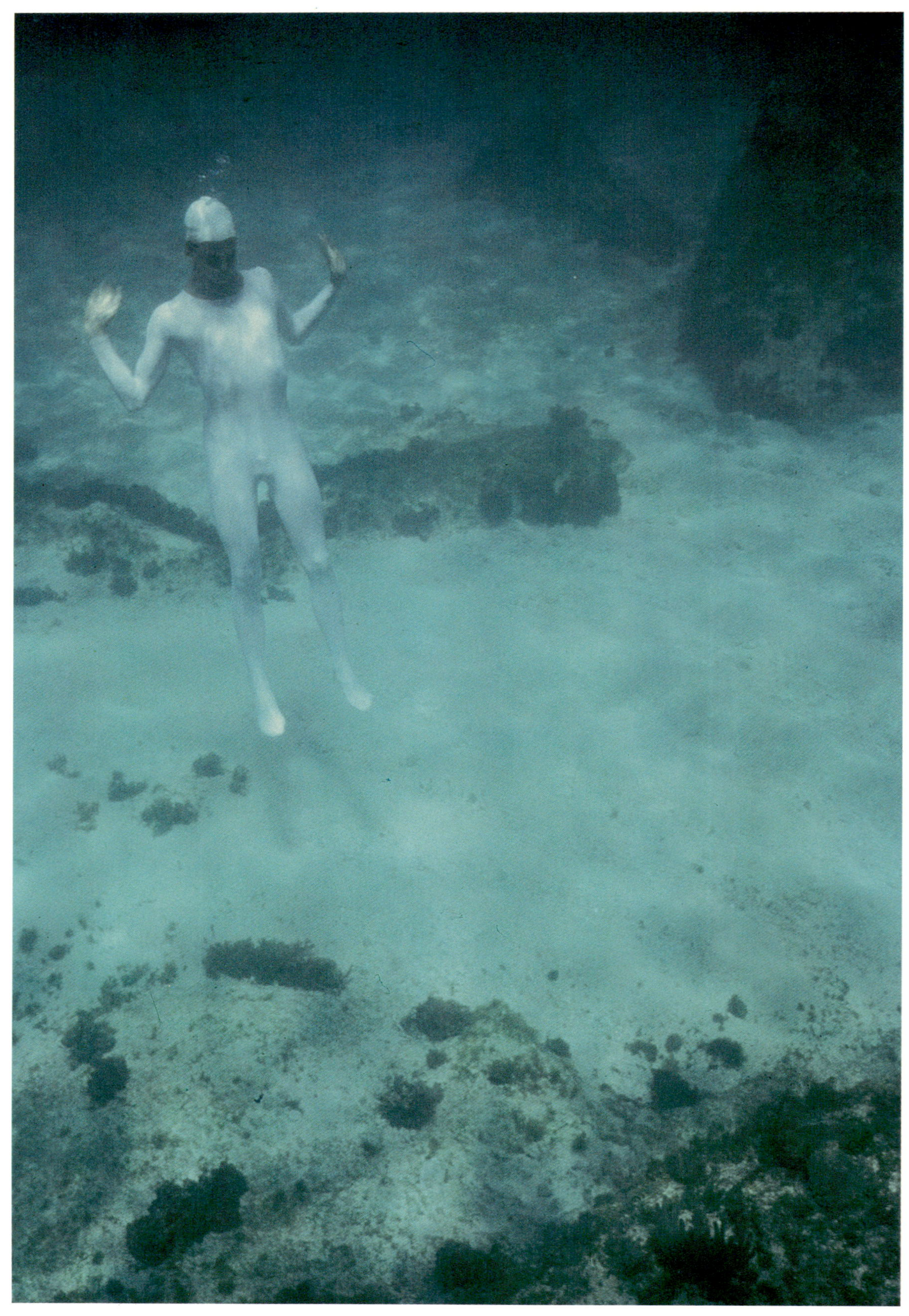

194 · Laurie Simmons · **Whiteman Coming** · 1981

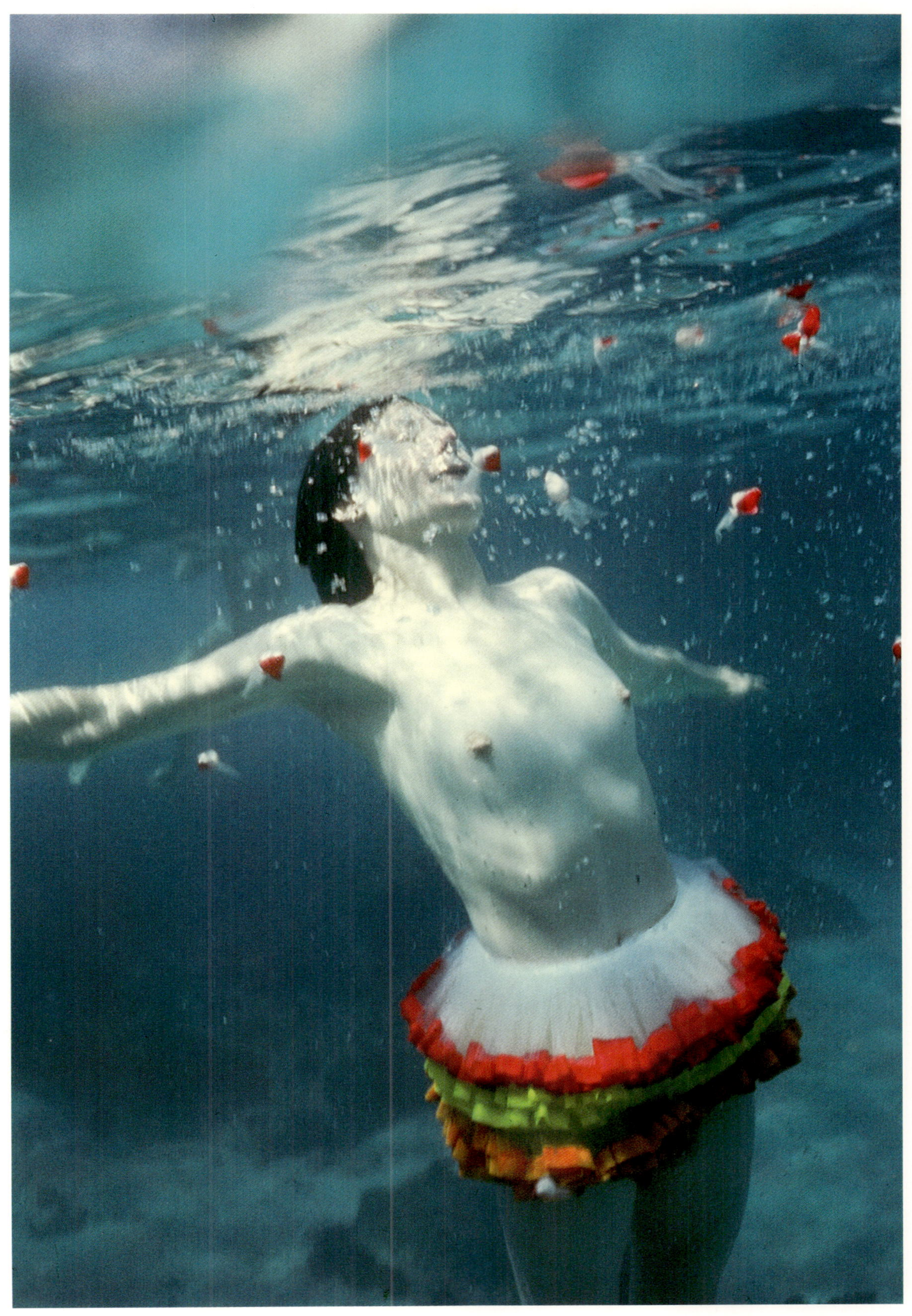

195 · Laurie Simmons · **Vertical Water Ballet** · 1981

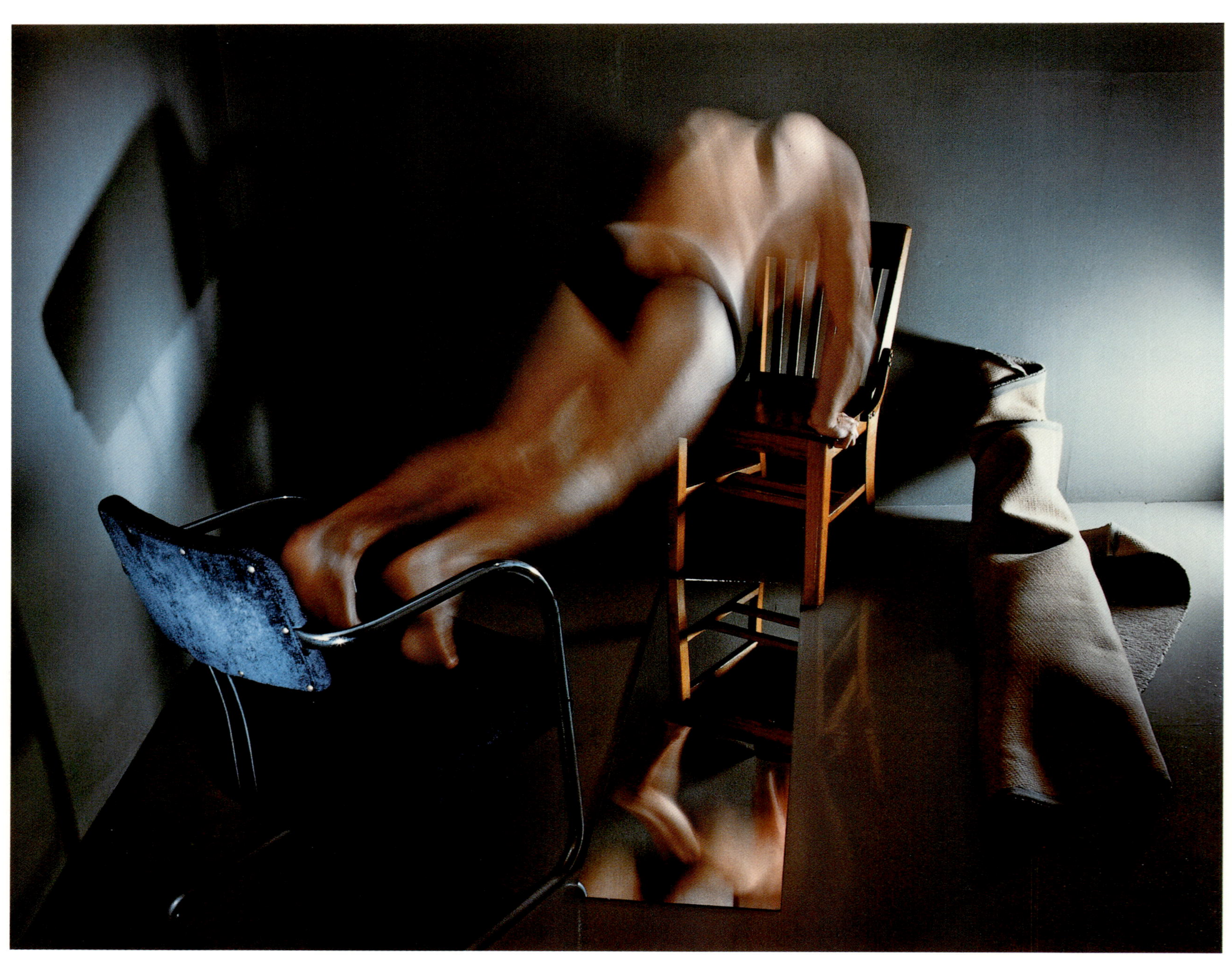

196 · Jo Ann Callis · **Man doing Pushups** · 1984–85

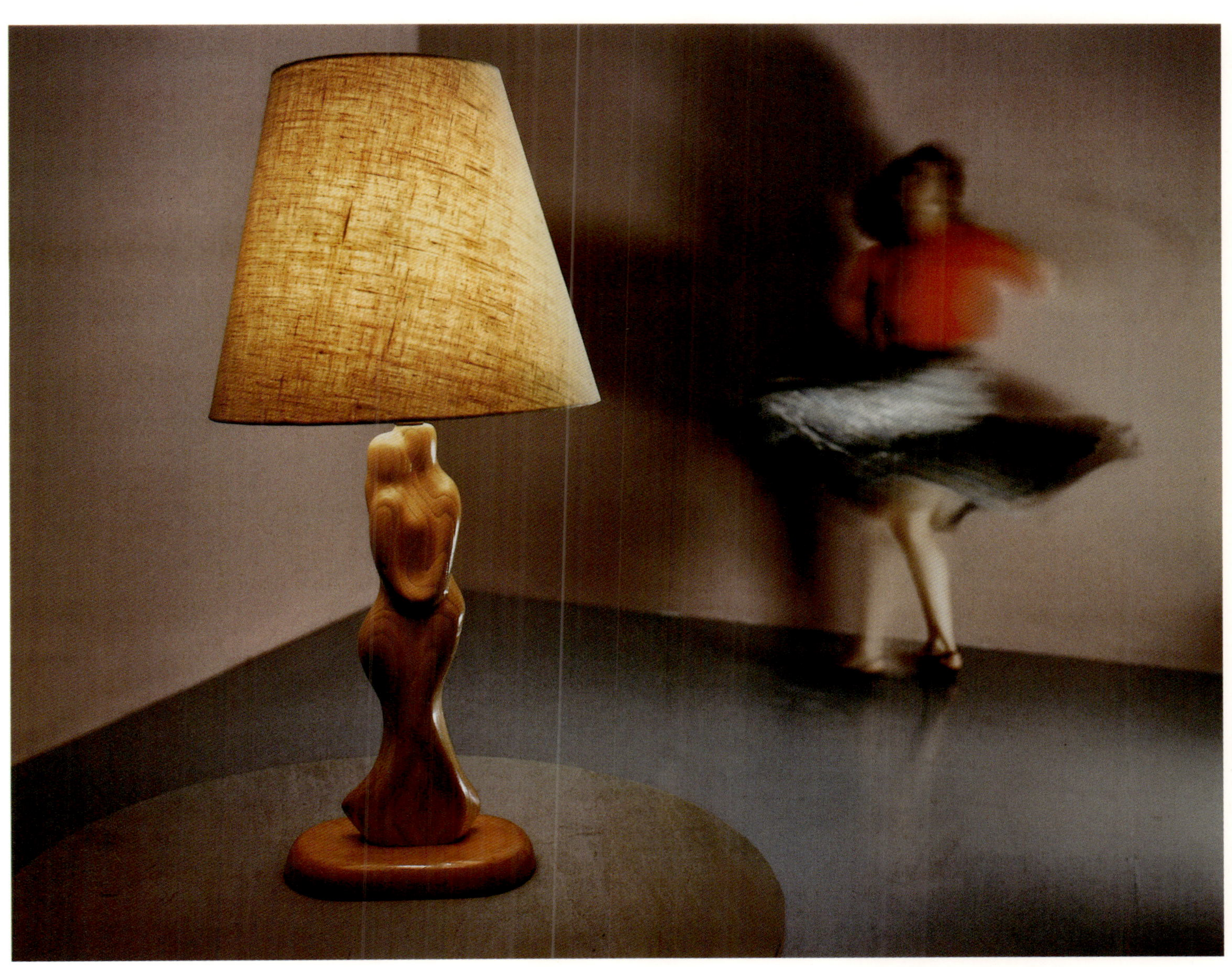

197 · Jo Ann Callis · **Woman Twirling** · 1984

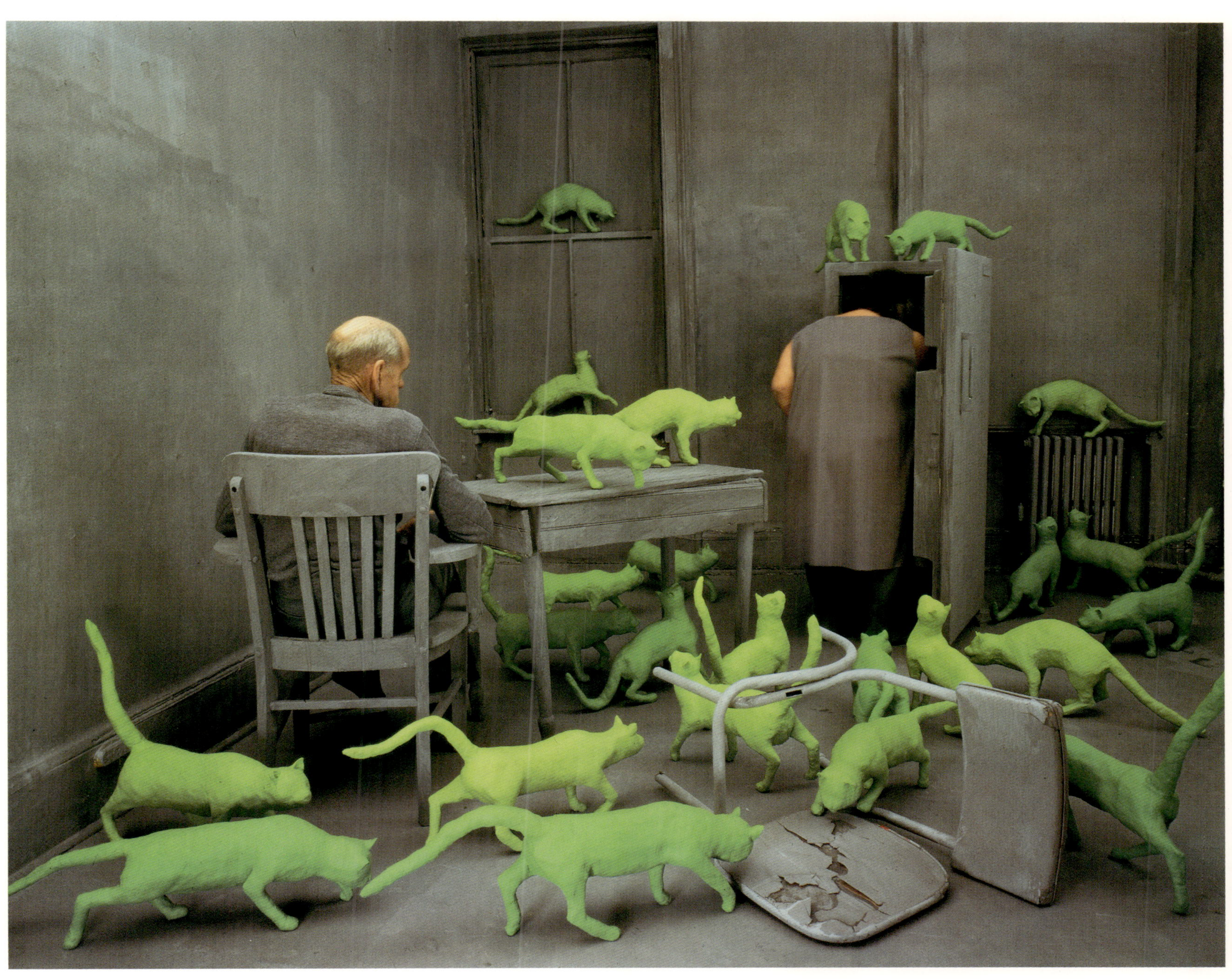

198 · Sandy Skoglund · **Radioactive Cats** · 1980

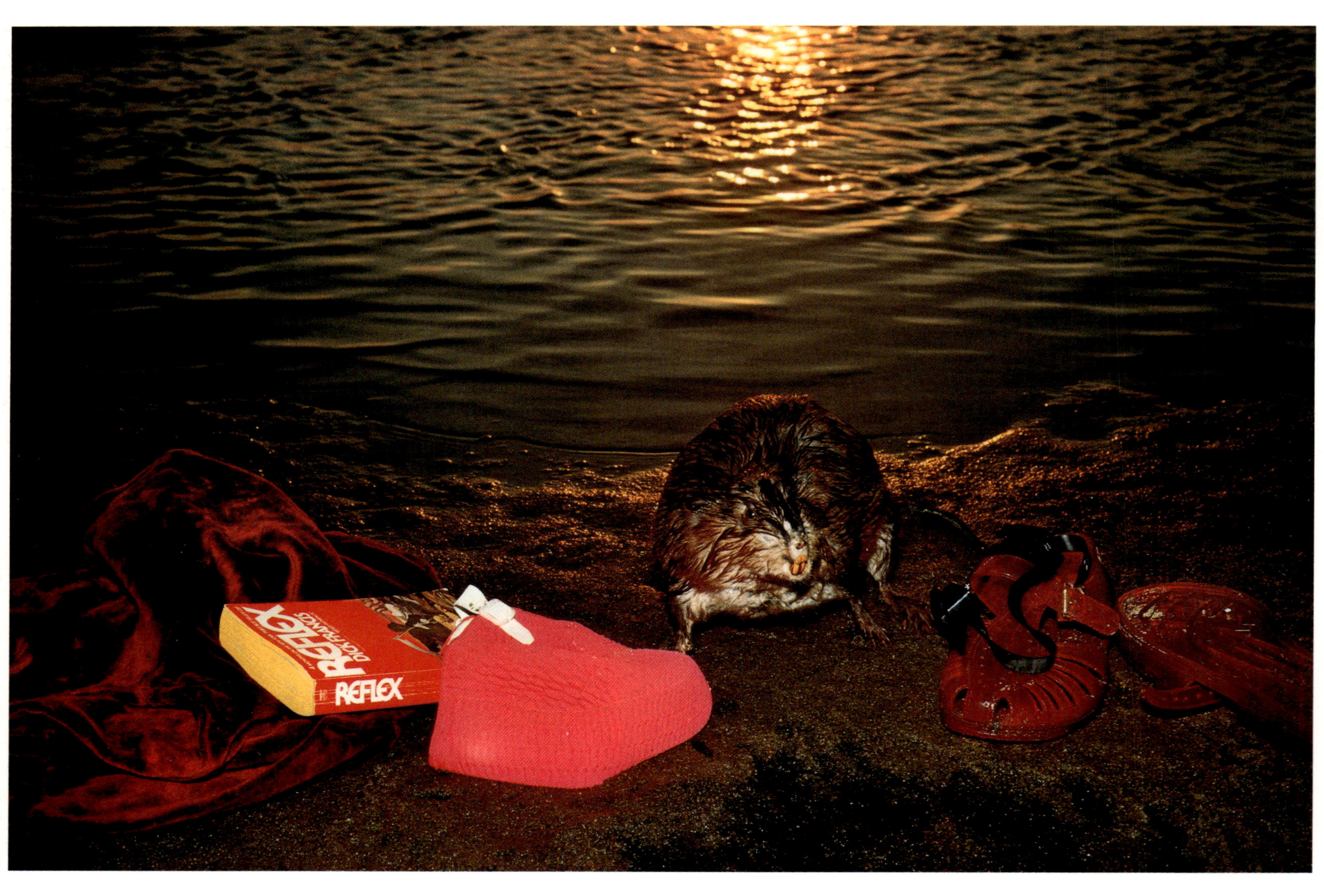

199 · Barbara Norfleet · **Muskrat and Dick Francis: Black Point Pond, MA** · 1985

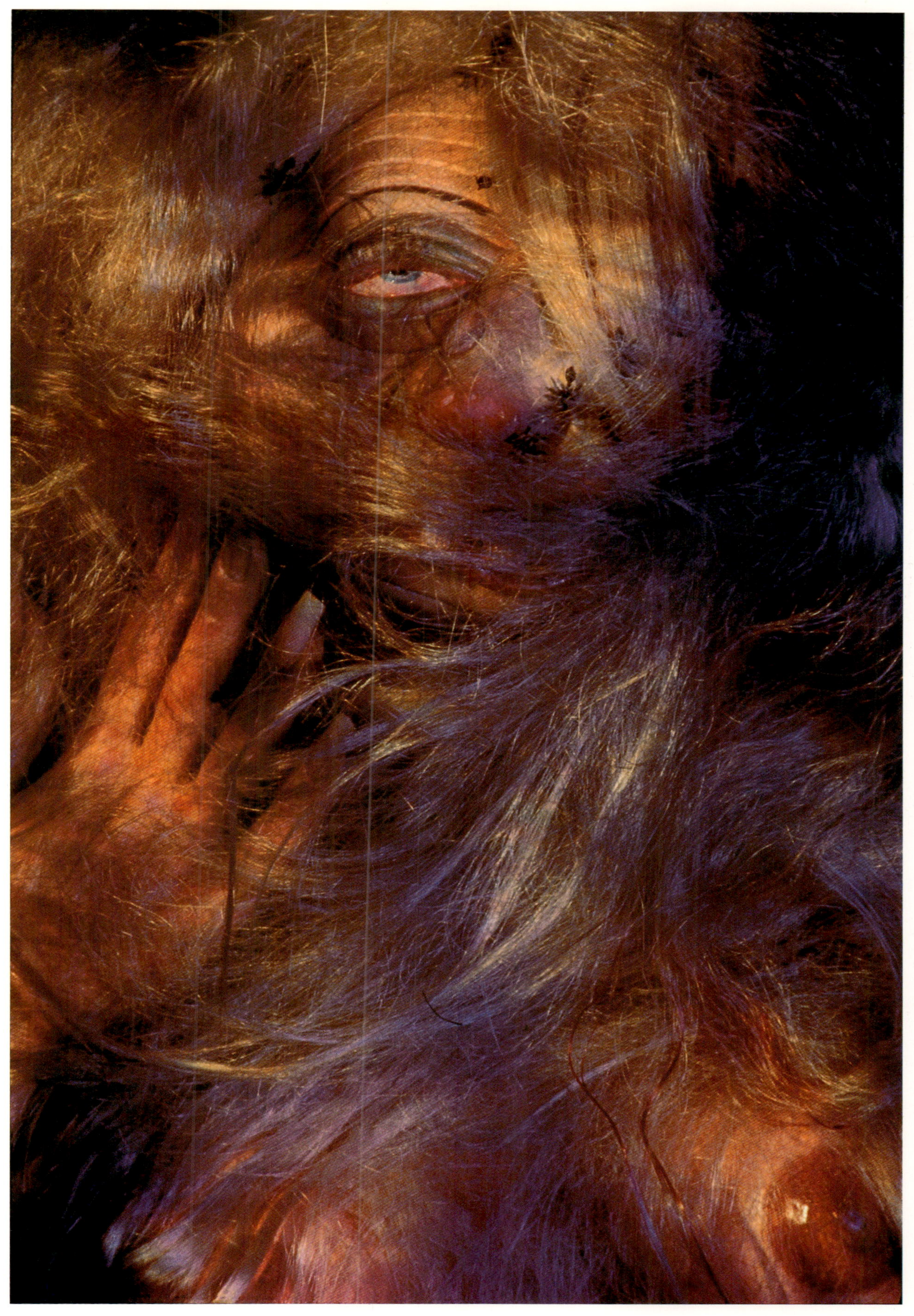

200 · Cindy Sherman · Untitled · 1989

ACKNOWLEDGMENTS

I am especially indebted to certain experts in the field who offered ideas, advice, and criticism. Susan Ehrens generously shared with me her research and extensive knowledge about significant photography by women. The passionate eye that shaped her remarkable photography collection influenced this selection. Jane Livingston, Jill Quasha, and Thomas Walther each brought their particular sensibility and keen observations about the medium to our numerous conversations.

These collectors, gallery administrators, museum curators, executors of estates, and directors of corporate and state collections made work available for consideration and publication. Gordon L. Bennett, San Francisco; Werner Bokelberg, Hambourg, West Germany; Janet Borden, New York; Eleanor Caponigro, Sante Fe; William Clift, Santa Fe; Thomas and Shirley Davis, California; Susan Ehrens, Berkeley, California; Paul M. Hertzmann, San Francisco; The Kolodny Collection, Princeton, New Jersey; Hans P. Kraus, Jr., New York; Janet Lehr, New York; Jan Leonard and Jerrold Peil, San Francisco; Gérard Lévy, Paris; Harvey S. Shipley Miller and Randy Plummer, Philadelphia; Merrily and Tony Page, San Francisco; Anne Peterson, Washington, DC; Marcuse Pfeifer, New York; Jill Quasha, New York; Leland Rice, Berkeley, California; Jill Rose, New York; Sean Thackery, The Rubel Collection, Thackery & Robertson, San Francisco; Paul Walter, New York; Thomas Walther, New York; Ann and Jürgen Wilde, Zülpich-Mülheim, West Germany; Jim Moffat, Art & Commerce, New York; Susan Morgan, Benteler-Morgan Galleries, Houston; Sheryl Finley and Ron Kurtz, Commerce Graphics Ltd., East Rutherford, New Jersey; Carol Ehlers and Shashi Caudill, Ehlers Caudill Gallery, Chicago; Jeffrey Fraenkel, Fraenkel Gallery, San Francisco; Marie Martin, Martin Gallery, Washington, DC; Howard Greenberg, Photofind, New York; Edwynn Houk, Edwynn Houk Gallery, Chicago; Jan Kesner Fine Arts, Los Angeles; Robert Klein Gallery, Boston; Nancy Lieberman and Julie Saul, Lieberman and Saul Gallery, New York; Susan Lorence and Robert Monk, Lorence Monk Gallery, New York; Gordon Veneklasen, Curt Marcus Gallery, New York; Katherine Chermayeff, Magnum Photos, New York; Helene Weiner, Metro Pictures, New York; George Hemphill, Middendorf Gallery, Washington, DC; Laurence Miller, Laurence Miller Gallery, New York; Howard Read, Robert Miller Gallery, New York; Peter MacGill and Linda Fiske, Pace/MacGill Gallery, New York; Alan Klotz, Photocollect, New York; Wendy Olsoff and Penny Pilkington, P.P.O.W. Gallery, New York; Anthony Slayter-Ralph, Anthony Ralph Gallery, New York; Gerd Sander, Sander Gallery, New York; Tartt Gallery, Washington, DC; Tom Southall, Amon Carter Museum of Western Art, Fort. Worth, Texas; Paula Pergament, David Travis, and Colin Westerbeck, Art Institute of Chicago; Jay Fischer and Jan Howard, Baltimore Museum of Art; Marguerite Lavin and Barbara Millstein, Brooklyn Art Museum; Laurie Gross, Canadian Centre for Architecture, Montreal; James Enyeart, Victor LaViola, and Terence Pitts, Center for Creative Photography, University of Arizona, Tucson; Tom Hinson, Cleveland Museum of Art; Weston J. Naef and Louise Stover, The J. Paul Getty Museum, Malibu, California; Gery Lofty and Pat Kattenhorn, India Office Library, London; International Museum of Photography at George Eastman House, Rochester, New York; Maria Morris Hambourg and Ellen Handy, Department of Prints and Photographs, The Metropolitan Museum of Art, New York; Clifford Ackley, Museum of Fine Arts, Boston; Kara Gustafson and Anne Tucker, Museum of Fine Arts, Houston; Bonnie Yochelson, Museum of the City of New York; Gina Guy and Susan Kismaric, The Museum of Modern Art, New York; Ann Thomas, National Gallery of Canada, Ottawa; Julia Van Haften, New York Public Library; Therese Heyman, The Oakland Museum; Pam Roberts, The Royal Photographic Society, Bath, England; Diana DuPont, Sandra Philips, and Lisa Taylor, San Francisco Museum of Modern Art; Mark Haworth-Booth, Victoria and Albert Museum, London; Mary Drugan, Estate of Diane Arbus, New York; Rondal Partridge, The Imogen Cunningham Trust, Berkeley, California; Antony Penrose, Lee Miller Archives, Chiddingly, East Sussex, England; Bowdoin College Museum of Art, Brunswick, Maine; Columbia University, Rare Book and Manuscript Library, New York; Phil Linhares, Mills College Art Gallery, Oakland, California; Kevin Donovan, University Art Museum, University of New Mexico, Albuquerque; Patty Carr Black and Hank Holmes, Mississippi State Historical Museum, Department of Archives, Jackson; Pierre Apraxine and Lee Marks, Gilman Paper Company, New York; and Keith Davis, Fine Arts Collection, Hallmark Cards, Inc., Kansas City, Missouri.

This project would not have been possible without the commitment of Eelco Wolf and Gary Moss at Polaroid Corporation.

Most of all, thanks to the photographers who made these pictures and lent their work and support.

Constance Sullivan

LIST OF PLATES

1. Maria Chambefort (French, active c. 1850). **Stéphanie Poyet, agée de 7 ans.** c. 1850. Daguerreotype, $5\frac{1}{2}$ x $3\frac{15}{16}$ in. (14 x 10 cm). Collection Gérard Lévy, Paris

2. Anna Atkins (British, 1799–1871). **Polypodium aureum (Jamaica).** c. 1854. Cyanotype, $13\frac{9}{16}$ x $9\frac{11}{16}$ in. (34.5 x 24.7 cm). The J. Paul Getty Museum, Malibu

3. Anna Atkins. **Iris pseudacorus.** c. 1861. Cyanotype, $13\frac{3}{4}$ x $9\frac{5}{8}$ in. (35 x 24.5 cm). Collection Dr. and Mrs. William Fielder, Atherton, California

4. Lady Filmer (British, c. 1840–1903), Untitled. c. 1864. Watercolor with collaged photographs, $11\frac{1}{4}$ x 9 in. (28.7 x 23 cm). University Art Museum, University of New Mexico, Albuquerque

5. Lucy Fleming (British, active 1860s). **Interior, Castle Hedington, Essex.** c. 1864. Albumen print from wet-collodion glass-plate negative, $8\frac{3}{8}$ x $10\frac{3}{8}$ in. (21.3 x 26.4 cm). Collection Gordon L. Bennett, San Francisco

6. Louise Deshong Woodbridge (American, 1848–1925). **Ladies' Pool.** c. 1890. Platinum print, $4\frac{1}{2}$ x $6\frac{1}{2}$ in. (11.4 x 16.5 cm). Janet Lehr, Inc., New York

7. Lady Clementina Hawarden (British, 1822–1865). Photographic study. c. 1862–63. Albumen print from wet-collodion glass-plate negative, 9 x $8\frac{1}{4}$ in. (23 x 21 cm). The Victoria and Albert Museum, London

8. Lady Clementina Hawarden. Photographic study. Early 1860s. Albumen print from wet-collodion glass-plate negative, $3\frac{1}{4}$ x $2\frac{9}{16}$ in. (8.2 x 6.5 cm). Collection Gilman Paper Company, New York

9. Lady Clementina Hawarden. Photographic study. Early 1860s. Albumen print from wet-collodion glass-plate negative, $7\frac{7}{8}$ x $5\frac{1}{16}$ in. (20 x 12.9 cm). Collection Gilman Paper Company, New York

10. Julia Margaret Cameron (British, 1815–1879). **Rev. J. Isaacson, Rector of Freshwater.** 1864. Albumen print, $10\frac{3}{16}$ x $8\frac{1}{4}$ in. (25.9 x 20.9 cm). The J. Paul Getty Museum, Malibu

11. Julia Margaret Cameron. **Hallam Tennyson.** 1867. Albumen print, $12\frac{13}{16}$ x $10\frac{7}{16}$ in. (32.6 x 26.5 cm). The J. Paul Getty Museum, Malibu

12. Julia Margaret Cameron. **Prayer and Praise/Freshwater.** 1865. Albumen print, $11\frac{1}{16}$ x $8\frac{15}{16}$ in. (28.1 x 22.7 cm). The J. Paul Getty Museum, Malibu

13. Julia Margaret Cameron. **Stella.** 1869. Albumen print, $9\frac{7}{8}$ x $8\frac{1}{4}$ in. (25 x 21 cm). The Rubel Collection, San Francisco

14. Julia Margaret Cameron. **Cassiopeia.** 1866. Albumen print, $13\frac{3}{4}$ x $10\frac{7}{8}$ in. (35 x 27.5 cm). The Rubel Collection, San Francisco

15. Anne Brigman (American, 1869–1950). **A Study in Radiation.** 1924. Gelatin-silver print, $9\frac{5}{8}$ x $7\frac{5}{8}$ in. (24.4 x 19.4 cm). Anthony Ralph Gallery, New York

16. Anne Brigman. **Saga—The Golden Fleece.** 1924. Gelatin-silver print, $9\frac{3}{4}$ x $7\frac{5}{8}$ in. (24.8 x 19.4 cm). Courtesy Susan Ehrens, Berkeley, California

17. Anne Brigman. Untitled. 1922. Gelatin-silver print, $9\frac{3}{4}$ x $7\frac{3}{4}$ in. (24.8 x 19.7 cm). Courtesy Susan Ehrens, Berkeley, California

18. Gertrude Käsebier (American, 1852–1934). **Miss Dix.** n.d. Platinum print, $8\frac{1}{16}$ x $6\frac{1}{8}$ in. (20.5 x 15.6 cm). Gift of Mina Turner. © 1989 The Art Institute of Chicago. All rights reserved

19. Gertrude Käsebier. **Indian Portrait.** c. 1905. Gum-bichromate print, $13\frac{3}{16}$ x $10\frac{1}{16}$ in. (33.5 x 25.6 cm). Gift of Mina Turner. © 1989 The Art Institute of Chicago. All Rights Reserved

20. Gertrude Käsebier. **Gertrude and Charles O'Malley, Newport, Rhode Island: A Triptych.** 1902. Platinum print, $7\frac{3}{8}$ x $5\frac{7}{8}$ in.; $7\frac{9}{16}$ x $5\frac{5}{8}$ in.; $7\frac{7}{16}$ x $5\frac{13}{16}$ in. (18.8 x 14.9 cm; 19.2 x 14.3 cm; 18.9 x 14.8 cm). The J. Paul Getty Museum, Malibu

21. Gertrude Käsebier. **Gertrude Käsebier O'Malley at Billiards.** c. 1909. Platinum print, $7\frac{11}{16}$ x $9\frac{11}{16}$ in. (19.6 x 24.7 cm). The J. Paul Getty Museum, Malibu

22. Frances Benjamin Johnston (American, 1864–1952). **Stairway of Treasurer's Residence. Students at Work,** plate from an album of The Hampton Institute. 1899–1900. Platinum print, $7\frac{1}{2}$ x $9\frac{1}{2}$ in. (19 x 24.1 cm). The Museum of Modern Art, New York. Gift of Lincoln Kirstein

23. Frances Benjamin Johnston. **Agriculture Mixing Fertilizer,** plate from an album of The Hampton Institute. 1899–1900. Platinum print, $7\frac{1}{2}$ x $9\frac{1}{2}$ in. (19 x 24.1 cm). The Museum of Modern Art, New York. Gift of Lincoln Kirstein

24. Jessie Tarbox Beals (American, 1871–1942). **Man and Children in Tenement Back Yard, New York.** n.d. Gelatin-silver print, $7\frac{1}{4}$ x $9\frac{7}{16}$ in. (18.5 x 24 cm). Community Service Society Papers, Rare Book and Manuscript Library, Columbia University

25. Jessie Tarbox Beals. **Children with Burlap Sacks and Wheelbarrow.** n.d. Gelatin-silver print, 4½ x 6½ in. (11.5 x 16.5 cm). Community Service Society Papers, Rare Book and Manuscript Library, Columbia University

26. Doris Ulmann (American, 1884–1934). **Woman Seated on Steps.** c. 1930. Platinum print, 7 15/16 x 5 15/16 in. (20.2 x 15.1 cm). University Art Museum, University of New Mexico, Albuquerque. Purchased through the Julius Rolshoven Memorial Fund

27. Doris Ulmann. **Laundress, Peterken Farm, South Carolina.** 1929. Platinum print, 8¼ x 6 in. (21 x 15.2 cm). Collection Caroline Zinsser, New York. Courtesy Anthony Ralph Gallery, New York

28. Doris Ulmann. **Baptism, South Carolina.** c. 1930. Gravure, 8⅜ x 6½ in. (21.3 x 16.5 cm). Collection William Clift, Santa Fe, New Mexico

29. Doris Ulmann. **Bell Ringer, South Carolina.** c. 1930. Platinum print, 7⅞ x 5⅞ in. (20 x 14.9 cm). Collection William Clift, Santa Fe, New Mexico

30. Laura Gilpin (American, 1891–1979). **Sunrise, San Luis Desert.** 1921. Platinum print, 7⅝ x 9⅜ in. (19.4 x 23.8 cm) © 1981 Laura Gilpin Collection, Amon Carter Museum, Fort Worth, Texas

31. Laura Gilpin. **Cottonwoods, Taos Pueblo.** 1923. Platinum print, 7½ x 9½ in. (19 x 24.1 cm). Collection Eleanor Caponigro, Santa Fe, New Mexico

32. Laura Gilpin. **The Tall Man at the Circus.** c. 1920s. Platinum print, 9 5/16 x 7¼ in. (23.7 x 18.4 cm). Collection Leland Rice, Berkeley, California

33. Margaret Watkins (Canadian, 1884–1969). **Still-life— Shower Hose.** 1919. Gelatin-silver print; image and sheet, 8 5/16 x 6¼ in. (21.2 x 15.9 cm). National Gallery of Canada, Ottawa

34. Margaret Watkins. **The Kitchen Sink.** c. 1919. Palladium print; image and sheet, 8⅜ x 6 7/16 in. (21.3 x 16.4 cm). National Gallery of Canada, Ottawa

35. Margaret Watkins. **Domestic Symphony.** 1919. Palladium print; image and mount, 8⅜ x 6 7/16 in. (21.3 x 16.4 cm). National Gallery of Canada, Ottawa

36. Imogen Cunningham (American, 1883–1976). **Triangles.** 1928. Gelatin-silver print, 2¾ x 3¾ in. (7 x 9.5 cm). Collection Thomas Walther, New York. © The Imogen Cunningham Trust

37. Imogen Cunningham. **Snake in Bucket.** 1929. Gelatin-silver print, 6 5/16 x 8¼ in. (16 x 21 cm). Collection Werner Bokelberg, Hambourg, West Germany. © The Imogen Cunningham Trust

38. Imogen Cunningham. **Nude.** 1932. Gelatin-silver print, 2¾ x 3 9/16 in. (7 x 9 cm). Collection Leland Rice, Berkeley, California. © The Imogen Cunningham Trust

39. Imogen Cunningham. **Breast.** c. 1927. Vintage gelatin-silver print, 8 x 6¼ in. (20.3 x 15.9 cm). Paul M. Hertzmann, Inc., San Francisco. © The Imogen Cunningham Trust

40. Imogen Cunningham. **Aloe Bud.** c. 1926. Gelatin-silver print, 11⅞ x 8 11/16 in. (30.2 x 22 cm). Collection Susan Ehrens, Berkeley, California. © The Imogen Cunningham Trust

41. Imogen Cunningham. Untitled (Portia Hume). c. 1930. Gelatin-silver print, 3⅝ x 4⅜ in. (9.2 x 11.1 cm). Collection Susan Ehrens, Berkeley, California. © The Imogen Cunningham Trust

42. Imogen Cunningham. **Calla.** c. 1929. Gelatin-silver print, 11¾ x 8⅞ in. (29.8 x 22.5 cm). Collection Leland Rice, Berkeley, California. © The Imogen Cunningham Trust

43. Dorothea Lange (American, 1895–1965). **Torso, San Francisco.** 1923. Vintage gelatin-silver print, 4½ x 3½ in. (11.4 x 8.9 cm). Edwynn Houk Gallery, Chicago

44. Tina Modotti (Mexican, b. Italy 1896–1942). **Roses.** 1924. Gelatin-silver print, 8½ x 7½ in. (21.6 x 19 cm). Private collection

45. Tina Modotti. **Experiment in Related Forms.** 1924. Platinum print, 7 x 9⅜ in. (17.8 x 23.8 cm). Mills College Collection, California

46. Tina Modotti. **Interior of Church Tower, Tepotzotlan, Mexico.** 1924. Platinum print, 6½ x 8¾ in. (16.5 x 22.2 cm). Collection Merrily and Tony Page, San Francisco

47. Tina Modotti. **Stairs, Mexico City.** 1923–26. Gelatin-silver print, 7⅛ x 9⅜ in. (18 x 23.8 cm). Collection Thomas Walther, New York

48. Tina Modotti. **Telephone Wire Composition, Mexico.** 1925. Gelatin-silver print, 9 x 6 5/16 in. (22.9 x 16 cm). The Baltimore Museum of Art

49. Tina Modotti. **Hands of a Marionette Player.** Mexico, 1926. Gelatin-silver print, 7½ x 9⅜ in. (19 x 23.8 cm). Collection Thomas Walther, New York

50. Tina Modotti. **Demonstrations by Campesinos, Mexico.** c. 1928. Gelatin-silver print, 7½ x 9½ in. (19.1 x 24.1 cm). The J. Paul Getty Museum, Malibu

51. Consuelo Kanaga (American, 1894–1978). **Girl in Straw Hat.** c. 1940. Gelatin-silver print, 7¾ x 5½ in. (19.7 x 14 cm). Photocollect, New York

52. Consuelo Kanaga. **The Girl with a Flower (Francis).** 1928. Gelatin-silver print, 9 11/16 x 7 11/16 in. (24.6 x 19.5 cm). Photocollect, New York

53. Alma Lavenson (American, 1897–1989). **Child with Doll.** 1932. Gelatin-silver print 7 9/16 x 9½ in. (19.2 x 24.1 cm). Courtesy Susan Ehrens, Berkeley, California. © Alma Lavenson

54. Alma Lavenson. **Egg Box.** 1931. Gelatin-silver print, $9\frac{9}{16}$ x $7\frac{9}{16}$ in. (24.3 x 19.2 cm). Courtesy Susan Ehrens, Berkeley, California. © Alma Lavenson

55. Alma Lavenson. **Calaveras Dam II.** 1932. Gelatin-silver print, $9\frac{7}{8}$ x $7\frac{9}{16}$ in. (25 x 19.2 cm). Edwynn Houk Gallery, Chicago. © Alma Lavenson

56. Margaret Bourke-White (American, 1904–1971). **George Washington Bridge.** c. 1930s. Gelatin-silver print, $8\frac{3}{4}$ x $13\frac{3}{4}$ in. (22.2 x 34.9 cm). Collection Merrily and Tony Page, San Francisco

57. Margaret Bourke-White. Untitled. Late 1920s. Gelatin-silver print, $12\frac{7}{8}$ x $9\frac{1}{4}$ in. (32.6 x 23.5 cm). Museum of Fine Arts, Houston. Museum purchase with funds provided by The Mundy Companies

58. Margaret Bourke-White. **Hydro Generators, Niagara Falls Power Co.** 1928. Gelatin-silver print, $17\frac{3}{4}$ x $13\frac{1}{8}$ in. (45 x 33.3 cm). Private collection, Washington, DC

59. Ilse Bing. **Paris.** 1932. Gelatin-silver print, $8\frac{3}{4}$ x $11\frac{1}{8}$ in. (22.2 x 28.3 cm). Collection Susan Ehrens, Berkeley, California

60. Ilse Bing. **Can-Can Dancers at the Moulin Rouge.** Paris, 1931. Vintage gelatin-silver print, 6 x $8\frac{7}{8}$ in. (15.2 x 22.5 cm). Edwynn Houk Gallery, Chicago

61. Ilse Bing. **Street Organ.** Amsterdam, 1933. Gelatin-silver print, $8\frac{5}{8}$ x $13\frac{1}{4}$ in. (21.9 x 33.6 cm). Edwynn Houk Gallery, Chicago

62. Marjorie Content. **From 29 Washington Square.** c. 1928. Vintage gelatin-silver print, $3\frac{3}{4}$ x $2\frac{7}{8}$ in. (9.5 x 7.3 cm). Collection Jill Quasha, New York

63. Marjorie Content. Untitled. c. 1928. Vintage gelatin-silver print, 3 x 4 in. (7.6 x 10.2 cm). Collection Jill Quasha, New York

64. Florence Henri. **In der Strasse.** 1930. Gelatin-silver print, $11\frac{1}{16}$ x $14\frac{15}{16}$ in. (28 x 38 cm). Collection Ann and Jürgen Wilde, Zülpich-Mülheim, West Germany

65. Florence Henri. **Réclame pour Hotchkiss, Paris.** c. 1931. Gelatin-silver print, $11\frac{13}{16}$ x $7\frac{11}{16}$ in. (30 x 19.5 cm). Collection Ann and Jürgen Wilde, Zülpich-Mülheim, West Germany

66. Florence Henri (French, 1893–1982). Photomontage. Brittany, c. 1935. Gelatin-silver print, $9\frac{1}{4}$ x $10\frac{3}{4}$ in. (23.5 x 27.3 cm). Collection Thomas Walther, New York

67. Florence Henri. **Still Life.** 1929. Gelatin-silver print, $4\frac{3}{4}$ x $6\frac{11}{16}$ in. (12 x 17 cm). Collection Leland Rice, Berkeley, California

68. Florence Henri. **Woti Werner.** c. 1929. Gelatin-silver print, $11\frac{13}{16}$ x $9\frac{7}{16}$ in. (30 x 24 cm). Collection Ann and Jürgen Wilde, Zülpich-Mülheim, West Germany

69. Lee Miller (American, 1907–1977). **Nude** (Self-portrait). Paris, c. 1931. Gelatin-silver print, $6\frac{7}{8}$ x $8\frac{7}{8}$ in. (17.5 x 22.5 cm). Collection Thomas Walther, New York

70. Lee Miller. **Eiffel Tower.** c. 1931. Gelatin-silver print, $8\frac{1}{2}$ x $9\frac{5}{8}$ in. (21.6 x 24.4 cm). Collection Thomas Walther, New York

71. Lee Miller. **Man Standing Near Asphalt.** Paris, c. 1930. Gelatin-silver print, 9 x $11\frac{1}{2}$ in. (22.9 x 29.2 cm). Collection Thomas Walther, New York

72. Lee Miller. **Dead Prisoners, Dachau Concentration Camp, Germany.** April 30, 1945. Gelatin-silver print, 10 x 10 in. on 16 x 12 in. paper (25.4 x 25.4 cm). © Lee Miller Archives

73. Lee Miller. **Beaten Guards Begging for Mercy, Dachau Concentration Camp, Germany.** April 30, 1945. Gelatin-silver print, 10 x 10 in. on 16 x 12 in. paper (25.4 x 25.4 cm). © Lee Miller Archives

74. Studio Ringl & Pit. **The Smoker.** 1932. Gelatin-silver print, $8\frac{3}{16}$ x $6\frac{1}{8}$ in. (20.8 x 15.6 cm). The J. Paul Getty Museum, Malibu

75. Lotte Jacobi (American, b. Germany 1896–1975). **Franz Lederer** (Actor). Berlin, c. 1929. Gelatin-silver print, 6 x $8\frac{1}{2}$ in. (15.2 x 21.6 cm). Collection Thomas Walther, New York

76. Lotte Jacobi. **Head of a Dancer** (Niura Norskaya). c. 1929. Gelatin-silver print, $6\frac{3}{8}$ x $6\frac{7}{8}$ in. (16.2 x 17.4 cm). The Baltimore Museum of Art

77. Madame Yevonde (British, 1893–1975). **Florence Lambert (Mrs. Constant Lambert).** 1933. Bromide print, 12 x $11\frac{5}{8}$ in. (30.5 x 29.6 cm). The Royal Photographic Society of Great Britain, London

78. Madame Yevonde. **Medusa.** 1933. Vivex print, $14\frac{1}{4}$ x $11\frac{5}{8}$ in. (36.2 x 29.6 cm). The Royal Photographic Society of Great Britain, London

79. Margrethe Mather (American, 1885–1952). **Moon Kwan with Yib Kirn.** n.d. Platinum print, $9\frac{1}{2}$ x $7\frac{1}{2}$ in. (24.1 x 19 cm). Leonard/Peil Collection, San Francisco

80. Margrethe Mather. **Semi-Nude.** c. 1923. Platinum print, $3\frac{11}{16}$ x $4\frac{5}{8}$ in. (9.3 x 11.8 cm). Center for Creative Photography, University of Arizona, Tucson

81. Margrethe Mather. **Billy Justema, L.A.** c. 1922. Gelatin-silver print, $3\frac{13}{16}$ x $2\frac{13}{16}$ in. (9.7 x 7.2 cm). Center for Creative Photography, University of Arizona, Tucson

82. Berenice Abbott (American, b. 1898). **Jean Cocteau, Paris.** 1926. Gelatin-silver print, $6\frac{3}{4}$ x $8\frac{13}{16}$ in. (17.2 x 22.4 cm). Collection, Bowdoin College Museum of Art. Courtesy Berenice Abbott/Commerce Graphics Ltd, Inc.

83. Berenice Abbott. **Gwen Le Gallienne, Paris.** 1927. Vintage gelatin-silver print, $9\frac{1}{2}$ x $7\frac{3}{4}$ in. (24.3 x 19.5 cm). Boston Museum of Fine Arts, Gift of Mrs. G. Rowland. Courtesy Berenice Abbott/Commerce Graphics Ltd, Inc.

84. Berenice Abbott. **Deputy M. Scappini, Paris**. 1927. Gelatin-silver print, $9\frac{3}{4}$ x $6\frac{1}{8}$ in. (24.8 x 15.6 cm). Collection Robert Klein Gallery, Boston. Courtesy Berenice Abbott/Commerce Graphics Ltd, Inc.

85. Lucia Moholy (British, b. Czechoslovakia 1900). **Portrait of Franz Roh**. 1926. Gelatin-silver print, $4\frac{5}{16}$ x $3\frac{1}{8}$ in. (11 x 7.9 cm). The Metropolitan Museum of Art, Ford Motor Company Collection. Gift of Ford Motor Company and John C. Waddell, 1987

86. Lucia Moholy. **Portrait of László Moholy-Nagy**. 1925–26. Gelatin-silver print, $10\frac{1}{16}$ x $7\frac{7}{8}$ in. (25.6 x 20 cm). The Metropolitan Museum of Art, Ford Motor Company Collection. Gift of Ford Motor Company and John C. Waddell, 1987

87. Wanda Wulz (Italian, 1903–1984). **Lo & Gatto (I and Cat)**. 1932. Gelatin-silver print, $11\frac{9}{16}$ x $9\frac{1}{4}$ in. (29.4 x 23.2 cm). Collection Werner Bokelberg, Hambourg, West Germany

88. Hannah Höch. **Die Braut**. c. 1928. Collage (mixed media), approx. $5\frac{5}{8}$ x 6 in. (14.3 x 15.2 cm). Collection Thomas Walther, New York

89. Lotte Beese. **Portrait of Katt Both**. c. 1928. Gelatin-silver print, $3\frac{1}{8}$ x $3\frac{1}{2}$ in. (7.9 x 8.9 cm). Collection Susan Ehrens, Berkeley, California

90. Alice Lex-Nerlinger (German, 1893–1975). **Näherlin**. c. 1930. Gelatin-silver print, $6\frac{9}{16}$ x $4\frac{11}{16}$ in. (16.7 x 11.9 cm). © 1989 The Art Institute of Chicago. All rights reserved. The Julien Levy Collection. Gift of Jean Levy and the Estate of Julien Levy

91. Dora Maar (French, b. 1907). Untitled. c. 1940. Gelatin-silver print (photomontage), $8\frac{5}{8}$ x $10\frac{9}{16}$ in. (21.9 x 26.9 cm). San Francisco Museum of Modern Art, Fund of the 80s Purchase

92. Lotte Beese. **Beese's Studio in the Bauhaus**. c. 1927. Vintage gelatin-silver print, $4\frac{3}{4}$ x $3\frac{1}{2}$ in. (12 x 8.9 cm). Edwynn Houk Gallery, Chicago

93. Ellen Auerbach (German, b. 1906). **Kurfursterstr**. 1931. Gelatin-silver print, $4\frac{1}{4}$ x $3\frac{1}{4}$ in. (10.8 x 8.3 cm). Collection Leland Rice, Berkeley, California

94. Aenne Biermann (German, 1898–1933). **Portrait mit Champs-Elysées, Paris**. c. 1929. Silver gelatin, negative montage, $9\frac{1}{4}$ x $7\frac{15}{16}$ in. (23.5 x 17.7 cm). Collection Thomas and Shirley Davis, California

95. Aenne Biermann. **Sonnenbad**. c. 1929. Gelatin-silver print, 7 x $7\frac{7}{8}$ in. (17.8 x 20 cm). Collection Ann and Jürgen Wilde, Zülpich-Mülheim, West Germany

96. Aenne Biermann. **Aus dem Fahrenden Zug**. c. 1930. Gelatin-silver print, $7\frac{15}{16}$ x $9\frac{5}{16}$ in. (17.7 x 23.7 cm). Collection Ann and Jürgen Wilde, Zülpich-Mülheim, West Germany

97. Germaine Krull (French, 1897–1986). **Le Cinéma Paramount**. c. 1935. Vintage gelatin-silver print, $5\frac{7}{16}$ x $3\frac{9}{16}$ in. (13.8 x 9 cm). Collection Jill Quasha, New York

98. Germaine Krull. **Traffic in Paris**. 1926. Gelatin-silver print, 11 x $7\frac{1}{2}$ in. (28 x 19.2 cm). Collection Ann and Jürgen Wilde, Zülpich-Mülheim, West Germany

99. Germaine Krull. **Nude**. Paris, c. 1926. Gelatin-silver print, $6\frac{3}{4}$ x $8\frac{3}{4}$ in. (17.1 x 22.2 cm). Collection Thomas Walther, New York

100. Germaine Krull. Untitled. c. 1929. Gelatin-silver print, $7\frac{3}{4}$ x $6\frac{1}{4}$ in. (19.7 x 15.9 cm). Ehlers Caudill Gallery, Chicago

101. Germaine Krull. **Iron-Work, Pont à Mousson**. 1926. Gelatin-silver print, $9\frac{1}{4}$ x $6\frac{5}{16}$ in. (23.5 x 16 cm). Collection Ann and Jürgen Wilde, Zülpich-Mülheim, West Germany

102. Berenice Abbott. **Walkway, Manhattan Bridge, New York**. 1936. Vintage gelatin-silver print, 10 x 8 in. (25.4 x 20.3 cm). Edwynn Houk Gallery, Chicago and Berenice Abbott/ Commerce Graphics Ltd, Inc.

103. Berenice Abbott. Photomontage. New York, c. 1930. Gelatin-silver print, $4\frac{1}{4}$ x $8\frac{1}{8}$ in. (10.8 x 20.6 cm). Collection Thomas Walther, New York

104. Berenice Abbott. **53 Gannesvoort Street, Brooklyn, New York**. 1936 or later. Gelatin-silver print, $9\frac{1}{4}$ x $7\frac{1}{2}$ in. (23.5 x 19 cm). Centre Canadien d'Architecture/Canadian Centre for Architecture. Courtesy Berenice Abbott/Commerce Graphics Ltd, Inc.

105. Berenice Abbott. **Court of the First Model Tenements, New York**. 1936. Gelatin-silver print, $9\frac{15}{16}$ x $7\frac{15}{16}$ in. (25.2 x 20.2 cm). Baltimore Museum of Art, Friends of Photography Fund. Courtesy Berenice Abbott/Commerce Graphics Ltd, Inc.

106. Eudora Welty (American, b. 1909). **Bird Pageant Costumes**. Before 1935. Gelatin-silver print; negative, $2\frac{1}{2}$ x $4\frac{1}{4}$ in. (6.3 x 10.8 cm). Eudora Welty Collection, Mississippi Department of Archives and History

107. Eudora Welty. **Preacher and Leaders of the Holiness Church**. c. 1935–36. Gelatin-silver print; negative, 3 x 4 in. (7.6 x 10.2 cm). Eudora Welty Collection, Mississippi Department of Archives and History

108. Eudora Welty. **Saturday Off**. Before 1935. Gelatin-silver print; negative, $2\frac{1}{2}$ x $4\frac{1}{4}$ in. (6.3 x 10.8 cm). Eudora Welty Collection, Mississippi Department of Archives and History

109. Eudora Welty. **Staying Home**. Before 1935. Gelatin-silver print; negative, $2\frac{1}{2}$ x $4\frac{1}{4}$ in. (6.3 x 10.8 cm). Eudora Welty Collection, Mississippi Department of Archives and History

110. Eudora Welty. Untitled. Before 1935. Gelatin-silver print; negative, $2\frac{1}{2}$ x $4\frac{1}{4}$ in. (6.3 x 10.8 cm). Eudora Welty Collection, Mississippi Department of Archives and History

111. Eudora Welty. Untitled. c. 1935–36. Gelatin-silver print; negative, 3 x 4 in. (7.6 x 10.2 cm). Eudora Welty Collection, Mississippi Department of Archives and History

112. Eudora Welty. **Making a Date.** Before 1935. Gelatin-silver print; negative, $2\frac{1}{2}$ x $4\frac{1}{4}$ in. (6.3 x 10.8 cm). Eudora Welty Collection, Mississippi Department of Archives and History

113. Eudora Welty. Untitled. c. 1935–36. Gelatin-silver print; negative, 3 x 4 in. (7.6 x 10.2 cm). Eudora Welty Collection, Mississippi Department of Archives and History

114. Marion Post Wolcott (American, b. 1910). **The Whittler. An old Negro man (ex-slave), Camden, Alabama.** 1939. Gelatin-silver print, $6\frac{1}{4}$ x $8\frac{3}{8}$ in. (15.9 x 21.3 cm). Courtesy Susan Ehrens, Berkeley, California

115. Marion Post Wolcott. Guest being served his lunch at posh private beach club in Palm Beach, Florida. 1939. Gelatin-silver print, $6\frac{3}{8}$ x $9\frac{15}{16}$ in. (16.2 x 25.2 cm). Private collection

116. Marion Post Wolcott. Group of Day Laborers waiting to be paid for picking cotton, Marcella Plantation, Mileston, Mississippi. 1939. Gelatin-silver print, $10\frac{7}{16}$ x $13\frac{7}{16}$ in. (26.5 x 34.1 cm). Collection Leland Rice, Berkeley, California

117. Dorothea Lange. **White Angel Kitchen, San Francisco.** 1933. Vintage gelatin-silver print, $4\frac{9}{16}$ x $3\frac{1}{2}$ in. (11.6 x 8.9 cm). Collection Robert Morrow

118. Dorothea Lange. **San Francisco Waterfront.** 1933. Vintage gelatin-silver print, $9\frac{1}{2}$ x $7\frac{1}{2}$ in. (24.1 x 19 cm). The Quillan Collection, Courtesy Jill Quasha, New York

119. Dorothea Lange. **Damaged Child, Shacktown, Elm Grove, Oklahoma.** 1936. Vintage gelatin-silver print, $9\frac{3}{8}$ x $7\frac{1}{2}$ in. (23.8 x 19 cm). Edwynn Houk Gallery, Chicago

120. Dorothea Lange. **One of the Homeless Wandering Boys, Before the Civilian Conservation Corps.** 1933. Vintage gelatin-silver print, $9\frac{1}{4}$ x 7 in. (23.5 x 17.8 cm). Edwynn Houk Gallery, Chicago

121. Margaret Bourke-White. **Fazenda Rio des Preda.** 1930s. Gelatin-silver print, 10 x $13\frac{1}{8}$ in. (25.4 x 33.3 cm). Collection Merrily and Tony Page, San Francisco

122. Helen Levitt (American, b. 1913). **Children and Fire Hydrant.** c. 1945. Gelatin-silver print, $9\frac{1}{2}$ x $6\frac{3}{4}$ in. (24.1 x 17.1 cm). Robert Klein Gallery, Boston

123. Helen Levitt. **New York City.** 1945. Gelatin-silver print, 11 x 14 in. (27.9 x 35.6 cm). Collection Thomas Walther, New York

124. Helen Levitt. **New York.** c. 1942. Gelatin-silver print, $6\frac{3}{8}$ x $8\frac{3}{8}$ in. (16.2 x 21.3 cm). Hallmark Photographic Collection, Hallmark Cards, Inc., Kansas City, Missouri

125. Helen Levitt. **Mexico City.** 1941. Gelatin-silver print, 11 x 14 in. (27.9 x 35.6 cm). Laurence Miller Gallery, New York

126. Lisette Model (Austrian, 1906–1983). **Woman at Opera with Face Covered.** c. 1945. Gelatin-silver print, $13\frac{5}{8}$ x 11 in. (34.6 x 28 cm). Gerd Sander Gallery, New York

127. Lisette Model. **Sailor and Girl, Sammy's Bar, New York.** c. 1944 (before 1950). Gelatin-silver print, $13\frac{3}{4}$ x $10\frac{5}{8}$ in. (34.9 x 27 cm). National Gallery of Canada, Ottawa

128. Lisette Model. **Lower East Side.** 1940. Gelatin-silver print, $13\frac{1}{2}$ x $10\frac{1}{2}$ in. (34.3 x 26.8 cm). The Estate of Lisette Model, Center for Creative Photography, University of Arizona, Tucson

129. Lisette Model. **Black Dwarf, Lower East Side.** 1950. Gelatin-silver print, $13\frac{11}{16}$ x $10\frac{5}{16}$ in. (34.8 x 26.2 cm). The J. Paul Getty Museum, Malibu

130. Diane Arbus (American, 1923–1971). **Albino Sword Swallower at a Carnival, MD.** 1970. Gelatin-silver print, 20 x 16 in. (50.8 x 40.6 cm). © 1982 Estate of Diane Arbus. Robert Miller Gallery, New York

131. Diane Arbus. **Girl with Patterned Stockings.** c. 1965–69. Gelatin-silver print, $10\frac{1}{4}$ x $10\frac{1}{4}$ in. (26 x 26 cm). © 1980 Estate of Diane Arbus. Collection Merrily and Tony Page, San Francisco

132. Diane Arbus. **Girl in a Watch Cap, New York City.** 1965. Gelatin-silver print, 20 x 16 in. (50.8 x 40.6 cm). © 1980 Estate of Diane Arbus. Robert Miller Gallery, New York

133. Diane Arbus. Untitled (7). 1970–71. Gelatin-silver print, 20 x 16 in. (50.8 x 40.6 cm). © 1972 Estate of Diane Arbus. Robert Miller Gallery, New York

134. Rosalind Solomon (American, b. 1930). **Bathers, Guatemala.** 1979. Gelatin-silver print, $7\frac{1}{4}$ x $7\frac{1}{4}$ in. (18.4 x 18.4 cm). Courtesy of the artist

135. Rosalind Solomon. **Man at Swayamanboth Temple, Kathmandu, Nepal.** 1985. Gelatin-silver print, $7\frac{1}{4}$ x $7\frac{1}{4}$ in. (18.4 x 18.4 cm). Courtesy of the artist

136. Graciela Iturbide (Mexican, b. 1942). **Nuestra Señora de las Iguanas, Juchitán.** 1980. Gelatin-silver print, $9\frac{3}{16}$ x $11\frac{9}{16}$ in. (23.3 x 29.4 cm). Courtesy of the artist

137. Graciela Iturbide. **Laganto, Juchitán.** 1988. Gelatin-silver print, $8\frac{1}{8}$ x $12\frac{1}{4}$ in. (20.6 x 31.1 cm). Courtesy of the artist

138. Susan Meiselas (American, b. 1948). **Cuesta del Plomo. Hillside outside Managua, a well-known site of many assassinations carried out by the National Guard. People searched here daily for missing persons.** 1978–79. Cibachrome print, 16 x 20 in. (40.6 x 50.8 cm). © Susan Meiselas/ Magnum, New York

139. Susan Meiselas. **Children rescued from a house destroyed by a 1000-pound bomb dropped in Managua. They died shortly thereafter.** 1978–79. Cibachrome print, 16 x 20 in. (40.6 x 50.8 cm). © Susan Meiselas/Magnum, New York

140. Mary Ellen Mark (American, b. 1941). **Blind Orphan at Shishu Bhawan, Calcutta, India.** 1980. Gelatin-silver print, 16 x 20 in. (40.6 x 50.8 cm). Mary Ellen Mark Library, New York

141. Mary Ellen Mark. **Home for the Dying, Calcutta, India.** 1981. Gelatin-silver print, 16 x 20 in. (40.6 x 50.8 cm). Mary Ellen Mark Library, New York

142. Mary Ellen Mark. **Home for the Dying, Calcutta, India.** 1980. Gelatin-silver print, 16 x 20 in. (40.6 x 50.8 cm). Mary Ellen Mark Library, New York

143. Mary Ellen Mark. **Home for the Dying, Calcutta, India.** 1980. Gelatin-silver print, 16 x 20 in. (40.6 x 50.8 cm). Mary Ellen Mark Library, New York

144. Debbie Fleming Caffery (American, b. 1948). Untitled. 1984. Gelatin-silver print, 19 x 19 in. (48.3 x 48.3 cm). Benteler-Morgan Galleries, Houston, Texas

145. Debbie Fleming Caffery. **Enterprise Sugar Mill.** 1987. Gelatin-silver print, 19 x 19 in. (48.3 x 48.3 cm). Martin Gallery, Washington, DC

146. Sally Mann (American, b. 1951). **Tobacco Spit.** 1987. Gelatin-silver print, 20 x 24 in. (50.8 x 61 cm). Courtesy of the artist

147. Sally Mann. **Blowing Bubbles.** 1987. Gelatin-silver print, 20 x 24 in. (50.8 x 61 cm). Courtesy of the artist

148. Sally Mann. **Drying Morels.** 1988. Gelatin-silver print, 20 x 24 in. (50.8 x 61 cm). Courtesy of the artist

149. Sally Mann. **Jessie at Six.** 1988. Gelatin-silver print, 20 x 24 in. (50.8 x 61 cm). Courtesy of the artist

150. Andrea Modica (American, b. 1960). **Treadwell, New York.** 1986. Palladium print, 8 x 10 in. (20.3 x 25.4 cm). Lieberman and Saul Gallery, New York

151. Andrea Modica. **Treadwell, New York.** 1987. Palladium print, 8 x 10 in. (20.3 x 25.4 cm). Lieberman and Saul Gallery, New York

152. Judith Joy Ross (American, b. 1946). Untitled from **Eurana Park, Weatherly, PA.** 1982. Gelatin-silver print, $7\frac{5}{8}$ x $9\frac{5}{8}$ in. (19.4 x 24.4 cm). Courtesy of the artist

153. Judith Joy Ross. Untitled from **Portraits at the Vietnam Veterans Memorial, Washington, DC.** 1983–84. Gelatin-silver print, $9\frac{5}{8}$ x $7\frac{5}{8}$ in. (24.4 x 19.4 cm). Courtesy of the artist

154. Nan Goldin (American, b. 1953). **Patrick Fox and Teri Toye on their Wedding Night, New York City.** 1987. Cibachrome print, 20 x 24 in. (50.8 x 61 cm). © Nan Goldin, Courtesy Pace/ MacGill Gallery, New York

155. Nan Goldin. **Brian on the Phone, New York City.** 1981. Cibachrome print, 20 x 24 in. (50.8 x 61 cm). © Nan Goldin, Courtesy Pace/MacGill Gallery, New York

156. Nan Goldin. **Cookie at Tin Pan Alley, New York City.** 1983. Cibachrome print, 20 x 24 in. (50.8 x 61 cm). © Nan Goldin, Courtesy Pace/MacGill Gallery, New York

157. Cindy Sherman (American, b. 1954). Untitled. 1981. Type C print, 24 x 48 in. (61 x 121.9 cm). Metro Pictures, New York

158. Tina Barney (American, b. 1945). **The Landscape.** 1988. Ektacolor Plus photograph, 48 x 60 in. (121.9 x 152.4 cm). Janet Borden, Inc., New York

159. Tina Barney. **The Graham Cracker Box.** 1983. Ektacolor Plus photograph, 48 x 60 in. (121.9 x 152.4 cm). Janet Borden, Inc., New York

160. Annie Leibovitz (American, b. 1950). **Randy Travis, Nashville.** 1987. Color, $2\frac{5}{16}$ x $2\frac{3}{4}$ in. (6 x 7 cm). © Annie Leibovitz. Courtesy of the artist

161. Annie Leibovitz. **David Byrne, Los Angeles.** 1989. Color, $2\frac{5}{16}$ x $2\frac{3}{4}$ in. (6 x 7 cm). © Annie Leibovitz. Courtesy of the artist

162. Maude Schuyler Clay (American, b. 1953). **Langdon and Anna Clay, near Rome, 1988.** Type C print, 14 x 14 in. image on 16 x 20 in. paper (35.6 x 35.6 cm). Courtesy of the artist

163. Maude Schuyler Clay. **William Eggleston, Memphis, 1988.** Type C print, 14 x 14 in. image on 16 x 20 in. paper (35.6 x 35.6 cm). Courtesy of the artist

164. W. Snyder MacNeil (American, b. 1943). **Jazimina.** 1985–87. Palladium-platinum print on tracing vellum, 20 x 24 in. (50.8 x 61 cm). Courtesy of the artist

165. W. Snyder MacNeil. **Jazimina and Ronald,** from the **Nuclear Portrait** series. 1987–89. Cibachrome print, 40 x 50 in. (101.6 x 127 cm). Courtesy of the artist

166. W. Snyder MacNeil. **Ezra Sesto.** 1977–88. Platinum-palladium print on tracing vellum, 20 x 24 in. (50.8 x 61 cm). Fraenkel Gallery, San Francisco

167. W. Snyder MacNeil. **Adrian Sesto.** 1977–88. Platinum-palladium print on tracing vellum, 20 x 24 in. (50.8 x 61 cm). Fraenkel Gallery, San Francisco

168. Nancy Hellebrand (American, b. 1944). **Mary Lee.** 1983. Gelatin-silver prints (series of 6). Each, 8 x 10 in. (20.3 x 25.4 cm). © Nancy Hellebrand, Courtesy Pace/MacGill Gallery, New York

169. Holly Wright (American, b. 1941). Untitled, from the **Vanity** series. 1988. Gelatin-silver print, 18 x 26 in. (45.7 x 66 cm). Courtesy of the artist

170. Holly Wright. Untitled, from the **Vanity** series. 1986. Gelatin-silver print, 18 x 26 in. (45.7 x 66 cm). Courtesy of the artist

171. Jan Groover (American, b. 1943). Untitled. 1983. Toned printing-out-paper contact print, 8 x 10 in. (20.3 x 25.4 cm). Robert Miller Gallery, New York

172. Jan Groover. Untitled. 1983. Palladium contact print, 8 x 10 in. (20.3 x 25.4 cm). Robert Miller Gallery, New York

173. Jan Groover. Untitled. 1984. Palladium contact print, 8 x 10 in. (20.3 x 25.4 cm). Robert Miller Gallery, New York

174. Jan Groover. Untitled. 1988. Ektacolor print, 18 x 22 in. (45.7 x 55.9 cm). Robert Miller Gallery, New York

175. Lynne Cohen (American, b. 1944). **Lecture Hall**. n.d. Gelatin-silver print, 20 x 24 in. (50.8 x 61 cm). P.P.O.W., New York

176. Lynne Cohen. **Observation Room**. n.d. Gelatin-silver print, 20 x 24 in. (50.8 x 61 cm). P.P.O.W., New York

177. Catherine Wagner (American, b. 1953). **Vista from Monorail, Wonderwall, Louisiana World Exposition, New Orleans, Louisiana**. 1984. Gelatin-silver print, 16 x 20 in. (40.6 x 50.8 cm). Fraenkel Gallery, San Francisco

178. Catherine Wagner. **Northwestern Corner with Sawhorse and Cement Mixer, George Moscone Site, San Francisco, California**. 1981. Gelatin-silver print, 16 x 20 in. (40.6 x 50.8 cm). Fraenkel Gallery, San Francisco

179. Patty Carroll (American, b. 1946). **Xmas Tree in Window**, Pompano Beach, Florida. 1976. Cibachrome print, 16 x 20 in. (40.6 x 50.8 cm). Ehlers Caudill Gallery, Chicago

180. Patty Carroll. **Motel in Hell**, Michigan. 1975. Cibachrome print, 16 x 20 in. (40.6 x 50.8 cm). Ehlers Caudill Gallery, Chicago

181. Barbara Kasten. **Puye Cliff Dwelling**. 1990. Cibachrome print, 30 x 40 in. (76.2 x 101.6 cm). Courtesy of the artist

182. Karen Halverson (American, b. 1941). **Lake Powell, near Wahweap Marina, Utah, 1987**. Ektacolor print, $11\frac{1}{2}$ x 23 in. (29.2 x 58.4 cm). Courtesy of the artist

183. Karen Halverson. **Hite Crossing, Lake Powell, Utah, 1988**. Ektacolor print, $11\frac{1}{2}$ x 23 in. (29.2 x 58.4 cm). Courtesy of the artist

184. Lois Conner (American, b. 1951). **Beijing, China**. 1988. Platinum-palladium contact print, $16\frac{7}{8}$ x $6\frac{3}{8}$ in. (42.9 x 16.2 cm). Laurence Miller Gallery, New York

185. Lois Conner. **Buddha, Le Shan, Szechuan, China**. 1986. Platinum-palladium contact print, $6\frac{3}{8}$ x $16\frac{7}{8}$ in. (16.2 x 42.9 cm). Laurence Miller Gallery, New York

186. Linda Connor (American, b. 1944). **Chörten, Ladakh, India**. 1985. Gelatin-silver print, 8 x 10 in. (20.3 x 25.4 cm). Courtesy of the artist

187. Linda Connor. **Prayer Flag with Chörtens, Ladakh, India**. 1988. Gelatin-silver print, 8 x 10 in. (20.3 x 25.4 cm). Courtesy of the artist

188. Linda Connor. **Monks, Phiyang Monastery, Ladakh, India**. 1985. Gelatin-silver print, 8 x 10 in. (20.3 x 25.4 cm). Courtesy of the artist

189. Linda Connor. **The Oracle of Sabu in Trance, Ladakh, India**. 1988. Gelatin-silver print, 8 x 10 in. (20.3 x 25.4 cm). Courtesy of the artist

190. Ruth Thorne Thomsen (American, b. 1943). **Cones**, from the **Expedition** series. c. 1982. Toned silver-emulsion photograph, contact printed from paper negative, approximately $3\frac{3}{4}$ x $4\frac{1}{4}$ in. (9.5 x 10.8 cm). Ehlers Caudill Gallery, Chicago

191. Ruth Thorne Thomsen. **Head with Plane**, from the **Expedition** series. Illinois, 1979. Toned silver-emulsion photograph, contact printed from paper negative, approximately $3\frac{3}{4}$ x $4\frac{1}{2}$ in. (9.5 x 11.4 cm). Ehlers Caudill Gallery, Chicago

192. Barbara Ess (American, b. 1948). Untitled, from the **Food for the Moon** series. 1986. Monochrome color photo, 30 x 40 in. (76.2 x 101.6 cm). Curt Marcus Gallery, Inc., New York

193. Barbara Ess. Untitled. 1988. Monochrome color photo, 34 x 73 in. (86.4 x 185.4 cm). Curt Marcus Gallery, Inc., New York

194. Laurie Simmons (American, b. 1949). **Whiteman Coming**. 1981. Cibachrome print, 11 x 14 in. (27.9 x 35.6 cm). Metro Pictures, New York

195. Laurie Simmons. **Vertical Water Ballet**. 1981. Cibachrome print, 16 x 20 in. (40.6 x 50.8 cm). Metro Pictures, New York

196. Jo Ann Callis (American, b 1940). **Man doing Pushups**. 1984–85. Cibachrome print, 24 x 30 in. (61 x 76.2 cm). Jan Kesner Fine Arts, Los Angeles

197. Jo Ann Callis. **Woman Twirling**. 1984. Cibachrome print, 30 x 40 in. (76.2 x 101.6 cm). Jan Kesner Fine Arts, Los Angeles

198. Sandy Skoglund (American, b. 1946). **Radioactive Cats**. 1980. Cibachrome print, 30 x 40 in. (76.2 x 101.6 cm). Lorence Monk Gallery, New York

199. Barbara Norfleet (American, b. 1926). **Muskrat and Dick Francis: Black Point Pond, MA**. 1985. Cibachrome print, 19 x $12\frac{3}{4}$ in. (48.3 x 32.4 cm). Courtesy of the artist

200. Cindy Sherman. Untitled. 1989. Type C print, 90 x 60 in. (228.6 x 152.4 cm). Metro Pictures, New York

WOMEN PHOTOGRAPHERS

was edited by Constance Sullivan.

Editorial preparation and production were coordinated by

Alicia Hathaway, Abigail Hutchinson, and Laurie Sokolsky.

The book was designed by Katy Homans.

Type was set in Monotype Gill Sans by Michael & Winifred Bixler.

Printing and binding were done by Benziger AG,

with color separations by Schwitter AG, Switzerland.

Tritone separations were made by Robert Hennessey.